The Triune God

The Triune God

A Historical Study
of the Doctrine of the Trinity

Edmund J. Fortman

BAKER BOOK HOUSE
Grand Rapids, Michigan 49506

PHOTOLITHOPRINTED BY CUSHING - MALLOY, INC.
ANN ARBOR, MICHIGAN, UNITED STATES OF AMERICA

Glory to the Father
and to the Son
and to the Holy Spirit

Contents

PART FIVE

PROTESTANT TRINITARIAN DOCTRINE
FROM LUTHER TO THE PRESENT

x

Contents

PART SIX

ORTHODOX TRINITARIAN DOCTRINE

CHAPTER EIGHTEEN

FROM PHOTIUS TO THE PRESENT ... 275

Cerularius and Psellos 275
The Second Council of Lyons 276
Hesychasm 276
The Council of Florence and Its Aftermath 276
Symbolic Books and Synods 277
Efforts at Reunion 278
20th-Century Orthodox Theologians 279

PART SEVEN

CATHOLIC TRINITARIAN DOCTRINE FROM THE 15TH CENTURY TO THE PRESENT

CHAPTER NINETEEN

PRINCIPAL TRINITARIAN THEOLOGIANS ... 287

CHAPTER TWENTY

OUR KNOWLEDGE OF THE TRINITY ... 289

CHAPTER TWENTY-ONE

THE DIVINE PROCESSIONS, RELATIONS, PERSONS, AND UNITY ... 292

Processions 292
Relations 293
Persons 295
Unity 300

CHAPTER TWENTY-TWO

DIVINE MISSIONS AND INHABITATION ... 303

Missions 303
Divine Inhabitation 308
Summary of Catholic Trinitarian Doctrine 313

CONCLUSION ... 316

NOTES ... 319

BIBLIOGRAPHY ... 347

ADDITIONAL BIBLIOGRAPHY ... 355

GLOSSARY ... 359

INDEX ... 367

Abbreviations

Standard abbreviations are used for the books of the Bible and for the works of the Fathers and Doctors of the church.

ArchHistDoctLitMA	*Archives d'histoire doctrinale et littéraire du moyen-âge. Paris, 1926–*.
BiblFranSchMa	*Bibliotheca franciscana scholastica medii aevi.* Quaracchi–Florence, 1903–.
BKV	*Bibliothek der Kirchenvater.* Kempten, 1911–.
ConOecDecr	*Conciliorum oecumenicorum decreta.* Bologna–Freiburg, 1962–.
Denz	H. Denzinger, *Enchiridion symbolorum.* Edited by A. Schönmetzer. 32nd ed. Freiburg, 1963–.
DTC	*Dictionnaire de théologie catholique.* Edited by A. Vacant et al. 15 vols. Paris, 1903–56. Indexes 1951.
EChurchQ	*The Eastern Churches Quarterly.* Ramsgate, 1936–.
EphemThLov	*Ephemerides theologicae lovanienses.* Bruges, 1924–.
FrancStudies	*Franciscan Studies.* St. Bonaventure, N.Y. 1940–.
JournEcumStud	*Journal of Ecumenical Studies.* Pittsburgh, Philadelphia, 1962–.
JTS	*Journal of Theological Studies.* London 1899–.

Mansi	J. D. Mansi, *Sacrorum conciliorum nova et amplissima collectio.* 31 vols. Florence–Venice 1757–98; reprinted and continued by L. Petit and J. B. Martin. 60 vols. Paris, 1889–1927.
MedSt	*Medieval Studies.* New York–London, 1939–.
NCE	*New Catholic Encyclopedia.* 15 vols. New York, 1967.
NicPNicChFath	*A Select Library of the Nicene and Post-Nicene Fathers.* Edited by P. Schaff, 14 vols. New York, 1866–1900. Second series, edited by P. Schaff and H. Wace, 1890–1900.
PG	*Patrologia graeca.* Edited by J. P. Migne. 161 vols. Paris, 1857–66.
PL	*Patrologia latina.* Edited by J. P. Migne, 217 vols; indexes, 4 vols. Paris, 1878–90.
RechScRel	*Recherches de science religieuse.* Paris, 1910–.
RechThMed	*Recherches de théologie ancienne et médiévale.* Louvain, 1929–.
RHE	*Revue d'histoire ecclésiastique.* Louvain, 1900–.
SBMünch	*Sitzungsberichte der Bayerischen akademie der Wissenschaften zu München.* Munich, 1860–.
SpicSacLov	*Spicilegium sacrum lovaniense.* Louvain, 1922–.
ThSt	*Theological Studies.* Woodstock, Md., 1940–.
ZTheolKirch	*Zeitschrift für Theologie und Kirche.* Tübingen, 1891–.

General Editors' Foreword

There is perhaps no more striking illustration of the situation of Christian doctrine today than the status of the dogma of the Trinity. The formulation of this dogma was the most important theological achievement of the first five centuries of the Church. It provided the conceptual framework and the vocabulary for the other major development of that period, the dogma of the person of Christ. Augustine, despite his historic significance for the doctrine of grace, entitled his masterpiece of speculative theology *De Trinitate*. Yet this monumental dogma, celebrated in the liturgy by the recitation of the Nicene Creed, seems to many even within the Church to be a museum piece, with little or no relevance to the crucial problems of contemporary life and thought. And to those outside the Church, the trinitarian dogma is a fine illustration of the absurd lengths to which theology has been carried, a bizarre formula of 'sacred arithmetic.'

The Triune God is an effort to probe the depths of this situation, both the meaning of the traditional doctrine and the reasons for its current predicament. On the basis of a careful analysis of the language of the Bible, it shows that although there is no single passage of Scripture setting forth the entire doctrine, it was the intent of the early creeds and councils to pull together the teaching of the New Testament (and, through it, of the Old Testament) about the mystery of the one God. Here it becomes clear that, far from being the cryptopolytheism it is often called, the trinitarian dogma was a way of preserving the confession of the oneness of God and yet of saying about Jesus Christ and the Holy Spirit what Christian experience and faith obliged the Church to say. Refusing to be put off by the Hellenized terminology of *ousia* and *hypostasis*, the author expounds the quite un-Hellenized motif of the terminology: the central reality of Christian revelation, that the God who has come in Christ to save the world is the Lord of heaven and earth.

But *The Triune God* is content neither with a Biblical-historical study nor with a summary of the traditional teaching. Instead, Father Fortman looks squarely at the obstacles to trinitarian theology today and shows why it is impossible simply to repeat conventional dogmatic language, if the trinitarian message is to be presented intelligibly to contemporary men. Although he is well aware of the hazards in any attempt at modern restatement, he shows himself willing to take the necessary risk of pressing for an objectively adequate reformulation that will be more meaningful today. Critical readers will not unanimously accept his proposals, but they will find themselves obliged to think about the problem of the Trinity with a new sense of urgency. Those who have been satisfied with the *status quo* will have their contentment shaken, and those who have felt able to dismiss the orthodox tradition can take a fresh look at it and can learn from it. Orthodoxy and relevance need not be set in opposition, as the facile but shallow advocates of each would often have us believe, but they must be combined if either is to be achieved. *The Triune God* is a serious and responsible effort at such a combination.

J.P.W.
J.P.

Introduction

The aim of this book is simple—to trace the historical development of trinitarian doctrine from its written beginnings to its contemporary status among Protestant, Orthodox and Catholic theologians. As a Catholic and a firm believer in the Triune God my belief will inevitably affect to some extent my selection, interpretation and presentation of the documents and writings that manifest the historical development of this doctrine, but hopefully it will not substantially distort these. This is not an exhaustive and definitive study but it is meant to be more than a superficial survey, and it is hoped it may stimulate other fuller studies.

The doctrine of the Triune God has had an amazing history. Convinced that this doctrine is a Christian doctrine that did and could originate only from divine revelation, I start the study from the authentic record of divine revelation that is found in the sacred writings of the Old and New Testaments.

What does the Old Testament tell us of God? It tells us there is one God, a wonderful God of life and love and righteousness and power and glory and mystery, who is the creator and lord of the whole universe, who is intensely concerned with the tiny people of Israel. It tells us of His Word, Wisdom, Spirit, of the Messiah He will send, of a Son of Man and a Suffering Servant to come. But it tells us nothing explicitly or by necessary implication of a Triune God who is Father, Son and Holy Spirit.

If we take the New Testament writers together they tell us there is only one God, the creator and lord of the universe, who is the Father of Jesus. They call Jesus the Son of God, Messiah, Lord, Savior, Word, Wisdom. They assign Him the divine functions of creation, salvation, judgment. Sometimes they call Him God explicitly. They do not speak as fully and clearly of the Holy Spirit as they do of the Son, but at times they coordinate Him with the Father and the Son and put Him on a level with them as far as divinity and personality are concerned. They give us in their writings a triadic ground plan and triadic formulas. They do not speak in abstract terms of nature, substance, person, relation, circumincession, mission, but they present in their own ways the ideas that are behind these terms. They give us no formal or formulated doctrine of the Trinity, no explicit teaching that in one God there are three co-equal divine persons. But they do give us an elemental trinitarianism, the data from which such a formal doctrine of the Triune God may be formulated.

To study the gradual transition from an unformulated Biblical witness to the Father, Son and Holy Spirit to a dogmatic formulation of a doctrine of the Triune God, we look first to the Eastern Church where most of this development took place.

The Apostolic Fathers were witnesses to the Biblical data and the traditional faith rather than theologians, but they furnished useful insights into the lines along which the Church's unconscious theology was developing. Most of them indicated quite clearly a belief in the divinity of Christ, less clearly a belief in the distinct personality and divinity of the Holy Spirit. They gave solid evidence of a belief in three pre-existent 'beings,' but they furnished no trinitarian doctrine, no awareness of a trinitarian problem.

The Apologists were, in a sense, the Church's first theologians: the first to attempt a sketch of trinitarian doctrine and an intellectually satisfying explanation of Christ's relation to God the Father. To set forth the truths handed down to them from the Apostles they used the terminology and philosophy that were then current, and in the process they christianized Hellenism to some extent. They manifested a belief in the unity of God and in some sort of 'trinity of divinity,' even though they had as yet no distinct conception of 'divine person' and 'divine nature.' They identified Christ with God, with the Logos, with the Son of God, but they seemed to count His Sonship not from eternity but from the moment of his pre-creational generation. In thus using a two-stage theory of a pre-existent Logos to explain the Son's divine status and His relation to the Father, they probably did not realize that this theory had a built-in 'inferiorizing principle' that would win for them the accusation of 'subordinationism.'

Origen, the greatest theologian of the East, rejected this two-stage theory and maintained the eternal generation of the Son. But to reconcile the eternity of the Son with a strict monotheism, he resorted to a Platonic hierarchical framework for the Father, Son and Holy Spirit, and ended up by also making the Son and Holy Spirit not precisely creatures but 'diminished gods.'

Thus two currents of thought and belief began to stand out. One read the Biblical witness to God as affirming that Father, Son and Holy Spirit are three who are equally God and somehow one God. The other read the Biblical witness differently and concluded that Christ, although divine to some extent, was not equal to the Father in divinity but somehow an 'inferior god.'

This set the stage for Arius, one of the pivotal figures in the development of trinitarian dogma. The idea of a 'diminished god' he found repugnant. Christ, he declared, must be either God or creature. But since God is and must be uncreated, unoriginated, unbegotten, and the Son is and must be originated and begotten, He cannot be God but must be a creature. And thus the subordinationist tendency in the Apologists and Origen reached full term.

Now the Church had to make its faith and its position clear, and it did this at the Council of Nicea in 325, the first ecumenical council. There it rejected Arius' doctrine that the Son is not true God but is a creature, and declared solemnly: 'We believe . . . that Jesus Christ is the Son of God, born of the Father, i.e., of the substance of the Father, true God from true God; begotten not created, consubstantial with the Father; through him all things were made.'

The significance of the Nicene definition is obvious. It gave a definitive answer to a question of vital importance for the Christian faith of the Church. It did not describe, it defined. It defined what the Son is in Himself and in His relation to the one God, the Father. And it defined this, 'not in the empirical categories of experience, not in the relational category of presence, not even in the dynamic categories of power and function, but in the ontological category of substance, which is a category of being.' By doing this it 'sanctioned the principle of development of doctrine, of growth in understanding of the primitive affirmations contained in the New Testament revelation.'

Arianism had received its dogmatic deathblow but it did not die immediately. Many years would pass before the Nicene symbol would be fully accepted. Shortly after Nicea a powerful Anti-Nicene group developed which for years refused to accept the *homoousion* as the test of orthodoxy. Against these Anti-Nicenes a smaller group, headed by Athanasius, battled tenaciously for the Nicene *homoousion* and put forth a sound trinitarian doctrine. But this doctrine left unsolved many questions about the divine persons, their definition and distinction and relation to one another and to the godhead.

The Cappadocians to some extent answered many of these questions. They built their doctrine mainly on the data of Scripture as Athanasius had done, but they made a greater use of philosophy to refute Arian rationalism. They chose hypostasis as the word best fitted to express the idea of person, and made 'one ousia in three hypostases' their formula for expressing God's triunity. They not only affirmed the Holy Spirit's divinity but even explicitly called Him God. They made the trinity of hypostases their methodical starting point and so thoroughly established the identity of substance for Father, Son and Holy Spirit, that they practically put an end to subordinationism. They differentiated the three hypostases metaphysically in terms of cause, relation, modes of existence, and tried to differentiate the Son's origination as image of the Father from the Holy Spirit's origination as breath of the Father. They attempted to answer the perplexing question how God can be at once objectively one and three, in terms of 'relation of cause and caused' and 'modes of being' but they seemed hardly aware of the question why there were only three hypostases in God. They made great contributions, both terminological and doctrinal, to the development of trinitarian theology; they laid down many, if not most, of the main lines of later trinitarian theology and helped give Eastern trinitarian theology the approach and method it was to use for a long, long time. But a great deal of dogmatic and theological development was still to come.

The Council of Nicea had merely declared, 'And we believe in the Holy Spirit.' It had thus implied the divinity of the Holy Spirit. The Creed that came out of the Council of Constantinople in 381 made this declaration of the Holy Spirit's divinity much more explicit by adding, 'the Lord and Giver of Life, who proceeds from the Father, who together with the Father and Son is adored and glorified, who spoke through the prophets.' And thus another step was taken toward the formulation of the dogma of the Trinity.

In the 8th century John of Damascus magnificently summed up the trinitarian doctrine of his great predecessors but did not greatly deepen or amplify it. In the 9th century Photius became the most famous opponent of what he called the *Filioque* 'innovation of some Latins,' and stirred up a bitter controversy between East and West that would provoke an endless theological literature out of all proportion to the matter itself. But it was the Cappadocians who brought Greek trinitarian doctrine to its highest point of speculative development.

Turning to the Western Church we find a modest beginning of trinitarian doctrine in 1 Clement and Hermas and a more developed doctrine in Justin. Irenaeus, 'the most important of the second century theologians,' although he abstained from speculation and developed no technical language and formulas, still made a significant contribution to Western trinitarian theology by his careful presentation and defence of the traditional doctrine that there is one God the Creator and Lord of all, who is Father, Son and Holy Spirit.

Tertullian, who has been called the 'founder of theology in the West,' went beyond Irenaeus in many respects. He was the first in the West to use the word *trinity* and he indicated clearly enough that the 'trinity of one divinity' was not just an economic trinity but also an immanent trinity. He was perhaps the first to stress the term *person* and to understand it in the metaphysical sense of a concrete individual, a self. When he affirmed that the three are 'one in substance' he seemed to understand by 'divine substance' a rarefied form of spiritual matter. Tertullian was guilty of serious doctrinal defects but his theological contribution outstripped these.

The Churches of Lyons and Africa, through Irenaeus and Tertullian, made great contributions to Western trinitarian doctrine. The early Church of Rome made no such great contributions. It fostered no great school like that of Alexandria, and it produced no theologian to rank with Origen or the Cappadocians nor even with Irenaeus and Tertullian. Two anti-popes, Hippolytus and Novatian, wrote vigorously against modalistic trinitarianism. Pope Dionysius in the 3rd century condemned Sabellianism and Tritheism and even Arianism by anticipation and he clearly affirmed the divine trinity and unity as the authentic teaching of Scripture and tradition. Pope Damasus in the 4th century put forth a solid trinitarian doctrine in full accord with the Creeds of Nicea and Constantinople. Thus already in the 3rd and 4th centuries Roman bishops felt quite competent to present traditional trinitarian doctrine authoritatively and to condemn bluntly errors opposed to it.

In the 4th century the outstanding names in trinitarian theology were two bishops, Hilary of Poitiers and Ambrose of Milan, and a layman, Marius Victorinus. Hilary, 'the Athanasius of the West,' wrote twelve books on the Trinity which have been regarded as one of the finest products of the Arian controversy. Victorinus, by his effort to present the Trinity 'in the more general categories of ontology,' showed 'himself to be the precursor, not only of St. Augustine, but of the boldest schoolmen.' Ambrose was, after Hilary, the most important opponent of Arianism and Macedonianism.

It was Augustine, however, 'the greatest doctor of the Church,'

who 'gave the Western tradition its mature and final expression,'
so that 'what Origen had been for the scientific theology of the 3rd
and 4th centuries, Augustine became in a much purer and more
profitable way for the whole life of the Church of the following
centuries until modern times.' In the fifteen books of his magnificent
De Trinitate he was at once thoroughly traditional and intensely
personal. Where the Greeks, in starting from the trinity of persons
and moving to the unity of nature, had faced the danger of Subordinationism, Augustine took a different approach that immediately
eliminated Subordinationism and Tritheism but laid him open to
the danger of Modalism. Instead of starting from the Father, considered as the source of the other two persons, he began with the
one simple divine essence that is the Trinity. This new approach
would dominate nearly all subsequent Western trinitarian teaching.
There can be little doubt that Augustine produced a more comprehensive and stimulating synthesis of trinitarian doctrine than anyone else before him in the West or East. He summed up the work of
his predecessors and laid the foundation for subsequent trinitarian
theology in the West. But Augustine's theology left many questions
unanswered: What is the nature of the two processions? How do
they differ? Why are there only two processions and only three
persons? These questions would fascinate theologians down the
centuries, and would find a full if extremely rarefied metaphysical
answer only in the writings of Thomas Aquinas.

A very important document of the 5th–6th centuries is the so-
called 'Athanasian Creed.' Nowhere else previously can we encounter a formula so balanced, so precise, so elaborate and so ingeniously
contrived. What is most amazing is the way in which this 'Creed'
achieved dogmatic value in the Western Church equal to that of the
Apostles' and Nicene Creeds, and then retained this value even after
it was realized that there was no certainty about its author or date
or birthplace. Even in recent dogmatic manuals in the West it was
treated as a dogmatic formula of 'divine and catholic faith.'

Between Augustine in the 5th century and Anselm in the 12th,
two men stood out for their trinitarian contributions, Boethius
(d. 524) and Eriugena (d. 877 *c*.). Boethius was the first to use Aristotelian philosophy in the analysis, definition and explanation of
trinitarian and christological data, and he thus laid a foundation on
which Scholastics would erect their more systematic expositions.
But he is best known for his definition of 'person,' a definition that
would be widely adopted, highly praised, strongly criticized and
would lead some of its adherents into heretical deviations. Eriugena
produced a bold and original philosophical-theological synthesis

that led some interpreters to charge him with pantheism, others with rationalism.

When we come to the Middle Ages we meet that remarkable group of men called 'Scholastics,' who were intent on producing a harmonious and systematic union of revelation and reason, of faith and knowledge, of the Word of God and the words of men. There were many important trinitarian writers in the 12th century. One, Anselm of Canterbury, was one of the West's most original thinkers and applied dialectic to Augustinian premises. Two, Abelard and Gilbert de la Porrée, were 'liberals' who ran foul of Bernard of Clairvaux, a strong 'traditionalist.' Two, Hugh and Richard of St. Victor, tried to 'demonstrate' the Trinity. Two, Peter Lombard and Joachim of Flora, battled over a divine 'quaternity.'

In the 13th century Dominicans and Franciscans made the greatest contributions to trinitarian systematization that the Western Church would ever see. Four men stood out, Thomas Aquinas, Alexander of Hales, Bonaventure, Duns Scotus, and the greatest of these by far was Aquinas. Augustine had left many trinitarian questions unanswered. One of these was: Why are there two and only two processions in God? Aquinas answered that the divine processions are grounded in immanent actions, and since there are only two of these in God, understanding and willing, only two processions are possible, that of the Word and that of Love. Augustine had found it impossible to say why the Second Person is generated but the Third Person is not. Thomas answered that the Second Person proceeds by way of intelligible action which is a likeness-producing operation and thus is generation, but the Third Person proceeds by way of dilection which is not a likeness-producing operation and hence is not generation. Augustine had not been able to give a clear-cut intrinsic reason why there are only three persons in God. Thomas suggested that there are only three persons because there are only two productive processions, of Word and Love, and hence only three distinct, subsistent, incommunicable relations—paternity, filiation and passive spiration. Scotus, in his synthesis of Hales and Bonaventure, gave a slightly different solution. There are only two processions, he said, because there are only two divine ways of producing, by way of nature and by way of will. Since only the production of the Word is by way of nature, only this is generation. With Aquinas and Scotus we have reached the high point of speculative trinitarian theology. Both the Thomist and the Scotist syntheses will find devoted, tenacious and disputatious followers and perdure down the years. Today both syntheses are in almost total eclipse.

There were three great trinitarian councils in the 13th and 15th centuries, Lateran IV, Lyons II and Florence. Lateran IV in 1215 was the first ecumenical council to define that the Holy Spirit proceeds from both the Father and the Son, and in its trinitarian declarations it went well beyond Nicea I and Constantinople I. It explicitly affirmed the consubstantiality, co-eternity, co-equality, co-omnipotence of the three Persons, their distinction from one another and their identity of nature, and it explicitly rejected a quaternity in God. Lyons II, an ecumenical and reunion council in 1274, went somewhat beyond Lateran IV, for it not only explicitly affirmed the *Filioque* but added that the Holy Spirit proceeds from the Father and Son as from one principle and by one spiration, and that this has always been the teaching of the Roman Church and the true judgment of both Greek and Latin orthodox Fathers and Doctors. In the 15th century Florence, another ecumenical and reunion council, amplified the declarations of Lateran IV and Lyons II by declaring that the patristic doctrine of the procession of the Holy Spirit from the Father through the Son is substantially equivalent to the *Filioque*; by defining that the *Filioque* had been lawfully added to the Creed; and by declaring that in God everything is one where opposition of relation does not intervene. This last point is extremely important for it represented the explicational climax of a long patristic and theological reflection on the root of distinction in the one simple God. With this Council the Church's solemn formulation of its trinitarian faith had now reached its climax.

In 1453 the great schism between the Latin and the Orthodox Churches became permanent. In the 16th century the Protestant Reformation brought about another break-away from the Roman Catholic Church. From then on we have three currents of ecclesial, religious, theological life, one Protestant, one Orthodox, one Roman Catholic.

The trinitarian doctrine of the Reformers was that of the early Church and the traditional Creeds, that God is one in essence and three in person. In the 17th century Protestant theologians began to take different attitudes toward traditional trinitarian doctrine. In Europe some opted for Scholasticism and its systematic theology, some for Pietism and its stress on spiritual experience, some for Socinianism and its rejection of the Trinity. In England some chose Deism and its naturalistic opposition to revealed religion. The 18th century was the Age of Enlightenment, with naturalism as its ideal and rationalism as its method. Kant, by his *Critiques*, put an end to the Enlightenment; he rejected both orthodox and rationalist views of religion, regarded the doctrine of the Trinity as of no practical value, and opened the way to the modern theological mood. The 19th century offered Protestants new options: Schleiermacher's theology of experience, Hegel's idealistic theology, and the Ritschl-Harnack liberal theology that rejected the whole metaphysical background of ecclesial Christology and cut away the Hellenistic overlay to reach the simple essence of Christianity. The 20th century has produced strong theological protests against the theologies of Schleiermacher, Hegel and the Liberals. But it has also produced notable developments of its own, especially in the areas of Biblical criticism and existential philosophy, which have deeply affected theological reflection on traditional trinitarian doctrine. The most eminent trinitarian theologians in this century are Karl Barth, Emil Brunner, Rudolf Bultmann and Paul Tillich, who all drew on the lonely genius of 19th-century Søren Kierkegaard.

Of the *De Fide Orthodoxa* of John of Damascus, an Orthodox theologian wrote recently that it 'has remained the summation of Greek theology, to which nothing was added and in which little change was made in subsequent centuries.' The great schism between the Orthodox East and the Catholic West still continues. Orthodox opposition to the *Filioque* was interrupted briefly at the reunion Councils of Lyons II in 1274 and Florence in 1439. In the 18th and 19th centuries there were two attempts to effect a union between the Orthodox East and Western Protestants, and one effort to restore communion between Rome and the East. Today, Orthodox trinitarianism is substantially the doctrine of the great Greek Fathers and of the first seven Ecumenical Councils, with the addition of Photianism and Palamism. Anthimus VII, the Orthodox Patriarch, wrote to Pope Leo XIII that it is the *Filioque*, both as doctrine and as addition to the Creed, that really divides the two Churches in trinitarian doctrine. Must it always? Does the Triune God they both love want this fraternal division to continue?

When we look at Roman Catholic trinitarian doctrine since the Council of Florence, the only notable dogmatic contribution that we encounter is Vatican I's definition of mysteries. But there were many interesting theological developments. Some theologians sought new ways of discerning the New Testament revelation of the Trinity, ways that led them to an elemental rather than a formal trinitarianism. In the matter of the divine processions some theologians assigned the psychological analogy little or no value as an index of the inner reality of the Triune God and thus approached agreement with modern Orthodoxy on this point. Most theologians still seemed to think that although the word *person* was not ideal today, since today 'person' means a 'center of consciousness,' yet the word should be retained since 'no other word . . . would be really better, more generally understandable and less exposed to misconceptions.' The most attractive trinitarian topic became the indwelling of the three, and the question of the just man's special relation to each of the divine persons. While the basic trinitarian dogmas are still substantially accepted, some theologians feel they need a reappraisal. For they see problems everywhere and tensions: tensions between the outlook of the Biblical writer and that of the trinitarian theologian; tensions between the rigid Hellenic thought patterns of trinitarian theology and the much more relevant thought patterns of modern philosophy and psychology with their heavy stress on function and evolution, and process and relativity and contingency; tensions between the old ontological view of person in trinitarian theology and the modern psychological view of the human person as always in process of becoming more fully an authentic person; tensions between the classical, metaphysical, 'dead' way of presenting the doctrine of the Trinity and the modern tendency to see value only in knowledge that is 'alive' and immediately relevant to modern man's way of thinking and living. That 'Catholic theology at present is at a critical juncture' is widely admitted.

But this is not the first time the Church has been in tension. It was in extreme tension at the time of Arius, and under the inspiration of the Holy Spirit it started at Nicea to formulate the doctrine of the Trinity. That same Holy Spirit is just as much alive today and just as capable of inspiring and directing whatever reformulation and re-expression He may consider necessary to meet the needs of the people of God today and tomorrow.

Preface

The Catholic faith is this, that we worship one God in Trinity and Trinity in unity, neither confounding the persons nor dividing the Substance. . . . The Father and the Son and the Holy Spirit have one divinity, equal glory, and coeternal majesty. . . . The Father is not made by anyone, or created by anyone, or generated by anyone. The Son is not made or created, but he is generated by the Father alone. The Holy Spirit is not made or created or generated, but proceeds from the Father and the Son. . . . The entire three persons are coeternal and coequal with one another, so that . . . we worship complete unity in the Trinity and the Trinity in unity (Denz 75).

This is the way a Creed long ago proclaimed the faith of Christians. This faith is at the center of Christian life, for Christ without a Triune God is only 'a noisy gong or a clanging cymbal' (1 Cor 13.1). From earliest times this faith in the Triune God permeated the Christian's sacramental and liturgical life. The early martyrs confessed it with their blood. The driving thrust of the Christian's hope for eternal life is to 'see clearly the Triune God himself, just as he is' (Denz 1305).

The doctrine of the Triune God is mysterious in its origin and its content. It deals with the supreme truth and reality revealed to men by 'the only Son, who is in the bosom of the Father' (Jn 1.18). It is a doctrine that revolves about a mystery that has fascinated and challenged the minds of men down the centuries. The New Testament writers first expressed it in their own inspired and distinctive ways. Then Fathers of the Church, councils, bishops, popes studied, formulated, and transmitted it. Theologians pondered,

developed, and systematized it. Men rose up to proclaim it, to distort it, to deny it, to accept it, to live by it. Today it is being challenged by many as unintelligible and irrelevant to modern man in
its traditional formulation and presentation.

This doctrine has had an amazing history. And it is the aim of
this book to deal with this history, to set forth the origin and development of this doctrine and its present status, and to indicate to
some extent the impact of this doctrine on believers and unbelievers
through the years, as well as today. To do this we will first look at
the Biblical witness to God in the Old Testament and the New Testament, then at the witness of the early Church in the East and in the
West, then at the development of trinitarian thought and trinitarian
controversy in the Middle Ages, at the time of the Reformation, and
in modern and contemporary times. A fuller outline of this procedure will be found in the *Contents*.

PART ONE

The Biblical
Witness to God

An eminent historian of the dogma of the Trinity has said that 'what
he has looked for in the inspired books of both Testaments is not
the rule of our faith, but the expression of the faith of their authors;
the excerpts are not quoted as if they were juridical texts to decide
a debate, but as historical documents to mark the development of a
doctrine.'[1] Our purpose is substantially the same. We do not intend
to seek in the Old Testament and in the New Testament what is not
there, a formal statement of trinitarian doctrine. Our aim is to
gather together the Biblical concepts that lie behind the doctrine of
the Trinity and to find what the sacred writers say and imply about
God that could lay the foundations for a later formulation of the
doctrine of the Triune God. From the Biblical writings we plan to
select what seems most relevant and important for our purpose and
to evaluate this as objectively as possible.

CHAPTER ONE

The Old Testament
Witness to God

The Old Testament writers tell us a great deal about God. For them He is the living God and the giver of life, all powerful, eternal, transcendent. He is the one and only God, the creator and lord of the whole universe and all its peoples, the Holy One *par excellence*. Glory is the radiance of His mysterious holiness, His hidden divinity (Gen 17.1; Dt 4.35; Is 5.24, 6.3, 40.22–30; Jer 10.10, 38.16; Mal 3.6). He is present everywhere (Ps 139.7–12). To Israel, however, He is specially present. He has chosen Israel to be His people and He has a special predilection for Israel. He is their God and they are His people, and with them He has made an everlasting covenant (Ex 19.3–5; Dt 7.6–8; Is 54.9–10; Jer 31.31–34). His amazing choice of Israel is not grounded in anything that Israel has or was but in His free and unlimited love (Dt 7.6–8). As He saved Israel in the exodus so He will save Israel in the future, by a messianic salvation that will be eternal (Is 45.17) and will mean a new Israel and a new world.

He has many names, El and Elohim, Shaddai and Adonai, but His proper name is Yahweh, for He is the great 'I am,' the one who causes everything to be (Gen 4.26, 17.1, 33.20, 49.25; Ex 3.13–16; Mal 3.1). This God of the Old Testament is a wonderful God, a God of life, love, wisdom, holiness, and righteousness, a God both immanent and transcendent, a God of power, glory, and majesty. But most of all He is a God of mystery.

PATERNITY AND FILIATION

The title 'Father' is found in many cults of the Gentile world, in Indian religion, in traditional Greek religion, in the mystery reli-

gions. Complementary to this belief that God is Father is the belief
that there are sons of God.

'Father' is not a common title of God in the Old Testament, but
it occurs in many writings and at different stages of Hebrew history.
At times God is called Father because He is the creator (Dt 32.6), at
times because of His mercy (Ps 103.13). Usually He is called the
Father of Israel (Jer 31.9), of the nation collectively (Ex 4.22).
Hosea stresses His fatherly love for Israel (11.1, 3, 4). He is also
described as Father of the king (2 Sam 7.14) and sometimes of
Israelites taken singly (Mal 2.10).

At first the 'son of God,' the 'first-born' of God, is the people as
a whole, for God has freely chosen Israel to be His son, the object
of His paternal care and providence. This communal perspective
continues until toward the dawn of the Christian era, when the
divine paternity is focused more on the individual person (Mal 2.10).
It is uncertain whether 'son of God' was used of the Messiah before
the time of Jesus. It was if Ps 2.7 is messianic. Not too long ago
some exegetes saw insinuations of a strictly divine filiation in Is 9.6
and Ps 2.7. More recent scholars find no evidence in the Old Testament that any sacred writer believed in or suspected the existence
of a divine paternity and filiation within the Godhead itself.

WORD

An important aspect of God in the Old Testament is His 'word.'
We meet the divine utterance at the very beginning of the Old Testa-
ment, and again at the deluge, at the call of Abraham, Moses, and
Samuel, at the election of Saul and David. It comes to the prophet
(Gen 1:3, 6.7, 12.1; Ex 3; I Sam 3.1–14, 9.17, 16.12; Ezek 1.3).

The word of Yahweh effects what it signifies: 'so shall my word
be that goes forth from my mouth; it shall not return to me empty,
but it shall accomplish that which I purpose' (Is 55.11).[1] The word
of Yahweh is a creative agent, and it is fulfilled in the visible creation that results from it (Genesis ch. 1). Nature as well as history is
a word that reveals Yahweh who speaks it, but the word of Yahweh
is also the written law. 'By His Word Yahweh lighted the way for
His people, marked out their path, indicated His will to them, gave
them the meaning of their past history and set the direction for the
future.'[2]

In one remarkable passage: 'For while peaceful silence en-
wrapped all things, and night in her own swiftness was in mid-course,
thine all-powerful word leaped into the midst of the doomed land,
bearing as a sharp sword thine unfeigned commandment' (Wis

18.15–16), there is such a vivid personification of the Logos that some interpreters suppose that the Logos is here hypostatized as in Philo and John. This supposition is unwarranted. The most that can be said is that 'although it is impossible to speak of any hypostasis of the word in the canonical books of the Old Testament, it must be recognized that many of the affirmations point in that direction.'[3] Nowhere in the Old Testament is there any solid evidence that a sacred writer viewed the word of Yahweh as a personal being distinct from Yahweh, and thus had intimations of plurality within the Godhead. The word of Yahweh is only Yahweh acting, or the means by which He revealed His will to men.

WISDOM

There is a famous passage in the book of Proverbs that represents wisdom as a child playing in front of its father and lord: 'The Lord created me at the beginning of his work. . . . Ages ago I was set up. . . . When there were no depths I was brought forth. . . . I was beside him . . . rejoicing before him always . . . and delighting in the sons of men' (8.22–31). It has been much discussed down the centuries. Jewish speculation saw in it the affirmation of the pre-existence of the Law, which was easily identified with the wisdom of God. Paul applied it to the Son of God. The Apologists used it to prove to Gentile and Jew the pre-existence of the Word and His role in creation. The Arians found in it a strong argument to show that Christ was but a creature.[4]

In the Wisdom literature of the Old Testament wisdom is a very complex concept. Wisdom 'came out of the mouth of the Most High, the first born before all creatures' (Sir 24.5). It has been created before all things' (Sir 1.4) and 'reaches from end to end mightily and orders all things sweetly' (Wis 8.1). Wisdom is 'the brightness of eternal light' (Wis 7.26), 'a breath of the power of God, a clear effluence of the glory of the Almighty . . . and an image of His goodness' (Wis 7.25–26), the 'worker of all things' (Wis 7.21).

If we ask what wisdom is in itself, it can seem that wisdom is a person, a conscious agent. For wisdom can do all things, orders all things, chooses among the works of God, praises and glorifies itself, guides men with instruction and advice and leads the Chosen People with powerful and kindly solicitude (Wis 7.27, 8.1, 4; Sir 24.1, 2; Wisdom, ch. 10–11). The people of the Old Testament, however, did not see wisdom as a person to be addressed. Today scholars agree with them and see in wisdom only God's own activity,[5] or an attribute of God,⁶ or just a personification,⁷ or an extension of the divine personality that suggests there is plurality in the Godhead.⁸

SPIRIT

Spirit in the Old Testament was originally wind and breath. To the ancient Israelite it meant the breath of life, and since Yahweh was the living God and the giver of life He was called spirit. And just as the wind and the breath of life can transform earth and flesh, so the spirit of Yahweh can animate man's spirit and give him new knowledge and energy.

The spirit of Yahweh has many functions. It is a creative force and a spirit of judgment (Job 33.4; Is 4.4). It is Yahweh's saving power and His all-pervading presence (Zech 4.6; Ps 139.7). The spirit of Yahweh is a charismatic spirit imparted to judges, to kings, to the messianic king, to the servant of Yahweh (Jg 3.10; 1 Sam 11.6; Is 11.2, 42.1). It is a passing charisma in the judges and in Saul but it reposes permanently upon David and the messianic king (1 Sam 11.6, 16.13; Is 11.2). It renews man inwardly (Ezek 36.26). It is a prophetic spirit, and the true instruments of the spirit were the prophets. To Amos, Hosea, Isaiah, and Jeremiah the spirit brought God's word and gave light to understand it and strength to proclaim it. 'By His Spirit . . . He infiltrated hearts in order to transform them, to open them up to His word.'⁹

At times the spirit of Yahweh seems linked with the Messiah: 'And the Spirit of the Lord shall rest upon him, the spirit of wisdom and understanding. . . .' (Is 11.2). In the messianic age there will be a special outpouring of the prophetic spirit upon the whole people: 'And it shall come to pass afterward, that I will pour out my spirit on all flesh; your sons and your daughters shall prophesy, your old men shall dream dreams, and your young men shall see visions' (Jl 2.28).

The spirit of Yahweh was often described in personal terms. The spirit was grieved, guided men, instructed them, caused them to rest (Ps 143.10; Neh 9.20; Is 63.10, 14). But it seems quite clear that the Jews never regarded the spirit as a person; nor is there any solid evidence that any Old Testament writer held this view. A few scholars today maintain, however, that even though the spirit is usually presented as an impersonal divine force, there is an underlying assumption that the spirit was a conscious agent, which 'provided a climate in which plurality within the Godhead was conceivable.'¹⁰

MESSIAH

Side by side with the doctrines of word, wisdom, and spirit there developed an expectation of the coming of a messianic age and a Messiah that would tie in intimately with the definitive establishment of the kingdom of God on earth in the final age of the world. The Old Testament writers saw the beginnings of this messianic expectation in the promises made by the Lord in the garden of Eden and later to Abraham and the other Patriarchs, and then in the Sinaitic covenant (Gen 3.15, 12.1–3, 26.2–5, 24, 28.1–4; Ex 19.3–6). They expressed its development in the Royal Psalms (2; 20; 21; 45; 72; 89; 101; 110), and in the pre-exilic, exilic, and post-exilic prophets (Is 6–9; Mic 5.1–5; Jer 23.5–8; Ezek 34.23, 37.24–28; Zech 6.9–15).

Thus there was a gradual development of the idea of a messianic kingdom of the future to be established by Yahweh in Israel and to be extended to all men. Salvation would be achieved only through the intervention of Yahweh, peace only through submission to the will of Yahweh. The messianic hope was based on the unshakable conviction that Yahweh would make good His promises to His people, establish His rule on earth, confirm Israel in well-being, and bring His and her enemies to their knees. In this messianic expectation there were two principal elements, the messianic kingdom and the Messiah as a person. But the contemporaries of Christ, while expecting a personal Messiah, seem to have been more concerned with the establishment of the messianic kingdom.

In spite of the name the messianic expectation did not always include the idea of a Messiah, a future king or deliverer. At times there was Messianism without a Messiah; at times the whole nation was pictured in the role of a Messiah mediating blessings to all the world. In a whole series of writings that speak of the messianic expectation (Daniel; 1 and 2 Maccabees; Tobias; Wisdom; Judith; Sirach) the Messiah does not appear. In other writings the Messiah occupies only a secondary place.[11] If the Messiah was commonly regarded as initiating the end of days, it was really Yahweh in His majesty and power who effectively caused salvation.

The most widespread idea about the Messiah was that he would be a king descended from David: 'My servant David shall be king over them . . . for ever' (Ezek 37.24–25). Three passages in the prophetic books seem to give a vivid description of this Davidic ruler. The first says: 'For to us a child is born, to us a son is given; and the government will be upon his shoulder, and his name will be called "Wonderful Counselor, Mighty God, Everlasting Father,

Prince of Peace" ' (Is 9.6). The second passage gives more detail:
'There shall come forth a shoot from the stump of Jesse, and a
branch shall grow out of his roots. And the Spirit of the Lord shall
rest upon him' (Is 11.1–2). The third bids Jerusalem rejoice at the
coming of its king: 'Rejoice greatly, O daughter of Zion . . . Lo, your
king comes to you; triumphant and victorious is he, humble and
riding on an ass, on a colt the foal of an ass' (Zech 9.9).

With this Davidic king Daniel's mysterious 'son of man'
was identified by many Jews: 'behold, with the clouds of heaven
there came one like a son of man . . . that all peoples, nations, and
languages should serve him; his dominion is an everlasting dominion'
(Dan 7.13–14). But the Messiah does not seem to have been identified with the 'suffering Servant of Yahweh' who 'had no form or
comeliness. . . . He was despised and rejected by men; a man of
sorrows . . . he was bruised for our iniquities' (Is 53.2, 3, 5). For to
the Jews this suffering and death were the exact opposite of what
they felt to be characteristic of the Anointed of the Lord.

From all this it seems quite clear that there was no expectation
in Judaism of a divine Messiah. However great the person and work
of the Anointed One were to be, he was certainly to be a creature.
Whether the Jews viewed the Messiah as the pre-existent son of man
or the richly endowed but purely human son of David, they saw in
him only a creature, only Yahweh's administrator, vested with
powers from Him but wholly subordinate to Him. It is in Yahweh
Himself that the messianic kingdom centers.

SUMMARY

To the Old Testament writers God is a God of life, love, wisdom,
and holiness, a God of righteousness, a God both immanent and
transcendent, a God of power, glory, and majesty, the one and only
God, the creator and lord of the universe.

Sometimes they call Him Father, especially of Israel. They give
the title 'son of God' not only to Israel collectively but also to the
king, to the judges, to the upright Jew, and perhaps to the Messiah.
There is no evidence that any sacred writer even suspected the existence of a divine paternity and filiation within the Godhead.

They write of the word of God and regard it as revelatory and
creative, as instructive and illuminative. If at times they seem to
show a slight tendency to hypostatize the word of God, nowhere do
they present the word of God as a personal divine being distinct
from Yahweh.

They write much of the wisdom of God that was 'created before all things' and is the 'worker of all things.' But to the people of the Old Testament the wisdom of God was never a person to be addressed but only a personification of an attribute or activity of Yahweh.

The spirit of Yahweh is a creative force, a saving power, a spirit of judgment, a charismatic spirit, a spirit of life and of inward renewal, a prophetic spirit. Although this spirit is often described in personal terms, it seems quite clear that the sacred writers never conceived or presented this spirit as a distinct person.

Many of the sacred writers spoke of a Messiah who was to be Yahweh's agent in establishing the kingdom of Yahweh in the messianic age. However, they regarded the Messiah not as a divine person but as a creature, a charismatic leader, a Davidic king.

Thus the Old Testament writings about God neither express nor imply any idea of or belief in a plurality or trinity of persons within the one Godhead. Even to see in them suggestions or foreshadowings or 'veiled signs' of the trinity of persons, is to go beyond the words and intent of the sacred writers. Perhaps it can be said that some of these writings about word and wisdom and spirit did provide a climate in which plurality within the Godhead was conceivable to Jews. However, these writers definitely do give us the words that the New Testament uses to express the trinity of persons, Father, Son, Word, Wisdom, Spirit. And their way of understanding these words helps us to see how the revelation of God in the New Testament goes beyond the revelation of God in the Old Testament.

CHAPTER TWO

The New Testament
Witness to God

In the first chapter we studied the writers of the Old Testament and found in them a majestic description of God and His activity, but nothing to indicate that they were aware of a plurality or trinity of persons within the one Godhead. We now turn to the writings of the New Testament, to the Synoptics and Acts, to Paul and John, to study their witness to the living God.

THE SYNOPTICS AND ACTS

The Synoptists give clear witness to a belief in one God (Mk 12.29), who at times is called 'Father' (Mt 5.44–45). This God, who is the Father of men, has a paternal love for them (Mt 6.5–8); but if men are 'sons of the Father who is in heaven,' Jesus is His own Son in a unique sense.

Son of God

There can be no doubt that in the Synoptic Gospels Jesus has a unique relationship with the Father. He speaks of the Father with an intimacy that appears nowhere in the Old Testament. He talks with God in a way that is utterly new and unique, as simply, intimately, securely as a child speaks with his father, and in His prayer He uses the Aramaic word *abba* that was too familiar to be used in Jewish prayer.[1] He speaks differently of the Father in relation to Himself and to His disciples: 'my heavenly Father' and 'your Father who is in heaven' (Mt 15.13; 5.44–45). In Matthew and Luke we hear Him say: 'no one knows the Son except the Father, and no one

10

knows the Father except the Son and any one to whom the Son chooses to reveal him' (Mt 11.27; Lk 10.22). In the Lucan infancy narrative the angel says that Jesus 'will be called the Son of the Most High. . . . holy, the Son of God' (Lk 1.32, 35). In the Synoptic accounts of His baptism a voice from heaven says of Him, 'This is my beloved Son' (Mt 3.17; Mk 1.11; Lk 3.22). In the accounts of His transfiguration a voice out of the cloud says, 'This is my beloved Son' (Mt 17.5; Mk 9.6; Lk 9.35). In the Matthean account of the Petrine confession Peter says of Jesus, 'You are the Christ, the Son of the living God' (Mt 16.16). Mark himself testifies that Jesus is 'the Son of God' (1.1). Thus there can be no doubt that for the Synoptists Jesus' sonship is unique. But what is the nature of this unique sonship?

Some scholars claim that Jesus' sonship is merely messianic, and discern this messianic sonship in the Lucan infancy narrative and in the baptism and transfiguration passages. But in the Matthean account of the Petrine confession the sonship of Jesus is definitely more than a merely messianic sonship, for Peter says 'You are the Christ, the Son of the living God' (Mt 16.16). In Mark's account of Jesus' condemnation the high priest asks: 'Are you the Christ, the Son of the Blessed,' and Jesus answers 'I am; and you will see the Son of Man sitting at the right hand of Power, and coming with the clouds of heaven' (14.61, 62). Here the high priest's question and Jesus' answer signify more than a merely messianic sonship.

At times in the Synoptics this sonship of Jesus involves some subordination of Jesus to the Father. There were things that the Son did not know: 'But of that day or that hour no one knows, not even the angels in heaven, nor the Son, but only the Father' (Mk 13.32). Again in Mark we hear Jesus saying: 'Why do you call me good? No one is good but God alone' (10.18).

In other passages, however, Jesus' sonship is presented as strictly divine. In the parable of the vineyard (Mk 12.1–8; Lk 20.9–16; Mt 21.33–41) Jesus definitely seems to be alluding to His own sonship, and He presents it as a natural sonship and hence by implication as a strictly divine sonship. Again when Jesus talks of the mutual reciprocal knowledge of Father and Son (Mt 11.27; Lk 10.22) it is extremely difficult to see anything else than equality of Son and Father in divine knowledge, and hence by implication the Son's sonship must be strictly divine. In Matthew's account of Jesus' baptismal command, 'baptizing them in the name of the Father and of the Son and of the Holy Spirit' (28.19), the Son is placed on the very same level as the Father and thus by implication His sonship would be as strictly divine as the Father's paternity.

Son of Man

If the title 'Son of God' is rarely used by or applied to Jesus in the
Synoptics and Acts, the title 'Son of Man' is used 70 times and
always by Jesus. In the Old Testament 'Son of Man' commonly
meant an individual man with the emphasis on his weakness in contrast to God's strength. In Daniel (7.13–14) the title is applied to an
apocalyptic figure that represents the messianic kingdom.

In the Synoptics Jesus uses the title in various contexts. In one
the Son of Man will come in glory on the clouds of heaven accompanied by angels (Mt 10.23). In another Jesus the Son of Man has
the power to forgive sins and is lord of the Sabbath (Mt 9.6, 12.8).
In the context of His messianic mission Jesus the Son of Man is 'he
who sows the good seed' (Mt 13.37), who seeks and saves the lost
(Lk 19.10). In the context of His passion and death Jesus the 'Son
of Man is to be betrayed into the hands of men, and they will kill
him; and on the third day he will rise again' (Mt 17.21). Thus in
Jesus two missions are united, the suffering of the Servant of the
Lord and the glory of the Son of Man (Is 53; Dan 7.13–14; Mk 10.45;
Lk 17.24–25). Jesus did not invent the expression 'Son of Man,' but
He did give it a new meaning.

Does the title 'Son of Man' affirm Jesus' divinity? No; but in the
Synoptics Jesus the Son of Man claims the power to forgive sins
and to be lord of the Sabbath. These are more than traditional
messianic powers. Since they were regarded as strictly divine
powers, it seems that Jesus the Son of Man claimed to be endowed
with strictly divine powers.

Lord

The Synoptists only rarely apply the title 'Lord' to Jesus. In Mark
and Matthew the Lord is usually God Himself, as is the case in the
Old Testament. When the title is applied to Jesus it is often only a
courtesy title and means no more than 'Sir,' 'Master.' But if Mk
12.35–37 is a genuine saying of Jesus, then in it Jesus says the
Messiah is not only David's son but also David's Lord, and hence
possesses an authority that is greater than David's.

Acts is fond of the title *kyrios* and applies it both to God the
Father and to Jesus Christ. In his speech in chapter 2, Peter says
that Jesus was made Lord and Christ at His exaltation, and he
quotes for this the words of Ps 110.1, which Jesus Himself had used
in Mk 12.35–37. The title as used by Peter here indicates that Jesus
is now an exalted heavenly Lord, but it does not seem to affirm or
imply that Jesus is God. However, Peter makes a further quotation

from the prophet Joel, and in the final verse of the quotation we read: 'And it shall be, that whosoever shall call on the name of the Lord shall be saved' (Acts 2.21). What does 'Lord' mean here? If in quoting Ps 110.1, which refers to a messianic lordship, Peter and the sacred writer meant to ascribe to the risen Jesus a messianic lordship, it seems quite probable that in quoting Jl 2.32, which refers to a divine lordship, they meant to ascribe to Jesus not merely a messianic lordship but a strictly divine lordship.

There are other indications in Acts that a more than messianic lordship was ascribed to the risen Jesus. In another speech Peter gives Jesus the title 'Lord of all' (10.36). And in Stephen's dying cry we hear: 'Lord Jesus, receive my spirit. . . . Lord, lay not this sin to their charge' (Acts 7.59, 60). For Stephen Jesus was thus more than a merely exalted Messiah; He was the recipient of prayer, a strictly divine Lord.

It has been objected that when Peter says, 'This Jesus God raised up . . . and made both Lord and Christ' (Acts 2.32, 36) he indicates that both the title and the power of 'Lord' are a gift bestowed by God on Jesus in virtue of His resurrection. This is a probable interpretation of what Peter said and meant. But it is also probable that Peter meant that God then 'established' Jesus in the exercise of the lordship that always belonged to Him.[2] In either case the author of Acts tried to indicate the transcendent mystery of Jesus the Lord, who in some ways seemed equal and in other ways subordinate to the Father. And we may well expect that this tension-presentation of the mystery of Jesus will recur in other New Testament writings.

Holy Spirit

The Spirit is encountered less frequently in the Synoptics than in Acts. The Holy Spirit is mentioned prominently in the Lucan infancy account as filling the Baptist 'even from his mother's womb,' as going to 'come upon' Mary, as filling Elizabeth and Zechariah, as revealing to Simeon (Lk 1.15, 35, 41, 67; 2.25–26). The Matthean infancy narrative states that Mary 'was found to be with child by the Holy Spirit' (Mt 1.18). All the Synoptists present the theophany at the baptism of Jesus as a revelation of the Father in a voice, of the Son in the flesh, and of the Spirit in a dove. This theophany of the Spirit has no parallel elsewhere in the inspired writings. Later in the Synoptics we find that Jesus is 'led up by the Spirit into the wilderness' (Mt 4.1), returns 'in the power of the Spirit into Galilee' (Lk 4.14), warns that 'there will be no forgiveness for the man who blasphemes against the Holy Spirit' (Lk 12.10), and after his resurrection gives the baptismal command to 'go . . . baptizing them in the name of the Father and of the Son and of the Holy Spirit' (Mt 28.19).

What is this Holy Spirit? In the Old Testament the spirit of Yahweh was a mysterious divine force that produced peculiar effects on or in men. Rarely in the Synoptics does the Holy Spirit seem to be presented as more than this mysterious divine force. But in the baptismal theophany and at the baptismal command where the Synoptists coordinate the Spirit with the Father and the Son they seem to ascribe to Him a distinct personal existence.

The Spirit dominates the book of Acts. Pentecost marks the opening of the new era of the Holy Spirit. When the Spirit comes upon the disciples, they are empowered to become witnesses of Jesus throughout the world, and their transformation marks the birth of the Church. Under the impetus of the Spirit the disciples leave the Upper Room and boldly preach Christ crucified (4.13, 29). The Spirit sends Peter to the Gentiles (10). Saul, 'filled with the Holy Spirit . . . began to preach that Jesus is the Son of God' (9.17, 20). The Spirit calls men to missionary service (13.2) and gives guidance as to the proper sphere of labor (16.6). Through such phenomena as the gift of tongues and prophecy the Spirit manifests His presence externally (2.4; 4.31).

To one scholar the Spirit in Acts is only 'a dynamic force, the charismatic spirit of the OT, which moves the apostles to preach and witness Jesus and empowers them to feats of courage and eloquence which are entirely beyond the personal capacities of these men as they appear in the Gospels.'[3] To another He is more than this. For in 18 of the 62 references to the Holy Spirit in Acts he finds the Holy Spirit described 'in terms which suggest that he is a person, who speaks (1.16; 8.29), forbids (16.6), thinks good (15.28), appoints (20.28), sends (13.4), bears witness (5.32), snatches (8.39), prevents (16.7), is lied to (5.3), tempted (5.9) and resisted (7.51).' And although most of the other references do not for themselves imply that the Spirit is a person, 'they do not contradict the impression given by the other passages.'[4]

Trinity

Obviously there is no trinitarian doctrine in the Synoptics or Acts. But there are traces of the triadic pattern of Father, Son, and Holy Spirit in both. In Luke there are several such traces: in the infancy narrative (1.35), in the baptismal theophany (3.22) and in the narrative of the temptation (4.1–14). In the beginning of Acts we read of Jesus and 'the Father' and 'the Holy Spirit' (1.1–6). In Peter's speech at Pentecost there is a deliberate presentation of the Three and their activity (2.33; 38–39). And in a few other passages it is possible to see traces of the triadic pattern (9.17–20; 10.38).

In Matthew there are several traces of this threefold pattern. A faint trace seems to be present in the infancy narrative (1.18–23). A clearer trace is evident in the baptismal theophany (3.16–17). The clearest form of this pattern to be found anywhere in the Synoptics is met with in the baptismal command after the resurrection (28.19). Whether these are the very words of Jesus or derive from an early baptismal formula based on the general teaching of Jesus is open to discussion. But it is hard to see how a contemporary interpreter can affirm so categorically that 'this formula was never used by Jesus in his earthly life.'[5] Or how another can say so absolutely, 'This formula has itself no trinitarian doctrinal implication.'[6] Could the evangelist put the Father, Son, and Spirit together in this way without insinuating or implying that for him the Son and Holy Spirit are distinct from the Father and on the same level with the Father, who is obviously God? Can it really be denied that the sacred writer here presents the three as at once a triad and a unity? And if it is true that Matthew's Gospel is a carefully planned Gospel, is it not extremely significant that he puts this triadic formula at the very end of his Gospel, when he might have chosen very different endings? Putting it there would be bound to make it stand out bluntly and indicate that for him it had very great, if not supreme, importance.

Summary

The Synoptics and Acts clearly indicate that there is a unique relationship between Jesus and the Father and that Jesus' sonship transcends other sonships. At times this sonship is presented in such a way that it seems to be really divine and to imply equality with the Father in terms of divine knowledge and power. In the Synoptics Jesus often calls Himself Son of Man, and as Son of Man claims to have divine power to forgive sins and to be lord of the Sabbath. In Acts Jesus is often called Lord, and at times this title implies not only a messianic lordship but a really divine lordship. In Acts as in the Synoptics Jesus is presented sometimes as subordinate to the Father, sometimes as equal to Him in certain divine functions.

The Holy Spirit is usually presented in the Synoptics and in Acts as a divine force or power. But in a few passages the sacred writers leave a vivid impression that for them He was someone distinct from both Father and Son with a distinct personal existence.

In both Synoptics and Acts there are traces of the triadic pattern of Father, Son, and Holy Spirit. The clearest expression of this pattern is found in the baptismal formula where Matthew presents the three together as at once a triad and a unity. But nowhere do we find any trinitarian doctrine of three distinct subjects of divine life and activity in the same Godhead. And when the three are coordinated on the same divine level in a triadic pattern there seems to be no realization of the problem of the relationship between the three and of the three to the same Godhead.

In both the Synoptics and Acts there is a realization that Jesus' tremendous works—His salvific death, resurrection, and exaltation —indicate that He was and always had been more than a mere man and that only divine titles could properly describe Him. But is there in them any clear indication that a community in divine function meant a community of nature between Father and Son, so that they could say explicitly that Jesus is one same God with the Father? It seems not.

PAUL

God the Father

'Grace to you and peace from God our Father and from the Lord Jesus Christ' (Rom 1.7; 1 Cor 1.3) is the salutation with which Paul begins almost all his letters. And under the action of the spirit of Christ the word *abba* (Father) comes spontaneously to the lips of the Christian (Rom 8.15, 29; Gal 4.6).

God the Father is the 'creator of all things' (Eph 3.9) and the author of the salvific plan (1 Cor 1.21). His concern is our 'salvation through our Lord Jesus Christ' (1 Th 5.9). In virtue of His eternal plan He calls us to faith and glory (2 Th 2.13–14). He sent His Son to redeem those under the Law (Gal 4.4) 'that he might be the firstborn among many brethren' (Rom 8.29).

Paul presents God as the Father of all things and of Christian believers. But most often he describes Him as the Father of Jesus Christ, so that his readers will begin to ponder His unique and mysterious paternity with regard to Jesus.

Jesus as Christ

Whether Jesus is or is not the Messiah is the question in the Synoptics, and the Synoptists try to indicate how gradual was the recognition of Jesus as Messiah, 'the Christ,' the 'Anointed One.' But that Jesus is 'the Christ' is a simple fact for Paul. In his writings the formula 'Jesus the Christ' is supplanted by the complete title 'Our

Lord Jesus Christ' that was then in use in the Christian communities. The word Christ has taken on the value of a proper name (Rom 16.18).

Jesus as Son of God

Jesus is called 'Son of God' in many of the Pauline writings (Rom 1.4; Gal 2.20; Eph 4.13; 2 Cor 1.19; 1 Th 1.10), but not as often as He is called 'Lord' and 'Christ.' He is called 'Son of God' in various contexts: 'God sent his Son . . . to redeem' (Gal 4.4); 'we were reconciled to God by the death of his Son' (Rom 5.10); 'the Son of God, who loved me and gave himself for me' (Gal 2.20); 'his beloved Son . . . the image of the invisible God . . . all things were created through him and for him' (Col 1.13, 15, 16).

In the Hellenistic-Roman world the title 'Son of God' was given to the Roman emperor, to mythical heroes, and to historical persons such as Pythagoras and Plato, apparently in the belief that such persons had divine powers. In the Old Testament the title seemed to signify a sonship based on a divine election for a God-given task.[7]

When Paul calls Jesus 'Son of God' what kind of sonship has he in mind? Often it seems to be the Old Testament sonship of one divinely chosen for a divine mission.[8] Thus in these passages Jesus' sonship is a functional sonship connoting Jesus' soteriological function rather than His ontological relation to the Father.

At times, however, Paul presents Jesus' sonship as more than merely elective and functional. When he writes that 'when the time had fully come, God sent forth his Son' (Gal 4.4), when he calls this Son 'his Son' (1 Th 1.10), 'his own Son' (Rom 8.3, 32), when he tells us this Son is 'the image of the invisible God, the first-born of all creation . . . and all things were created through him' (Col 1.13, 15, 16) and adds that Christ Jesus 'was in the form of God' (Phil 2.6), it seems impossible to see in all this only an elective sonship. It must be an eternal sonship that puts the Son on the same divine level as the Father. The divine nature, divine origin, and divine power ascribed to Jesus cannot be the fruits of adoption. That is why Paul makes the pre-existence of Christ so explicit. For Paul the title 'Son of God' affirms the divinity of Jesus and differentiates Him from the Father, who is denominated by the title 'God.' And in all this Paul was not proposing an idea that he devised. The Church perceived that an eternal Father had to have an eternal Son.[9]

It has been maintained that Christ was born a man but divinized after His death, or as Paul put it, 'designated Son of God in power . . . by his resurrection from the dead' (Rom 1.4). All we have just said above contradicts this. For Paul, Jesus is 'revealed as the Son of

God in His resurrection; before this event men might question the title, but not after it.'[10] For Paul as for the early Christians 'the fact that Christ was the Son stands out and is made obvious by his resurrection and exaltation: it was not merely a decorative title which came into being at that moment.'[11]

At times Paul writes as if Christ were 'subordinate' to the Father. For he tells us that 'God sent forth his Son to redeem' (Gal 4.4) and 'did not spare his own Son but gave him up for us all' (Rom 8.32). And in a notable passage he declares that 'when all things are subjected to him, then the Son himself will also be subjected to him who put all things under him, that God may be everything to everyone' (1 Cor 15.28). Taken by themselves these passages might warrant the conclusion that Paul held a merely subordinationist view of Christ and did not place Him on the same divine level with the Father. But if they are taken together with the passages cited above in which Paul does put Christ on the same divine level as the Father by presenting Him as the creator of all things and the 'image of the invisible God' who was 'in the form of God' and equal to God, it becomes clear that Paul views Christ both as subordinate and equal to God the Father. Possibly he thus means merely to subordinate Christ in His humanity to the Father. But more probably he wishes to indicate that while Christ is truly divine and on the same divine level with the Father, yet there must be assigned to the Father a certain priority and superiority over the Son because He is the *Father* of the Son and *sends* the Son to redeem men, and there must be ascribed to the Son a certain subordination because He is the *Son* of the Father and is *sent* by the Father. Nowhere, however, does Paul say or imply that the Son is a creature, as the Arian subordinationists will say later on. On the contrary he makes it clear that the Son is not on the side of the creature but of the Creator and that through the Son all things are created. Paul is dealing with the mystery of Christ and is aware of the problem of his relationship with the Father. Perhaps his nearest approach to a solution of this problem turns not on the 'mission' of Christ by the Father but on the *kenosis* whereby being 'in the form of God . . . [he] emptied himself, taking the form of a servant' (Phil 2.6, 7).

Jesus as Lord

Paul calls Jesus 'Lord' more often than 'Son of God.' Although he also calls Yahweh 'Lord' when he quotes or explains Old Testament texts (1 Cor 3.20), 'the Lord' becomes his favorite title for Jesus. He uses *Kyrios* in various contexts. The mission of the apostles is to announce that Christ is Lord (2 Cor 4.5). Christians are slaves of the Lord and must serve and obey Him (Eph 6.5–8; Rom 12.11). The Lord assigns to apostles their mission and authority (1 Cor 3.5; 2 Cor 10.8). The Lord assigns to Christians their state in life (1 Cor 7.17) and they live and die for Him (Rom 14.8). Paul calls Jesus 'Lord' even during His life on earth: 'the Lord Jesus on the night when he was betrayed took bread' (1 Cor 11.23). But more often he connects the title 'Lord' with Jesus' resurrection and parousia: 'For to this end Christ died and rose again, that he might be Lord of the dead and of the living' (Rom 14.9). Does this manifest 'an Adoptionist emphasis'?[12] No, it rather indicates that in Paul's view Jesus attained to an exercise of lordship at His resurrection that He had not had during His earthly life.

Although 'Paul is not the creator of the idea that Jesus is Lord,'[13] this idea becomes the most concise epitome of his gospel: 'We preach not ourselves, but Jesus Christ as Lord' (2 Cor 4.5). As Lord Jesus 'is God's vice-gerent, exercising a power that belongs to God,'[14] a dominion over men and heavenly beings.[15]

For Paul 'Lord' is predominantly a functional title, but at times he gives it a deeper signification. By applying this title to Jesus he obviously intends to raise Him above the level of common humanity, for he connects the title with His resurrection and parousia. To the Lord Jesus he ascribes attributes and powers that are strictly divine. In the LXX *Kyrios* is the usual name for Yahweh; in giving this name to Jesus Paul also gives Him attributes and powers of Yahweh, dominion over creation, and a right to the adoration of all creation (Phil 2.9–10). Further, for the Hebrew mentality 'name' was very important since it corresponded to nature and not merely function. If then God has bestowed on Jesus 'the name which is above every name' (Phil 2.9), the name of *Kyrios*, the name of God Himself, must not this 'name' have divine value and denote both the divine nature and function of Christ?[16] Perhaps the divinity of Christ cannot be determined on the basis of this word alone, but the lordship that Paul ascribes to Christ certainly implies divinity and places Him in the same divine sphere as the Father.

Does this mean that Jesus was openly and directly identified with Yahweh? Again and again Paul puts an antithesis between God the Father and the Lord Jesus Christ, between *Theos* and *Kyrios*. He was reluctant to call Jesus 'God,' even though he gave Him a divine name and the attributes of divinity, and placed Him on the same level as the Father. He preferred to call Him Lord, for this title with its more flexible meaning would not so easily offend a monotheist. But if Paul so definitely ascribes divinity to Jesus,

will he never simply call Him 'God'? In three passages of the Pauline writings, Rom 9.5, Tit 2.13, Heb 1.8, it is quite probable that
Christ is called 'God' in the fullest sense of the word.[17]

Holy Spirit

In the Pauline writings the Holy Spirit receives a fuller treatment
than anywhere else in the New Testament, but the word *spirit* expresses so many diverse conceptions that it is very difficult to determine precisely the Pauline doctrine of the 'Holy Spirit.'

Where the author of Acts stressed the Spirit's extraordinary
activity Paul underlines the Spirit's activity in ordinary Christian
life. The Holy Spirit is prominent in every part of the Christian's
life. He is the Spirit that dwells in us (Rom 8.11), the Spirit of grace
(Heb 10.29), the Spirit of wisdom and revelation in the knowledge
of the Lord Jesus (Eph 1.17), the Spirit of life (Rom 8.2), the Spirit
of gentleness (Gal 6.1), the Spirit of power and love and self-control
(2 Tim 1.7). He is the Spirit of adoption (Gal 4.5–6), the Spirit of
sonship (Rom 8.15) and heirship (Eph 1.14), the guarantee of our
resurrection (Rom 8.11). Most of these Pauline conceptions can be
found in the Old Testament, for there also the Spirit is represented
as light, strength, life, and the source of extraordinary gifts and
interior renewal. But in Paul these doctrines are transformed so as to
manifest an unsuspected unity in Christ and in the glorified life of the
risen Christ.

Paul associates the Holy Spirit and Christ very closely in the
work of sanctification, so closely that he often attributes to them the
same functions and operations. Grace, charismata, filial adoption,
good works, salvation, eternal glory are referred sometimes to
Christ, sometimes to the Spirit. The Holy Spirit is the dispenser of
the charismata and yet these are conferred 'according to the measure
of the gift of Christ' (1 Cor 12.11; Eph 4.9). By Jesus Christ we
receive the adoption of sons, yet the Holy Spirit is the Spirit of
adoption (Eph 1.5; Rom 8.15). We are justified in the Spirit and
justified in the Lord (1 Cor 6.11; Gal 2.17), sanctified in the Spirit
and sanctified in Christ (1 Cor 1.2, 6.11). The love of God comes
to us from the Spirit and is given to us through the Lord (Rom 5.5,
8.39). It is the same with peace (Rom 14.17; Phil 4.7), liberty (2 Cor
3.17; Gal 2.4), life (2 Cor 3.6; Rom 8.2), and glory (2 Cor 3.8; Phil
4.19).

This does not mean that Paul identifies Christ and the Spirit.
He puts a very limited equivalence between them and never identifies the historical Christ with the Spirit. It is the glorified Christ in

His mystical life that he associates so closely with the Holy Spirit. Certain interior operations are attributed exclusively to the Spirit, such as prayer (Rom 8.26), assurance that we are children of God (Rom 8.16, 23), the infusion of wisdom (1 Cor 2.11, 14), the strengthening of man's innermost being (Eph 3.16). Paul exhorts Christians to 'put on Christ' and to 'conform to his image' (Rom 13.14; 2 Cor 3.18), but not to 'put on the Spirit' or to 'conform to the image of the Spirit.' The famous passage where Paul says 'the Lord is the Spirit' (2 Cor 3.17) is not conclusive; for even if 'the Lord' here signifies Christ and not Yahweh, the Spirit 'must mean the divine and heavenly level of being, which is proper to the risen Jesus.'[18] Paul does not identify Christ and the Spirit, but he does associate them often and intimately because their sphere of influence is the same and their fields of action blend. In several passages, however, he does not distinguish the Spirit from Christ clearly enough.[19]

What is the Holy Spirit for Paul? Many scholars seem convinced that in Paul the Holy Spirit is an impersonal divine force that is occasionally personified. And so many passages suggest just this that it seems correct to say that 'the spirit is not obviously and explicitly conceived as a distinct divine personal being in Paul.'[20] It must be noted, however, that an impersonal divine force does not necessarily signify that the Spirit is impersonal; for if the spirit of God in the Old Testament was the divine power of a personal God, the Spirit in Paul could just as well be the divine power of a personal Holy Spirit. But more than this, there is another series of texts that strongly suggests that the Holy Spirit is a person, for in these Paul says the Spirit is 'grieved,' 'bears witness,' 'cries,' 'leads,' 'makes intercession,' and 'comprehends the thoughts of God' (Rom 8.14, 16, 26; Gal 4.6; Eph 4.30; 1 Cor 2.11). There is the double mission of the Son and the Spirit of the Son (Gal 4.4–6). There are triadic texts that coordinate Father, Son, and Holy Spirit in a way that seems to put the three on the same level as far as divinity, distinction, personality are concerned (2 Cor 1.21–22; 1 Cor 2.7–16, 6.11, 12.4–6; Rom 5.1–5, 8.14–17; Eph 1.11–14, 17). In all these so many personal actions are attributed to the Spirit in diverse contexts, and he is presented in such close parallel to Christ that it is extremely difficult if not impossible to regard the Spirit as merely a divine impersonal force or personification.[21]

Trinity

Paul has many triadic texts that present God (or the Father), Christ (or the Son or Lord), and the Spirit side by side in closely balanced formulas: 'There is one body and one Spirit . . . one Lord, one faith, one baptism; one God and Father of us all' (Eph 4.4–6); 'God sent forth his Son, born of woman. . . . And because you are sons, God has sent the Spirit of his Son into our hearts' (Gal 4.4–6); 'God saved us . . . by the . . . renewal in the Holy Spirit, which he poured out upon us richly through Jesus Christ our Saviour' (Tit 3.4–6); 'Now there are varieties of gifts, but the same Spirit; and there are varieties of service, but the same Lord; and there are varieties of working, but it is the same God who inspires them all in everyone' (1 Cor 12.4–6).

These passages give no doctrine of the Trinity, but they show that Paul linked together Father, Son, and Holy Spirit. They give no trinitarian formula to compare with Mt 28.19, but they offer material for the later development of trinitarian doctrine. Usually they indicate only an 'economic' understanding of the three in the work of salvation, but in a few passages Paul seems to be groping toward a deeper understanding of the three (Gal 4.4–6; 1 Cor 2.7–16). It is not hard to see in the parallelism of God and Christ and Spirit the basis of later trinitarian doctrine and the presence of an elemental trinitarianism.

The threefold problem is never fully faced in the Pauline writings, but at times it seems to be touched tangentially. In Gal 3.13–14 when he indicates that Christ's crucifixion is to bring about the gift of the Spirit, Paul seems to be thinking about the relationship between the Spirit and Christ. In Gal 4.4–6 when he says that it was God who sent both the Son and the Spirit, he touches on the relationship of the three. When he traces the pattern of salvation in Rom 1–8, he fits his account of this plan into the threefold pattern, so that God the Father dominates the first section, Jesus Christ the second, and the Holy Spirit the third.

This does not mean that Paul clearly realized the problem of the interrelationship of the three and deliberately set himself to solve it. He accepted a threefold pattern of Father, Son, and Spirit to describe the activity of God, but he showed no clear awareness of a threefold problem within the Godhead. He did, however, seem aware of the problem of the unity of God and the divinity of Christ in 1 Cor 15.28, and especially in Phil 2.5–12 where he seems to focus on the very basis of Christ's equality with the Father. In the case of the Holy Spirit he does not go so far, perhaps because he had not clarified for himself the relation of the Spirit to the Father and the Son.

Summary

In Paul the Father is called 'God' (*ho theos*) and there is no question of His full divinity and distinct personality. Without doubt Paul attributes full divinity to Jesus, God's 'own Son,' the 'Lord of the living and the dead,' who was 'in the form of God' and 'before all things' and through whom 'all things were created.' He makes Christ's pre-existence very explicit. In the two 'Christological hymns' (Col 1.15–20; Phil 2.5–12) we see his view of the three stages of Jesus' life: the eternal pre-existence of the Son with the Father, His historical appearance on earth in the form of man, and His glorious exaltation as the risen Christ. Paul ascribes to Jesus a divine nature, origin, power, and sonship that put Him on the same divine level as the Father. Though at times he presents the Son as in some sense subordinate to the Father, he never makes the Son a creature. Paul's Christology is largely functional, although not entirely so,[22] for some of it has what will later be called 'metaphysical implications.' As one scholar has observed, 'it might be said that he came as near to asserting a metaphysical equality of community of natures as his non-metaphysical framework of thought permitted him to do.'[23] This was the reason why the Church later had to move on from a purely functional to an essential Christology.[24]

The Spirit plays a large if not always clear and consistent part in the Pauline writings. In the work of sanctification the Spirit and Christ are closely associated but not identified. Many passages suggest that the Spirit is an impersonal divine power; but in other passages so many personal activities are attributed to Him and He is presented in such close parallel to Christ that it is extremely difficult to regard Him as other than a distinct divine person. However, just as Paul was more concerned about the work of Christ than the person of Christ, so he is more concerned about the work of the Spirit than the person of the Spirit.

Paul has many triadic texts and in some of them he seems to present Christ and the Spirit as distinct from one another and from the Father and on the same divine level with the Father. He has no formal trinitarian doctrine and no clear-cut realization of a trinitarian problem, but he furnishes much material for the later development of a trinitarian doctrine.

God the Father

John makes the purpose of his Gospel quite clear: 'these are written that you may believe that Jesus is the Christ, the Son of God, and that believing you may have life in his name' (Jn 20.31).

John's favorite name for God is 'the Father,' and he presents Him almost entirely as the Father of Jesus. Jesus is the only begotten of the Father (1.14). The Father and Jesus are one (10.30) and Jesus alone knows the Father (1.18). The Father is in Jesus and Jesus is in the Father (10.38). No one can come to the Father except through Jesus (14.6). Jesus is sent by the Father and lives through the Father (6.57) and does the works of the Father (10.32). The Father is greater than Jesus (14.28) and yet 'all that the Father has is mine' (16.15). Unique, intimate, transcendent, mysterious is the relationship of the Father and Jesus.

Jesus as Word

In the beginning was the Word, and the Word was with God, and the Word was God. He was in the beginning with God; all things were made through him, and without him was not anything made that was made. . . . And the Word became flesh and dwelt among us, full of grace and truth; we have beheld his glory, glory as of the only Son from the Father. . . . No one has ever seen God; the only Son, who is in the bosom of the Father, he has made him known (1.1–3, 14, 18).

Jesus as the Word of the Father is the revelation of the Father and the embodiment of His power. He is thus a 'revelatory word.' But He is also a 'creative word,' and John emphasizes even more strongly than other New Testament writers the participation of the pre-existent Christ in creation. John's stress is on the functional aspect of the Word, on His creative and revelatory action rather than on His divine being. The Word is the self-revealing, self-giving God in action.

John, however, does not present merely the dynamic and functional aspect of the Word. In the very beginning of the Prologue he refers to the being of the Word with God even before the time of creation: 'the Word was with God' (1.1). The Word is not a creature, for 'all things were made through him.' He is not subordinate to God: He *is* God. He is not a second being beside God: He *is* God. And yet the Word and God are not simply identical, for 'the Word was *with* God.' Later the Church will express this in other words: the Word and the Father are two distinct divine persons in one divine nature or Godhead, or more simply, the Son is consubstantial with the Father.[25] In the prologue when John calls the Word, God, he means this literally. Toward the end of his Gospel there is 'the clearest example in the New Testament of the use of "God" for Jesus,'[26] when Thomas says 'My Lord and my God' (20.28); and thus, as John's story of Jesus began, so it ends.

The Prologue tells a great deal about the Word. It indicates His eternal pre-existence, 'In the beginning was the Word'; His personal distinction from the Father, 'the Word was with God,' 'the only Son who is in the bosom of the Father'; His divinity or divine nature, 'the Word was God'; His creative function, 'all things were made through him'; His incarnation, 'and the Word became flesh and dwelt among us'; and His revelatory function, 'No one has ever seen God; the only Son, who is in the bosom of the Father, he has made him known.' Undoubtedly this is the most exalted passage of the Fourth Gospel. And with it the term *Word* as a proper name disappears from the Gospel. It has served its purpose, to affirm the divine pre-existence of Jesus and to point Him out as the revelation of the Father.

Jesus as Son of God

Faith in the 'Son of God' is at the center of John's Gospel. In the Prologue we meet the Word who is the 'only-begotten Son of the Father.' Throughout the Gospel we continue to encounter this 'Son of God.' And toward the end of the Gospel John tells us, 'these are written that you may believe that Jesus is the Christ, the Son of God' (20.31).

The title 'Son of God' has a varying signification in John. Often it indicates the very intimate and unique union of Jesus with the Father. Jesus is 'his only Son' (3.16). 'The Father loves the Son, and shows him all that he himself is doing' (5.20). 'I do as the Father has commanded me, so that the world may know that I love the Father' (14.31). 'Whatever he does, that the Son does likewise' (5.19). 'That all may honor the Son, even as they honor the Father' (5.23). 'If a man loves me, he will keep my word, and my Father will love him, and we will come to him and make our home with him' (14.23).

At times 'Son of God' is a soteriological title connected with His divine mission: 'God sent the Son into the world that the world might be saved through him' (3.17). 'The Father has given all judgment to the Son' (5.22). The Son's mission is not to condemn the world but to give it eternal life (3.17, 16).

But the title has not only ethical and soteriological implications. It also has metaphysical implications. For Jesus is the utterly unique and pre-existent Son of God. He is unique functionally, in terms of His unique salvific mission (3.17); but could He efficaciously confer adoptive sonship on men (1.12) if He were merely an adoptive son of God Himself? He is unique ethically, in terms of His perfect oneness of will, purpose, and action with the Father (10.30; 17.20–23) and in terms of their mutual inexistence (10.38; 14.10–11); but does not such perfect oneness of action and mutual inexistence imply a unity of nature? He is unique because He is the only-begotten Son of God (1.14, 18; 3.16, 18; 1 Jn 4.19); but must He not be different, then, not only in degree but also in kind from all other 'sons of God'? And as begotten by the Father, must He not have the divine nature by derivation from the Father?

Jesus is also the Son who pre-existed with the Father from all eternity. The words 'God sent the Son into the world' (3.17), 'I came from the Father into the world' (16.28), 'my teaching is not mine, but his that sent me' (7.16) may not prove the Son's eternal existence with the Father, but they strongly suggest this. However, if 'glory' is the radiance of deity,[27] then the words 'the glory which I had with thee before the world was' (17.5) imply eternal existence with the Father. If there is any doubt left, the Son's words, 'before Abraham was, I am' (8.58), must remove it, for they imply: 'before Abraham came into existence, I eternally was, as now I am, and ever continue to be.'[28]

Thus 'for John, Jesus' sonship does indeed involve a metaphysical relationship with the Father'[29] and later theology will draw this out explicitly.

For some scholars,[30] as for the Arians, all the theology of the Fourth Gospel is dominated by the phrase, 'The Father is greater than I' (14.28). To them this signifies that the Son is dependent on the Father as a creature on the Creator.

What does it signify for John? It does not signify the dependence of creature on Creator, for the Son is the Word and the Word is God and through Him all things are created. Often it signifies the Son's dependence in His human life: 'I have not spoken on my own authority; the Father who sent me has himself given me commandment what to say and what to speak' (12.49; cf. 4.34; 8.29; 14.31; 15.10; 17.1–2). But at times it apparently refers to the Son in His pre-existence, in His eternal divine activity: 'Truly, truly, I say to you, the Son can do nothing of his own accord, but only what he sees the Father doing' (5.19); 'For as the Father has life in himself, so he has granted the Son also to have life in himself' (5.26). Can

John think that the eternal Father is greater than the eternal Son? It seems that he does, just 'as the father is always superior to his son, and the sender to the one sent.'[31] The Council of Florence will say much later: 'All that the Son is, and all that he has, he has from the Father' (Denz 1331). And later theologians will urge that this relation of origin and dependence within the Godhead alone enables us to distinguish between Father and Son who possess the same identical nature, and in consequence this dependence of the Son on the Father does not threaten the unity and equality of these persons but consecrates it and is the condition that enables us to conceive it.

John did not see or say all this. He was, however, aware of what later will be called the 'distinction of natures in the unity of the person' of Christ, inasmuch as this distinction is indicated when he says: 'And the Word was made flesh and dwelt among us' (1.14). But he made no explicit distinction between the divine and the human natures in Jesus or between these natures and the divine person. He saw Jesus as a unity, a totality, and he did not want to 'divide' Him.

Jesus as God

In the Synoptic Gospels there is one passage that could imply that Jesus is God: Mt 1.23.[32] In the Pauline writings there are three passages in which Jesus is probably called God: Rom 9.5, Tit 2.13, and Heb 1.8.[33] In the Johannine writings there are two passages in which Jesus is probably called God: Jn 1.18 and 1 Jn 5.20.[34] And there are two passages in which He is clearly called God: Jn 1.1 and Jn 20.20.[35] Thus John's Gospel not only ascribes to Jesus strictly divine functions that put Him on the same divine level as the Father, but it clearly calls Him God. As this Gospel opens we meet a sublime song of a Word who is God, and as it ends we echo the words of Thomas, 'My Lord and my God.'

Holy Spirit

In the Johannine writings there are numerous and striking statements about the Spirit. Most of them are thrown into the period after the death and resurrection of Jesus.

In the Gospel the Holy Spirit is regularly associated with Jesus. The Baptist 'saw the Spirit descend as a dove from heaven, and it remained on him' (1.32). To Nicodemus Jesus said, 'unless one is born of water and the Spirit, he cannot enter the kingdom of God' (3.5). Jesus said this 'about the Spirit, which those who believed in him were to receive' (7.39). After His resurrection Jesus 'said to them, "Receive the Holy Spirit. If you forgive the sins of any, they are forgiven" ' (20.22–23).

The fullest presentation of the Holy Spirit is found in the Paraclete passages (14.16, 17, 26; 15.26; 16.7–15), and no other passages in the New Testament contain such explicit teaching. He is 'another Paraclete' (14.16), 'the Spirit of truth' (14.17; 15.26; 16.13), who 'dwells with' the Apostles, 'whom the world cannot receive, because it neither sees him nor knows him' (14.17). He is sent by the Father and by Jesus (14.26; 15.26), and proceeds from the Father (15.27). 'He will teach you all things, and bring to your remembrance all that I have said to you' (14.26). 'He will bear witness to me' (15.26). He will guide you into all the truth . . . and will declare to you the things that are to come' (16.13). 'He will glorify me, for he will take what is mine and declare it to you' (16.14). He will 'be with you forever' (14.16).

What is the Holy Spirit in these passages? He is not merely a new operation of divine power in man or the spirit of Christ perpetuating itself in the lives of His disciples. The Spirit is a person distinct from the Father and the Son, and His distinct personal reality is more explicitly affirmed here than anywhere else in the New Testament.

That the Spirit is distinct from the Father is clear, for He is sent by the Father (14.26), given by the Father (14.16), and proceeds from the Father (15.26). That the Spirit is distinct from the Son is equally clear, for He is sent 'in the name of the Son' (14.26), sent by the Son (15.26), receives from the Son (16.14), and is 'another Paraclete' (14.16).

There can be no real question of the personality of the Holy Spirit here. He is not merely a divine gift or power, nor is He a metaphor for Jesus Himself. He is as much a living person as Jesus Himself and one whose action is so divine that His presence will, for the disciples, advantageously replace the visible presence of Jesus Himself. So clearly does John regard the Holy Spirit as a person that he uses a masculine pronoun for the Spirit, even though the Greek *pneuma* is neuter. What is even more decisive is the analogy between the Spirit and Jesus. The personality of Jesus is the measure of the personality of the Holy Spirit. They must both be denied or both be accepted. It is as the Paraclete that the Spirit is most characteristically presented by John; and Paraclete means 'Consoler,' 'Advocate,' 'Intercessor.' As the Paraclete He is the living, personal link between the Church of John's time and Jesus.

Although John's doctrine of the Holy Spirit is not so rich and full as Paul's, yet in it the relation of the Spirit to both Father and

Son is made clearer than it is in Paul's. But no more than Paul does John give any indication of the nature of the Spirit's distinct personality or of the way in which He is distinct from the Father and Son. John never calls the Spirit God or makes Him the object of worship or prayer. Possibly he meant to ascribe to the Spirit the divine function of 'judgment' in 16.8–11, but the text is too obscure to be helpful.

Trinity

In the Synoptics there is one amazing triadic formula in the Matthean baptismal command (28.19). In Paul there are many tripartite passages that indicated an 'economic' understanding of the three in the work of salvation, but little or no realization of a threefold problem within the Godhead.

In John there is no trinitarian formula like that in Matthew, nor many tripartite passages as in Paul. But there are four clear-cut instances of the triadic pattern (1.29–35; 14.16, 26; 16.15). John goes further than any other New Testament writer in awareness of the trinitarian problem. More clearly than any other does he present the divinity of the Son and the personality of the Spirit. More clearly than any other does he indicate the distinction of the Spirit from both the Father and the Son. More clearly than any other does he indicate the mission of the Spirit by both the Father and the Son, a point that will be stressed later in the *Filioque* controversy between the Latin and Greek Churches over the procession of the Holy Spirit.

In all this John is laying, unwittingly, the foundations for a doctrine of a co-equal Trinity and furnishing much material out of which such a doctrine might be formulated. He seems aware of the problem of the unity of God and the divinity of Christ, for he indicates that both are God and yet the Father is 'greater than' the Son. Although he gives no explicit explanation of this problem he perhaps insinuates an explanation in terms of generative procession by saying that while both are God, yet One is Father and One is Son; One sends the Son and One is sent by the Father. It will not be too difficult for later theology to infer this explanation from what John says and implies.

Summary

It is not hard to see the triadic pattern of John's Gospel. In the beginning was God, and the Word was with God. The Word was God and was the only-begotten Son of God in the bosom of the Father. The Word took part in the creation of the world. The Father sent His Son to the world, and the Word was made flesh and lived and died for us, rose and ascended into heaven. The Father and the Son sent the Holy Spirit to be the living link between the Church and Jesus.

The Father-Son relationship is stressed more in the Johannine writings than in any other New Testament work. 'Son' is the most prominent title for Christ: it is used 52 times in John's Gospel and Epistles and only 67 times in the rest of the New Testament. 'Father' is the most prominent title for God: it occurs 137 times in John's Gospel and Epistles and only 123 times in the rest of the New Testament.[36]

John comes closer to a trinitarian position than any other New Testament writer. He presents the divinity of the Son and the personality of the Spirit more clearly than any other. He stresses the divinity of Jesus and His unity with the Father more than any other writer and calls Jesus the Son of God more often than they do. Apparently he considered the Father-Son relationship best fitted to express the unity and interaction of the Father and Son within the Godhead and the priority of the Father over the Son. In the Paraclete passages he stresses the personality of the Holy Spirit, His distinction from the Father and the Son, and His mission by the Father and the Son, more than the other New Testament writers.

There seems little doubt that John was aware of the problem involved in the mysterious relationship of Jesus and the Father. For he made it clear that Jesus, the only-begotten Son, is one with the Father and God as well as the Father, and yet the Father sends the Son and is greater than the Son. To what extent he was aware of the problem of the Holy Spirit's relationship with the Father and the Son and with the one Godhead is not clear. He does not call the Holy Spirit 'God,' though he does regard Him as divine and puts Him on the same divine level with the Father and the Son in the Paraclete passages. More clearly than the other New Testament writers does he regard the Holy Spirit as a 'person' distinct from the Father and the Son and sent by the Father and by the Son. It has been pointed out that 'though with St. John we are still in the pre-dogmatic stage of the Trinitarian teaching, the sayings about the Paraclete carry us a degree farther than any other writing in the development of the NT doctrine of the Godhead.'[37]

SUMMARY OF NEW TESTAMENT WITNESS TO GOD

No more than the Old Testament writers do the New Testament writers set forth a systematic doctrine about God. For them, too, there is only one God, the creator and lord of the universe; and He is the God of Abraham, Isaac, and Jacob. He is the heavenly Father, but more especially the Father of Jesus. The New Testament writers also use the concepts of the Word of God, the Wisdom of God, and the Spirit of God, but now these are much more than mere personifications. The Messiah appears too, and He is Jesus of Nazareth.

In the New Testament writings Jesus is the Son of God, the Messiah, the Word of God, the Wisdom of God, and the Lord. To Him are ascribed the strictly divine functions of creation, salvation, and judgment, and sometimes He is explicitly called God. The New Testament writers attribute divinity to Him in different ways. The Synoptists usually assign to Him the powers and prerogatives of Yahweh in the work of salvation, and at times put Him on the same divine level with the Father in knowledge and power. Paul calls Him the image of God, Lord, Son of God, Christ, and Savior; he says that He subsists in the form of God and is equal to God; he assigns to Him the divine functions of creation, salvation, and judgment; and he probably also calls Him God explicitly. Paul makes Christ's eternal pre-existence more explicit than the Synoptists did. If at times he sees the Son as in some sense subordinate to the Father, yet he never makes Him a creature but always puts Him on the side of the creator. John calls Jesus the only-begotten Son and the Word, and says that the Word was with God in the beginning and that the Word was God and that through the Word all things were made. He adds that Jesus is one with the Father and is in the Father and yet is sent by the Father and the Father is greater than He.

Something of the mystery and paradox of Jesus, something of the basic trinitarian problem caught hold of the New Testament writers. Jesus is God and one with the Father and yet not the Father. One in what sense? One in function, operation, power? One in nature and being? These questions they did not answer, perhaps they did not even clearly formulate them. But John came closer to the heart of this problem than the other New Testament writers when he wrote that in the beginning 'the Word was with God' and 'the Word was God.'

Thus the New Testament writers were not adoptionists, although in a few passages they can seem to point in this direction. If they assigned to Jesus a messianic sonship and lordship at His resurrection and exaltation, they also assigned to Him a prior and deeper sonship and lordship that put Him on the same divine level as the Father. They did not attempt, however, to explain the nature of this unique divine sonship. Nor were they subordinationists in intention or words, if subordinationist is understood in the later Arian sense of the word; for they did not make the Son a creature but always put Him on the side of the creator.

The New Testament writers do not witness to the Holy Spirit as fully and clearly as they do to the Son. In the Matthean baptismal command the Holy Spirit is coordinated with the Father and the Son and put on a level with them as far as divinity and personality are concerned. The book of Acts so often attributes personal activities to the Holy Spirit as to leave a vivid impression that its author regarded the Holy Spirit as someone on a level with the Father and the Son and yet distinct from them. Paul often associates the Holy Spirit with the risen Christ in the work of sanctification, but he does not identify the two. At times he seems to view the Holy Spirit merely as a power and effluence of God, and not as a person. But at least some of the many triadic texts in which he brings together the Father, Son, and Holy Spirit do seem to indicate a distinct personality for the Holy Spirit. John, however, clearly distinguishes the Holy Spirit from the Father and the Son. If the New Testament writers nowhere explicitly call the Holy Spirit God and do not explicitly ascribe to Him the divine functions of creation, salvation, and judgment, still they do at times put the Holy Spirit on the same divine level as the Father and the Son, and ascribe to Him the divine functions of vivification, justification, and sanctification.

There is no formal doctrine of the Trinity in the New Testament writers, if this means an explicit teaching that in one God there are three co-equal divine persons. But the three are there, Father, Son, and Holy Spirit, and a triadic ground plan is there, and triadic formulas are there. The three are not considered in and for themselves but rather in terms of their roles and functions in the divine plan of salvation. Even if Christ and not the three is the center of the New Testament message of salvation, unless this Christ and His salvific activity are connected with the salvific activity of the Father and the Holy Spirit, the essence and the fullness of the New Testament message is lacking. This means that a trinitarian schema or ground plan is there and must be there. And it seems clear that some of the New Testament writers not only deliberately coordinated the three in triadic formulas, but also to some extent were aware of the trinitarian problem that this involved, namely, the relationship of Christ and the Holy Spirit to the Godhead. Only Paul and John seem to have attempted something of a solution of this problem, in terms of mission and economic trinity, and possibly something deeper. But where Paul only insinuates that the Holy Spirit is sent by both the Father and the Son, John clearly states this, and thus seems to put 'relational opposition' as a basis for the distinction of the three in the economic trinity. Did he realize all this? It is difficult to say. But later theologians will take the hint and expand it into a coherent theology of the inner divine life where the unity of the three is rooted in identity of nature and the distinction of the three persons turns on their relative opposition.

The New Testament writers do not speak in abstract terms of nature, substance, person, relation, circumincession, mission; but they present the ideas that are back of these terms in their own Biblical modes of expression. John says simply but correctly 'the Word was with God and the Word was God,' the 'Word was made flesh and dwelt among us,' 'the Father and I are one,' 'the Son is in the Father and the Father is in the Son,' 'the Father sends the Son,' 'the Father and the Son send the Holy Spirit.'

In the following centuries when heretics rise up to contest the divinity of the Son or of the Holy Spirit, the Fathers will be forced to reflect more deeply on the Biblical truths and to find more precise terms in which to express them, so that they can present and explain these truths of their faith in a way that will be intelligible and relevant to the men of their day. Their work will be necessary and invaluable, but it will add nothing essentially new to the Biblical witness to God. It will only give this witness a new mode of expression.

PART TWO

The Triune God in the Early Eastern Church

The Biblical witness to God, as we have seen, did not contain any formal or formulated doctrine of the Trinity, any explicit teaching that in one God there are three co-equal divine persons. Rather it contained the data from which a doctrine of this kind could be formulated. And it would take three centuries of gradual assimilation of the Biblical witness to God before the formulation of the dogma of one God in three distinct persons would be achieved.

To observe this gradual transition from an unformulated Biblical witness to a dogmatic formulation of a doctrine of the Triune God, it is first necessary to look to the Eastern Church where most of this development took place and study its witness to the Triune God in three phases: the pre-Nicene, the Nicene, and the post-Nicene.

CHAPTER THREE

The Pre-Nicene Phase

THE APOSTOLIC FATHERS

The Apostolic Fathers were Christian writers of the 1st and early 2d centuries whose teaching may be considered a fairly immediate echo or application of the teaching of the Apostles. Though not numbered among the inspired canonical writers, at one time some of their writings were regarded as Scripture or almost Scripture. These writers appear as witnesses to the traditional faith rather than as theologians, but they furnish useful insights into the lines along which the Church's unconscious theology was developing. They wrote not for outsiders but for those within the community of the Church.

There are varying enumerations of Apostolic Fathers.[1] Here we consider 1 Clement, 2 Clement, Ignatius of Antioch, the Martyrdom of Polycarp, the Letter of Barnabas, the Didache, and the Shepherd of Hermas.

1 Clement

This letter[2] is among the most important documents of sub-apostolic times. It speaks of God the Father, of Christ His Son, and of the Holy Spirit and coordinates the three in an oath.

God is 'the Father and Creator of the whole universe' (19.2), the 'Creator and Lord of the universe' (20.11). He is all holy, and He gives men 'life in immortality' (35.1–2). His name is made known to Christians through Jesus Christ (59.2). To Him 'be glory and majesty forever and ever. Amen' (20.12).

God is God, but Jesus Christ is His child (59.4) and the scepter of His greatness (16.2). Jesus is most commonly called 'Christ' or the 'Lord Jesus Christ.' He is God's servant (59.2–4) but also His Son

37

(36.4). He is above the angels, the splendor of divine majesty, begotten of God, sitting at His right hand (36.1–5).

The Holy Spirit is mentioned often, and the function most commonly attributed to Him is inspiration: 'You have studied the Holy Scriptures, which are true and inspired by the Holy Spirit' (45.2; cf. 13.1; 16.2; 42.3; 47.3). It has been maintained that where Clement says 'for Christ Himself calls us through the Holy Spirit' (22.1), by implication 'a pre-existent Christ is identified with the Holy Spirit.'[3] But if there is question here of a pre-existent Christ, it rather seems that He is not identified with but distinguished from the Holy Spirit, since He 'calls us through the Holy Spirit.' Thus there are not two pre-existents but three: the Father, Christ, and the Holy Spirit.

The three are coordinated in an oath: 'As God lives, and the Lord Jesus Christ lives, and the Holy Spirit' (58.2). The three are mentioned in connection with the mission of the Apostles: 'being filled with confidence because of the Resurrection of the Lord Jesus Christ, and confirmed in the word of God, with full assurance of the Holy Spirit' (42.3). The three stand out in an account of our calling in Christ: 'Do we not have one God and one Christ, and one Spirit of Grace poured out upon us—one calling in Christ?' (46.6). Here there is a clear trace of trinitarian belief, in which the undivided Trinity is a type of Christian unity, and Basil will point to it later to show that the Godhead of the Holy Spirit belonged to the oldest tradition of the Church (*De Sp. S.* 29.72).

Christ is not called God, but His divinity is implied by His coordination with God in the oath. Whether He is viewed as Son of God from eternity is not clear. The Holy Spirit is not called God, but His divinity and personality are implied by His coordination with the Father and Son in the oath as the object of the faith and hope of the elect and in the attribution to Him of the divine function of inspiration.

There is, however, no stress on the three. The stress is on Christ, and only rarely are the three mentioned together. There is obviously no doctrine of the Trinity, no explicit affirmation of the divinity of the Son and Holy Spirit but only an echo of the data of Scripture.

Ignatius of Antioch

Ignatius delves more deeply into some matters than do the other Apostolic Fathers and adds his personal reflections but without developing any systematic theology.[4]

The core of his thought is the divine 'economy' in the universe. God wished to save the world and humanity from the despotism of the prince of this world. And so He 'manifested Himself in Jesus Christ His Son, who is His Word proceeding from silence, and who in all things was pleasing to Him who sent Him' (*Magn.* 8.2). 'Our God, Jesus the Christ, was born of Mary . . . of the seed of David and of the Holy Spirit' (*Eph.* 18.2). He 'was truly crucified and died . . . and was truly raised from the dead when His Father raised Him' (*Trall.* 9).

For Ignatius God is Father, and by 'Father' he means primarily 'Father of Jesus Christ': 'There is one God, who has manifested Himself by Jesus Christ His Son' (Magn. 8.2). Jesus is called 'God' 14 times (*Eph. inscr.* 1.1, 7.2, 15.3, 17.2, 18.2, 19.3; *Trall.* 7.1; *Rom. inscr.* 3.3, 6.3; *Smyrn.* 1.1; *Polyc.* 8.3). He is the Father's Word (*Magn.* 8.2), 'the mind of the Father' (*Eph.* 3.3), and 'the mouth through which the Father truly spoke' (*Rom.* 8.2). He is 'His only Son' (*Rom. inscr.*), 'generate and ingenerate, God in man . . . son of Mary and Son of God . . . Jesus Christ our Lord' (*Eph.* 7.2). He is the one 'who is beyond time the Eternal the Invisible who became visible for our sake, the Impalpable, the Impassible who suffered for our sake' (*Polyc.* 3.2).

It has been said that for Ignatius Jesus' 'divine Sonship dates from the incarnation,'[5] and that he 'seems rather to ascribe the divine sonship of Jesus to the fact that Mary conceived by the operation of the Holy Spirit.'[6] If he did date Jesus' sonship from the incarnation he did not thereby deny His pre-existence. For he declared very definitely that Jesus Christ 'from eternity was with the Father and at last appeared to us' (*Magn.* 6.1) and that He 'came forth from one Father in whom He is and to whom He has returned' (*Magn.* 7.2). But just how He was distinct from the Father, since both are God, Ignatius does not say. Perhaps he hints at an answer when he says that Christ is the Father's 'thought' (*Eph.* 3.2).

While Ignatius concentrated most of his thought on Christ, he did not ignore the Holy Spirit. The Holy Spirit was the principle of the Lord's virginal conception (*Eph.* 18.2). Through the Holy Spirit Christ 'confirmed . . . in stability the officers of the Church' (*Phil. inscr.*). This Spirit spoke through Ignatius himself (*Phil.* 7.1).

Ignatius does not cite the Matthean baptismal formula, but he does sometimes mention Father, Son, and Holy Spirit together. He urges the Magnesians to 'be eager . . . to be confirmed in the commandments of our Lord and His apostles, so that "whatever you do may prosper" . . . in the Son and Father and Spirit' (*Magn.* 13.2). And in one of his most famous passages he declares: 'Like the stones of a temple, cut for a building of God the Father, you have been lifted up to the top by the crane of Jesus Christ, which is the

Cross, and the rope of the Holy Spirit' (*Eph.* 9.1). Thus although there is nothing remotely resembling a doctrine of the Trinity in Ignatius, the triadic pattern of thought is there, and two of its members, the Father and Jesus Christ, are clearly and often designated as God.

It has been urged[7] that for Ignatius there is no Trinity before the birth of Jesus, but that before the birth there was only God and a pre-existent Christ, who is called either Logos or Holy Spirit. There is, however, no solid evidence that Ignatius either in intention or in words made any such identification either in his letter to the Smyrnaeans (*inscr.*) or in that to the Magnesians (13.1, 2). On the contrary, when Ignatius writes that 'our God, Jesus Christ, was born of Mary . . . and of the Holy Spirit' (*Eph.* 18.2), he seems to indicate that before this birth both 'our God Jesus Christ' and the Holy Spirit pre-existed distinctly and that thus there was a Trinity before His birth.

Hermas

The doctrine of Hermas[8] on the unity of God and on creation is clear enough: 'First of all, believe that there is one God, that He created all things and set them in order, that He caused all things to pass from non-existence to existence' (*Mand.* 1).

In his Christology Hermas is far from clear, probably because of his infelicitous attempt to combine diverse Christologies, such as an Angel-Christology, a Son-of-God-Christology, a Spirit-Christology, and a Name-Christology.[9] He never used the term Logos or the name Jesus Christ. He invariably calls the Savior Son of God or Lord, but at times he seems to call Him the 'servant' and 'the glorious angel.' But his conception of the Son of God is baffling, both in relation to 'the glorious angel,' 'the servant,' and the 'Holy Spirit.' The Son of God is older than the angels: 'The Son of God is born before all His creation and, so, is counsellor to His Father in His creation' (*Sim.* 9.12.2). There is, however, a 'glorious' or 'most reverend' angel (*Sim.* 9.1.3; *Mand.* 5.1.7) who decides about the righteous and sinners and grants admission to the Church (*Sim.* 8.1.1–2). It seems that this high angelic figure is meant to be Christ, but suddenly we learn that this glorious angel is Michael (*Sim.* 8.1.2). And then Hermas ascribes the same functions to the glorious angel, to Michael, and to the Son of God (*Sim.* 8.2.5; 9.7.1.2; 8.3.3). Does he mean to identify Christ and the glorious angel and Michael and the Son of God? The variety of answers given to this question by scholars down the years is fascinating and indicates that there is no immediate prospect of a 'consensus-interpretation.'

If we read Hermas to find out who or what was the Son of God, the situation is equally baffling. In one section he says that the Son of God 'is the law of God, given to the whole world,' and that 'the great and glorious angel Michael . . . inspires the law in the hearts of believers' (*Sim.* 8.3). Somewhat later he adds that the 'Holy Spirit is the Son of God' (*Sim.* 9.1). But if the Holy Spirit is the Son of God, what is the Savior? In *Sim.* 5.2 he seems to be the faithful 'servant' in the vineyard of the Lord, whom the Lord proposes to reward for his work by making him joint heir with his Son (*Sim.* 5.2; cf. Mk 12.1–12). If Christ is this servant, as He seems to be, then He is only an adopted Son of God (*Sim.* 5.2.3). For alongside this Servant-Son of God there appears to be a further Son of God, the Holy Spirit, to whom the incarnation is ascribed (*Sim.* 5.6.5–7).

It is not surprising that Hermas has been variously interpreted. Some consider him a strict adoptionist.[10] Others regard him as a mitigated adoptionist; for what was 'adopted' was what the Holy Spirit dwelt in, and this was only 'this flesh' (*Sim.* 5.5.2). Others consider him a binitarian who, by identifying the Son of God and the Holy Spirit, posited only two pre-existent divine persons.[11]

It seems probable that as far as explicit doctrine is concerned Hermas posits only two pre-existent divine persons before the birth of Jesus, the Father and the Son of God who is the Holy Spirit. But it is not clear whether this was his deliberate intention or merely due to terminological confusion.

Didache

The *Didache*[12] is an important document of the sub-apostolic period. It has recently been called a 'semiheretical book,'[13] but in the early Church it was venerated by some almost as Scripture and cited with respect by Clement of Alexandria and Origen.

In it there are quite a few references to God. He is the creator (1.2), the God of David (10.6) whose word has gone forth (4.1), who exercises judgment on His prophetic agents (11.11). He is called 'Almighty Master' (10.3) and 'Father' both in prayers (8.2; 10.2.8) and in the 'trinitarian' formulas (7.1.3).

For Jesus the favorite title is 'Lord' (8.2; 9.5). The title 'Son' is applied to Him only in the trinitarian formulas. Jesus is not called God, and nowhere is He pictured as creator, revealer, or savior. The Holy Spirit as a divine agent is hardly to be found apart from the trinitarian formulas. In its teaching regarding baptism the *Didache* gives the trinitarian formula twice: 'Baptize in the name of the Father, and of the Son, and of the Holy Spirit' (7.1.3).

The Martyrdom of Polycarp

The Epistle of St. Polycarp is weak in doctrinal detail, but the Martyrdom of Polycarp is much richer in this respect.[14] In the third part of this document a precise trinitarian doxology is put into the mouth of the dying martyr: 'For this and for all benefits I praise thee, I bless thee, I glorify thee, through the eternal and heavenly high priest, Jesus Christ, thy beloved Son, through whom be to thee with him and the Holy Spirit glory, now and for all the ages to come. Amen' (14.3). Clearly enough this implies a belief in the divinity of Jesus and of the Holy Spirit, for the same glory is attributed to the three. The divinity of Christ is stressed again in chapters 17 and 18, which point out the difference between the worship paid to Jesus Christ and the love shown to the saints and their relics.

The Epistle of Barnabas

This is a letter only in appearance.[15] Actually it is a theological treatise whose chief interest lies in the prominence it gives to Christ's pre-existence: 'He is the Lord of the whole world, to whom God said at the foundation of the world: "Let us make man in our image and likeness" ' (5.5). Christ talked with Moses (14.3) and before the incarnation received from the Father the command to redeem us (14.5).

God is the creator of the universe and man (2.10) and is the true Lord of all men (19.7) He is also called the 'Father' (2.9; 12.8) and 'Master' (1.7; 4.3). He has sent His Son Jesus for man's salvation (14.7). Jesus is no ordinary man or prophet. He is 'Son of God' and 'Lord' who has been active in creation (5.5.10) and will ultimately judge (5.7; 7.2.9). Jesus most frequently is called 'Lord,' although the same title is used for God. Both the divinity of Jesus and His distinction from the Father are stressed.

While there are no passages that unambiguously refer to the Holy Spirit as a divine person, some point in that direction: 'those whom the Spirit of the Lord foresaw' (6.14); 'the Spirit speaks to the heart of Moses' (12.2); 'those whom the Spirit prepared' (19.7).

There is no evidence that Barnabas identifies the pre-existent Spirit with the pre-existent Lord and Son of God but rather the opposite. To the Son he ascribes the divine functions of creation and judgment, but to the Spirit those of inspiration and prophecy. Thus before the birth of Christ there was a trinity of God the Father, Christ the Son of God and Lord, and the Spirit of the Lord.[16]

2 Clement

This is not a work of Clement of Rome, nor is it a letter, but rather an exhortation to repentance and salvation.[17] Two passages stand out, the opening verse: 'Brethren, we must think of Jesus Christ as of God, as the Judge of the living and the dead' (1.1); and the concluding doxology: 'To the only invisible God, the Father of truth, who sent to us the Savior and Prince of immortality, through whom also He disclosed to us the truth and heavenly life—to Him be glory for ever and ever. Amen' (20.5). Here we have an affirmation of the divinity of Christ; and since through Christ we know the Father, Christ and the Father are clearly distinct.

But whether Christ and the Holy Spirit are really distinct is not so clear. Chapter 9 states: 'If Christ the Lord, who saved us, being spirit at first, became flesh and so called us.' Chapter 14 states: 'If we say that the flesh is the Church and the Spirit is Christ, then he who has abused the flesh has abused the Church. Such a one, accordingly, will not share in the Spirit, which is Christ' (14.3.4). It is possible that 2 Clement is here confusing Christ with the Holy Spirit, as Hermas did.[18] But it is also possible that by Spirit he meant not the Holy Spirit but rather 'the principle of deity,' 'the stuff of the divine nature.'[19] Then, unlike Hermas, 2 Clement would not identify the pre-existent Christ with the pre-existent Holy Spirit but would merely stress the divine 'nature' of Christ.

Summary

The Apostolic Fathers fall far short of Paul and John in their doctrine of God. For all of them there is one God who is the creator, ruler, judge, Father of the universe and in a special sense of Christ.

All, except perhaps Hermas, subscribe to the divinity of Christ. 1 Clement coordinates Christ with the Father and the Holy Spirit in an oath. Ignatius calls Christ God 14 times. In the *Didache* the Son is coordinated with the Father and the Holy Spirit in the baptismal formula, and in the Martyrdom of Polycarp He is given glory equally with the Father and the Holy Spirit. In the Epistle of Barnabas He is the Lord of the whole world and pre-existent with God at the foundation of the world. 2 Clement says we must think of Christ as God.

The Apostolic Fathers do not call the Holy Spirit God, but most of them indicate adequately their belief in His distinct personality and divinity. For they coordinate Him with the Father and the Son in an oath and in the baptismal formula, give Him equal glory with the Father and the Son, and ascribe to Him the strictly divine function of inspiration.

It is incorrect, then, to say that 'by the end of the period of the Apostolic Fathers there was no belief in a pre-existent Trinity, and that before the birth of Christ there were only two pre-existent beings, God and the Holy Spirit.'[20] Only for Hermas was this probably true, and possibly for 2 Clement. In the other Apostolic Fathers there is solid evidence of a belief in three pre-existent beings, both from their actual words and more especially from the fact that they ascribed strict divinity to the Father, Christ, and the Holy Spirit. There is in them, of course, no trinitarian doctrine and no awareness of a trinitarian problem.

THE APOLOGISTS

These Christian writers of the later 2d century aimed at vindicating Christianity and extending its influence. They directed their apologies against pagans and Jews. As defenders of the faith they stressed points of contact between Christianity and reason, such as the unity of God, the moral law and its sanctions. As teachers of the faith they dealt with distinctively Christian truths such as the divinity of Christ. They hoped to present Christianity as a form of wisdom immeasurably above Greek philosophy.

They were in a sense the Church's first theologians. They did not produce a systematic treatment of the whole body of revelation but only an initial formal study of some theological doctrines. They were the first to attempt an intellectually satisfying explanation of the relation of Christ to God the Father, and in them there is the first sketch of a trinitarian doctrine. These Greek Apologists used the terminology and philosophy that were then current to set forth the Christian truths that had come down to them from the Apostles, and in the process they Christianized Hellenism to some extent. Various authors have been included in the list of Apologists,[21] but here we consider only Justin, Tatian, Athenagoras, and Theophilus of Antioch.

Justin

Justin is considered the most important apologist of the 2d century.[22] In his *First Apology* he gives proofs of the divinity of Christ from Old Testament prophecies. In his *Dialogue with the Jew Trypho* he shows that the worship of Jesus is not contrary to monotheism.

Justin considers God both biblically and philosophically. Biblically, God is a living God, alone having life in Himself (*Dial*. 6). He is 'the Father and Maker of all' (1 *Apol*. 8; *Dial*. 14). He created the world out of goodness for man's sake (1 *Apol*. 10; 2 *Apol*. 4), and it was in accord with His counsel that Christ came (2 *Apol*. 6).

From a more philosophical aspect Justin presents God as transcendent, unchangeable (1 *Apol*. 13), eternal, passionless (1 *Apol*. 12). Though He can be said to be 'in the heavens' or 'above heaven' or 'above the universe' (*Dial*. 127.5; 56.1; 60.5), He is not really located in space at all (*Dial*. 127.3). God has no name. His appellations 'Father,' 'God,' 'Creator,' 'Lord,' 'Master' are derived from His relations with man and the cosmos (1 *Apol*. 10; 2 *Apol*. 6).

Since God is transcendent, the Logos bridges the abyss between God and man. Before the coming of Christ every man possessed in his reason a seed of the Logos (1 *Apol*. 32.8). Hence men like Socrates who 'lived with reason' were in a sense Christians before Christ (1 *Apol*. 46.3). As among the pagans the Logos spoke by the philosophers, so among the Jews He showed Himself in theophanies and spoke by the prophets. But only in Jesus Christ did the Logos become incarnate in His entirety (1 *Apol*. 5.4; 2 *Apol*. 10.1).

The Logos is with the Father before all creatures and is divine: 'He is adorable, He is God' (*Dial*. 63.5). He is the Father's intelligence or rational thought or rational consciousness (1 *Apol*. 46; 2 *Apol*. 13). He is distinct from the Father not only in name but 'numerically distinct too' (*Dial*. 128.4). And this distinctness, this otherness, 'which meant for Justin "different in person," '[23] Justin proceeded to 'prove' from the Logos' theophanies in the Old Testament (*Dial*. 60.2), from the 'divine dialogue' passages of the Old Testament, and from the great wisdom texts (*Dial*. 62.2; 129.3). In calling the preexistent Logos the Father's intelligence or rational consciousness, did Justin conceive the Logos as proceeding from the Father within the Godhead while remaining inseparable from the Father and the Godhead? And did he use this processional picture to give some theological indication of how the Logos can be one with the Father and still other than the Father? Perhaps. But this depends on just how the Logos and the Father are related in Justin's thought.

At first glance the relation of the Logos to the Father seems quite clear. Is not Christ, for Justin, from all eternity Logos, and Son of God, and God, and numerically distinct from the Father? On a more careful view, however, there are elements of obscurity. It is not clear whether the eternal Logos is eternally a distinct divine person, as some scholars think,[24] or originally a power in God that only becomes a divine person shortly before creation of the world when He emanates to create the world, as others believe.[25] Nor is it clear whether Justin held an eternal generation of the Son, as some maintain,[26] or merely an 'economic' emission of the Son in order to be creator, as others hold.[27]

That Justin regarded the Logos as God and as the unique Son of God prior to creation is clear. But whether he regarded the Logos as a distinct divine 'person' from all eternity is debatable. And whether he regarded the Logos as eternally the Son of God, the issue of an eternal generation, is likewise debatable.

Was Justin then a subordinationist? He was not a subordinationist in the full Arian sense of the term, for he regarded the Logos-Son not as a thing made, a creature but as God born of the Father. But if, as is quite probable, the Logos for him was not a divine person from eternity but only became one when He was generated as Son of God shortly before creation in order to be the Father's instrument of creation and revelation, then to this extent the Logos-Son was subordinate to God both as to His person, which was not eternal, and to His office, which was instrumental.

No great blame should attach to Justin for this. He was a pioneer grappling with a tremendous mystery, that of the relationship of Christ, the Word made flesh, the only-begotten Son, with the eternal God and Father of the Lord Jesus Christ. He believed that Christ was God, was the Son of God, was the Word of God distinct from the Father, and that there was but one God. To express this in an intellectually satisfying way he used to the best of his ability the terminology and philosophy that seemed most suited to his purpose. It was almost inevitable that he should stray somewhat from the straight line of later orthodoxy. When he is content to affirm the Christian teachings, he expresses them well enough. But when he tries to explain these teachings rationally and to harmonize God's transcendence and unity with the divinity of the Son, his expressions are less adequate.

Justin's conception of the Holy Spirit is not easy to determine, and it has been variously interpreted. It has even been maintained that for Justin Logos and Spirit were ultimately but two names for the same conception.[28]

References to the Spirit abound. Sometimes Justin even called the Spirit Logos or God, but most frequently 'Holy Spirit' or 'Prophetic Spirit.'[29] For Justin the Holy Spirit was not only the inspirer of the prophets', but also the guide of spiritual endeavor, the source of the spiritual gifts found in the Church. At times he seems to have regarded the Spirit as a power of God (1 *Apol.* 33.6).

Was the Spirit for Justin a person distinct from the Logos or simply an aspect of the activity of the Logos? Much of his language about the Holy Spirit has a sub-personal sound, but it becomes more personal when he speaks of 'the prophetic spirit.' In a passage on the annunciation he definitely seems to use Spirit and Logos as two names for the same person (1 *Apol*. 33.6), and to identify them as regards function. But in other passages he seems just as clearly to distinguish the Logos and the Spirit: 'For he gives the second place to the Word who is with God . . . and the third to the Spirit which was said to be borne over the water' (1 *Apol*. 60.6–7). Elsewhere he says that Christians honor Jesus Christ in the second place after God and the prophetic Spirit in the third rank (1 *Apol*. 13.3). And four times he quotes the formula, 'In the name of the Father and of the Son and of the Holy Spirit' (1 *Apol*. 61.3, 13; 65.2; 67.2).

On several occasions Justin coordinates the three persons, sometimes citing formulas derived from baptism and the eucharist, sometimes echoing official catechetical teaching. He worshipped the Father as supreme in the universe; he worshipped the Logos or Son as divine but in the second place; he worshipped the Holy Spirit in the third place. But he has no real doctrine of the Trinity, for he says nothing of the relations of the three to one another and to the Godhead.

Tatian

Tatian was a disciple of Justin.[30] He also maintained the unity of God (*Suppl*. 10). 'Let no one,' he adds, 'count it absurd that God His rationality and then being generated by an act of His will (*Orat*. 5.1). He stressed the Word's essential unity with the Father: 'the birth of the Logos involves a distribution but no severance' (*ibid*.). To illustrate this he used the same image of light kindled from light that Justin had used and that the Council of Nicea would use later on in its definition (Denz 125).

Tatian set forth even more bluntly than Justin the two states of the Logos, immanent and expressed. Before creation God was alone. Then the Logos was immanent in Him as His potentiality for creating all things. At the moment of creation He leaped forth from the Father as His primordial work. Once born as 'rationality from rational power,' He served as the Father's instrument in creating and governing the universe, in making men in the divine image (*Orat*. 5.1; 7.1–3). It is very difficult to escape the impression that for Tatian the creation of the world marks the beginning of personal existence for the Word.

Tatian hardly speaks of the Holy Spirit, except to say that the Spirit of God is not in all men 'but in some who live justly' (*Orat*. 13). A little later he calls the Holy Spirit the minister of God who has suffered. Perhaps this indicates the personality of the Holy Spirit (*Orat*. 7.12.13).

Athenagoras

Athenagoras, an Athenian Christian philosopher,[31] was the first to try to prove monotheism scientifically (*Suppl.* 8). And he proves, as Justin did, that Christians are not atheists by their worship of the Father, Son, and Spirit (*Suppl.* 10).

The eternal, unoriginate, invisible God, he declares, has created and governs the universe by His Word, and this Word is the Son of God (*Suppl.* 10). 'Let no one,' he adds, 'count it absurd that God should have a Son ... The Son is the Word of God the Father, both in thought and also in working: from Him and through Him all things had their beginning, the Father and the Son being one. The Son is in the Father and the Father in the Son by the unity and power of the Spirit; whence the Son of God is the Father's Mind and Word' (*Suppl.* 10). But while He is God's Son He never actually came into being, 'for God from the beginning, being eternal intelligence, had His Word in Himself being eternally instinct with Logos [*logikos*]' (*ibid.*).

That the Word was with God eternally is clear. But it is not so clear that this Word eternally had His distinct personality, and eternally was Son of God. Some scholars affirm this.[32] Others think Athenagoras maintained that the Word existed distinctly from eternity but that His 'generation' and thus His eligibility for the title 'Son' dates only from His emission for the purpose of creation, revelation, and redemption.[33]

Just as Justin and Tatian, so Athenagoras gives much less attention to the Holy Spirit than to the Logos-Son. He regarded the Spirit as inspiring the prophets and defined Him as 'an effluence of God, flowing forth and returning to Him like a ray of the sun' (*Suppl.* 10). He did not seem to realize the work of the Spirit upon the members of the living Church.

He has several trinitarian passages: 'We affirm that God and His Word or Son and the Holy Spirit are one in power ... The Son, the Mind, Word, Wisdom of the Father, and the Spirit an effluence from Him as light from fire' (*Suppl.* 24); 'we ... believe in a God who made all things by His Word and holds them together by the Spirit that comes from Him' (*Suppl.* 6); 'who then can fail to be astonished when he hears the name of atheists given to men who hold the Father to be God, and the Son God, and the Holy Spirit, and declare their power in union and their distinction in order' (*Suppl.* 10). But one text stands out: 'The one ambition that urges us Christians on is the desire to know the true God and the Word that is from Him—what is the unity of the Son with the Father, what the fellowship of the Father with the Son, what is the Spirit; what is the unity of these mighty Powers, and the distinction that exists between them, united as they are—the Spirit, the Son, the Father' (*Suppl.* 12).

The interest with which he regards the problems presented by the relation of the Son to the Father and the Spirit to the Father and the Son is most remarkable. There is no mention of 'essence' or 'person,' but there is more than a hint of the later doctrine of circum-incession. Here there seems to be not just an 'economic' trinity but indications of an eternal immanent Trinity. To have reached such an approximation to later trinitarian dogma before the year 180 is most remarkable and marks a great advance in the development of trinitarian thought. As Swete notes:

It is impossible not to observe how near Athenagoras comes to the Catholic dogma of the Holy Trinity as it is ultimately defined. . . . He sees that plurality of Persons in God is not inconsistent with the idea of 'monarchy' but complementary to it. There is unity in the divine life and there is also diversity. The unity consists in the possession of the same divine power, the diversity in a distinction of rank or order.[34]

Theophilus of Antioch

Theophilus[35] agrees with the other Greek Apologists in affirming the unity of God and identifying Christ with the Son of God and the Logos. He, too, maintains the eternal existence of the Logos: the Logos 'always exists, residing within the heart of God, for before anything came into being He had Him as a counsellor, being His own mind and thought' (*Autol.* 2.22). He is the first Apologist to distinguish bluntly the immanent (*endiathetos*) and the uttered (*prophorikos*) Logos: 'God, then, having His own Word internal (*logon endiatheton*) within His own bowels begot Him, emitting Him along with wisdom before all things. . . . He begot the Logos, uttered (*prophorikos*), the first-born of all creation' (*Autol.* 2.10.22).

Where Justin identified wisdom with the Logos, Theophilus identified wisdom with the Spirit, and the Spirit of God or wisdom issued from God before the world was made, just as the Word did (*Autol.* 2.10). In the next sentence the Word seems identified with the Spirit, but a little further on the distinction reappears. For Theophilus, as for the other writers of his age, the Spirit is the Spirit of prophecy (*Autol.* 1.14).

Theophilus was the first to apply the term *trinity* (*trias*) to the Godhead, stating that the three days that preceded the creation of sun and moon were types of the 'trinity,' that is, 'of God and of His Word and of His Wisdom' (*Autol.* 2.15). But he spoils the effect by adding: 'the fourth day finds its antitype in Man, who is in need of light; so we get the series, God, the Word, Wisdom, Man' (*ibid.*). His trinitarian doctrine was still a far cry from the precision of later dogmatic formulations.

Summary

In the Apologists we see a belief in the unity of God and in a trinity of divine 'persons,' Father, Son, and Holy Spirit, although there is as yet no distinct conception of divine person and divine nature. There is an identification of Christ with the Son of God, with the Logos and with God.

To the Logos they ascribe a divine pre-existence that is not only pre-creational but also strictly eternal. Did they conceive this as a distinct personal existence of the Logos? To some extent they did, for they viewed the eternal Logos as Someone with whom the Father could commune and take counsel. Probably no more could be expected at this early stage of theological development when the concepts of person and nature were as yet undefined.

If God must have His Logos from eternity, must He also have His Son? Later theology and dogma will say yes unequivocally. But the Apologists are not quite clear on this point and rather seem to say no. For them, if the origination of the Logos from God is eternal, the generation of the Logos as Son seems rather to be pre-creational but not eternal, and it is effected by the will of the Father. This view, if compared with later theology and dogma, will smack of a subordination or 'minoration' of the Son of God. This subordination of the Son was not precisely the formal intent of the Apologists. Their problem was how to reconcile monotheism with their belief in the divinity of Christ and with a concept of His divine sonship that they derived from the Old Testament. For to their minds Prov 8.22 and other texts seemed to ascribe to Christ not precisely an eternal origination but rather a pre-creational generation for the purpose of creation. So they ascribed to Christ the title and reality of divine Logos from eternity, and to the Logos the title and reality of divine Son not from eternity but from the moment of this pre-creational generation.

The Apologists contributed much less with regard to the Holy Spirit, although Justin and Athenagoras did try to find a place for the Spirit in the theology of the Church. Justin sometimes coordinated the Holy Spirit with the Father and Son in baptismal and eucharistic formulas. Athenagoras regarded the Holy Spirit as 'an effluence of God.' Theophilus identified the Holy Spirit with Wisdom and coordinated 'God and His Word and His Wisdom.' But aside from ascribing to the Holy Spirit the inspiration of the Prophets, the Apologists seem to have been very vague about His function in the work of salvation, and still more vague about His relations to the Father and Son within the Godhead. At times they tended to confuse the use of 'Spirit' to express the pre-existent nature of Christ with its use as the name of the Third Person in God. But none of them spoke of the Spirit of God as one of the creatures.

There are many more clear-cut trinitarian passages in the Apologists than in the Apostolic Fathers. Theophilus was the first to speak of the 'trinity of God and of His Word and of His Wisdom.' Four times Justin gives the formula, 'In the name of the Father and of the Son and of the Holy Spirit,' but elsewhere he says Christians honor Jesus Christ in the second place after God and the prophetic Spirit in the third rank. Athenagoras has one of the clearest trinitarian passages: 'men who speak of God the Father and of God the Son and of the Holy Spirit and declare both their power in union and their distinction in order' (*Suppl.* 10). The Apologists do not take the Sabellian road of a merely nominal trinity of persons but hold to a real distinction of the three, a distinction that is not in name only, not only in thought but in number. They base their distinction on rank or order. They realize there is a trinitarian problem and try to solve it for the Son in terms of an eternal Logos, for the Holy Spirit in terms of 'an effluence of God.'

They stress the unity of God as well as the trinity of persons. To the question, what kind of unity is there between these three who are really distinct and yet only one God, they answer: a unity of power, a unity of rule. Thus Justin speaks of 'the monarchy' of God (*Dial.* 1), Tatian about 'the rule of one' (*Orat.* 14), Theophilus about the 'monarchy of God' (*Autol.* 2.35.38), while Athenagoras states that God, the Logos, and the Holy Spirit are 'united in power' (*Suppl.* 24). Do they conceive any deeper unity than this? They seem vaguely aware of a unity based on the fact that both the Son and the Holy Spirit somehow have their origin from the Father and not by way of creation. And since they hold that although they originate from the Father, they are not divided or separated from the Father, they seem to conceive them as one in essence or fundamental being with the Father. But they did not say this in explicit terms. Only later will this deeper unity come to be expressed as a unity of 'substance' or 'essence' in a trinity of 'persons.'

Toward A.D. 200 there were signs of a new development in the Church. The Apologists had laid the foundations of Christian theology, but no Christian author had yet attempted to make a systematic presentation of the entire body of belief. There was a need for an orderly and comprehensive exposition of the tenets of the Christian religion that could be used for the instruction of catechumens. Thus were created the theological schools that became the cradles of sacred science. The oldest and most famous of these was at Alexandria in Egypt.[36]

At Alexandria the Septuagint was produced, and Philo developed his synthesis of the teaching of the Old Testament and of Greek speculation. The Christian school of Alexandria counted among its students and teachers Clement, Origen, Dionysius, Athanasius, Didymus, Cyril. This school was characterized by its interest in a more metaphysical investigation of the content of the faith, by its leaning to the philosophy of Plato, and an allegorical interpretation of sacred Scripture. It brought about a fertile contact of revelation and Greek philosophy.

Clement

Clement was a pioneer who aimed to protect and deepen faith by using philosophy to set up a true and Christian gnosis in which faith would be the beginning and foundation of philosophy.[37]

For Clement God is indeed the God of Christians, real and concrete, eminently holy and kind, who watches over men and wills their salvation (*Str.* 2.2; 5.10; 7.12; 6.17). But He is also a God conceived in the Platonic fashion, who is so transcendent that He is above the whole world and all causes, above the One and the Monad (*Paed.* 1.8; *Str.* 5.10, 11, 12; 7.1). He cannot be assigned 'genus, differentia, species, individual, number, accident, subject of accident' (*Str.* 5.12.82). He is one and incomprehensible, infinite and unnameable. He cannot be known by the work of human reason but only by divine grace (*Str.* 5.82.4), in the revelation of the Son (*Str.* 4.156.1).

Logos-Son

God's Logos or Son is His image and inseparable from Him, His mind or rationality. The incarnate Logos as Logos retains the transcendence He has in common with the Father, and here Clement goes beyond Justin and the Apologists who based the possibility of a mission of the Logos in His diminished transcendence. In the incarnation the Logos begets Himself (*Str.* 5.39.2; 16.5), without thereby becoming twofold. He is one and the same who is begotten of the Father in eternity and who becomes flesh (*Exc. Theod.* 7.4; 8.1). And in one notable passage (*Quis div* 37.1–4) Clement sees in the Father's 'love the origin of the generation of the Son.'[38] Clement clearly identifies the personal pre-existent Logos with the historical Christ, but like the early writers leaves unexplained the relationship between the inner generation of the Logos in God from eternity and his incarnational generation in time.

Clement's system and religious thinking center on the Logos. The Logos is the creator of the universe. He manifested God in the Law of the Old Testament, in the philosophy of the Greeks, and finally in His incarnation. He is not only the teacher of the world and the divine law-giver but also the savior of the human race and the founder of a new life that begins with faith, moves to knowledge and contemplation, and leads through love and charity to immortality and deification. As the incarnate Logos Christ is God and man, and through Him we rise to divine life (*Prot.* 11.88.114).

It has been the general opinion of scholars[39] that Clement affirms directly the eternal generation of the Son, and there is a great deal of solid evidence to this effect. For Clement says of the Son that 'He is wholly mind, wholly the Father's light' (*Str.* 8.2.5); that He is the 'eternal Son' (*Prot.* 12.121); that His generation from the Father is without beginning, for 'the Father is not without His Son' (*Str.* 4.162.5; 5.1.3), 'the Father [does not] exist without the Son' (*Str.* 5.1.1); that He is essentially one with the Father since the Father is in Him and He is in the Father (*Paed.* 1.24.3); that He is truly God as the Father, since to both prayers are offered and both are one and the same God (*Paed.* 1.8, 7; *Str.* 5.6; 7.12). In fact, Clement so stresses the unity of the Father and Son that he sometimes seems very close to Modalism (*Paed.* 1.8).

To find, then, in all these and other statements 'no evidence to prove a belief in the single stage theory' of the eternal generation of the Son[40] is somewhat baffling. And to see instead evidence pointing to a belief in the twofold stage theory in such statements as: 'Now the Logos coming forth was the cause of creation; then also He generated Himself, when the Logos had become flesh, that He might be seen' (*Str.* 5.3.16), when this clearly enough refers to the Logos' incarnational generation of Himself and not to the Father's eternal generation of the Son, seems to indicate something less than an objective approach to the matter.

Holy Spirit

Clement speaks quite freely of the Holy Spirit. The Spirit is the
light issuing from the Word that illumines the faithful, and the
power of the Word that attracts men to God; and He comes third in
order after the Father and the Son (*Str.* 6.138.1–3; 7.9.4). He is the
inspirer of the Scriptures so that in the words of the Old Testament
and the New Testament His voice is heard (*Paed.* 1.5.15; *Str.*
7.16.99). The true gnostic 'is united to the Spirit through the love
that knows no bounds' (*Paed.* 2.2.20; *Str.* 7.7.44), and 'we who are
baptized have the eye of the spirit, by which alone we can see God,
free from obstruction, the Holy Spirit flowing in upon us from
heaven' (*Paed.* 1.6.28). Like a magnet He attracts men to higher or
lower mansions according to their characters (*Str.* 7.2.9). He is the
holy anointing oil that Christ prepared for His friends (*Paed.* 2.8.65),
the royal gold that makes Christians what they are (*Str.* 5.14.99).

Trinity

Clement knows and adores the Trinity. He calls it a 'wondrous mystery. One is the Father of all, one also the Logos of all, and the Holy
Spirit is one and the same everywhere' (*Paed.* 1.6.42.1).

Some scholars have seen in his writings traces of subordinationism, and in some passages there seems to be foundation for the
charge that he subordinated the Son to the Father and made Him a
creature (*Str.* 4.25; 7.1; 7.2; 8.2.5). But elsewhere we find a negation
of subordination, for he tells us that the Son is generated 'without
beginning,' is 'true God without controversy, equal with the Lord of
the universe, since He was His Son' (*Prot.* 10.110.1), is in the Father
as the Father is in Him, so that they are one and the same God
(*Paed.* 1.62.4; 1.8, 7; *Str.* 5.6). It seems better to conclude that
Clement's theology is far from being a finished system and that it
therefore includes elements that he has failed to bring into proper
harmony.[41]

Origen

Origen, born at Alexandria about 185,[42] was the greatest and most
influential theologian of the East. His greatest theological work, *On
First Principles*, in which he tried to systematize all his doctrine,
might be called the first *Summa* ever composed in the Church.

God for Origen, as for Clement, is largely the somewhat abstract
God of Platonism. God is a spirit, free of all matter, 'an uncom-
pounded intellectual nature . . . altogether *monad*, and so to speak,
henad, and the mind and source from which all intellectual nature
or mind takes its beginning' (*Princ.* 1.1, 6). He alone is unbegotten,

the absolute principle of the world and personally active as its creator, sustainer, and ruler. This monad is *trias*: it contains three hypostases, the Father, the Son, and the Holy Spirit (*Jo.* 2.6).

Son-Logos

At the apex of his system Origen puts God the Father. He alone is God in the strict sense (*Jo.* 2.6; *Princ.* 1.1.6). To mediate between His absolute unity and the multiplicity of coeternal spiritual beings brought into existence by Him, He has His Son, His express image. The Father begets the Son by an eternal act, and the Son proceeds from the Father not by a process of division but in the way the will proceeds from reason:

> The Son . . . is born of Him, like an act of His will proceeding from the mind. . . . As an act of the will proceeds from the understanding, and neither cuts off any part nor is separated or divided from it, so after some such fashion is the Father to be supposed as having begotten the Son, His own image; so that, as He is Himself invisible by nature, He also begot an image that was invisible. For the Son is the Word, and therefore we are not to understand that anything in Him is cognizable by the senses (*Princ.* 1.2.6; 4.28).

> Light without splendor is unthinkable. But if this is true, there is never a time when the Son was not the Son. . . . He will be the splendor of the unbegotten light. . . . there was not a time when He was not. Thus Wisdom, too, since it proceeds from God, is generated out of the divine substance itself . . . it . . . is called 'a sort of clean and pure outflow of omnipotent glory' (Wis 7.25). Both these similes manifestly show the community of substance between Son and Father. For an outflow seems *homoousios*, i.e. of one substance with that body of which it is the outflow or exhalation. (*Frag. Heb.* 24.359).

Several points stand out in these passages that will have an immense influence on later trinitarian theology. The first is the clear-cut affirmation of the eternal generation of the Son: 'It is an eternal and ceaseless generation, as radiance is generated from light' (*Princ.* 1.2.4); 'the Father did not generate the Son and dismiss Him after He was generated, but He is always generating Him' (*Hom.* 9.4 *in Jer.*). This means a definitive rejection of the twofold stage theory of the pre-existent Logos. And when Origen says 'there never was a time when the Son was not,' this is an anticipatory negation of a basic Arian principle that 'there was a time when the Son was not.'

The second point is the procession of the Son from the mind of the Father, as 'will proceeds from understanding.' Here is one of the earliest presentations of an immanent intellectual procession of the Son from the Father that excludes all materiality from the Father and Son and marks out a line of thought that will reach its crest in the theology of Aquinas. The third point is the appearance of the word *homoousios*. If the text is authentic, and there 'seems to be no cogent reason why it should not be,'[43] then Origen is here the first to use the word *homoousios* in speaking of the Son's basic relation with the Father. What did he mean by 'consubstantial'? Basically *homoousios* meant 'of the same stuff' or 'substance.'[44] However, 'of the same substance' might mean 'of generically the same substance' or 'of identically the same substance.' In later theology 'consubstantial' will mean that the Son is 'of identically the same substance as the Father,' possesses the same identical substance as the Father, and thus is God in the strictest sense as much as the Father. But in the light of Origen's subordinationism it would seem that he understood consubstantial only in its generic sense, even though his monotheism should point toward 'identity of substance.'

Was Origen a subordinationist? The answer must be both no and yes. He was not a subordinationist in the later Arian sense, for he did not consider the Son a creature, produced out of nothing and in such a way that there was a moment when the Son was not. Verbally at times he called the Son a creature (*ktisma*) and created, but only because he with many others understood Prov 8.22 of the Son. But he always taught that the Son issued from the Father by way of unitive eternal generation and not by way of separative production *ad extra*.

In other ways, however, he was definitely subordinationist, for he made the Son inferior to and subordinate to the Father. For only the Father was God in the strict sense, *ho theos*, *autotheos*. The Son was only *theos*, a 'secondary God,' who possessed the Godhead only by participation or derivation. He did not see the oneness of Father and Son as an identity of substance but rather as a moral union of virtually identical wills or a union like that of man and wife to form one flesh or like that of a righteous man and Christ to form one spirit. He considered the Son the Father's minister and said 'we should not pray to any generate being, not even to Christ, but only to the God and Father of the universe' (*Or.* 15.1; *Cels.* 8.13). He said openly that the Son was inferior to the Father: 'we ... declare that the Son is not mightier than the Father but inferior to Him' (*Cels.* 8.15); 'we say that the Savior and the Holy Spirit are very much superior to all things that are made, but also that the Father is even more above them than they are themselves above creatures even the highest' (*Jo.* 13.25).

Origen tried to build a harmonious synthesis of strict monotheism and a Platonic hierarchical order in the Trinity—and failed. Along with a great deal of excellent theology he handed down an unfortunate mixture of truth and error that would exert an unhappy influence on Greek theology for a long time.

Holy Spirit

The status and the origin of the Holy Spirit baffled Origen. He felt that the matter had been left open by the Church (*Princ.* 1), but owing to the lack of Biblical and traditional data he did not know what to think.

At times he seems to affirm the divinity of the Holy Spirit quite clearly, for he says that everything was made except the nature of the Father, the Son, and the Holy Spirit, and that nowhere is it stated that the Holy Spirit is a creature (*Princ.* 1.3.3; 2.2.1). The Spirit 'is ever with the Father and the Son; like the Father and the Son He always is, and was, and will be' (*Ep. ad Rom.* 6.7). He is 'associated in honor and dignity with the Father and the Son' (*Princ. praef.* 4).

In other passages, however, the Spirit is definitely inferior to the Son (*Jo.* 2.6), and where the Father's action extends to all beings, the Son's to all rational creatures, the Holy Spirit's only extends to the saints (*Princ.* 1.3.1–8).

What disturbed Origen most was the origin of the Holy Spirit: was He born like the Son or created (*Princ. praef.* 4.3). Since 'all things were made by' the Word, the Holy Spirit too must be His work (*Jo.* 2.6). Origen had reason to be disturbed, for he was facing one of the deepest aspects of the trinitarian mystery, the eternal origin and distinction of the Son and of the Holy Spirit. In one passage: 'God the Father from whom both the Son is born and the Holy Spirit proceeds' (*Princ.* 1.2.13), Origen expressed the origin of the Holy Spirit as procession from the Father, as St. John had expressed it and the Greek Church would continue to express it. But elsewhere he saw only two real possibilities for the Holy Spirit, that He was born or that He was made. He could not accept the Holy Spirit's origination as generation, and so he chose to view the Holy Spirit as 'made by the Father through the Son' (*Jo.* 2.6). He was moving dimly toward a third type of origination that is neither generation nor creation but which will later be called 'spiration' by the Council of Lyons (Denz 850).

Trinity

Origen is trinitarian in his thought: 'We, however, are persuaded that there are really three persons [*treis hypostaseis*], the Father, the Son and the Holy Spirit' (*Jo.* 2.6). For him 'statements made regarding Father, Son, and Holy Spirit are to be understood as transcending all time, all ages, and all eternity' (*Princ.* 4.28), and there is 'nothing which was not made, save the nature of the Father, and the Son, and the Holy Spirit' (*Princ.* 4.35). 'Moreover, nothing in the Trinity can be called greater or less' (*Princ.* 1.3.7).

Other writers before Origen had regarded the three as distinct, but often they looked to this distinction only as manifested in the economy. Origen, however, clearly maintains that each of the three is a distinct hypostasis, an individual existent from all eternity and not just as manifested in the economy. This is one of his most important contributions to Greek theology and stems directly from his belief in the eternal generation of the Son.

Dionysius of Alexandria

Origen had many followers. Some of these followed his stress on the Son's essential kinship to the Father, such as Theognostus and Gregory Thaumaturgus.[45] Others followed his subordinationist trend, such as his pupil Dionysius, bishop of Alexandria.[46]

When Dionysius became bishop he found that Sabellianism had spread in the Pentapolis. This was a form of Modalism, named after Sabellius who was excommunicated at Rome by Pope Callistus. It maintained in substance that Father, Son, and Holy Spirit were not three really distinct divine Persons but merely modes or manifestations of one and the same Person, who is God.

To refute this Sabellianism Dionysius wrote letters to the bishops of Pentapolis in which he strongly stressed the personal distinction of the Father and the Son. In fact, he stressed this so strongly that he was related to the pope at Rome, who was also named Dionysius. He was charged with separating the Son from the Father, with failing to describe the Son as *homoousios* with the Father, with denying the Son's eternity and making Him a creature and only an adopted son.[47]

The pope sent back two letters, one for the patriarch alone asking him to explain his position, the other to the public to set out the true doctrine. In the second he condemned the Sabellian blasphemy 'that the Son is the Father, and the Father the Son' (Denz 112), the Tritheists who preach 'three gods since they divide the sacred unity into three different hypostases completely separate from one another' (Denz 112), and the anticipatory 'Arians' who affirm that 'the Son was made' and 'there was a time when He did not exist' (Denz 113). He then declared that 'it is right to believe in God the Father almighty, and in Christ Jesus his Son, and in the Holy Spirit. . . . This is the way to keep intact the sacred preaching of the divine Trinity and unity' (Denz 115). He said nothing of the *homoousios*, but he seemed very disturbed by the Origen-inspired doctrine of three hypostases, which appeared to him to be virtual tritheism.

Dionysius of Alexandria in his reply to the pope restated his position more carefully. He admitted that he had used some unsuitable comparisons to illustrate the relations of the Father and the Son; but he denied that he had separated the three, since each necessarily implied the others. Nor had he denied the eternity of the Son. For if God is eternally Father, He must have an eternal Son; and if He is eternal light, He must have an eternal Son as the eternal radiance of that light. As to the word *homoousios*, he had not used it because he had not found it in Scripture.[48]

Different judgments have been passed on Dionysius of Alexandria, a mild one by Athanasius (*De sent. Dion.* 4–12), a more severe one by Basil (*Ep.* 9.2). There is no doubt that some of his comparisons and expressions were, to say the least, imprudent and unfortunate, whatever may have been his intention in using them.

This encounter between East and West made several important contributions to the development of trinitarian doctrine, both in terminology and proper emphasis. It made it clear that while three hypostases meant three persons for Origenists, for Pope Dionysius they rather meant three substances and hence three divinities. It showed that in trinitarian doctrine the East stressed the divine plurality, whereas the West stressed the divine unity. It pointed out the lurking dangers of Sabellianism, Tritheism, and 'Arianism' in inaccurate presentations of trinitarian doctrine, and the necessity of more accurate and precise concepts, terms, and distinctions for a proper exposition of the divine trinity and unity. But much time would elapse before all this would be achieved to the satisfaction of both East and West.

Summary

It will be helpful to recapitulate the flow of trinitarian thought thus far so as to see what its status was on the eve of the Nicene conflict that was to play such a tremendous part in the further development of trinitarian thought and dogma.

In the New Testament writings Jesus was called the 'Son of God,' 'Lord,' and 'Word' and was assigned the divine functions of creation, salvation, and judgment. He was explicitly said to be God and with God from eternity, to be one with the Father and in the Father. The Holy Spirit was not explicitly called God, but at times He was put on a level with the Father and Son in terms of divinity and personality. To Him were ascribed the divine functions of inspiration, vivification, justification, sanctification. There was no formal doctrine of one God in three co-equal persons, but the elements of this doctrine were there.

The Apostolic Fathers maintained that there was only one God. They affirmed the divinity and distinct personality of Christ quite clearly and that of the Holy Spirit less clearly. They offered no trinitarian doctrine and saw no trinitarian problem.

The Apologists went further. They affirmed that God is one but also triadic. To Christ they ascribed divinity and personality explicitly, to the Holy Spirit only implicitly. To try to express Christ's mysterious relationship with God, they used the concept of a pre-existing Logos somehow originating in and inseparable from the Godhead, which was generated or emitted for the purposes of creation and revelation. Thus they had what is called a 'two-stage theory of the pre-existent Logos,' or a Logos *endiathetos* and a Logos *prophorikos*. But in describing the origin of the Logos-Son, they sometimes presented the personality of the Logos and the generation of the Son so obscurely as to leave a strong impression that the Logos-Son was a non-eternal divine person, a diminished God drastically subordinate to the Father. But they did not go as far as the later Arians would and make the Son only a creature and an adopted son of God.

The Alexandrines made further contributions to the development of trinitarian thought. Clement affirmed one God and adored the trinity of Father, Word, and Holy Spirit. Although he has some subordinationist passages, his general doctrine is that the Son is eternally generated by the Father and is one and the same God with the Father. But how the three are one and the same God he does not explain.

Origen maintained the eternal generation of the Son and thus abandoned 'the twofold stage theory of the pre-existent Logos' and substituted 'for it a single stage theory.'[49]

While other writers had spoken of the three, they had not answered the question, 'Three what'? Origen answered it by saying they were 'three hypostases' (*Jo.* 2.6), and thus seems to have been the first to apply to the Trinity this word that Greek theology ultimately accepted as the technical description of what the Latins called the *personae* of God.[50] He made it clear also that these three hypostases were not only 'economically' distinct, but essentially and eternally.

In some of his commentaries (*Num.* 12.1; *Lev.* 13.4) he apparently applies 'the conception of a single *ousia* to the divine triad' and contends that there 'is a single substance and nature of the triad,'[51] and in one passage he seems to say the Son is *homoousios* with the Father. But he probably meant He was only generically, not identically, consubstantial.

To some extent Origen was a subordinationist, for his attempt to synthesize strict monotheism with a Platonic hierarchical order in the Trinity could have—and did have—only a subordinationist result. He openly declared that the Son was inferior to the Father and the Holy Spirit to the Son. But he was not an Arian subordinationist for he did not make the Son a creature and an adopted son of God.

Bishop Dionysius of Alexandria made a notable, if unintended, contribution to the developing crisis by bringing into prominence the three basic trinitarian deviations that are known to history as Sabellianism, Subordinationism, and Tritheism, and the urgent need of precise trinitarian concepts, terms, and distinctions. His encounter with the Pope of Rome also turned a strong light on the term *homoousios* that was soon to occupy the center of the stage at Nicea.

CHAPTER FOUR

The Nicene Phase

In the 4th century a new phase of trinitarian thought developed in the Church, a phase of controversy, initial definition, clarification, and fuller formulation. Before this there had been doctrinal conflicts within the Church. But now there developed what have been called the 'great heresies,' which brought with them great disturbances, strong champions of opposing views, and the intervention of the Church through ecumenical councils of its bishops. The opening controversy was with 'Arianism' over the full divinity of Jesus Christ and His relation to the Father, and the initial definition of His divine status was made at the Council of Nicea in 325.

Some scholars maintain that Arianism, even though it was first taught at Alexandria, was an Antiochene rather than an Alexandrian heresy, and derived less from Origen than from Paul of Samosata and Lucian of Antioch.[1] The actual doctrines of Paul and Lucian are too obscure to confirm this judgment. Though we know practically nothing of Lucian's doctrine, we have the testimony of St. Epiphanius (*Haer.* 76.3), St. Alexander of Alexandria (Thdt. *Hist. eccl.* 1.4), and, it seems, of Arius himself (*ibid.* 1.5.4) that there was a close relationship between Arianism and Lucian. The nature of Paul's theology is not clear, but scholars consider it to have been 'Monarchian' and 'Adoptionist.'[2] The Council of Antioch, which condemned Paul in 268, also condemned the use of the word *homoousios* for reasons that are not clear.[3] Less than ten years before this Dionysius of Alexandria had been criticized for not using this word. Fifty years later Nicea will canonize the same term.

If Arianism derived from Subordinationism rather than from Monarchianism,[4] and it probably did, then it drew great support from Origen and the Apologists. These writers had taught both the divinity of the Son and His subordination to the Father, but without making the Son a creature. They had held that the Son was truly God yet inferior to the Father, convinced that only thus could the divine monarchy be maintained. Now theologians were going to be forced to determine the compatibility of these two propositions, 'truly divine' and yet 'inferior,' and to decide once for all whether the Son was God or creature. For if He was 'truly divine,' then He must be consubstantial with the Father; and if He was not strictly consubstantial with the Father, then He was a creature. The days of an 'inferior' God, a 'diminished' God were running out.

And the one who would force the theologians to make this decision and in a sense force the Church to define the Son's divine status and His relationship to the Father was Arius.

ARIUS

Arius, a priest of Alexandria, began to air his views concerning the nature of Christ about 318. Our chief sources of information regarding his views are some letters of his own and such fragments of his *Thalia* as Athanasius has preserved in his own writings.[5]

The basic principle of Arius' system is simple. God must be and is uncreated, unbegotten, unoriginated. The immediate conclusion is simple but devastating: since the Son is begotten by the Father, He is not God but only a creature.

For Arius there is only one God. He alone is unbegotten, eternal, without beginning, truly God. He cannot communicate His being or substance since this would imply that He is divisible and mutable. If anything else is to exist, it must come into existence not by any communication of God's being but by an act of creation that produces it out of nothing (*Ep. Alex.* in Ath. *De syn.* 16).

God resolved to create the world, and so He created first a superior being, which we call the Son or Word, destined to be the instrument of creation. The Son occupies a place intermediate between God and the world, for He is neither God nor part of the world-system. He is before all creatures and the instrument of their creation (*Thal.* in Ath. *C. Ar. Or.* 1.5)

He is a creature, produced from nothing by the Father by an act of His will (*ibid.*). Although He is a creature, the Son is a perfect creature, so perfect that God can produce no creature that surpasses Him (*Ep. Alex.* in Ath. *De syn.* 16). He is not of the substance of God and in His substance is unlike the substance of the Father: 'The Unbegun made the Son a beginning of things originated; and advanced Him as a Son to Himself by adoption. He has nothing

proper to God in proper subsistence. For He is not equal, nor one
in essence with Him' (*Thal.* in Ath. *De syn.* 15). The Son is not eternal for 'there was when He was not' (*Thal.* in Ath. *C. Ar. Or.* 1.5).
The words of Arius are clear: 'We are persecuted because we say
that the Son had a beginning, but that God was without beginning
. . . and likewise because we say that He is from nothing. And this
we say because He is neither part of God, nor of any subjacent
matter' (*Ep. Eus.* in Epiph. *Haer.* 69.6).

Although He is a creature, the Son is the immediate author of
creation. He is also the agent of redemption, and for this purpose
He became incarnate. He cannot comprehend the infinite God: 'The
Father remains ineffable to the Son, and the Word can neither see
nor know the Father perfectly and accurately . . . but . . . propor-
tionately to His capacity, just as our knowledge is adapted to our
powers' (Ath. *Ep. Aeg. Lib.* 12). If He is called 'God' and 'Son of
God,' it is only by participation in grace that He is so designated
(Ath. *C. Ar.* 1.5, 6).

Arius relied heavily on Biblical argumentation. He emphasized
three distinct hypostases. But they are three entirely different beings,
not sharing in any way the same nature or essence (*Ep. Alex.* in Ath.
De syn. 16; Ath. *C. Ar. Or.* 1.6). The Holy Spirit possesses neither
the same substance nor the same glory as the Father or the Son. He
is probably a creature of the Son (*Thal.* in Ath. *C. Ar. Or.* 1.6).

Arius relied heavily on biblical argumentation. He emphasized
the Old Testament texts in which wisdom is a creature or a divine
attribute (Prov 8.22). In the New Testament his favorite texts were
those that said that 'the Father is greater than I' (Jn 14.28) and that
Jesus was established or enthroned as Lord for having completed
the work of salvation (Acts 2.36; Rom 8.29; Col 1.15; Heb 3.2).

Yet Arius made a great contribution to the development of trinitarian theology and dogma. He went to the heart of the problem of
the relationship of Christ and God. He cut through metaphor and
Platonist speculation and put his question bluntly in ontological
categories, and in the Hebraic-Christian categories of Creator and
creature: 'Is the Son God or not,' 'Is the Son of the order of the
Creator, who is God, or of the order of creature, who is not God?'
And his answer was just as blunt: 'The Son is not God, He is a
creature.'[6]

The Christology of the New Testament was largely functional,
intent on showing what Jesus as Son, Lord, Savior, Word, Messiah
had done for our salvation. It did not explicitly define what Jesus
is, what His relation to the Father *is*. Arius changed the scriptural
state of the question and asked whether the Son *is* God or not. He

put his question and answer not in functional categories but in the ontological categories of Creator and creature, of being and substance. This was legitimate, for these ontological categories 'were undeniably scriptural. If the Old Testament and the New Testament affirm anything at all, they affirm that the Creator *is* God and the creature *is* a creature. These two categories, Creator and creature, are classifications of being.'[7]

ALEXANDER

Alexander was bishop of Alexandria from 313 to 328 and one of the key figures at the Council of Nicea.[8] He first tried kindness with Arius and attempted to show him that his views were contrary to tradition. When Arius and his followers stuck to their position, nearly 100 bishops joined Alexander in a synod in 318 that excommunicated both Arius and his adherents. When this too proved ineffectual, the Council of Nicea was convened in 325, and Arius was finally condemned.

In an encyclical letter, Alexander gives a summary of the Arian doctrine:

> God was not always the Father. . . .. The Word of God was not always, but was made from things that are not . . . wherefore there was a time when He was not. For the Son is a thing created, and a thing made; nor is He like to the Father in substance; nor is He the true and natural Word of the Father . . . He is by His very nature changeable and mutable . . . The Word, too, is alien and separate from the substance of God. The Father also is ineffable to the Son; for neither does the Word perfectly and accurately know the Father, neither can He perfectly see Him (*Ep. enc.* in Socr. *Hist. eccl.* 1.6).

Alexander himself maintains on the authority of Scripture that the Son is eternal, not created but generated by the Father without beginning; and so He is the Son of God not by adoption but by nature. He was not made 'from things which are not,' and there was no 'time when He was not.' He was generated by the Father and 'is always being generated,' and equally with the Father is unchangeable and immutable and wanting in nothing. He does not use the word *homoousios* but he does say the Son 'was begotten of the Father Himself,' a formula almost identical with the phrase that Nicea will use (*Ep. Alex.* in Thdt. *Hist. eccl.* 1.3, 4).

In 325 a Council was convoked by Constantine the emperor at Nicea in Bithynia.[9] The names of over 220 of those in attendance are known. Most of these came from the East. Five or six came from the West, among these Hosius of Cordova and the priests Vitus and Vincent, who represented Pope Sylvester. There is no record of the acts of the Council. Only its Creed, 20 canons, and a synodal letter condemning Arius are extant (Denz 125–130).

The Nicene Creed says simply:

> We believe in one God, the Father almighty, creator of all things both visible and invisible. And in one Lord Jesus Christ, the Son of God, the only-begotten born of the Father, that is, of the substance of the Father; God from God, light from light, true God from true God; begotten, not created, consubstantial with the Father; through Him all things were made, those in heaven and those on earth as well. . . . And we believe in the Holy Spirit. As for those who say: 'There was a time when He did not exist' and 'before He was begotten, He did not exist' and 'He was made from nothing, or from another hypostasis or essence,' alleging that the Son of God is mutable or subject to change—such persons the Catholic and apostolic Church condemns (Denz 125–126).

What the Creed rejected is clear enough. It was Arius' doctrine that the Son is not true God but a creature, that He was not begotten of the substance of the Father but was made from nothing, that He was not eternal but rather that 'there was a time when He did not exist.' What was affirmed was a belief in one God, the Father almighty, creator of all things; and in one Lord Jesus Christ, through whom all things were made and who is the Son of God, the only-begotten of the Father, born of the substance of the Father, true God from true God, begotten not created, consubstantial with the Father; and in the Holy Spirit. The Holy Spirit is merely mentioned together with the Son and the Father, to indicate belief in the Triad of Father and Son and Holy Spirit, but He is given no further attention. All the conciliar stress was on the Son, His status, and His relation to the Father. Somewhat surprisingly the Council still used the words *ousia* and *hypostasis* as synonyms.

Several points stand out. The Council Fathers did not use the term *Logos* for Christ but the more evangelical word *Son*. They stressed that He was not created but begotten, not made from nothing but born from the substance of the Father, thus indicating that His was not a metaphorical or adoptive sonship but a real, metaphysical sonship that entailed consubstantiality or community of divine nature between the Father and the Son. They emphasized His divinity by saying He was not only born of the Father and not created but also was eternal and was God from God, true God from true God.

But the word that has continued to stand out most of all is the word *consubstantial* or *homoousios*. What does it mean in the Nicene Creed? Before Nicea it generally meant 'of generically the same substance.'[10] For later Catholic theologians it means 'of identically the same substance.' For a long time it had been widely assumed that the specific teaching of Nicea was that the Son as consubstantial with the Father had identically the same substance as the Father, and that the Council had thus taught not only the divinity of the Son but also His numerical identity of substance with the Father. But in recent years there has developed a growing tendency to question and reject this assumption.

It is clear that the Council did not explicitly affirm that the Son, as 'consubstantial with the Father' had the one same identical divine substance as the Father, and hence this was not its specific or formal teaching. But when it said the Son was 'consubstantial with the Father,' it meant at least that He is 'utterly like the Father in substance,' 'utterly unlike creatures in substance,' that He is 'of the Father's substance' and 'of no other substance.'[11]

But if the Council did not explicitly affirm numerical consubstantiality of Son and Father, was the idea of numerical consubstantiality prominent in the minds of the Nicene Fathers? Today there is a tendency to doubt or deny this also, and for a variety of reasons.[12] It is urged that if the word *consubstantial* up to Nicea had only meant generic identity or likeness of substance, it would not suddenly be accepted as meaning numerical identity of substance, and if it had been so understood then the Eusebians would have cried out 'Sabellianism.' Further, it is argued that since the great issue at Nicea was the Son's full divinity and coeternity and not the unity of the Godhead, the word *consubstantial* would have been understood to signify the Son's full divinity, His total likeness in substance to the Father and total unlikeness to creatures in substance. It is pointed out also that later on when the numerical identity of substance was fully acknowledged, some orthodox theologians still used the word *consubstantial* in the sense of generic unity.

All this seems to make an impressive case for the view that the Nicene Fathers generally understood 'consubstantiality' as likeness in substance. But perhaps an even stronger case can be made for the traditional view that they understood consubstantiality as identity of substance. Could they have failed to realize that if the Son was 'of the Father's substance,' then He must be like the Father in substance? Why, then, would they add consubstantial if it merely meant 'like the Father in substance'? Again, it would seem to be unnatural[13] for monotheists to admit two divine *ousiai*. And yet the Fathers must have realized that they would be doing just that if they said the Son was only 'like the Father in *ousia*.' Further, why is it logical to say that the Fathers used 'consubstantial' in its Origenist sense[14] of 'like the Father,' when they must have known that for Origen it meant 'like but inferior to the Father,' while they were intent on affirming the Son's equality with the Father? Again, why should the Fathers be unready to accept a new meaning instead of the traditional meaning of this term, if they were ready to use this 'new' term itself instead of a traditional Biblical term? Again, if Hosius of Cordova influenced the adoption of the term,[15] would he have failed to indicate to the Nicene Fathers that for him and the West it signified 'identity of substance'? Finally, to all this we might add Athanasius' declaration that it *was* the intention of the Nicene decree to go beyond mere likeness and touch identity (*De decr. nic. syn.* 20).[16]

SUMMARY

In the New Testament the eternity and divinity of the Son and the Holy Spirit were indicated clearly enough but nowhere formally declared. There was no formal doctrine about Christ's origin, nature, relation to the Father and to the Holy Spirit. There was no formal doctrine about a Triune God. But the elements for such a doctrine were there.

In their somewhat infelicitous attempts to explain the Son's divine status and His relation to the Father by a two-stage theory of a pre-existent Logos, the Apologists obscured if they did not deny the eternal personality and the eternal generation of the Son.

Clement and Origen rejected the two-stage theory of the Apologists and maintained the eternal generation of the Son. But Origen, in his attempt to combine strict monotheism with a hierarchical order in the Trinity, ended up by making the Son and the Holy Spirit not precisely creatures but 'diminished gods,' inferior to the Father who alone was God in the strict sense.

The stage was set for Arius. He saw in Scripture, the Apologists, and especially Origen two interwoven ideas, one that the Son was God, the other that the Son was subordinate and inferior to the

Father in divinity. He saw a tension between these two ideas that
the Father alone was God in the strict sense and that the Son was a
'diminished god' but not a creature, and he was not satisfied with the
tension. He felt it must be resolved, and so he put a blunt question:
Is the Son God or creature? He answered his question just as
bluntly: The Son is not God, He is a perfect creature, not eternal but
made by the Father out of nothing. And thus the subordinationist
tendency in the Apologists and in Origen had reached full term.

The question that Arius put and answered so bluntly was a 'live'
question, of vital importance to the Christian and trinitarian faith
of the Church and one that was deeply disturbing. The Church had
to face up to the Arian question and go on record for or against the
Arian answer. It did this at Nicea.

Though there may be doubt about the understanding of 'consubstantial' at Nicea, there can be no doubt about the historical and
dogmatic importance of the Council itself. For there the Church
definitively rejected the answer that Arius gave to the question he
put: Is the Son God or creature? The Council firmly rejected Arius'
contention that the Son was a creature, not eternal, and made out of
nothing. It firmly declared that He was begotten, not made, was
born of the Father's substance, was true God from true God, was
consubstantial with the Father.

It did more. In the New Testament affirmations about the Son
were largely functional and soteriological, and stressed what the
Son is to us. Arians willingly recited these affirmations but read into
them their own meaning. To preclude this Arian abuse of the Scripture affirmations Nicea transposed these Biblical affirmations into
ontological formulas, and gathered the multiplicity of scriptural
affirmations, titles, symbols, images, and predicates about the Son
into a single affirmation that the Son is not made but born of the
Father, true God from true God, and consubstantial with the Father.

A definitive answer was given to the question of Arius

> not in the empirical categories of experience, the relational
> category of presence, or even the dynamic categories of power
> and function but in the ontological category of substance, which
> is a category of being. Nicaea did not describe; it defined. It
> defined what the Son is, in himself and in his relation to the one
> God the Father. The Son is from the Father in a singular, un-
> shared way, begotten as Son, not made as a creature. The Son
> is all that the Father is, except for the Name of Father. This is
> what homoousion means. This is what the Son is. . . . The
> Nicene definition . . . formally established the statute of the onto-
> logical mentality within the Church. It was the precedent for the

Councils of Ephesus and Chalcedon, which resolved the issue of
the internal constitution of Christ, the Son Incarnate, in the
ontological categories of nature and person. . . . By its passage
from the historical-existential categories of Scripture to the ontological or explanatory categories exhibited in the homoousion
Nicaea sanctioned the principle of the development of doctrine
. . . of growth in understanding of the primitive affirmations
contained in the New Testament revelation.[17]

CHAPTER FIVE

The Post-Nicene Phase

The Council of Nicea was over, but many years would pass before the Nicene Creed would be fully established and accepted. Arianism, although driven underground, was far from dead. When Arius, Eusebius of Nicomedia, and other exiled leaders of the Arian faction returned, Eusebius quickly began to form an Anti-Nicene party.[1]

The Anti-Nicene group was, in fact, much larger than the Pro-Nicene group, and it included Anomoians such as Aetius and Eunomius, Homoians such as Acacius of Caesarea, Eusebius of Emesa and George of Laodicea, as well as Ursacius and Valens, and Homoiousians such as Basil of Ancyra and Eustatius of Sebaste.[2] Only a small minority of these was fully Arian, but all rejected the Nicene *homoousion* both because it was not scriptural and because it seemed to them to connote Sabellianism and to threaten their doctrine of three hypostases. The Homoiousians are usually called Semi-Arians,[3] but it would be more accurate to apply this title to the Homoians, who agreed with the strict Arians in making Christ a creature yet held, unlike the Anomoians, that He was like the Father. The designation Semi-Arians could also be accurately applied to the Pneumatomachi, and in fact was so applied by the Council of Constantinople (Denz 151).

In a long series of synods the Anti-Nicene group produced a variety of creeds that were intended to replace or modify the Nicene symbol and to do away with the Nicene phrases 'consubstantial with the Father' and 'begotten of the Father's substance' as tests of orthodoxy.[4] Among these creeds was the 'Long-lined Creed' issued at Antioch and sent to Milan in 345 to explain the Eastern viewpoint.[5] It omitted the terms *ousia*, *hypostasis*, and *homoousios*, called the Father, Son, and Spirit three *prosopa*, rejected the Arian view of

71

the non-eternal production of the Son out of nothing, and said that the Son is 'perfect and true God in nature.' In 357 the second synod at Sirmium in Pannonia put out a thoroughly Arian creed that was later called the 'Sirmium blasphemy' (Hilary, *de syn.* 11).[6] It declared that the Son was neither 'of the same substance' (*homoousios*) nor 'of like substance' (*homoiousios*) with the Father, but was unlike (*anomoios*) the Father in all things.[7] A synod at Ancyra in 358 opted for Homoiousianism and condemned all who used *homoousios tautousios* of the Son and the Father because of its resemblance to Sabellianism (Epiphanius, *Haer.* 73, 3–11). In 359 a council at Nice in Thrace used the term *homoios* of Christ but indicated that He was a creature with only a moral resemblance to the Father (Thdt. *Hist. eccl.* 2, 21, 3–7; Ath. *de syn.* 30). In the same year at Seleucia the Acacians rejected *homoousios, homoiousios,* and *anomoios* and declared merely that the Son is like the Father in the sense of Col 1.15.[8]

Ranged against this large Anti-Nicene party was a small group headed by Athanasius and strongly dedicated to the Nicene symbol and to *homoousios* as the best term to express the traditional faith that Father and Son have the same Godhead and thus are identical in substance. But not until the Council of Constantinople will the Nicene faith be securely established.

ATHANASIUS

Athanasius, who was to become the great defender of the Nicene faith and symbol, was born at Alexandria about 295.[9] He accompanied Bishop Alexander of Alexandria to the Council of Nicea and succeeded him as Patriarch of Alexandria. He met intense opposition from the Arians and was banished from his see five times. In his chief dogmatic work, the *Orations against the Arians* (hereafter abbreviated *Ar.*), he summarized the Arian doctrine and defended the Nicene formula. His *Letter concerning the Decrees of the Council of Nicea* (hereafter *De decret.*) described the proceedings at Nicea and defended the Council's use of non-Biblical terms. His tract *On Synods* (*De syn.*) aimed at bringing about a reconciliation with the Homoiousians. In his *Letters to Serapion* (*Ep. Serap.*) he solidly developed his doctrine of the Holy Spirit.[10]

Athanasius produced a well-rounded doctrine of the Trinity. He maintained just as strongly as Arius that there is only one God: 'we confess God to be one through the Triad, and . . . entertain a belief of the One Godhead in a Triad . . . for there is but one form of Godhead' (*Ar.* 3, 15). But unlike Arius he sees that the Word is

God, and not a creature: 'there is but one form of Godhead, which is also in the Word . . . for the Word is God . . . wherefore neither is the Son another God . . . for if the Son be other as an offspring, still He is the same as God; and He and the Father are one . . . in the identity of the one Godhead' (*Ar*. 3, 15, 16, 4). The Father is eternally Father and the Son is eternally Son: 'He is God's offspring, and as being proper Son of God, who is ever, He exists eternally' (*Ar*. 1, 14), 'the eternal offspring of His essence' (*Ar*. 2, 34). The generation of the Son is a mysterious process that man should not seek to fathom: 'nor again is it right to seek how . . . God begets, and what is the manner of His begetting' (*Ar*. 2, 36).

Is this generation voluntary on the Father's part? Has the Word been generated by the will of the Father? How could He be, asks Athanasius, 'since He is the Father's living counsel' (*Ar*. 3, 63). And if the Arians say 'of will He came to be,' this implies 'that once He was not . . . that the Father could even not will the Son' (*Ar*. 3, 66). But this is impossible since the Father is eternally Father and 'always generative by nature' (*Ar*. 3, 66). But if this generation is not by will, by what is it? It is by nature, Athanasius replies, for He is 'truly Father of the Son by nature and not by will' (*Ar*. 3, 62). Is it then 'by necessity and not at His pleasure' (*Ar*. 3, 62)? No, it is not 'by necessity' for 'who is it then who imposes necessity on Him' (*Ar*. 3, 62)? But if the Son 'is by nature and not by will, is He without the pleasure of the Father and not with the Father's will' (*Ar*. 3, 66)? No, 'the Son is with the pleasure of the Father . . . for the Father has love and good pleasure toward His Son who is His own by nature,' just as 'the Son has love and good pleasure toward the Father' (*Ar*. 3, 66), but 'let no one, with Valentinus, introduce a precedent will' (*Ar*. 3, 66). Much later the Eleventh Council of Toledo in Spain will declare that 'God the Father must be believed to have generated neither by will nor by necessity' (Denz 526).

That Athanasius maintained strict consubstantiality of the Father and Son, strict identity of substance, is beyond doubt. For he declares that 'the divinity of the Father is the same as that of the Son . . . and thus there is one God' (*Ar*. 1, 61), and he adds that 'there is but one form of Godhead, which is also in the Word . . . for if the Son be other as offspring, still He is the same as God, and He and the Father are one . . . in the identity of the one Godhead' (*Ar*. 3, 15, 16, 4). What is more, in his fundamental principle that 'the same things are said of the Son, which are said of the Father, except His being said to be Father' (*Ar*. 3, 4), we can see the Athanasian summary of the scriptural evidence for the consubstantiality of the Father and the Son.[11]

Since Athanasius held identity of substance for Father and Son and was such a staunch defender of the Nicene symbol, we might have expected him to use the term *homoousion* ceaselessly. But he did not. In his earlier works he employed it infrequently, perhaps to indicate that orthodox doctrine need not be expressed by this term. At times he says that Father and Son are 'like in substance,' to stress their distinction and to point out that as the Father's image the Son is 'like the Father' (*Ar.* 3, 4). But when he finds the Homoians and the Homoiousians using the phrase 'like in substance' he begins to stress *homoousion* as the word best fitted to express the traditional faith against Arians. We meet the word once in his *Orations against the Arians* (1, 9), and again in his *Letter to the African Bishops* (8, 9). But in his *Letter on Synods* we find him trying hard to persuade the Homoiousians, who already admitted that the Son was 'of the Father's substance,' to take the last step:

> but since they say that He is 'of the substance' and 'like-in-substance,' what do they signify by these but 'consubstantial'? . . . And accordingly they themselves . . . have called the Son the Radiance of the Eternal Light, and the Offspring from the Fountain. . . . But the Radiance from the Light, and Offspring from the Fountain and Son from Father, how can these be so fitly expressed as by 'consubstantial' (*De syn.* 41; cf. 37, 39, 40, 42, 43, 44, 45)?

In his *Letters to Serapion*[12] Athanasius developed his doctrine of the Holy Spirit against the 'Tropici,'[13] who considered the Holy Spirit to be a creature and said that He 'must be counted with the angels' (*Ep. Serap.* 1, 10; 1, 2). He insisted that the Holy Spirit 'is not a creature' but belongs to the indivisible 'holy Triad,' and that 'the whole Triad is one God' (*ibid.*, 1, 17). If He is 'no creature' but comes from God, and is immutable and omnipresent, and sanctifies, vivifies, and deifies us (*ibid.*, 1, 22–27); if He 'is one with the Son as the Son is one with the Father . . . is glorified with the Father and the Son . . . is confessed as God with the Word . . . is active in the works which the Father works through the Son' (*ibid.*, 1, 31), then He must be as fully divine, Athanasius argues, as the Father and the Son. He must be 'proper to God who is one and consubstantial with Him' (*ibid.*, 1, 27). Thus Athanasius goes well beyond the Nicene formula in explicitly maintaining the full divinity and consubstantiality of the Holy Spirit, even though he 'never applies to Him the title *theos.*'[14]

Thus Athanasius' conception of the Trinity is sound enough but goes little farther than the Biblical data. The one divine *ousia*, infinite, simple, and indivisible, is at once Father, Son, and Holy Spirit, a truly consubstantial Triad. The three possess one identical and indivisible substance or essence and have one and the same activity so that the 'Father accomplishes all things through the Word in the Holy Spirit' (*Ep. Serap.* 1, 28). Since the Son is in the Father as the Spirit is in the Son (*ibid.*, 1, 21), there is in the Trinity a mysterious union of nature and operation quite unlike the moral union of creatures.[15] Although Athanasius insisted again and again that the three are really distinct and that the Father's distinctive property is *agennesia*, the Son's *gennesis*, and Holy Spirit's *ekporeusis*, he investigated neither the meaning nor the distinction of these properties.[16] And even though he wrote that the Holy Spirit was the Spirit of the Son and that 'all things whatsoever the Father hath . . . are in the Spirit also through the Son' (*Ep. Serap.*, 3, 1), he did not seem to see in this what later will be called the Holy Spirit's procession from the Father through the Son. 'Yet if we regard what is implicit, rather than what is explicit, in these letters, we are justified in claiming that the procession of the Spirit through the Son is a necessary corollary of his whole argument.'[17]

He had no proper term for *person*, for he found both *prosopon* and *hypostasis* unsatisfactory. He regularly identified *ousia* and *hypostasis* (*De decret.* 27; *De syn.* 41; *Tom. ad Ant.* 6); even as late as 369 he still wrote that '*hypostasis* is the same as *ousia*, signifying nothing other than being itself' (*Ep. ad Afr.* 4). But in the council of Alexandria in 362 he agreed that the formula 'three hypostases' could be used legitimately to express the distinct subsistence of the three in the consubstantial Triad, provided that it did not carry the Arian connotation of three alien and separate substances (*Tom. ad Ant.* 6).[18]

The inner nature of the trinitarian life he always considered a mystery to be respected but not curiously investigated (*Ar.* 2, 36). He was not a speculative systematic theologian, and he lacked a well-constructed vocabulary of terms and definitions. He left unanswered many, many questions that later Fathers and theologians would be forced to ponder and answer in ways that would be relevant to the needs of their times.

THE CAPPADOCIANS

Athanasius had left unsolved many questions about the divine persons, their definition and distinction and relation to one another and to the Godhead. Here the Cappadocians, Basil the Great (d. 379), his brother Gregory of Nyssa (d. 394), and Gregory of Nazianzus (d. *c.* 390)[19] made important contributions, both terminological and doctrinal, to the development of trinitarian theology and helped to give Eastern trinitarian theology the approach and method it was to use for a very long time. Mainly they built their doctrine on the data of Scripture as Athanasius had done, but they made a greater use of philosophy in their efforts to refute Arian rationalism.

Basil's chief trinitarian works were his treatise *Against Eunomius*, the Anomoian rationalist who held that the essence of God was innascibility, and his tract *On the Holy Spirit* in which he maintained the full divinity of the Holy Spirit against the Pneumatomachi, who regarded Him as only a creature. In his most important trinitarian work, *Theological Orations*, Gregory of Nazianzus defended the divinity and consubstantiality of the Son against Eunomius and the full divinity of the Holy Spirit against the Pneumatomachi. Gregory of Nyssa was the author of several trinitarian works, *That There Are not Three Gods, To the Greeks, Concerning the Deity of the Son and Holy Spirit*, and an important treatise *Against Eunomius*. In his *Great Catechetical Oration* he put forth the only *Summa theologiae* to be found in the East between Origen's *On Principles* and Damascene's *On the Orthodox Faith*. When death put an end to their trinitarian labors, the overthrow of Arianism and the victory of the faith of Nicea was in sight.

Where Athanasius had stressed the unity of the divine nature the Cappadocians emphasized the trinity of the divine hypostases and the primacy of the Father as the fontal principle in the consubstantial Triad, since in their milieu this seemed to them the capital question. The Father is He out of whom and toward whom the Son and Holy Spirit are reckoned, and by the communication of His nature He makes the unity of the Trinity. If He is said to be greater than the Son, it is not because He is so by nature, but because ideally the principle is conceived as superior to what flows from it.

Against Eunomius they vigorously maintained the full divinity of the Son and His consubstantiality with the Father. Basil wrote simply: 'the Father, God in substance, who begot the Son, God in substance' (*Ep.* 8.3), and added that 'the Son is eternally begotten of the Father, born of His substance, without any division of this substance' (*Hom.* 24.4). He declared that 'the Son is second from the Father in order, since He is from Him, and in dignity since He is His origin and cause . . . but He is not second in nature, since in both there is one deity' (*Eun.* 3.1). The Son differs from creatures in that He is 'eternally begotten of the Father, not made from the outside, but born of His substance' (*Hom.* 24.4). Gregory of Nazianzus expressed this distinction by saying that the Son 'is the maker of time and is not subject to time' (*Or*. 39.12).

Nowhere do the Cappadocians call the Son's generation an intellectual generation, but all three mention 'mind' in connection with this generation. Basil asks why the Son is called 'Word' and answers 'so that it be clear that He proceeded from the mind . . . because He is the image of His generator, showing in Himself the entire generator' (*Hom*. 16.3). Gregory of Nazianzus writes that the Son is called Word

> because He is related to the Father as word to mind; not only on account of His passionless generation, but also because of the union, and of His declaratory function. . . . Perhaps too this relation might be compared to that between the definition and the thing defined since this also is called *logos* . . . and the Son is a concise demonstration and easy setting forth of the Father's nature. For everything that is begotten is a silent word of him that begot it (*Or*. 30.20).

Gregory of Nyssa writes along similar lines, though less explicitly (*Or. Cat*. 1). Nowhere do the Cappadocians say or imply that the Son's generation is by way of intellect, but they do ascribe to the generation of the Word a relation to the Father's intellect that they do not ascribe to the Spirit's procession from the Father, and they do this not merely to illustrate the 'passionless . . . incorporeal' nature of the Son's generation. It need not appear too surprising, then, that Western theologians will later seize on the relation of the Word to the mind of the Father to indicate why the Son's origin from the Father is by way of generation and the Spirit's is not.

The Cappadocians do not present the Son's generation as the result of an antecedent free act of the Father's will, but Gregory of Nyssa, like Athanasius, seems to admit in the generation of the Word what Cyril of Alexandria will later call a 'concurrent will' of the Father (*Eun*. 8.2).

Though Athanasius had maintained the full divinity and consubstantiality of the Holy Spirit, this doctrine was not universally accepted. As late as 380 Gregory of Nazianzus declared (*Or*. 31.5) that some regarded the Holy Spirit as a force, others as a creature, others as divine but with a lesser degree of divinity than the Father and the Son, while of those who considered Him to be fully divine some held this as a private opinion while others proclaimed it publicly. Those who opposed the full deity of the Holy Spirit were known as Macedonians or Pneumatomachi.[20]

All three Cappadocians affirmed the full divinity of the Holy

Spirit, sometimes arguing from the Holy Spirit's credal inseparability from the Father and the Son, sometimes from His coequal adoration or consubstantiality with the Father and the Son, sometimes from His deifying operation. In his treatise *On the Holy Spirit* Basil did not explicitly call the Spirit God nor explicitly affirm that He was consubstantial with the Father, and for this he was strongly censured,[21] but he fully demonstrated the divinity of the Holy Spirit as One who is fully coordinate with the Father and the Son, completes the adorable and blessed Trinity, and must be adored with the Father and the Son and not below them (*De Sp. S.* 41–47; 58–64; 71–75). Gregory of Nyssa substantially repeats this doctrine but does not seem to have called the Holy Spirit 'God' explicitly in his treatise *On the Holy Spirit*, although he emphasizes the oneness of nature of the three (*Or. Cat.* 1–4). Gregory of Nazianzus declares explicitly that the Holy Spirit is God and consubstantial, when he argues that if the Holy Spirit deifies us in baptism then He is to be adored, and if He is to be adored, is He not God? Then he asks 'Is the Spirit God? Most certainly. Is He then consubstantial? Yes, since He is God' (*Or.* 31.28, 10).

Arians had objected that if the Holy Spirit were consubstantial with the Son, then He must be a 'Son' and the Father must have two 'Sons.' In the light of the Biblical and Nicene doctrine of an 'only-begotten Son,' the Cappadocians strenuously rejected these conclusions. But they were then faced with a problem they found insoluble: how to differentiate the origin of the Holy Spirit from that of the Son. Gregory of Nazianzus declared 'that the Holy Spirit is truly Spirit, coming forth from the Father indeed, but not after the manner of the Son, for it is not by generation but by procession since I must coin a word for the sake of clearness' (*Or.* 39.12). But in what precisely this 'procession' consisted Gregory admitted he could not explain, any more than his opponents could explain in what precisely the Son's generation consisted. Basil merely said that the Holy Spirit 'comes forth as a breath from the mouth of the Father' (*De Sp. S.* 46), in a manner unutterable. Gregory of Nyssa saw a difference in the fact that the Holy Spirit proceeds from the Father and receives from the Son, but the intimate nature of this 'procession' baffled him also (*C. Maced.* 2, 10, 12, 24). Although the Cappadocians ascribed to the generation of the Word a relation to the Father's intellect that they did not ascribe to the Holy Spirit's procession from the Father, they did not seem to see in this any answer to their problem.

Just as the Cappadocians nowhere said the Holy Spirit 'proceeds' (*ekporeuetai*) from the Son but always that He 'proceeds' (*ekporeuetai*) from the Father, so nowhere did they say any more than John the Evangelist that the Holy Spirit 'proceeds from the Father alone.' But they do assign to the Son some role in the origination of the Holy Spirit. Basil says that 'goodness . . . holiness . . . royal dignity extend from the Father through the Only-begotten to the Spirit,' that the Son alone joins the Spirit to the Father and that the Holy Spirit has the same relation with the Son that the Son has with the Father (*De Sp. S.* 47, 45, 43). Gregory of Nyssa writes that the Holy Spirit is out of God and is of Christ and he compares the Father, Son, and Holy Spirit to three torches, the first of which imparts its light to the second and through the second to the third (*C. Maced.* 2, 5). In another passage (*Eun.* 1.42) he seems to speak of the Holy Spirit as caused by the Son: 'the Holy Spirit is in touch with the Only-begotten, who is conceived of as before the Spirit's subsistence only in the theoretical light of a cause' (fin.) He adds to this that 'in respect of cause, and that which is caused . . . one Person is distinguished from another . . . For one is directly from the First Cause, and another by that which is directly from the First Cause' (*Quod non sint*: ad fin.). While Gregory clearly insists mainly on the Father's causal role in the production of the Holy Spirit, yet he seems to insinuate that the Son too has a functional or causal role in this production, and this without detriment to the Father's primordial role.

Athanasius had maintained that the three—Father, Son, and Holy Spirit—were really distinct but he had no satisfactory word to answer the question 'Three what'? *Prosopon* did not satisfy him, and with the Council of Nicea he identified *ousia* and *hypostasis*. Because of its Sabellian use Basil viewed *prosopon* with reserve (*Ep.* 210.5), but Gregory of Nazianzus held that it could be used for the Trinity, if the meaning of a mere tragic or comic personage were set aside (*Or.* 42.16). *Hypostasis*, however, was the term the Cappadocians preferred, and Basil was one of the first, if not the first, to insist on the distinction between *ousia* and *hypostasis* in God and to hold that the only acceptable formula is *mia ousia, treis hypostaseis*. Origen had distinguished *ousia* and *hypostasis* and had said that there were three hypostases in the Godhead (*Jo.* 2.10.75). The Cappadocians accepted his distinction and his terms but differed radically from him in making the Son and the Holy Spirit not 'diminished gods' but as fully divine as the Father: 'the Godhead is one in Three and the Three are one, in whom the Godhead is, or to speak more accurately, who are the Godhead' (Gr. Naz. *Or.* 39.11).

They tried, too, with some success, to define hypostasis. In his letter to Terentius Basil pointed out that '*ousia* has the same relation to *hypostasis* as common has to the particular' (*Ep.* 214.4). And in Letter 236 we are told that

> the distinction between *ousia* and *hypostasis* is the same as that between the general and the particular. . . . Wherefore, in the case of the Godhead, we confess one essence or substance . . . but we confess a particular *hypostasis*, in order that our conception of Father, Son, and Holy Spirit may be without confusion and clear. If we have no distinct perception of the separate characteristics, namely, fatherhood, sonship, and sanctification, but form our conception of God from the general idea of existence, we cannot possibly give a sound account of our faith. We must, therefore, confess the faith by adding the particular to the common' (6).

As a scientific definition of a 'person' this left much to be desired, for it actually defined an 'individual,' it failed to mention the intellectual element that is distinctive of a person, and it seems to be applied univocally to divine and human persons, and thus could easily lead to the conclusion that the three divine persons were no more one than three human persons, or that the three divine persons must be three divine *ousiai*. But the Cappadocians were aware that the comparison of the divine *ousia* and *hypostases* with a universal and its particulars was defective, and they made it abundantly clear elsewhere that the three divine hypostases were essentially different from three human hypostases in that they were one concrete identical divine *ousia*. They thought, however, that in using *hypostasis* to designate what was proper to each of the three in the one divine *ousia*, they were on the right track. And they were, and from a deeper analysis of what is 'proper' to each of the three would come later on a more adequate definition of a divine person.

The Cappadocians made a further contribution to trinitarian theology by studying the intrinsic differentiation of the divine hypostases. Each divine person, they declared, is distinct from the others in virtue of a distinctive property that belongs to Him. For Basil these distinctive properties are 'fatherhood, sonship, and sanctification' (*Ep.* 236.6); for Gregory of Nazianzus they are ingenerateness (*agennesia*), generateness (*gennesis*), and procession (*ekporeusis*) (*Or.* 25.16; 26.19; 29.2). They make it clear, too, that these are relative properties. Thus Basil says that 'the Father precedes the Son according to the relation of causes to the things which proceed from them' (*Eun.* 1.20), and adds that 'it is clear to one thinking over the names *father* and *son*, that when they are said alone, they indicate only a mutual relation' (*Eun.* 2.22). Gregory of Nyssa also points out that the distinction between the three turns on their mutual relations of cause and caused (*Quod non sint.* ad fin.). Gregory of Nazianzus, in refuting a Eunomian objection that the name *Father* either says essence or action, replied that 'the name of Father is neither a name of essence nor of action, but it indicates a relation, the relation the Father has to the Son or the Son to the Father' (*Or.* 29.16). When he indicates that there is complete identity among the three divine persons except for their relations of origin (*Or.* 34.10; 31.8, 9), it is not hard to see in germ the doctrine that the Council of Florence will later summarize in the sentence: 'In God everything is one where the opposition of relation does not intervene' (Denz 1330).

If the three divine hypostases are thus relationally distinct, what are they? Clearly, they are not three substances, not three Gods, for 'God is one and the same even though . . . each is called a subsisting substance and God' (Gr. Nyssa, *De comm. not.*). For Basil the Holy Spirit is a 'mode of the ineffable existence' (*De Sp S.* 46), while for Gregory of Nyssa both the Son and the Holy Spirit are described in terms of 'mode of existence' (*Eun.* PG 45.632D, 316C, 404B–C). This metaphysical view of the divine hypostases as 'modes of existence' will find favor much later on in the West with Karl Barth and others.[22] But for the Cappadocians the three were not merely three relationally distinct metaphysical realities who were one identical God; they were also three really distinct subjects of divine life, who know, love, live, and operate divinely.

In Basil's Letter 38, of which Gregory of Nyssa may really be the author, we find a statement about the mutual inexistence of the divine Persons: 'the whole Son is in the Father and has all the Father in Himself' (8). Later on John Damascene will speak of this as the *perichoresis* of the three.

The Cappadocians have been called Neo-Nicenes in contradistinction to the primitive Nicenes like Athanasius, on the ground that they accepted the Nicene *homoousios* but understood it to mean only likeness and not identity of substance.[23] But like Athanasius they not only affirmed the consubstantiality of the three; they also signified by this consubstantiality not just likeness but identity of substance. Thus Basil wrote that 'while confessing the Father and the Son, we confess also the identity of their substance' (*Hom.* 24, 3, 4), and added that 'we in accordance with the true doctrine speak of the Son as neither like nor unlike the Father. Each of these terms is equally impossible, for like and unlike are predicated in relation to quality, and the divine is free from quality. We, on the contrary, confess identity of nature and accept consubstantiality and reject composition' (*Ep.* 8.3). Gregory of Nazianzus affirmed that 'the Godhead is one in Three and the Three are one . . . who are the Godhead' (*Or.* 39.11), and he added that there is 'one sole God because one sole divinity. . . . Each of the persons is also one with that which joins it . . . because of the identity of substance and of power' (*Or.* 31.14, 16). Gregory of Nyssa declared that 'of the Jewish conception, let the unity of the nature stand; and of the Hellenistic, only the distinction as to persons' (*Or. Cat.* 1.3), and he added that 'the divine, simple, and unchanging nature, that it may be one, rejects all diversity in essence' (*Quod non sint.* PG 45.133A). And Basil confirmed all this by arguing from unity of action to unity of nature when he wrote: 'grant, then, that we perceive the operation of Father, Son, and Holy Spirit to be one and the same; in no respect showing difference or variation; from this identity of operation we necessarily infer the unity of the nature' (*Ep.* 189.6).

Thus the Cappadocians definitely maintained the triunity of God, one *ousia* in three hypostases. They were not unaware of the problem that this posed: how could God be both one and three without open contradiction? They found no perfect solution of course, for this is impossible here below, but they tackled the problem in terms of cause and relation and existence, in much the same way that Western theologians will later on. Sometimes they approach it from the angle of the divine names, and point out that these names signify only mutual relations, and hence do not imply a multiplication of the divine substance (Bas. *Eun.* 2.9; Gr. Naz. *Or.* 31.9). At times they declare that these names signify cause and caused, and hence do not divide the nature. So Gregory of Nyssa wrote:

> when we speak of a cause and that which depends on it, we do not by these words refer to nature. For no one would hold that cause and nature are identical. Rather do we indicate a difference in manner of existence. For in saying the one is caused, the other uncaused, we do not divide the nature by the principle of causality, but only explain that the Son does not exist without generation, nor the Father by nativity and generation (*Quod non sint*; PG 45.133C-D).

Sometimes they speak of the three in terms of their 'mode of existence' (Bas. *De Sp. S.* 46; Gr. Nyss. *Eun.* PG 45.632D, 316C, 404B–C) to indicate that these hypostatic modes of existence do not divide or multiply the one single divine being (Gr. Nyss. *Quod non sint.* PG 45.133A). Obviously their answers leave much to be desired, but by indicating that God was not one and three under the very same real aspect, they did to a considerable extent achieve their purpose of showing that their opponents' rationalistic affirmations of evident contradiction in the Triune God were not as cogent as they appeared to be.

Athanasius had done much toward the development of trinitarian doctrine by his vigorous defense of the real distinction of the Father, Son, and Holy Spirit, and of their identity of substance. But he had no word or definition for *person*, no formula to express God's triunity, and he had made little or no attempt to face up to the trinitarian problem of how God can be at the same time objectively one and three.

In all these neglected areas the Cappadocians made important contributions. They chose *hypostasis* as the word best fitted to express *person*, and their formula for expressing God's triunity was 'one *ousia* in three hypostases.' Where Athanasius had stressed the unity of God, they stressed the trinity of hypostases, and made this their methodical starting point. They not only affirmed the Holy Spirit's full divinity, but explicitly called him 'God.' They so thoroughly established the identity of substance for Father, Son, and Holy Spirit that they practically put an end to Subordinationism. They studied the three hypostases and differentiated them metaphysically in terms of cause, relation, modes of existence, and thus laid the foundations of the later theology of the divine persons. They tried to differentiate the Son's origination from the Father by way of generation as the Father's image from the Holy Spirit's origination from the Father through the Son as the breath of the Father, and thus laid the groundwork of later divine-procession theology. They pondered the trinitarian problem of God's triunity, how can He be at once objectively one and three, and attempted something of an answer in terms of 'relations of caused and cause,' 'modes of being and being,' and so contributed considerably to later divine-triunity theology. They stressed the real distinction of the three, but they hardly touched on or were aware of the question why there were only three hypostases in God.

Thus they laid down many, if not most of the main lines of later trinitarian theology, but a great deal of further development was still to come.

THE COUNCIL OF CONSTANTINOPLE

Athanasius had worked hard to secure the universal acceptance of the Nicene faith and the consubstantiality of the Son and of the

Holy Spirit with the Father. The Cappadocians added their powerful defense of this faith so that there might be no lingering traces of
subordinationism.

But 56 years after Nicea there still were! And so in 381 the
emperor Theodosius I convened a council at Constantinople to put
an end to the heresies and schisms that were disturbing Church and
State. The pope was not invited to it nor was any Western bishop
present or represented, and only much later was this synod accepted
as an Ecumenical Council in the West.[24] Of the 186 bishops who
attended, 36 were Pneumatomachi, and they quickly left when they
were asked to accept the faith of Nicea. The synod drew up several
canons and a 'Tome' or exposition of doctrine. It also promulgated,
it seems, a symbol that came to be called the Nicene-Constantinopolitan Creed and that affirmed the divinity of the Holy Spirit much
more fully than the Nicene symbol. This symbol of Constantinople
'became the sole baptismal confession of the East and the eucharistic creed of Christendom.'[25]

Of the 7 canons attributed to this council[26] the first four are
definitely authentic. Canon 1 is important for trinitarian dogma in
that it condemned those who rejected the consubstantiality or the
real distinction of the Three Persons. It said that 'the confession of
faith of the 318 Fathers, who were assembled at Nicea in Bithynia,
shall not be violated but shall remain firm and stable, and every
heresy shall be anathematized, especially that of the Eunomians or
Anomoians, of the Arians or Eudoxians, of the Semi-Arians or
Pneumatomachi, of the Sabellians, Marcellians, Photinians and
Appollinarians' (Denz 151).

The 'Tome' that the Fathers of the Council drew up is no longer
extant.[27] It is mentioned in the Synodical Letter sent by the synod
of Constantinople of 382 'to the honorable . . . lords, brothers and
coministers, Damasus . . . and the other holy bishops gathered in
greatest Rome' as 'the tome which was last year published by the
ecumenical council held at Constantinople.'[28] It seems probable that
what this Tome condemned was what Canon 1 condemned, and
what it affirmed is summarized in this Synodical Letter of 382.[29]

The most influential credal product of the late fourth century
was the symbol that is called the Nicene-Constantinopolitan Creed.
At the Council of Chalcedon in 451 this symbol was recited after
the Nicene Creed and 'it was incorporated along with the Nicene
creed in the definition adopted by the council.'[30] Though its origin
is still uncertain and its precise connection with the council of Constantinople of 381 is disputed,[31] it has been accepted as a symbol of
the faith not only in the ecumenical councils of Chalcedon[32] and

Constantinople III[33] but also 'admitted as authoritative in East and West alike from 451.'[34]

Its doctrine about the Son is substantially identical with that of Nicea, for it declares: 'We believe . . . in one Lord Jesus Christ, the only-begotten Son of God, born of the Father before all time; light from light, true God from true God begotten, not created, consubstantial with the Father; through Him all things were made. . . .' (Denz 150). But it omits the Nicene phrase 'of the substance of the Father' and 'God from God' (Denz 125), and because of this omission and its doctrine about the Holy Spirit Harnack concluded that this creed can be 'taken simply as a formula of union between orthodox, Semi-Arians, and Pneumatomachi.'[35] But if this creed was promulgated by the Council, then its intent can be judged by that of the Council's first canon, and that intent was definitely not unitive and not Semi-Arian. Why, then, were these phrases omitted? Probably because it was now understood that they were adequately contained in the phrases 'born of the Father,' 'consubstantial with the Father' and 'true God from true God' (Denz 125).

The Nicene symbol only implied the divinity of the Holy Spirit when it said, 'We believe . . . in the Holy Spirit.' The symbol of Constantinople went further for it added to the Holy Spirit, 'the Lord and Giver of life, who proceeds from the Father, who together with the Father and Son is adored and glorified, who spoke through the prophets' (Denz 150). Thus it ascribed to the Holy Spirit strictly divine names and functions, and by co-enumerating the Holy Spirit with the Father and the Son as object of the same faith and worship it definitely put Him on the very same divine level as the Father and Son. It clearly affirmed His divinity but it did not explicitly give Him the name of 'God.' The *Quicunque* would do that in the West (Denz 75).

In 382, as noted previously, much the same group of bishops gathered again in Constantinople and sent a Synodical Letter to Pope Damasus. In this letter they referred to the council held at Constantinople the year before and then gave a brief summary of the 'ancient faith . . . that teaches us to believe in the name of the Father, of the Son, and of the Spirit. We believe in one divinity, power, and substance of the Father and Son and Holy Spirit; and in their equal honor, dignity, and co-eternal majesty; in three most perfect hypostases or three perfect prosopa.' They added that they rejected Sabellian, Eunomian, Arian, and Pneumatomachian denials of the 'uncreated, consubstantial and coeternal Trinity.'[36]

Terminologically, if not doctrinally also, this 'faith . . . in' an 'uncreated, consubstantial and coeternal Trinity,' 'in three most perfect hypostases' goes beyond the creed of Constantinople and is reminiscent of the Cappadocians. Whether this summary of faith substantially represents the doctrine of the lost 'Tome' of 381,[37] or not, in any case it gives a valuable witness to what the Church of Constantinople thought was 'of faith' in 382 and can be considered an important testimony to what might be called dogmatic development.

CYRIL OF ALEXANDRIA

Cyril of Alexandria (d. 444) is eminent for his trinitarian as well as for his christological contributions to theology. His chief trinitarian writings, *Thesaurus on the Holy and Consubstantial Trinity* and *On the Holy and Consubstantial Trinity*, constitute something of a *Summa* of theology, with 'proofs' from Scripture and the Fathers and reason, and an exposition and refutation of Arian objections. Perhaps his most notable contributions are in the areas of divine circumincession, procession, indwelling, and sanctification.

In his writings circumincession and consubstantiality are very closely connected, but circumincession seems to be based on consubstantiality rather than vice versa.[38] He touches on the Holy Spirit's inexistence in the Father and the Son when he writes, 'the Spirit is God of and in God' (*Thesaur*. 34. col. 592), 'naturally exists in God' (*ibid*. 577), 'is joined to the Father according to essence and is from Him and in Him' (*ibid*. 577), 'is not alien to the essence of the Son, but is in Him and from Him' (*ibid*. 581). He affirms and tries to explain the mutual inexistence of Father and Son when he writes that 'the Father is in the Son and the Son in the Father . . . but the Son is in the Father, as the splendor that is emitted from the sun, proceeds from it . . . yet exists one in nature with it' (*Thesaur*. 11. col. 100). Continuing, he says, 'since the Son is the peculiar property of the Father's essence, He carries within Himself the Father entire, and is Himself entire in the Father according to the identity of *ousia*' (*Thesaur*. 12. col. 185); 'the Son is in the Father as in a font . . . existing in the Father's substance, and shining out from it . . . always coexisting and radiating from Him according to the ineffable manner of divine generation' (*In Jo*. I, c. I. col. 28); 'the Father in turn is in the Son, as in His consubstantial offspring, connaturally distinct . . . as . . . the sun . . . in its splendor' (*ibid*. c. V. col. 82): He adds that 'since each naturally and necessarily is in the other, when the Father operates of course the Son operates . . . and when the Son operates the Father also operates' (*ibid*. col. 81, 84).

The Son's procession from the Father is by way of eternal generation, for the Son is Word and Wisdom, and 'the Word is coeternal with the Father, born of Him and issuing from the paternal essence as from a font' (*Thesaur.* 4. col. 49); 'if the Son is truth and wisdom, when was He not in the Father? For wisdom and truth were always in God and the Father' (*ibid.* col. 49, 51). This generation is utterly incorporeal, for 'if God is incorporeal, then He generates without division or section of Himself' (*ibid.* col. 44), and so 'the Father produced the Son from Himself without division or interval, as the sun produces the splendor it emits' (*Thesaur.* 6. col. 80). No deliberation or counsel or will precedes this generation (*ibid.* 7. col. 88), for since the Son is God and the wisdom and will of the Father (*ibid.* col. 85), the Word is in the Father spontaneously and without deliberation (*ibid*) col. 89). This generation is neither by nor without nor against the Father's will, but rather according to His concurrent will, for the Father is generator not 'without or from will, but rather by nature and substantially. For that which is naturally, is not outside the will, since to will to be what one is accompanies one's nature' (*De Trin.* dial. II. PG 75. 780AB). Is this generation, then, by way of intellect? Cyril can seem to hint at this when he writes that 'Word and wisdom is He called, because He is from the mind and in the mind proximately and indivisibly' (*In Jo.* I. c. V. col. 82). But does he mean 'mind' as 'intellect' or as 'essence,' mind as generating word, or does he use the word merely to suggest a passionless, spiritual immanent procession of Son from Father? It is impossible to be sure, especially since his overriding thought seems to be that the Son's generation is 'an utterly ineffable and non-intelligible mode of generation' (*De Trin.* Dial. II. col. 757; *Thesaur.* 6. col. 76, 77).

Cyril's teaching about the Holy Spirit's origination is enigmatic. He declares that 'you will discern the Father as the supreme root beyond which there is utterly nothing; you will confess to be the Son Him who proceeds from the supreme root and is generated . . . you will call the Holy Spirit Him who flows forth from the Father through the Son naturally' (*De Trin.* Dial. II. col. 721). Regularly he says that the Holy Spirit 'proceeds from' (*ekporeuetai*) (*Thesaur.* 34, col. 589), is caused by the Father. But does he mean that the Father is the exclusive cause or only the primordial cause of the Holy Spirit? He does not say. Greek and Latin interpreters continue to argue about his precise thought on this matter. He does not say that the Holy Spirit 'proceeds' (*ekporeuetai*) from the Son or is caused by the Son. But he says many things that can easily seem to imply that the Son also has a causal role in the production of the Holy Spirit. Thus he says that 'it is necessary to confess that the Spirit is from the essence of the Son. For naturally existing from

Him and being sent from Him upon the creature, He works its renovation' (*Thesaur*. 34. col. 608). Again, he says that the Holy Spirit 'is from the Father and the Son' (*ibid*., col. 585) and that 'He is the Spirit both of the Father and of the Son, seeing that He is poured forth substantially from both, or in other words, from the Father through the Son' (*De ador*. 1. 147). He declares that the Holy Spirit is 'consubstantial with the Son, and proceeds through Him in a way that fits God' (*In Jo*. XI. 1.449), that the Spirit 'proceeds through Him naturally, in that He is proper to Him' (*ibid*.). The Spirit is 'the Son's own Spirit' (*Adv. Nestor*. IV. 3.184), 'the Spirit that is from the Son and in Him' (*De Trin*. Dial. VIII. col. 1120). Again, the relation of the Spirit to the Son is that of the Son to the Father (*In Joel*. XXXV. 377). In his comparisons he represents the Holy Spirit as a sort of emanation from the Son, like perfume from a flower (*De Trin*. Dial. VI. col. 1012), sweetness from honey (*Thesaur*. 34.588), a ray or heat from light (*ibid*. 34.589), and coolness from water (*ibid*.).

Obviously there is question here not only of the Holy Spirit's mission to creatures but of His origination within the Godhead also. And this eternal origination is clearly from the Father, and from the Father as the primordial principle of divine life. But it is also somehow from or through the Son, for otherwise these words and comparisons are empty indeed. It seems impossible to see in these passages a relation of the Holy Spirit to the Son only in terms of consubstantiality and not also of causal origination. Verbally Cyril does not affirm that the Holy Spirit proceeds from the Father and the Son, but logically and contextually his words and comparisons at least tend in that direction.

Cyril has a magnificent doctrine on the sanctification and divine filiation of the Christian and the presence of the Holy Spirit in his soul. The Word of God is made man to divinize men, and in Christ, the new Adam, there is restored to man the divine image that was lost. At baptism the Holy Spirit is given to make men sons of God and to form Christ in them. The three persons inhabit the just, for 'advent' and 'operation' are common to the Three by reason of their natural unity (*De Trin*. Dial. VIII. col. 1093). But the Holy Spirit is stressed:

> Truly, if the one Spirit abides in all of us, then the one Father of all will be God within us, and through His Son He will bring into unity . . . those who participate of the Spirit. . . . Since we all receive within us the one Spirit . . . we are mingled, so to speak, both with one another and with God. For, although we are distinct one from the other . . . the Spirit of the Father and of the

Son dwells in each one individually . . . and . . . joins our many distinct spirits into unity and somehow makes them one spirit in Himself. . . . We are all one, in the Father, and in the Son, and in the Holy Spirit (*In Jo*. XI. col. 561).

The sanctifying activity of the Holy Spirit has many facets. The Holy Spirit deifies us (*Thesaur*. 34.592), vivifies us (*ibid*. 664), regenerates us (*ibid*. 592), strengthens us and makes us wise (*ibid*. 661), operates divine gifts in us (*ibid*. 660). The sanctification lost in Adam and recovered in Christ consists in the recovery of our conformity with the Son and the Father through the Holy Spirit, for 'the Spirit is the perfect image of the substance of the Son. . . . He makes those in whom He abides like to the Father's image, which is the Son. And so all things are brought back by the Son to Him from whom He proceeds, that is to the Father, through the Spirit' (*In Jo*. XI. col. 541). Thus 'our return to the Father is effected through Christ our Savior only by means of the participation and the sanctification of the Spirit. The Spirit it is who elevates us to the Son and so unites us to God. When we receive the Spirit we become sharers and partakers of the divine nature. But we receive the Spirit through the Son, and in the Son we receive the Father' (*In Jo*. XI. 545).

Two points in the Cyrillan doctrine of sanctification have been found to be especially enigmatic and controversial, our filiative union with Christ and our deifying union with the Holy Spirit. For Cyril seems to posit a mysterious dual filiation of men and a very special, almost hypostatic, union of the just with the Holy Spirit. Thus he writes: 'Christ is at once the only Son and the first-born Son. He is only Son as God; He is the first-born through the salutary union which He established between Himself and us by becoming man. By this union, in Him and through Him we are made sons of God both by nature and by grace. By nature we are sons in Him and in Him alone; through and in the Spirit, we are sons by participation and by grace' (*De recta fide ad Theodos*. col. 1177). And again he declares that we 'are in Him and through Him sons of God naturally and according to grace, through Him, in the Spirit' (*De Incarn. Unig*. col. 1229). Does this 'natural' filiation mean a 'collective incarnation that would replace the individual incarnation of Christ'?[39] No. Rather, it has been thought that for Cyril Christ has, because of the incarnation, 'a relation of the ontological order with humanity in its entirety' which involves 'only a sort of potential, radical, fundamental filiation.' But our strictly supernatural filiation is effected by the grace of baptism and of the Eucharist so that 'Christ sanctifies us corporally as man by the Eucharist, and spiritually as God by the communication of His Spirit in baptism.'[40]

Cyril argues, as do many other Fathers, that as the Holy Spirit is sanctity itself and directly sanctifies and deifies us He must be God. But in some of the passages cited above and in others he seems to assign to the Holy Spirit a special and proper role in our sanctification, to refer all sanctification to our union with the Holy Spirit, and to affirm that only in and by the Spirit do the Father and Son communicate themselves to us. Thus he writes: 'the Holy Spirit by Himself operates in us, truly sanctifying and uniting us to Himself and by conjoining . . . us with Himself makes us partakers of the divine nature' (*Thesaur.* 34.597): 'our return to the Father is effected through Christ our Savior only by means of the participation and sanctification of the Spirit' (*In Jo.* XI. 545); 'the Spirit . . . regenerates the saints into unity with God, because He dwells in them and makes them partakers of His nature' (*Thesaur.* 34.592). Just what precise role Cyril assigns to the Holy Spirit in our sanctification is difficult to say. Petavius much later will see in Cyril the view that sanctification belongs to the Holy Spirit as properly as paternity to the Father and filiation to the Son and that the Holy Spirit sanctifies by a communication of Himself or a union of Himself with the just soul that while not strictly hypostatic still is little less proper to the Spirit than union with His humanity is proper to the Word.[41] Others, however, will maintain that the special role Cyril assigns to the Holy Spirit in our sanctification is only one of appropriation, since inhabitation and sanctification are works common to the three persons by reason of their 'natural unity.'[42]

Although Cyril is preeminently the Doctor of the Incarnation, it is not hard to see in his trinitarian doctrine part of the reason why 'he ranks as one of the three great lights of the Church with Athanasius and Augustine.'[43]

JOHN OF DAMASCUS

John of Damascus (d. *c.* 749) took over the trinitarian doctrine of his great predecessors and achieved eminence as the last great representative of Greek theology. His most important work, *The Source of Knowledge,* is divided into three parts, and the last part, entitled *De Fide Orthodoxa* is often presented as a work complete in itself. It is a valuable *Summa* of Greek theology but it lacks the philosophical and theological profundity and genius of the *Summa* of Aquinas. In his doctrine about God one and triune Damascene leans heavily on the Pseudo-Areopagite and on the Cappadocians.

He declares that 'the knowledge of the existence of God is

implanted in us by nature' and that 'even the very continuity of the creation, and its preservation and government, teach us that there does exist a Deity, who supports and maintains and preserves and ever provides for this universe' (*De Fide Orth.* I. 3). But he stresses God's transcendence and incomprehensibility (*ibid.*) and adds that we cannot understand or express what is the essence of God' (I. 2). Moving into the area of faith he says, 'we believe, then, in one God, one principle having no principle . . . one substance, one divinity, one power, one will, one operation . . . but so that He is known in three perfect persons (*hypostaseis*) and adored with one adoration' (I. 8). Because the Father is the principle of the Son He is said to be greater than the Son, and not because the Son is in any way inferior in nature to the Father (I. 8). Echoing the Nicene symbol and substantially reproducing the teaching of his predecessors, he goes on to say that we believe

> in one Father . . . alone without cause or generation, the creator of all things, but by nature the Father of only one, His only-begotten Son and our Lord and Savior Jesus Christ, and Producer of the most Holy Spirit; and in one Son of God, the only-begotten, our Lord, Jesus Christ, begotten of the Father before all ages, Light of Light, true God of true God, begotten, not made, consubstantial with the Father, through whom all things are made . . . and in one Holy Spirit, the Lord and Giver of Life, who proceeds from the Father and rests in the Son, the object of equal adoration and glorification with the Father and Son, since He is consubstantial and coeternal . . . Lord of all creation . . . deifying . . . sanctifying . . . proceeding from the Father and communicated through the Son . . . derived from the Father, yet not after the manner of generation, but after that of procession (I. 8).

He sees a difference between generation and creation, for 'generation means that the begetter produces out of his essence offspring similar in essence, but creation and making mean that the creator and maker produces from that which is external, and not out of his own essence, a creation of an absolutely dissimilar nature' (I. 8). But the difference between generation and procession is beyond him: 'we have learned that there is a difference between generation and procession, but the nature of that difference we in no wise understand' (I. 8).

Damascene calls only the Father 'the Producer of the Holy Spirit' and says, 'we do not speak of the Son as cause (*aition*) or Father, but we speak of Him both as from the Father, and as the Son of the

Father. And we speak likewise of the Holy Spirit as from the Father, and call Him the Spirit of the Father. And we do not speak of the Spirit as from the Son but yet we call Him the Spirit of the Son . . . and we confess that He is manifested and imparted to us through the Son' (I. 8). Did he mean that the Son was in no sense cause of the Holy Spirit, or only not the primordial cause? It is hard to say, but it seems more probable that he assigned to the Son no causal role in the production of the Spirit.

There is no doubt that Damascene holds a strictly consubstantial Triad, for he says that the persons are coeternal 'and their essence is the same . . . and their will, authority, power, goodness is the same. I did not say likeness but identity . . . One and the same are Father and Son and Holy Spirit, except that the Father is unbegotten, the Son begotten, and the Holy Spirit proceeds. . . . We know one God; only in the properties of paternity, filiation and procession, and as regards cause and caused and perfection of hypostasis, that is mode of existing, do we understand distinction' (I. 8). For all 'that the Son has the Holy Spirit also has from the Father, even that which He is. . . . And because of the Father, that is, because the Father exists, both the Son and the Holy Spirit exist. And because of the Father, that is, because the Father has these things, so also do the Son and Holy Spirit have whatever they have' (I. 8).

Thus Damascene views the persons metaphysically as 'modes of existence, in much the same way as the Cappadocians. But he forestalls any accusation of Sabellianism by declaring that 'the persons dwell in one another, in no wise confused but cleaving together . . . for . . . they are made one not so as to commingle, but so as to cleave to each other, and they have their being in each other without any coalescence or commingling' (I. 8). Just as Basil maintained a unity of *ousia* and a unity of rule, so Damascene says that owing to the fact that the three persons have 'the same substance and dwell in one another, and have the same will and operation and power and authority and movement, so to speak, we recognize the indivisibility and the unity of God. For verily there is one God, and His Word and Spirit' (I. 8).

Nowhere does Damascene explicitly try to solve the problem of the divine Triunity, how three perfect hypostases can be identical in substance and rule and yet really distinct and subsistent in themselves, but perhaps he hints at a solution when he presents the three hypostases as three modes of existence of the one divine *ousia*, which are really but only relationally or causally distinct.

Damascene may not have greatly deepened or extended the trinitarian doctrine of his predecessors, but he gave us a most clear and simple and effective summary of that doctrine. In its way his *De Fide Orthodoxa* is a minor masterpiece.

Photius (d. *c.* 897) was 'a learned humanist,'[44] a master of languages with an amazing learning in varied fields. He has been called 'the greatest scholar of his day.'[45] He was twice appointed to the patriarchal see of Constantinople, first by Emperor Michael III in 858 after the emperor had deposed Ignatius from this see, then by the next emperor, Basil the Macedonian, after the death of Ignatius. In 867 Photius convened a synod at Constantinople which declared Pope Nicholas I 'a heretic' and deposed and excommunicated him. In 869 another council at Constantinople, presided over by three papal legates, condemned Photius as 'an intruder,' excommunicated him and annulled all his acts and synods. This Council the West later on regarded as the Eighth General Council. In 879–880 still another synod, called the Synod of Rehabilitation, was held at Constantinople, which reinstated Photius as the legitimate patriarch of Constantinople. This last synod some Orthodox Greeks have regarded as the Eighth General Council, but it has never been officially declared such by the Byzantine Church.[46] In a letter to Photius in 880 Pope John VIII wrote that 'we also approve what has been mercifully done in Constantinople by the synodal decree of your reinstatement.'[47] At this time, it seems, Photius resumed communion with Rome.[48] While his fellow Orientals have regarded Photius as 'apostolic ecumenical doctor' and 'saint,' Western historians have painted a very black picture of him.[49] But 'for the past several decades a number of Western scholars have been endeavoring not without opposition to vindicate him, not only as a great scholar, but also as a noble-minded ecclesiastic.'[50]

Photius' writings on dogma, Biblical exegesis, canon law, literary criticism and philology cover almost 4 volumes of Migne's *Greek Patrology* (vols. 101–104). His *Mystagogia Spiritus sancti* (PG 102.279–391) is of capital importance for fixing the doctrine that he opposed to what he considered the *Filioque* 'innovation' of some Latins. This work has served for hundreds of years as the arsenal of Greek polemicists in their controversy with the Latins over the *Filioque*.

His basic thesis is that just as the Son is born of the Father alone, so the Holy Spirit proceeds from the Father alone, but this Spirit is called Spirit of the Son because He is sent by the Son and is consubstantial with the Son (*Myst. Sp. S.*, inscr.). He draws his Biblical argument chiefly from Johannine texts, especially the one that says that the Holy Spirit 'proceeds' (*ekporeuetai*) from the Father (Jn 15.26). This he understands to mean 'from the Father alone.' For if the Son here declares that the Holy Spirit proceeds from the Father, it would be impious to say that the Holy Spirit proceeds from the Son (*Myst. Sp. S.* 2). So when Christ says that the Holy Spirit 'will receive of what is mine' (Jn 16.14), He does not imply that the Holy Spirit proceeds from the Son but only that He is consubstantial, identical in nature and equal in dignity with the Son (*Myst. Sp. S.* 27, 28). And when Paul calls the Holy Spirit the Spirit of the Son (Gal 4.6) he in no way means that He is caused by the Son (*Myst. Sp. S.* 50–58), but only that He is consubstantial with the Son. When in Isaiah the Holy Spirit is called 'the Spirit of the Lord' (Is 61.1), this once again is because He is consubstantial with the Son and anoints Him (*Myst. Sp. S.* 93). Thus his scriptural argument is simple. Only one text signifies the eternal procession of the Holy Spirit, the one in which it is said that He 'proceeds from the Father' (Jn 15.26). Those that relate Him to the Son signify His consubstantiality with or mission by the Son. It hardly needs to be noted that such an interpretation of the Biblical data is extremely subjective.

His patristic argumentation is like that from Scripture: 'neither in the divine words of Scripture nor in the human words of the holy Fathers was it ever verbally enunciated that the Spirit proceeds from the Son' (*Myst. Sp. S.* 91). To the objection that Ambrose and Augustine and Jerome taught that the Holy Spirit proceeds from the Son, he replied that they were fallible and so it would be better to gloss over their error and not glory in it (*ibid.*, 66–72). And what if Ambrose did say that the Holy Spirit proceeds from the Son, he added. The Roman Pontiffs Celestine, Leo the Great, Vigilius, Agatho, Gregory the Great, Hadrian I, Leo III, Benedict III, John VIII, and Hadrian III (*ibid.*, 79–89) held that the Holy Spirit proceeds from the Father, and so did six of the seven universal synods (*ibid.*, 5). But what Photius did not and could not show was that these taught that the Holy Spirit proceeds from the Father alone. Nor did he point out that Leo III wrote explicitly to 'all oriental churches: This symbol of the orthodox faith we send you. . . . We believe . . . in the holy Trinity, i.e., Father, Son, and Holy Spirit, the Father from Himself and not from another, the Son generated by the Father, the Holy Spirit proceeding equally from the Father and the Son, consubstantial and coeternal with the Father and the Son.'[51]

To his Biblical, patristic, pontifical, and conciliar argumentation he added a most impressive series of dialectical arguments. If we say that the Son produces the Holy Spirit, must we not also say that the Holy Spirit produces the Son (*Myst. Sp. S.* 3)? If the Holy Spirit subsists by a twofold cause and a twofold procession, must there not be composition in the Trinity (*ibid.*, 4)? What can the Holy Spirit receive by proceeding from the Son that He has not already by His procession from the Father (*ibid.*, 7)? If the Holy Spirit proceeds from the Father and the Son would this not imply a Sabellian confusion of Father and Son (*ibid.*, 9)? If two principles are admitted in the Trinity, must this not involve the destruction of the monarchy and the introduction of polytheism (*ibid.*, 11)? If two principles are admitted in the monarchical Trinity, why not three (*ibid.*, 12)? If the Father is the cause of the persons who proceed from Him by reason of His person and not His nature, then since His person does not include the Son, how can the Son be the cause of the Holy Spirit (*ibid.*, 15)? If the production of the Holy Spirit is a hypostatic property of the Father, how can the Son also have it (*ibid.*, 19)? If the Spirit's procession from the Father is perfect, what can His procession from the Son add to this (*ibid.*, 31)? If everything in the Trinity is either common to the three or proper to one person, then must not the production of the Holy Spirit be proper to the Father alone (*ibid.*, 36)?

Many of these Photian arguments are impressive, and it is not hard to see how they came to form the basis of the dogmatic teaching of subsequent Orthodox theologians. Latin theologians will reject them on the basis of a more objective and contextual exegesis and a more accurate metaphysical analysis of the concepts of nature, person, and principle as regards the inner life of the Trinity. But the *Filioque* controversy will go on and on, provoking an endless literature out of all proportion to its importance. The theological energies of East and West could be much better spent in a unified ecumenical effort to make the doctrine of the Trinity and the fact of the Trinity more intelligible to men and more influential in their lives.

SUMMARY

If we look back over the years from the New Testament writers to Photius, the flow of Greek trinitarian thought becomes clearer. In the New Testament the eternity and divinity of the Son and the Holy Spirit were indicated clearly enough, but nowhere formally declared. There was no formal doctrine about Christ's origin, nature, and relation to the Father and to the Holy Spirit. There was no formal doctrine about a triune God. But the elements for such a doctrine were there.

The Apostolic Fathers maintained only one God and affirmed

the divinity and distinct personality of Christ quite clearly, but that of the Holy Spirit less clearly. The Apologists went further. They were the first to try to give an intellectually satisfying explanation of the relation between Christ and God. For this purpose they adopted a philosophical framework, a two-stage theory of the pre-existent Logos, that obscured if it did not deny the eternal personality and the eternal generation of the Son. Perhaps they did not realize that this theory had a built-in 'inferiorizing principle.' Origen rejected the two-stage theory of the Apologists and maintained the eternal generation of the Son. But to reconcile this with a strict monotheism, he resorted to another philosophical framework, a Platonic hierarchical framework, and ended up by making the Son and the Holy Spirit not precisely creatures but 'diminished gods,' inferior to the Father who alone was God in the strict sense. Once again the philosophical framework had a built-in inferiorizing principle. But he still made an important contribution to the development of trinitarian doctrine by being the first to speak of God as 'three hypostases' and 'one *ousia*' and of the Son as *homoousios* with the Father, for these will come to be the accepted terms for expressing God's triunity in the Eastern Church.

Now the stage was set for Arius. He wanted no 'inferior God.' Either the Son was God or He was a creature. How determine this? Simply: God must be uncreated, unoriginated, unbegotten. But the Son is originated, is begotten. Hence He is not God but creature. The subordinationist tendency in the Apologists and in Origen had thus reached full term.

As Arius had put his question in ontological categories, so the Church at Nicea had to answer it in ontological categories. In the New Testament affirmations about the Son were largely functional and stressed what the Son does for and is to us. Arians willingly recited these affirmations but read into them their own meaning. To preclude this Arian abuse of the Scripture affirmations Nicea transposed these Biblical affirmations into ontological formulas, and gathered the multiplicity of scriptural affirmations about the Son into a single affirmation that the Son is not made but born eternally of the Father's substance, that He is true God from true God and consubstantial with the Father. Nicea thus defined what the Son is in Himself and in relation to the Father: He is all that the Father is, except for the name of Father. Herein lies the historical and dogmatic importance of Nicea. And by passing from the historical-existential categories of Scripture to the ontological or explanatory categories exhibited in the *homoousion* it sanctioned the principle of the development of doctrine, of growth in understanding of the primitive affirmations of the New Testament revelation and furnished the precedent for Ephesus and Chalcedon.

At the end of the Nicene Council Arianism was driven underground but it was not dead. A very large Anti-Nicene party developed, which refused to accept the *homoousion* as the test of orthodoxy. Athanasius became the great defender of the Nicene faith against the Anti-Nicenes in the East. He presented a solid trinitarian doctrine that maintained strict consubstantiality of the Son and Holy Spirit with the Father, but he felt that the inner nature of the Trinity was not to be curiously investigated. Had he had an adequate vocabulary of terms and definitions he could have coped better with his opposition. He left many questions for later Fathers to ponder and answer.

The Cappadocians made the most important contribution to the development of Greek trinitarian doctrine. Athanasius had had no term or definition for person, no formula to express God's triunity, and he had made little or no attempt to deal with the trinitarian problem of how God can be at the same time objectively one and three. The Cappadocians chose *hypostasis* as the word best fitted to express person, and their formula for expressing God's triunity was 'one *ousia* in three hypostases.' They made the trinity of hypostases their methodological starting point. They not only affirmed the Holy Spirit's full divinity but explicitly called Him 'God.' They so thoroughly established the identity of substance for Father, Son, and Holy Spirit that they effectively put an end to subordinationism. They differentiated the three hypostases metaphysically in terms of cause, relation, modes of existence. They tried to differentiate the Holy Spirit's origination from the Father through the Son as breath from the Son's generation by the Father alone as image. They tried to answer the problem of God's triunity in terms of 'relations of caused and cause,' 'modes of being and being' that accounted for the distinction of hypostases without multiplying the *ousia*. They developed or touched most all the main lines of later trinitarian theology and brought Greek trinitarian doctrine to its highest point of speculative development.

In 381 the emperor Theodosius convoked at Constantinople what has come to be called the Second Ecumenical Council. Out of it came a creed that is admitted as authoritative in East and West. Its doctrine about the Son is substantially identical with that of Nicea but it goes beyond Nicea in affirming belief in the Holy Spirit as 'the Lord and Giver of life, who proceeds from the Father, who together with the Father and Son is adored and glorified, who spoke through the prophets.' It thus defines the divinity of the Holy Spirit

without explicitly calling Him 'God' or 'consubstantial' with Father
and Son.

Cyril of Alexandria made important contributions to trinitarian
doctrine in the areas of divine circumincession, procession, indwelling, sanctification. He teaches the inexistence of the Holy Spirit in
the Father and the Son and the mutual inexistence of Father and
Son by reason of consubstantiality. He perhaps hints that the Son's
generation is intellectual and that the Spirit is caused by the Son as
well as by the Father. He teaches that the Trinity inhabits the just but
stresses the presence of the Holy Spirit. In the matter of sanctification he seems to posit a mysterious dual filiative union with Christ
and a very special, almost hypostatic, union of the just with the
Holy Spirit.

John of Damascus summed up the trinitarian doctrine of his
great predecessors. He held to a strictly consubstantial Triad and
viewed the persons metaphysically as 'modes of being.' He is able to
differentiate generation from creation but not from procession, and
he seems to have assigned the Son no causal role in the production
of the Holy Spirit. He did not greatly deepen or extend the trinitarian doctrine of his predecessors but in his clear and effective
summary of it he left us a minor masterpiece.

Photius, who has been called 'the greatest scholar of his day,' is
notable in the West mainly for his opposition to what he considered
the *Filioque* innovation of some Latins. The basic thesis of his
Mystagogia Spiritus sancti is that just as the Son is born of the Father
alone, so the Holy Spirit proceeds from the Father alone. He backs
up his thesis with an impressive array of Biblical, patristic, pontifical, conciliar, and dialectical arguments, which served for centuries
as the arsenal of Greek polemicists. The *Filioque* controversy that
he stimulated will go on and on, provoking an endless theological
literature out of all proportion to its importance.

PART THREE

The Triune God in the early Western Church

When the faith was first preached at Rome in the 1st century, the primitive Christian community was made up predominantly of Easterners. Greek became the official language of the Church and of its liturgy. The shift to Latin as the official language of the Church would not take place until about A.D. 250.

Of the writings of the Apostolic Fathers only *1 Clement* and *The Shepherd of Hermas* are considered to be of Western and Roman provenance.[1] *1 Clement* presents no doctrine of the Trinity, but it speaks of God the Father, of Christ His Son, and of the Holy Spirit and coordinates the three in an oath. The doctrine of Hermas about Christ and the Holy Spirit is so obscure that he has been called an adoptionist and a binitarian. Probably he presented explicitly only two pre-existent divine persons before the birth of Jesus, namely the Father and the Son of God who is the Holy Spirit. But it is not clear whether this was his deliberate intention or merely due to terminological confusion.

Of the Apologists only Justin is properly ascribed to the Early Western Church, for he 'founded a school in Rome.'[2] In Justin's writings we find a belief in the unity of God and in a trinity of divine persons, Father, Son, and Holy Spirit, although there is as yet no distinct conception of 'divine person' and 'divine nature.' Justin identifies Christ with the Son of God, with the Logos, and with God. To the Logos he ascribes a divine pre-existence that is not only pre-creational but also strictly eternal, and he probably viewed this eternal Logos as Someone with whom the Father could commune and take counsel. But the generation of the Logos as Son seems rather to be pre-creational but not eternal and is effected by the will of the Father for the purpose of creation. Thus Justin is counted among those who subscribed to the 'Twofold Stage Theory of the Logos,'³ and to some extent he was a subordinationist, though not in the full later Arian sense of the term, for he regarded the Logos-Son not as a thing made, a creature, but as God born of the Father. There is some obscurity in Justin's presentation of the Holy Spirit, so that some have thought that he identified the Logos and the Holy Spirit, while others have judged that he regarded the Holy Spirit as sub-personal rather than fully personal. But in more than one passage he clearly distinguishes the Holy Spirit from the Logos and appears to regard Him as a distinct person. He calls the unity of the three 'the monarchy of God' and regards it as a unity of power and rule, but not as a unity of substance. Thus he offers no systematic trinitarian doctrine but an interesting and valuable, if imperfect, attempt to give an intellectually satisfying explanation of some aspects of trinitarian belief, which will exercise a degree of influence on Irenaeus and other Western theologians.

CHAPTER SIX

The Pre-Augustinian Phase

IRENAEUS

Irenaeus of Lyons (d. *c.* 202) has been called 'one of the greatest figures of the first ages of the Church'[1] and 'the most important of the 2d century theologians.'[2] Though he was born in the East, he accomplished his great pastoral and theological work in the West as bishop of Lyons. He was 'not an exact and systematic writer'[3] but he was undoubtedly 'the first constructive theologian of historical Christianity after the Apostolic age.'[4] He wrote in Greek, not in Latin.

His *Demonstration of the Apostolic Preaching* is a summary presentation of Catholic doctrine. His chief work, *Detection and Overthrow of the Pretended but False Gnosis*, usually called *Adversus Haereses*,[5] gives a history of Gnosticism and then a refutation of it from reason, from the doctrine of the Church and from the sayings of the Lord.

For many Gnostics[6] there is one supreme God infinitely remote from the world of matter and men, and between this God and matter there is a pleroma of intermediary beings or aeons, which become less and less perfect as they recede from God. Among aeons one is the Demiurge who is the God of the Jews and the Creator of man and of the material world; other aeons for 'Christian' Gnostics are Christ, Jesus, and the Holy Spirit. Irenaeus presents some of the different views of Christ and the Holy Spirit that were held by 'Christian' Gnostics such as Basilides, the Valentinians, the Ophites.

According to Irenaeus Basilides

sets forth that Nous was first born of the unborn Father, that from him was born Logos, from Logos Phronesis, from Phronesis Sophia and Dynamis, and from Dynamis and Sophia, the powers, and principalities, and angels, whom he also calls the first; and that by them the first heaven was made. Then other powers, being formed by emanation from these, created another heaven similar to the first; and in like manner . . . more and more principalities and angels were formed, and three hundred and sixty-five heavens. . . . Those angels who occupy the lowest heaven, that, namely, which is visible to us, formed all the things which are in the world. . . . The chief of them is he who is thought to be the God of the Jews; and inasmuch as he desired to render the other nations subject to his own people . . . all other nations were at enmity with his nation. But the Father without birth and without name, perceiving that they would be destroyed, sent his own first-begotten Nous (he it is who is called Christ) to bestow deliverance on them that believe in him, from the power of those who made the world. He appeared, then, on earth as a man, to the nations of these powers, and wrought miracles. Wherefore he did not himself suffer death, but Simon, a certain man of Cyrene, being compelled, bore the cross in his stead; so that this latter being transfigured by him, that he might be thought to be Jesus, was crucified, through ignorance and error, while Jesus himself received the form of Simon, and, standing by, laughed at them (*Haer*. I. 24–34).

Irenaeus adds that according

to the disciples of Ptolemaeus, whose school may be described as a bud from that of Valentinus . . . Monogenes, acting in accordance with the prudent forethought of the Father, gave origin to another conjugal pair, namely Christ and the Holy Spirit. . . . Then out of gratitude for the great benefit which had been conferred on them, the whole Pleroma of the Aeons . . . with the concurrence of Christ and the Holy Spirit, their Father also setting the seal of His approval on their conduct . . . produced to the honor and glory of Bythus, a being of most perfect beauty, the very star of the Pleroma, and the perfect fruit [of it], namely Jesus (*Haer*.I. pref. I. 5–6)

Others again (Ophites)

declare that there exists, in the power of Bythus, a certain primary light . . . this is the Father of all, and is styled the first man. They also maintain that his Ennoea, going forth from him, produced a son, and that this is the son of man—the second man. Below these, again, is the Holy Spirit . . . the first woman. Afterwards, they maintain, the first man with his son, delighting over the beauty of the Spirit—that is, of the woman—begat by her an incorruptible light, the third man, whom they call Christ—the son of the first and second man, and of the Holy Spirit, the first woman (*Haer.* I. 30.1).

Against these fantastic speculations Irenaeus sets forth with solid argumentation the doctrine that there is but one God the Father, Lord and Creator of heaven and earth (*Haer.* II. 1.1), who formed all things by His Son and Spirit who were always with Him (*Haer.* IV. 20.1).

For Irenaeus there is no doubt that Jesus is Christ, is Savior, is the Son of God and the Word of God, the Lord and God: 'For Christ did not at that time descend upon Jesus, neither was Christ one and Jesus another: but the Word of God, who is the Savior of all and the ruler of heaven and earth, who is Jesus and did also take upon Him flesh and was anointed by the Spirit from the Father—was made Jesus Christ . . . the Word of God was man from the root of Jesse and . . . He was God' (*Haer.* III.9.3). He declares that 'this, therefore, was the knowledge of salvation; but [it did not consist in] another God, nor another Father, nor Bythus, nor the Pleroma of thirty Aeons, nor the Mother of the [lower] Ogdoad: but the knowledge of salvation was the knowledge of the Son of God, who is both called and actually is, salvation and Savior, and salutary. . . . He is indeed Savior, as being the Son and Word of God. . . . This knowledge of salvation did John impart' (*Haer.* III. 10.2). He insists that Christ as well as the Father is Lord and God: 'no other is named as God, or is called Lord, except Him who is God and Lord of all . . . and His Son Jesus Christ our Lord' (*Haer.* III. 6.2); 'all things . . . were both established and created by Him who is God over all, through His Word . . . so that He indeed who made all things can alone, together with His Word, properly be termed God and Lord' (*Haer.* III. 8.3); 'since, therefore, the Father is truly Lord, and the Son truly Lord . . . for the Spirit designates both by the name of God—both Him who is anointed as Son, and Him who does anoint, that is, the Father. . . . The Church . . . is the synagogue of God, which God—that is, the Son Himself—has gathered by Himself' (*Haer.* III. 6.10).

Did Irenaeus hold the eternal generation of the Son? It has been argued that he did not, since 'he nowhere mentions the doctrine as such' and it would be hard to square it' with the framework of ideas he inherited from the Apologists' and 'in his usage "Son" was little more than a synonym for "Word." '[7] But this argumentation is weak. For Irenaeus 'prefers generally the name of *Son* to that of *Word*.'[8] He certainly speaks of that generation when he writes, that 'if anyone, therefore, says to us, "How then was the Son produced by the Father?" we reply to him, that no man understands that production or generation . . . but the Father only who begat, and the Son who was begotten' (*Haer.* II. 28.6). And he clearly enough indicates that this generation was eternal when he writes: 'He is the father of our Lord Jesus Christ: through His Word, who is His Son, through Him He is revealed. . . . But the Son, eternally co-existing with the Father, from of old, yea, from the beginning, always reveals the Father to Angels, Archangels, Powers, Virtues and all to whom He wills that God should be revealed' (*Haer.* II. 30.9). He criticizes the Gnostics as 'those who transfer the generation of the uttered word of men to the eternal Word of God, assigning [to Him] a beginning of prolation and a genesis, even as they do to their own word' (*Haer.* II. 13.8). If he considers the Father to be Lord and God from eternity, must he not consider the Son as Son equally eternal when he writes, 'the Father is truly Lord, and the Son truly Lord. . . . For the Spirit designates both by the name of God' (*Haer.* III. 6.1). Nowhere does Irenaeus use the expressions that are characteristic of the twofold stage theory of the Apologists. Rather he rejects this theory in its Gnostic analogue when he writes that 'while they style Him unspeakable and unnameable, they nevertheless set forth the production and formation of His first generation, as if they themselves had assisted at His birth, thus assimilating Him to the word of mankind formed by emissions' (*Haer.* II. 28.6). Hence it seems clear that 'the twofold stage theory was, therefore, rejected by Irenaeus as something dangerous, as something which might lead the unwary to the false Gnostic view which assigns to the Logos "a beginning of prolation." '[9]

What place does the Holy Spirit hold in the theology of Irenaeus? Though Irenaeus' 'chief interest lies in the Incarnation of the Son . . . the doctrine of the Spirit is not overlooked, and for the first time it takes its place in an orderly scheme of Christian teaching.'[10] Irenaeus argues that, if God was rational and therefore had His Logos, He was also spiritual and so had His Spirit (*Dem.* 5). Though Irenaeus, following the example of the Scriptures, never calls the Holy Spirit 'God,' he clearly considered Him divine for he placed Him on the same divine level as the Son and the Father and equally eternal, for 'the breath, then, is temporal, but the Spirit eternal' (*Haer.* V. 12.2). With Theophilus Irenaeus identifies the Spirit with Wisdom and declares 'that the Word, i.e. the Son, was always with the Father has been shown at length; that Wisdom also, which is the Spirit, was with Him before all creation is taught by Solomon (Prov 3.19) (*Haer.* IV. 20.3–4). Irenaeus with the Church of the 2d century stressed faith in the Holy Spirit as the Spirit of the Old Testament Christological prophecy: 'the faith in one God, the Father Almighty . . . and in one Lord Jesus Christ, the Son of God . . . and in the Holy Spirit, that through the prophets preached the dispensations and the advents, and the birth from a virgin and the passion and the resurrection from the dead and the ascension' (*Haer*. I. 10.1). The Spirit's anointing of Jesus caught Irenaeus' attention: 'the Father anointed, the Son was anointed, the Spirit was the unction' (*Haer*. III. 18.3); 'the Word of God who took flesh and was anointed by the Father with the Spirit. The Spirit of God it was that descended on Jesus, the Spirit of Him who by the Prophets had promised to anoint Him; that receiving of the unction which overflows from Him we might be saved' (*Haer*. III. 9.2–3).

But it was in his exposition of the Spirit's work on the hearts and lives of men that Irenaeus was most in advance of other writers of the 2d century. Many are the functions he assigns to the Holy Spirit, 'to dwell in the race, and to rest in men and dwell in the creatures of God, working in them the Father's will, renewing them so that they pass from the old self into the newness of Christ' (*Haer*. III. 17.2), to bring about union and fellowship of God and man (*Haer*. V. 1.2), to cleanse man and elevate him to the life of God (*Haer*. V. 9.1), to perfect and prepare men for immortality, and to hold and carry God (*Haer*. V. 8.1). Without the Spirit the Word of God cannot be seen (*Dem*. 7), without the Spirit of God 'we cannot be saved' for 'where the Spirit of the Father is, there is a living man' (*Haer*. V. 36.2). And he adds, 'where the Church is, there is also the Spirit of God, and where the Spirit of God is, there is the Church and all grace; for the Spirit is truth' (*Haer*. III. 24.1). The Paraclete is 'the living water which the Lord grants to those who rightly believe in Him and love Him' (*Haer*. V. 18.2). And somewhat ecstatically Irenaeus adds, 'if hearts of flesh are now capable of receiving the Spirit, what wonder if in the resurrection they receive the life which is in the gift of the Spirit . . . what shall be done when, rising again, we shall see Him face to face . . . what will the whole grace of the Spirit do, which men will then receive from God? . . . it will make man after the image and likeness of God' (*Haer*. V. 13.4; V. 8.1).

Irenaeus does not use the term *trinity* that Theophilus used, but he does teach that God is an eternal Triad of Father, Son, and Spirit, who are distinct and equally divine. Thus he writes that 'His Word and His Wisdom, His Son and His Spirit, are always by Him, by whom and in whom, freely and spontaneously, He made all things, to whom also He speaks, saying, "Let us make man after our image and likeness" ' (*Haer*. IV. 20.1). The Church believes 'in one God, the Father Almighty . . . and in one Christ Jesus, the Son of God . . . and in the Holy Spirit, who proclaimed through the prophets the dispensations of God' (*Haer*. I. 10.1). 'There is therefore one God, who by the Word and Wisdom created and arranged all things' (*Haer*. IV. 20.4). He adds, 'let us not . . . seek after any other God besides Him who really exists . . . who created us, being most properly assured that the Scriptures are indeed perfect, since they were spoken by the Word of God and His Spirit' (*Haer*. II. 28.2).

At times Irenaeus seems to use subordinationist language. He often speaks of the Son and Spirit as the 'Hands' of God the Father: 'Now man . . . was formed after the likeness of God, and moulded by His hands, that is, by the Son and Holy Spirit, to whom also He said, "Let us make man" ' (*Haer*. IV. pref.4; cf. V. 6.1; IV. 20.1). Again he calls them the 'ministers' of the Father: 'for His offspring and His similitude do minister to Him in every respect; that is, the Son and the Holy Spirit, the Word and Wisdom' (*Haer*. IV. 7.4). And he describes 'the Father planning everything well and giving His commands, the Son carrying these into execution and performing the work of creating, and the Spirit nourishing and increasing . . . but man . . . ascending towards the perfect . . . the uncreated One . . . God' (*Haer*. IV. 38.3).

Taken literally these words can suggest subordinationism. But if we judge Irenaeus rather by his total thought and by his intention, he is not a subordinationist. For he does not regard the Son and Spirit as creatures but as just as eternal and divine as the Father, for they are the very Word of God and the Wisdom of God who belong to the very life of God and possess the divine, creative, revelative, and inspirative power of God. They are with the Father the one uncreated God. Why does he view the Father as planning, the Son as executing, the Spirit as nourishing? Probably because that was the view of St. Paul. Why does he call them 'ministers' of the Father? Probably because that mode of expression seemed to him to correspond with the New Testament doctrine of the Father's sending of the Son and the Spirit. Why did he call them the 'Two Hands' of God? Probably because of the Old Testament metaphor of the 'finger of God,' the 'hand of God.' But it was not his intention to subordinate them to the Father but to tell the Gnostics that the Supreme God is the Creator and none other, that the one true God who is Father, Son, and Spirit is the direct and immediate Creator of all that is and needs no mediating aeons or angels as His intermediary instruments of creation: 'For God did not stand in need of these [beings] . . . as if He did not possess His own hands. For with Him were always present the Word and Wisdom, the Son and the Spirit, by whom and in whom, freely and spontaneously He made all things' (*Haer.* IV. 20.1). It seems necessary to conclude, then, that 'there is no emanationism in the doctrine of "The Two Hands of God" nor is there any subordinationism. The "Hands" indeed serve God, but they are not thereby subordinate, for this service is God's own activity in the world. So also the Spirit may be described as a gift, but this does not place the Gift below the Giver, for that which God gives is Himself.'[11]

Are there modalist passages in Irenaeus? Some have maintained that there are, and one in particular has been singled out:[12] 'for the Father is the invisible of the Son, but the Son the visible of the Father' (*Haer.* IV. 6.6). But it is clear enough that neither here nor in the 'Two Hands' doctrine did Irenaeus actually intend modalism, for in this same Book IV in passages dealing with the 'Two Hands' he presents the Son and Spirit as eternally and 'personally' distinct from the Father: 'for God did not stand in need of these [aeons] . . . as if He did not possess His own hands. For with Him were always present the Word and Wisdom, the Son and Spirit, by whom and in whom . . . He made all things, to whom also He speaks, saying "Let Us make man after Our image and likeness" ' (*Haer.* IV. 20.1; cf. IV. pref. 4). Irenaeus believes in one God, Father, Son, and Holy Spirit but he finds the inner life of God inscrutable. To cast some tiny light on this mystery he calls the Son and Spirit 'The Two Hands of God' the Creator. How they are this he does not explain, and 'thus he was not a complete theologian, but in inward spirit he was the very opposite to a Modalist.'[13] He can well lay claim to having taught the doctrine of creation 'by the whole Trinity.'

Thus Irenaeus made a solid contribution to the development of Western theology. He abstained from speculation and was somewhat hostile to research. He developed no technical language and formulas to express trinitarian doctrine. But he presented and defended as well as he could the traditional doctrine he had received —that there is one sole God the Creator and Lord of all, who is Father, Son, and Spirit. That was enough for him. And that was a great deal for the Church.

TERTULLIAN

Tertullian (d. *c.* 220) has been called 'the greatest of the early Latin writers'[14] and the 'founder of theology in the West.'[15] It has been said that in him 'we first find the accurate definition and technical terms that passed over into Catholic theology, winning prompt acceptance in the West and securing—when the time came—the grudging but certain approval of the East.'[16] It has even been maintained that 'his place is secure as the last of the Greek Apologists' since 'he was profoundly influenced by previous Greek speculation, and, unlike almost all of the Latin Fathers, he read Greek with facility, and actually composed his earliest works in that language.'[17] His writings 'show us that he knew Athenagoras and Melito, Tatian and Minucius Felix, and Clement of Alexandria'[18] and he himself tells us that he used the writings of Justin, Irenaeus and Miltiades (*Adv. Valent.* 5).

Of his many works 'the treatise *De praescriptione contra haereticos* is, with the *Apologeticum* the work which has had the most brilliant and lasting fame.'[19] His 5 books *Against Marcion* 'may be taken as representing Tertullian's considered opinion on the faith . . . before the influence of Montanism seriously took effect, and serve to show how little difference the "new prophecy" made to the essentials of Christian belief.'[20] His work *Against the Valentinians* leans heavily on Irenaeus. His treatise *Against Praxeas* 'represents the most important contribution to the doctrine of the Trinity in the Ante-Nicene period.'[21]

The Apologists had tried to show how the Son and Spirit, who were revealed in the 'Economy' as other than the Father, were yet inseparably one with Him in His eternal being. But in the West a strongly unitarian reaction to this developed. It was called 'Monarchianism' because its supporters, as Tertullian puts it, 'shy at the economy' and say 'we hold to the monarchy' (*Adv. Prax.* 3). The term *monarchy* had been used by the Apologists as a protest against polytheism,[22] and in itself it was as unobjectionable as the term *unity*. It had originally the political sense of sovereignty, empire, imperial authority. But it was used later as a catchword by 'Unitarians' who denied the distinction of the Father, Son, and Spirit or rejected the true divinity of Christ and the personality of the Holy Spirit. Against them Tertullian points out that a monarchy is not divided and 'does not cease to be a monarchy, if the son also is assumed as partner in it' (*Adv. Prax.* 3).

Tertullian declares that Praxeas 'was the first to import to Rome out of Asia this kind of wrongheadedness' (*Adv. Prax.* 1) and that his unitarian monarchianism had a diabolical origin:

> In divers ways has the devil shown hostility to the Truth. . . . He is the champion of the one Lord, the Almighty, the creator of the world, so that he may make a heresy out of the unity. He says that the Father Himself came down into the virgin, Himself was born of her, Himself suffered, in short Himself is Jesus Christ.

. . . Nay but he himself rather is a liar from the beginning, and so is any man whom he has suborned . . . like Praxeas. . . . And so . . . a Father who was born, a Father who suffered, God Himself the Lord Almighty, is preached as Jesus Christ. . . . So . . . this wrongheadedness . . . thinks it impossible to believe in one God unless it says that both Father and Son and Holy Spirit are one and the same (*Adv.* Prax. 1–2).

Leaning on the principle 'that whatever is earliest is true and whatever is later is counterfeit' (*Adv. Prax.* 2), Tertullian sets out against Praxeas the 'Rule of the Faith' 'that has come down from the beginning of the Gospel, even before all former heretics, not to speak of Praxeas of yesterday' (*ibid.*). And according to this Rule, he declares:

We . . . believe that there is one only God, but under the following dispensation, or *oikonomia*, as it is called, that this one only God has also a Son, His Word, who proceeded from Himself, by whom all things were made and without whom nothing was made. Him [we believe] to have been sent by the Father into the Virgin, and to have been born of her . . . being both man and God, the Son of Man and the Son of God, and to have been called by the name of Jesus Christ; [we believe] Him to have suffered, died, and been buried, according to the Scriptures, and, after He had been raised by the Father and taken back to heaven to be sitting at the right hand of the Father, [and] that He will come to judge the quick and the dead; who sent also from heaven from the Father, according to His own promise, the Holy Spirit, the Paraclete, the Sanctifier of the faith of those who believe in the Father, and in the Son, and in the Holy Spirit (*ibid.*).

Tertullian gives a similar Rule of Faith in two other works (*De praescr.* 13; *De virg. vel.* 2). He says that this Rule of Faith is 'constant,' 'immovable and irreformable' (*De virg. vel.* 1) but there are variations in his three forms of it and between his forms and those of Irenaeus (*Haer.* I. 10.1; *Dem.* 6). Yet in terms of central truths there is substantial agreement among all these forms, so that it can be said that Tertullian adopted the Rule of Faith 'in essentials from his predecessors, but he added to it, the chief additions being the priority of the Son to all creatures, and His agency in the work of creation, and the qualification of the assertion of the unity of God by the introduction of the notion of the divine economy.'[23]

Thus, for Tertullian, there is one only God, 'but . . . this one only God has also a Son, His Word, who proceeded from Himself, by

whom all things were made' (*Adv. Prax.* 2). But is this Word eternally a Person? Is this Son eternally generated? The Apologists by
reason of their twofold stage theory of the Logos seem to have
answered both questions in the negative, although it is probable that
for Justin the Word was a Person from eternity with whom the
Father took counsel. Tertullian seems to agree with the Apologists,[24]
for he writes:

> certain people affirm that in Hebrew Genesis begins, 'In the be-
> ginning God made for Himself a son.' Against the ratification of
> this I am persuaded by other arguments from God's ordinance
> in which He was before the foundation of the world until the
> generation of the Son. For before all things God was alone . . .
> because there was nothing external beside Him. Yet not even
> then was He alone: for He had with Him that Reason (*Rationem*)
> which He had in Himself—His own, of course. For God is
> rational, and Reason is primarily in Him . . . and that Reason is
> His consciousness (*sensus*). This the Greeks call *Logos*, which
> we designate Word (*sermonem*). . . . For although God had not
> yet uttered His Word, He always had it within Himself along
> with and in His Reason, while He silently thought out and
> ordained with Himself the things which He was shortly to say
> by the agency of the Word: for while thinking out and ordain-
> ing them in company of His Reason, He converted into Word
> that which He was discussing in discourse. . . . So . . . even then,
> before the establishment of the universe, God was not alone,
> seeing He continually had in Himself Reason, and in Reason
> Word, which He made another beside Himself by activity with-
> in Himself (*Adv. Prax.* 5).

That God thus eternally had in Himself Reason and in Reason Word
(*Logos*) is clear enough. But is it possible to see in this eternal Logos
another Person? Obviously this Logos is not clearly and fully per-
sonalized, but perhaps we can see a hint that Tertullian regards this
Logos as at least initially a person when he says God made His Word
'second to Himself by agitating it within Himself' and declares that
'in a certain sense, the word is a second person within you' and then
adds 'how much more fully is all this transacted in God' (*Adv. Prax.*
5).

Tertullian tells of the generation of the Son:

> so listen also to Wisdom, established as a second person (Prov
> 8.22–31). . . . For when first God's will was to produce in their
> own substances and species those things which in company of
> Wisdom and Reason and Word He had ordained within Him-

self, He first brought Word. . . . At that point therefore Word also itself receives its manifestation and equipment, namely sound and voice, when God says, 'Let there be light' (Gen. 1.3). This is the complete nativity of Word, when it comes forth from God . . . thereafter causing Him to be His Father by proceeding from whom He became Son. . . . Whatever therefore the substance of the Word (*substantia sermonis*) was, that I call a Person, and for it I claim the name of Son: and while I acknowledge Him as Son I maintain He is another (*secundum*) beside the Father (*Adv. Prax.* 6–7).

In another work he repeats this even more bluntly: 'God is in like manner a Father, and He is also a Judge; but He has not always been Father and Judge, merely on the ground of His having always been God. For He could not have been the Father previous to the Son, nor a Judge previous to sin. There was, however, a time when neither sin existed with Him, nor the Son' (*Adv. Hermog.* 3).

Thus the Son was generated, not from eternity but before and for creation, and then became a second Person. Once again, as in the Apologists, a wrong interpretation of the famous Proverbs text has been influential in establishing the non-eternal generation of the Son. And if what is not eternal is not divine in the strict sense, then the Son is not divine. But if the possession of 'divine substance' is a norm of divinity, then perhaps the Son will still be divine in Tertullian's theology. And so it is. For he writes: 'we have been taught that He proceeds forth from God, and in that procession He is generated; so that He is the Son of God, and is called God from unity of substance with God. . . . Thus Christ is God of God, as light of light is enkindled . . . so, too, that which has come forth out of God is at once God and the Son and God, and the two are one' (*Apol.* 21).

Tertullian's teaching on the Holy Spirit is notable, for he is the first and only one before Athanasius to affirm the Holy Spirit's 'divinity in an express, clear and precise manner.'[25] In his 'Montanist'[26] work *Against Praxeas* he says that the Holy Spirit is 'closely joined with the Father in His substance' (3), 'proceeds from the Father through the Son' (4), 'is third with God and [his] Son' (8), is one God with the Father and the Son (2) and 'is God' (13). Further on in this work he writes of 'the Holy Spirit, the third name of the deity and the third sequence of the majesty, the preacher of one monarchy and also the interpreter of the economy for those who admit the words of His new prophecy, and the leader into all the truth which is in the Father and the Son and the Holy Spirit according to the Christian mystery' (30). In his tract *On Modesty* he writes: 'but again, what is the power? The Spirit, and the Spirit is God.

What did He teach? That we should have no fellowship with the works of darkness' (21). In his treatise *On Baptism* he says, 'not that in the waters we obtain the Holy Spirit; but in the water . . . we are cleansed and prepared for the Holy Spirit . . . who is about to come upon us, by the washing away of sins, which faith, sealed in the Father, and the Son, and the Holy Spirit, obtains' (6). And in his work *On Repentance* he says 'among brethren . . . there is a common hope . . . because there is a common Spirit from a common Lord and Father' (10). These last two works probably belong to his Pre-Montanist period[27] and yet in all three we find the same trinitarian coordination of the Spirit with the Father and the Son, the same belief in the Holy Spirit as the Third in the Godhead.

As the 'word "triad," with reference to the godhead, appears first in Theophilus'[28] in the East, so in the West the word 'trinity' (*trinitas*) first appears in Tertullian.[29] Thus he writes: 'if the number of the Trinity still offends you . . .' (*Adv. Prax.* 12), 'a unity which derives from itself a trinity is not destroyed but administered by it' (*ibid.* 3); 'in like manner the Trinity, proceeding . . . from the Father . . . does not at all disturb the Monarchy, while it conserves the quality of the economy' (*ibid.* 8); so in these texts (Is 42.1; 43.1; 45.1; 49.6; 61.1; Pss 3.1; 71.18; 110.1; Jn 12.38; Rom 10.16) the distinctiveness of the Trinity is clearly expounded: for there is the Spirit Himself who makes the statement, the Father to whom He makes it, and the Son of whom He makes it' (*ibid.* 11). Again he writes of a 'trinity of one divinity, Father, Son and Holy Spirit' (*De pud.* 21).

In his refutation of the 'unitarian' doctrine of Praxeas he leaves no doubt that the three are numerically distinct among themselves: they are 'capable of being counted' (*Adv. Prax.* 2), for the Son is 'second' (*ibid.* 5) and the Holy Spirit is 'third' (*ibid.* 8); 'so the close series of the Father in the Son and the Son in the Paraclete makes three who cohere, the one attached to the other. And these three are *unum* and not *unus*, in respect of unity of substance, not of singularity of number' (*ibid.* 25); 'for we . . . specify two, the Father and the Son, and even three with the Holy Spirit, according to the principle of the divine economy which introduces number' (*ibid.* 13); 'setting forth Father and Son and Spirit as three, three however not in quality (*statu*) but in sequence (*gradu*), not in substance (*substantia*) but in aspect (*forma*), not in power (*potestate*) but in manifestation (*specie*), yet of one substance and one quality and one power' (*ibid.* 2); 'but that both the Father is God and the Son is God and the Holy Spirit is God and each several one is God' (*ibid.* 13).

What are the three to be called? Often Tertullian seems to prefer to call them simply 'the three,' but his most distinctive appellation for them is 'Person' (*persona*): 'there was already attached to him the Son, a second Person, His Word, and a third Person, the Spirit in the Word' (*ibid.* 12); 'how many Persons do you think there are, self-opinionated Praxeas, if not as many as there are voices? You have the Son on earth, you have the Father in heaven' (*ibid.* 23); 'therefore He also made manifest the conjunction of the two Persons . . . and it is apparent that each Person is Himself and none other' (*ibid.* 24).

It has been said that 'Tertullian is the first to use the term *persona*'[30] but it seems 'fairly certain that *persona* had penetrated the theological realm even before Tertullian,'[31] and 'it seems very probable that Hippolytus was the source from which his Latin contemporary adopted the term.'[32]

What does Tertullian mean when he calls the three 'Persons'? Harnack conjectured that in his use of this word 'Tertullian always continued to be influenced' 'by *juristic usage*'[33] but 'this view cannot be upheld.'[34] For Tertullian uses 'person' in many senses, in that of 'mask' (*De spect.* 23), that of 'face' (*Adv. Prax.* 14), in a quasi-dramatic sense (*ibid.* 11, 7, 22), in a sense equivalent to *homo* or *vir*, with no psychological or metaphysical or juristic reference (*De paenit.* 11; *De cor.* 1; *De monol.* 7; *Adv. Prax.* 14). And when he uses it with theological import 'there seems nowhere to be any sign of juristic usage.'[35] Thus 'in legal usage it could stand for the holder of the title to a property, but as employed by Tertullian it connoted the concrete presentation of an individual as such. In neither case . . . was the idea of self-consciousness nowadays associated with "person" and "personal" at all prominent.'[36] In the treatise *Against Praxeas persona* 'is much more the concrete presentation of an individual than, as is commonly alleged, the holder of the legal title to a hereditament.'[37]

It has been said that Tertullian knows as little of an immanent Trinity as the Apologists. But this statement is far from accurate, for if Tertullian stressed the economic Trinity, he also indicates that there is an immanent Trinity in the Godhead, when he speaks of a 'trinity of one divinity, Father, Son, and Holy Spirit,' of three who are 'of one substance and one quality and one power,' of a trinity proceeding from the Father [that] does not at all disturb the Monarchy,' of 'Three who cohere . . . and are *unum* . . . in respect of unity of substance,' such that 'the Father is God and the Son is God and the Holy Spirit is God.'

That Tertullian strongly emphasizes the 'unity of substance' of the three is evident, for he says that 'I always maintain one sub-

stance in three who cohere' (*Adv. Prax.* 12). But what does he mean
by 'substance'? He seems to mean 'body' or 'corporeity,' for he
writes: 'who will deny that God is a body, although "God is a
spirit"? For Spirit has a bodily substance of its own kind, in its own
form' (*ibid.* 7). Again he says 'the Father is the whole substance, while
the Son is a derivation and portion of the whole' (*ibid.* 9). He says
that 'God, too, is a Spirit,' and yet to illustrate the generation of the
Son he uses a material analogy and declares that 'even when the ray
is shot from the sun, it is still part of the parent mass . . . there is no
division of substance, but merely an extension. Thus Christ is Spirit
of Spirit, and God of God, as light of light is kindled' (*Apol.* 21).
And when he treats of the origin of the Spirit he again uses material
analogies: 'the Spirit indeed is third from God and the Son; just as
the fruit of the shoot is third from the root . . . or as the apex of the
beam is third from the sun' (*Adv. Prax.* 8).

It is not surprising, then, that interpreters disagree. Tixeront
says, 'it would probably be unfair to charge Tertullian with having
taught God's corporeity' since he 'more probably . . . used . . . the
word *corpus* as synonymous with *substantia*.'[38] And Evans declares
that when Tertullian 'says that God is *corpus* he means no more
than that he really exists: he cannot conceive of *substantia* except
as *corpus*.'[39] But other interpreters more correctly affirm that Tertullian 'regarded the divine spirit as a highly rarefied species of
matter,'[40] and understands by the substance of God 'a light, fine,
invisible matter which while being a unity is differentiated within
itself.'[41] And with keen insight Lonergan adds that if with Tertullian
you conceive the divine substance as a 'certain imagined spiritual
divine matter,' and 'if the Son is God because He has his substance
from the substance of the Father and not separated from the paternal substance, then divinity is not taken away from Him if He
originates temporally later and from the free will of the Father and
as ordered to creation and government.'[42]

Thus Tertullian's 3d-century trinitarian doctrine reached a
remarkably high stage of development for that early period of the
Church and in many respects went beyond the 2d-century doctrine
of Irenaeus. Where Irenaeus' work *Against Heresies* was aimed
chiefly at Valentinian Gnosticism, Tertullian's *Against Praxeas* was
directed against the Monarchianism of Praxeas. Tertullian gives the
same Rule of Faith substantially as Irenaeus but amplifies it somewhat. Where Irenaeus rejected the twofold stage theory of the
Logos, Tertullian seems to have accepted it and thus to have
affirmed the pre-creational but non-eternal generation of the Son
from the divine substance of the Father. Hence, if eternity is the norm

of divinity the Son is not divine, but if possession of the same divine substance as the Father's is the norm, as it seems to be for Tertullian, then the Son is divine and is God. Tertullian goes beyond Irenaeus in clearly expressing the divinity of the Holy Spirit, for he says that the Holy Spirit 'proceeds from the Father through the Son,' 'is third with God and His Son,' is one God with the Father and the Son, and 'is God.' Tertullian is the first in the West to use the word *trinity* and he indicates clearly enough that this 'trinity of one divinity' is not just an economic trinity but also an immanent trinity. He is one of the first, if not the first, to use the term *person* for the three and he seems to mean it not in the juristic sense of a title-holder but in the metaphysical sense of a concrete individual, of a self. When he says often that the three are 'one in substance' he seems to understand by 'divine substance' a rarefied form of spiritual matter. Many of Tertullian's affirmations about the Son will appear later in the Symbol of Nicea, such as these: 'the Son is of the Father's substance,' is 'one in substance with the Father,' is 'begotten,' is 'God of God,' is 'light of light.' His chief doctrinal defects lie in his materialistic view of the divine substance and in his acceptance of the non-eternal generation of the Son. But his doctrinal contributions far outstrip these defects and deservedly vindicate to him the title of founder of Latin theology.

THE ROMAN CHURCH

Through Irenaeus the Church of Lyons made a great contribution to the development of trinitarian doctrine in the West, and through Tertullian the Church of Africa made a still greater contribution. Now we turn to the Church in Rome when Latin is beginning to replace Greek as the official language of the Church and a Latin theological literature is starting to develop. The preeminence of the Roman Church did not give it a corresponding share in the development of trinitarian doctrine. It fostered no great school like that of Alexandria and it produced no theologian who would rank with Origen or the Cappadocians. Three writers stand out, Minucius Felix, Hippolytus, and Novatian.

Minucius Felix

Minucius Felix is notable for his *Octavius*, which was the only apology for Christianity written in Latin at Rome during the period of the persecutions. It has been called 'a masterpiece, not so much perhaps by the originality of the ideas as by their perfect expression and development.'[43] It gives a very imperfect idea of Christianity and a very simple Creed but it achieved its purpose of giving 'to Roman society an apology for Christianity which would fully satisfy their refined taste in literature.'[44] In ideas and expressions it so resembles Tertullian's *Apologeticum* that there can be little doubt that one of these works depends on the other. But the question of priority is still unsettled.

Hippolytus

Hippolytus (d. 235?) lived and worked in Rome as a presbyter, wrote in Greek, and ranks with Origen in the number but not the quality of his writings. He was elected 'antipope' to Callistus and remained in schism under Urban and Pontianus. He was occupied in the first period of his life with scriptural work, in the second period with defending the faith, and in the third period with personal controversies. He is venerated as a martyr and is considered to have been reconciled with the Church before his death.

The best sources of his trinitarian doctrine are his *Philosophumena* or *Refutation of all Heresies*, which was originally ascribed to Origen, and his *Against Noetus*, which is a part of his *Syntagma* or *Against All Heresies*.

In his *Philosophumena* he sets forth the 'heresy' of Noetus, and then accuses Popes Zephyrinus and Callistus of favoring it. He writes:

Now that Noetus affirms that the Son and Father are the same, no one is ignorant. But he makes his statement thus: 'When, indeed, then, the Father had not been born, He yet was justly styled Father; and when it pleased Him to undergo generation, having been begotten, He Himself became His own Son . . . and He is styled by name Father and Son, according to vicissitude of times . . . He is one who has . . . submitted to generation from a virgin, and as a man held converse among men. . . . This person suffered by being fastened to the tree, and having died to appearance. . . . He raised Himself up the third day (*Ref.* 9. 5).

Then Hippolytus adds:

Callistus attempted to confirm this heresy—a man cunning in wickedness—and moulded to his purpose Zephyrinus, an ignorant and illiterate individual, and one unskilled in ecclesiastical definitions. . . . Now Callistus brought forward Zephyrinus himself, and induced him publicly to avow the following sentiments: 'I know that there is one God, Jesus Christ; nor except Him do I know any other that is begotten and amenable to suffering.' And on another occasion . . . 'the Father did not die, but the Son.' . . . and he hurried headlong into folly . . . and called us worshippers of two gods. . . . And Callistus . . . after the death of Zephyrinus . . . excommunicated Sabellius, as not entertaining orthodox opinions. . . . This Callistus, not only on account of his publicly saying in the way of reproach to us, 'You are Ditheists,' but also on account of his being frequently accused by Sabellius . . . devised some such heresy as the following. Callistus alleges that the Logos Himself is Son, and Himself is Father. . . . And he maintains that the Father is not one person and the Son another, but that they are one and the same. . . . And he affirms that the Spirit, which became incarnate in the virgin, is not different from the Father, but one and the same. . . . 'For,' says Callistus, 'I will not profess belief in two Gods, Father and Son, but in one . . . so that Father and Son must be styled one God, and that this Person being one, cannot be two.' And in this way Callistus contends that the Father suffered along with the Son; for he does not wish to assert that the Father suffered (*Ref.* 9. 6, 7).

It is not easy to evaluate this accusation, for in it we read first that the Father and Son 'are one and the same' and then that 'the Father suffered along with the Son.' And if Callistus excommunicated Sabellius, how could he himself be the thoroughgoing Modalist that Hippolytus makes out? It seems impossible to determine the precise doctrinal positions of Zephyrinus and Callistus. But since Callistus fought for the unity of the divine essence against what he considered the 'ditheism' of Hippolytus, and for the trinity of persons against Sabellianism, he seems definitely to have been on the side of 'orthodoxy.' From what Hippolytus says it can seem that both Zephyrinus and Callistus were so fearful that the 'new' teaching about two or three *persons* would lead to ditheism or tritheism, that they leaned excessively toward Monarchianism, but Hippolytus is such an impassioned and hostile witness that it is difficult to accept his testimony as the simple truth.[45]

After castigating the Modalist errors Hippolytus sets out his own teaching on the relations of the Father and the Son in the Trinity, in a three-stage form of the two-stage theory of the Apologists.[46] In his treatise *Against Noetus* he wrote:

God, subsisting alone . . . determined to create the world. . . . Beside Him there was nothing; but He . . . yet existed in plurality. For He was neither without reason, nor wisdom, nor power, nor counsel. . . . And He begat the Word . . . and begetting Him

Light of Light, He set Him forth to the world as its Lord. . . . And thus there appeared another beside Himself. But when I say another, I do not mean that there are two Gods, but that it is only as light of light, or as water from a fountain, or as a ray from the sun. . . . Acting then in these [prophets] the Word spoke of Himself. . . . But . . . neither was the Word, prior to incarnation and when by Himself, yet perfect Son, although He was perfect Word, only-begotten. Nor could the flesh subsist by itself apart from the Word, because it has its subsistence in the Word. Thus, then, one perfect Son of God was manifested (10. 11. 12. 15).

In the first phase, then, the Logos (*endiathetos*) was eternally in the Father, but impersonally as divine intelligence and wisdom. In the second phase, God begot the Word to manifest God in creation, and thus God became Father and the Word became perfect Word and Person and Son, but not yet perfect Son. In the third phase the Word became incarnate and then became perfect Son.[47]

To the credit of Hippolytus it must be noted that the Logos, although He came into existence by the will of God, yet came into existence not by creation out of nothing but by generation and communication of the divine substance. On the other hand, there are very grave defects in his theory. The Logos was not a person nor Son from eternity, but only pre-creationally. The generation of the Son was not essential to God but only the result of a free decision of God. Hence God might have remained without a Son and thus might have remained only one Person. And yet Hippolytus made a clear distinction between creatures who are drawn from nothing, and the Logos 'who is from God himself; wherefore also the Logos is God, being the substance of God' (*Ref.* 10.29). Thus for Hippolytus, as for Tertullian, a norm of divinity seems to be the possession of divine substance and not eternal existence.

Hippolytus has a number of trinitarian passages in his tract *Against Noetus*:

a man, therefore . . . is compelled to acknowledge God the Father almighty, and Christ Jesus the Son of God, who, being God, became man . . . and the Holy Spirit; and that these therefore are three. But if he desires to learn how . . . there is one God, let him know that His power is one (8); we . . . know the Father by Him, and we believe in the Son, and worship the Holy Spirit (12); I will not say two Gods, but one only, but two Persons, and in the 'economy' a third rank, the grace of the Holy Spirit. For the Father indeed is One, but there are two Persons, because there is also the Son; and in the third place the Holy Spirit. . . . He who commands is the Father, He who obeys is the Son, He who gives understanding is the Holy Spirit. The Father is over all, the Son through all, the Holy Spirit in all. In no other way can we hold One God, but by really believing in Father, Son, and Holy Spirit. . . . Through this Trinity (*triados*) the Father is glorified; for what the Father wills, the Son translates into act, and the Spirit manifests (14); to Him be the glory and the power, with the Father and the Holy Spirit, in the holy Church both now and ever, and even for evermore. Amen (8).

In these passages Hippolytus rather deliberately seems to avoid putting the Holy Spirit on the same personal plane with the Father and the Son, and to regard Him more as a divine force than a divine person. Perhaps the Holy Spirit was outside the main thrust of his controversy with the Modalists and hence he felt little need to give a more precise doctrine about Him. But about this same time Tertullian was clearly calling the Holy Spirit both 'God' and 'a third Person.'

Novatian

Novatian (d. *c.* 257) was a priest who held a leading position among the clergy of Rome about the year 250. It seems that he had hoped to become Bishop of Rome, for when Cornelius was chosen bishop he had himself somehow consecrated bishop and then declared that he was the true successor of St. Peter.[48] He was the first theologian in Rome to write in Latin, and his writings indicate that he was well-trained in rhetoric, philosophy, and theology.

His most notable work, *On the Trinity*, systematically develops this doctrine according to the three chief articles of the Creed, so that he treats first of the Father (1–8), then of the Son (9–28), then of the Holy Spirit (29), and finally returns to the relationship between the Father and the Son (30–31). The treatise has such a wealth of Biblical proof and was developed with such clear order and method that it became something of a dogmatic *vade mecum* for the West.

Novatian begins with 'the Rule of truth' that 'requires that we should first of all believe in God the Father and omnipotent Lord . . . the absolutely perfect founder of all things, who has suspended the heavens in lofty sublimity, has established the earth with its lower mass, has diffused the seas with their fluent moisture . . . made man in the image of God . . . and willed that he alone should be free. . . . In higher regions . . . He previously ordained angels, He arranged spiritual powers' (*Trin.* 1).

'The same rule of truth,' Novatian continues, 'teaches us to

believe after the Father, also in the Son of God, Christ Jesus, the
Lord our God, but the Son of God' (*Trin.* 9). Against the heretics
who deny that Christ was truly man, Novatian insists that 'the Word
took on Him our flesh. And for this reason blood flowed forth from
His hands and feet, and from His very side, so that He might be
proved to be a sharer in our body by dying according to the laws of
our dissolution' (*Trin.* 10). But Novatian is even more intent on
showing that Christ is God, both from the Old Testament and the
New Testament. In the Old Testament he sees the divinity of Christ
indicated in Hosea's statement that 'I will save them by the Lord
their God' (Hos 1.7), and in Is 7.14; 35.3; and in Hab 3.3. In the New
Testament he turns most of all to Johannine texts, such as: 'In the
beginning was the Word, and the Word was with God, and the Word
was God' (Jn 1.1); 'Father, glorify thou me in thy own presence with
the glory which I had with thee before the world was made' (Jn
17.5); 'I and the Father are one' (10.30); 'my Lord and my God' (Jn
20.28). If Christ is only man, Novatian argues, how is it that Jesus
says in John's Gospel that 'whatever he [the Father] does, that the
Son does likewise' (Jn 5.19), and how can He say that 'as the Father
has life in himself, so he has granted the Son to have life in himself'
(Jn 5.26)? Again, he continues, how can Christ say that 'Not . . . any
one has seen the Father except him who is from God; he has seen the
Father' (Jn 6.46) and 'before Abraham was, I am' (Jn 8.58) if He is
only man ?

From the Son's divinity Novatian turns to His distinction from
the Father, for 'many heretics, moved by the magnitude and truth
of this divinity . . . have dared to announce or to think Him not the
Son, but God the Father Himself' (*Trin.* 23). 'Who does not acknowledge,' he argues,

> that the person of the Son is second after the Father, when he
> reads that it was said by the Father, consequently to the Son, 'Let
> us make man in our image and likeness' (Gen 1.26) . . . or when
> that beloved writer says 'the Lord said unto my Lord, Sit thou
> on my right hand' (Ps 110.1) . . . or when . . . he finds it written
> thus 'Thus saith the Lord to Christ my Lord' (Is 45.1) . . . or when
> he reads 'I came not down from heaven to do mine own will,
> but the will of him that sent me?' (J 6.38) . . . or when he finds
> it written 'because he who sent me is greater than I?' (Jn 14.28).
> And what can be so evident proof that this is not the Father, but
> the Son as that He is set forth as being obedient to God the
> Father (*Trin.* 26)?

Novatian aimed to exclude not only Modalism but also Ditheism, and so was concerned to refute the charge that 'if Christ be not the Father, because Christ is God the Son, there appear to be two Gods' (*Trin*. 30). Hence he insists that 'we . . . believe and maintain that God is one' (*Trin*. 30) and 'that Jesus Christ the Son of God is our Lord and God' (*ibid*.). He argues that 'if they do not think that it can by any means interfere with the truth that there is one Lord, that Christ also is Lord . . . let them understand that, from the fact that God is one, no obstruction arises to the truth that Christ also is declared to be God' (*ibid*.), for 'assuredly God proceeding from God, causing a person second to the Father as being the Son,' does not take 'from the Father that characteristic that He is one God' (*ibid*. 31), since 'He could not make two Gods, because He did not make two principles' (*ibid*. 31).

Novatian sees he must maintain unity in plurality, but he seems somewhat uncertain just how to present this unity, whereby Christ and the Father are 'one.' At times he presents it as a unity of concord[49] so that *unum* has reference 'to the agreement, and to the identity of judgment, and to the loving association itself, as reasonably the Father and Son are one in agreement, in love, and in affection' (*Trin*. 27). But again he seems to look beyond this moral union towards something more metaphysical, when he writes that this unity pertains 'to His divinity' (*ibid*. 15) and that 'the true and eternal Father is manifested as the one God, from whom alone this power of divinity is sent forth, and also given and directed upon the Son, and is again returned by the communion of substance to the Father' (*ibid*. 31). In this 'communion of substance' Novatian seems to find his deepest source of this unity, 'a communion of substance' whereby 'the deity bestowed by the Father on the Son for ever reverts to the Father . . . and there is no division of the divine nature.'[50]

Novatian makes it clear that the Son is distinct from the Father and is God and yet there is only one God. But what he holds about the Son's generation is not so clear. On the one hand, unlike Tertullian he seems to maintain that the Son was always in the Father and thus the Father was always Father, for he writes: 'He who is before all times must be said to have been always in the Father' (*Trin*. 31); 'He, then, since He was begotten of the Father, is always in the Father' (*ibid*.); 'He is always in the Father, lest the Father be not always Father' (*ibid*.). On the other hand he seems to affirm that the Father is before the Son, and when the Father willed it then the Son was born, for he writes: 'He is always in the Father . . . only that the Father also precedes Him in a certain sense since it is necessary in

some degree that He should be before He is Father. Because it is
essential that He who knows no origin must go before Him who has
an origin' (*ibid.*); 'thus God the Father . . . of whom, when He willed
it, the Son, the Word, was born' (*ibid.*); 'reasonably, He is before all
things, but after the Father . . . since He proceeded from Him' (*ibid.*).
Does this mean merely a logical priority of Father over Son?[51] Or
does it mean that in reality 'there was when the Son was not' and
that Novatian thus espoused the twofold stage theory of the Logos
as the Apologists did?[52]

Perhaps Novatian's thought is deeper than that of Tertullian or
of the Apologists. For he seems to make a distinction between the
Son's generation and His birth: 'He therefore is God, but generated
that He should be God. He is also Lord, but born that He might be
Lord' (*Trin.* 31). But does this mean that the Son was in the Father
from eternity as a second person? It seems not, for he writes: 'He is
always in the Father . . . although He has an origin in that He is
born. . . . He, then, when the Father willed it, proceeded from the
Father, and He who was in the Father came forth from the Father
. . . assuredly God proceeding from God, causing a person second
to the Father as being the Son' (*ibid.*). It is difficult to escape the
impression that Novatian is not clear about his own thought on this
matter.[53]

There are other traces of subordinationism in Novatian. For he
says that the Son, unlike the Father, is neither invisible nor incomprehensible (*Trin.* 31), that 'the Son does nothing of His own will
. . . but obeys all His Father's commands' (*ibid.*), and 'in receiving
sanctification from the Father, He is inferior to the Father' (*Trin.*
27). But perhaps this 'subordination of the Son' regards not the
divinity itself but creation,[54] for he seems to put the Son on the same
level of divinity as the Father when he writes: 'this power of divinity
is sent forth, and also given and directed upon the Son, and is again
returned by the communion of substance to the Father' (*Trin.* 31).

Novatian tells us more about the work of the Holy Spirit than
about the Holy Spirit Himself. Unlike Tertullian he does not call
Him 'God' or a 'third person.' But he indicates clearly enough that
he regards Him as a divine person. For he declares that 'the authority of faith admonishes us . . . to believe also in the Holy Spirit' . . .
who 'was in the prophets and apostles,' 'the illuminator of divine
things,' who 'effects with water the second birth, as a certain seed
of divine generation,' who 'can make us God's temple and fit us for
His house . . . an inhabitant given for our bodies and an effector of
their holiness,' and who 'can also produce our bodies at the resurrection of immortality, accustoming them to be allied with the

divine eternity of the Holy Spirit' (*Trin.* 29). He coordinates Him with the Father and the Son when he writes that 'concerning the Father, and the Son, and the Holy Spirit, let it be sufficient to have briefly said thus much' (*Trin.* 30). He seems bluntly to subordinate Him to Christ when he states that if the Paraclete 'has received from Christ what He may declare to us, Christ is greater than the Paraclete because the Paraclete would not receive from Christ unless He were less than Christ' (*Trin.* 16). Yet he seems to qualify this when he adds that the Paraclete is 'found to be in this economy less than Christ' (*ibid.*). And since he held that the statement, 'the Father is greater than I' meant that the entire divinity was common to Father and Son except that one gives and the other receives (*Trin.* 22), then this statement that the Son is greater than the Spirit merely means that all is common to Son and Spirit except that one gives and the other receives.[55]

It has been said by Jerome that Novatian summarized Tertullian's trinitarian doctrine (*De viris illust.* 70). This hardly seems to be true in what concerns the Holy Spirit. For Tertullian taught that the Holy Spirit proceeds from the Father through the Son, is third with God and His Son, is a third person, is one God with the Father and the Son, and is God. Novatian did not. His contribution to trinitarian doctrine is not nearly so great as that of Tertullian.

Other Early Roman Theologians

Dionysius of Rome (d. 268). At Rome Hippolytus and Novatian were easily the outstanding theologians in the third century. There is no evidence that any of the popes, Zephyrinus, Callistus, Cornelius, or Stephen showed any special competence in trinitarian doctrine. But we have a fragment of an epistle against Tritheists and Sabellians written by Pope Dionysius to Dionysius, the bishop of Alexandria, that deserves attention. In it he says:

> I would do right to speak against those who by their dividing and partitioning the one God into three separate powers and divinities destroy the monarchy of God, the most sacred teaching of the Church of God. . . . These men hold an opinion exactly opposite, I might say, to Sabellius's opinion. For Sabellius's blasphemy is that the Son is the Father, and the Father the Son. These men somehow preach three gods since they divide the sacred unity into three different hypostases completely separate from one another. It is necessary that the divine Word be united with the God of all and that the Holy Spirit remain in God and dwell in Him, and that thus the divine Trinity be brought to-

gether into one, as in one supreme point, that is the almighty God of all things. The teaching of the foolish Marcion who divides and separates the one God into three principles is a teaching from the devil, not the teaching of those who truly follow Christ and who are content with the teachings of the Savior. These latter clearly understand that the Sacred Scripture teaches the Trinity, but nowhere does the Old Testament or New Testament mention three gods. . . . Therefore the wonderful and divine unity is not to be separated into three divinities, and the excellence and vast greatness of God is not to be diminished by the word *making*: but we must believe in God the Father almighty, and in Christ Jesus his Son, and in the Holy Spirit and we must believe that the Word is united to the God of all. For He says, 'I and the Father are one' (Jn 10.30), and 'I am in the Father, and the Father is in me' (Jn. 14.10). Thus the divine Trinity and the sacred preaching of the monarchy will be kept intact (Denz 112, 115).

Dionysius adds, 'No less are those to be blamed, who think that the Son is a work and that the Lord was made . . . since the divine writings testify that He was not created or made but begotten. It is not a slight but a very great impiety to say that the Lord was somehow made. For if He was made, there was a time when He did not exist; and yet He always was . . .' (Denz 113).

Thus Dionysius condemns Sabellianism and Tritheism and even Arianism by anticipation, and although he does not attempt to reconcile them intellectually he yet clearly affirms the divine trinity and unity, not as his own opinion but as the authentic teaching of Scripture and preaching of the Church. This is no insignificant witness to trinitarian faith in the early Western Church.

Liberius (d. 366), at the beginning of his pontificate, firmly defended Athanasius and the Nicene faith against Constantius' Arian pressure, and in consequence was exiled to Thracia. In 358 he returned to Rome and 'was fairly energetic when the Nicene faith came into its own after the Emperor's death.'[56] But his conduct during his exile has been a matter of strong controversy, particularly because of his four so-called *Letters from Exile*.[57] For a time the authenticity of these letters was seriously questioned but today it is admitted.[58] Some Catholic critics, among them Mgr. Duchesne[59] and E. Amann,[60] have maintained, and it seems properly, that Liberius was derelict in his papal duty and failed to uphold Athanasius and the Nicene faith. It seems that he did subscribe to the first and third formulas of Sirmium (cf. Denz 137, 139), but these were only ambiguous; he did not subscribe to the second Sirmium formula, the 'Sirmium Blasphemy,' which was truly heretical. Papal infallibility, however, was not in question, since he signed under pressure and had no intention of doctrinally binding the whole Church in this matter. Unhappily, Liberius lacked the courage of Athanasius and Hilary.

Damasus (d. 384), the new pope, was of a stronger personality than his predecessor and worked hard to settle the Arian troubles that were disturbing the West and East. We have a few fragments of his letters, *De Trinitate divina* (Denz 144–145), *De incarnatione contra Apollinaristas* (Denz 146), *De Spiritu Sancto et de incarnatione Verbi* (Denz 147), *De incarnatione Verbi divini* (Denz 148) and *Damnatio Apollinarismi* (Denz 149). In these fragments Damasus declares that he holds 'in everything to the inviolable faith of the Nicene Council' (Denz 147), and believes in a coeternal Trinity of one essence (Denz 147) and in three Persons, Father, Son, and Holy Spirit 'of one power, one majesty, one divinity, one *ousia*' (Denz 144). Furthermore, in a letter to Paulinus Damasus gives a list of 24 anathemas of contemporary heresies (PL 13, 358–364; Denz 152–180), which has come to be called the 'Tome of Damasus.' It seems that Damasus presented this 'Tome' of Trinitarian, Christological, and especially Macedonian errors to a council that met in Rome in 382 and that this council condemned these errors. Some of these canons read as follows:

We anathematize: (1) those who do not proclaim with complete freedom that He [the Holy Spirit] is of one power and substance with the Father and the Son; (2) those who follow the error of Sabellius, saying that the Father is the same person as the Son; (3) Arius and Eunomius, who with the same ungodliness, though in different words, assert that the Son and the Holy Spirit are creatures; (4) the Macedonians, who come from the stock of Arius and have changed only the name and not the perfidy. . . . If anyone denies: (10) that the Father is eternal, the Son is eternal, the Holy Spirit is eternal: he is a heretic; (11) that the Son was born of the Father, that is, of his divine substance: he is a heretic; (12) that the Son of God is true God, just as the Father is true God, having all power, knowing all things, and equal to the Father: he is a heretic; (16) that the Holy Spirit is truly and properly from the Father, and, like the Son is of the divine substance and is true God: he is a heretic; (17) that the Holy Spirit has all power and knows all things, and is everywhere just as the Father and the Son: he is a heretic; (19) that the Father made all things through the Son and through His Holy Spirit . . . he is a heretic; (20) that the Father, Son and Holy Spirit have one divinity, authority, majesty, power, one glory, dominion, one kingdom and one will and truth: he is a heretic; (21) that the three persons, the Father, the Son, and the Holy Spirit, are true persons, equal, eternal . . . omnipotent: he is a heretic; (22) that the Holy Spirit must be adored by every creature, just as the Son and the Father: he is a heretic; (24) but if anyone, while saying that the Father is God and the Son is God and the Holy Spirit is God, makes a division and says that they are gods, and does not say that they are one God, precisely on account of the one divinity and power which we believe and know is possessed by the Father and the Son and the Holy Spirit . . . he is a heretic. . . . Therefore, this is the salvation of Christians: that believing in the Trinity, that is in the Father, Son and Holy Spirit, and being baptized in the Trinity, we may unhesitatingly believe that in the Trinity there is only one true divinity and power, majesty and substance.

This 'Tome' and these fragments give a vivid, clear-cut, negative, and positive presentation by a pope of sound and solid trinitarian doctrine that is in full agreement with the creeds of Nicea and Constantinople. Taken together with the letter of Pope Dionysius, this teaching of Pope Damasus clearly shows that in the 3d and 4th centuries the Roman bishops felt quite competent to present the traditional trinitarian doctrine of the Church authoritatively and to condemn bluntly the errors that were opposed to it.

HILARY OF POITIERS

Hilary of Poitiers (d. *c.* 367) has been ranked with Ambrose and Jerome[61] and called 'the leading theologian of his day.'[62] About 353 he was elected bishop of Poitiers and in 356 he was exiled to Phrygia by Constantius II for refusing to condemn Athanasius.[63] His four years of exile proved to be a theological blessing, for he tells us he had not even heard of the Nicene *homoousion* until 355 (*De syn* 91). Now he got first-hand information about the Eastern Church, its controversies over the divinity of Christ, its many Post-Nicene synods and creeds. There he wrote his *De Synodis* and wrote or completed his *De Trinitate*.[64] In 360 his exile ended and he returned to the West. There he worked strenuously against Arianism in the Church, where 'the fundamental difference of the Arian from the Catholic position was not generally recognised.'[65]

'His firm and courageous procedure against the Arian heresy, his fearless attitude in resisting secular interference in Church affairs, his fruitful exile, his influence on his contemporaries through his policy of conciliation and, especially, his masterful defense of the divinity of Christ, merited for him the title of 'the Athanasius of the West.'[66] He began an exegetical work in the West that Jerome would perfect.[67] He ranks not only as a positive theologian[68] but also as a speculative theologian.'[69] He is famed as an intermediary between the theology of the East and that of the West. He derived many of his ideas from the Greeks and expressed them in Latin terms and thus enriched Western theology 'with new and fecund elements and at the same time helped to make precise and to fix the dogmatic terminology of the future.'[70] But it is now thought that his sojourn in the East did not influence him as much as was formerly believed, for he 'refers only to Scripture . . . as the basis for his ideas [and] he makes no reference to the Greek Fathers in a way that would indicate he depended on them.'[71]

In his treatise *On the Councils* (*De Synodis*) he first sets forth the machinations of the Arians and Semi-Arians for the benefit of the bishops of Gaul and Britain and explains various creeds that had been drawn up in the East; then he addresses himself to the Homoiousian bishops of the East in an attempt to bring them to accept the Nicene *homoousion*.

It seems that the 12 books of *On the Trinity* were originally entitled *De Fide*.[72] This work 'is generally regarded as one of the finest writings that the Arian controversy produced,'[73] and it is considered Hilary's masterpiece.[74] It treats the divinity and consubstantiality of the Son (1–3), refutes objections against Christ's divinity (4–7), defends the eternal birth of the Son against the Arians (9), shows the harmony between Christ's divinity and His subordination in John and Paul (11) and the difference between divine and human birth (12).

Sabellius is often singled out in the treatise *On the Trinity* (1.25, 26; 2.4; 4.12; 6.5, 11; 7.3, 5). To refute him Hilary turned to the Gospels:

Let Sabellius, if he dare, confound Father and Son as two names with one meaning, making of them not Unity but One Person. He shall have a prompt answer from the Gospels, not once or twice, but often repeated, 'This is my beloved Son, in whom I am well pleased' (Mt 17.5). He shall hear the words, 'the Father is greater than I' (Jn 14.28), and 'I go to the Father' (Jn 14.12), and 'Father, I thank thee' (Jn 11.41), and 'glorify me, Father' (Jn 17.5), and 'Thou art the Son of the living God' (Mt 16.17).

But it was Arianism that was the main object of Hilary's attack, this 'mad' heresy that 'denies the mystery of the true faith by means of statements borrowed from our confession, which it employs for its godless ends' (*Trin.* 6.4). He feels that Arians are 'fanatics' (7.7) and 'their loud profession of the unity of God is a fraudulent imitation of the faith; their assertion that Christ is the Son of God a play upon words for the delusion of their hearers; their saying that He did not exist before He was born a bid for the support of the world's philosophers; their confession of God as incorporeal and immutable leads, by a display of fallacious logic, up to a denial of the birth of God from God' (7.1). They slight 'the Father by refusing to reverence the Son' (4.41); they teach 'a new Christ . . . as well as another God the Father' (11.4), they admit that Christ is 'greater than other adopted sons, and first in rank among the creatures because of the greater splendor which accompanied His creation' (4.3), and they maintain 'that the Son is not born from the Father, and is God not by nature but by appointment' (4.3). In their denial that Our Lord Jesus Christ is God

> they are accustomed to appeal to such words of our Lord as, 'why callest thou me good? None is good save One, even God' (Lk 18.19), 'and this is life eternal that they should know thee the only true God, and him whom thou didst send, Jesus Christ' (Jn 17.3), 'the Son can do nothing of himself, but what he hath seen the Father doing' (Jn 5.19), 'The Father is greater than I' (Jn 14.28), and 'but of that day and hour no one knows, neither the angels in heaven nor the Son, but God only' (Mk 18.32).

In reply Hilary points out (*Trin.* 1.30; 2.10–11) that the same Christ who said all this also said: 'I and the Father are one' (Jn 10.30), 'he that hath seen me hath seen the Father also' (Jn 14.9), 'Father, all things that are mine are thine, and thine are mine' (Jn 17.10), 'I in the Father and the Father in me' (Jn 14.11). Then he adds Paul's words, 'for in him dwelleth all the fulness of the Godhead bodily' (Col 2.9) and John's, 'and the Word was with God and the Word was God' and 'all things were made through him' (Jn 1.1, 3). When the Arians urged that Moses said, 'the Lord thy God is one' (Deut 6.4), Hilary points out (*Trin.* 4.15) that God said, 'let us make man after our image and likeness' (Gen 1.26). When they maintain that Christ is a creature because it is written that 'the Lord created me at the beginning of his work' (Prov 8.22 LXX), Hilary indicates (*Trin.* 12.35–37) that it is also written there that 'before he made the earth . . . he begat me' (Prov. 8.24–25), so as to signify not 'creation' but 'establishing.' When they insist that 'the Father is greater than the Son,' Hilary agrees both in terms of the Son's incarnation (*Trin.* 9.51) and of His divine birth, but so that the Father as the Unbegotten, the Father, the Sender, the one that wills is greater than the Begotten, the Sent, the one that obeys (*Trin.* 3.12), greater as principle and in authority but not in nature (*In Ps.* 138.17 CSEL 22.756) or divinity or honor (*Trin.* 11.12).

In his positive doctrine Hilary is chiefly concerned with the Father and the Son, for the Holy Spirit was not so directly involved in the Arian controversy. In his early work, his *Commentary on St. Matthew* (PL 9), he sets out the basic themes of his doctrine, the eternity of Christ (31.2; 23.8; 1.2; 16.4), His divine power (12.24; 23.8; 8.8), His true divinity (1.5; 12.8; 12.11; 14.2; 18.3; 27.8). He goes beyond predecessors in insisting on the identity of substance in the Father and the Son, declaring that the Son has received from the Father His own substance (8.8), holds His existence 'from the infinity of the paternal substance' (4.14), has received all that the Father is, 'the same eternity' (31.3) so that Father and Son are really one God (16.4). But he is not yet clear enough about the eternal generation of the Son, and the eternal distinction of the Persons.[75] That he considers the Holy Spirit not a creature but divine Hilary indicates variously, by associating Him with the Father and the Son in the matter of blasphemy (12.17), by presenting Him as the source of all graces (4.1; 12.15; 3.1; 14.19; 10.24; 2.4), and as dwelling in the faithful as in temples (25.1). Some have thought they discerned traces of Binitarism in Hilary, but it is hard to see how a dweller in a temple would be an impersonal divine force.[76]

In his later works Hilary presents a more perfect trinitarian doctrine but again centers it mostly on the Father and the Son. In the Old Testament he finds (*Trin.* 4–5) indications of two Persons who are equally God, in passages concerning the history of creation (Gen 1.6–7, 26–27), the theophanies (Gen 16.7–14; 17.1–22; Ex 3.2–22), the psalmist and Prophets (Ps 44.8; Is 43.10; 45.14). In the New Testament he finds (*Trin.* 6) the divine sonship of Christ revealed in the Father's witness to His beloved Son (Mt 3.17; 17.5), in Christ's words about 'my Father' (Mt 15.13; Jn. 2.16), in the Apostles' testimony that Christ is more than an adoptive Son of God (Mt 16.16; Jn 1.18; 20.31; 1 Jn 2.22; 5.20; Rom 8.32), in Christ's exclusive knowledge of the Father (Mt 11.27; Jn 7.29), in His procession and mission from the Father (Jn 8.42; 7.29; 16.28–29).

The focal point of Hilary's trinitarian doctrine is the Son's generation whereby He receives the very substance of the Father, for faith in this mystery of divine revelation is 'the foundation of the Church, the pledge of eternity' (*Trin.* 6.37). He sets out to prove that it is strictly divine. The Son does not originate from nothing, as the Arians maintain, but from the very substance of the Father, for His is 'the birth of a living nature from a living nature. It is God proceeding from God' (*Trin.* 6.35), so that 'our faith is the confession of God from God and God in God, by no bodily process but by divine power, by no transfusion from nature into nature but through the secret and mighty working of the One nature; God from God, not by division or extension or emanation, but by the operation of a nature which brings into existence, by means of birth, a nature One with itself' (*Trin.* 5.37). In His birth the Son receives what the Father has and what the Father is, the paternal substance itself: 'He has granted everything that is His without any loss to the giver' (*Trin.* 7.39), so that 'whatever is in the Father is also in the Son' (*Trin.* 3.4) and 'that which He Himself is has also been generated by the birth of God into God' (*Trin.* 8.54). Thus the Son is not a creature but God (*Syn.* 69), 'not a second God' (*Trin.* 7.12), 'not a false God, nor God by adoption, nor God by gift of the name, but true God . . . Creator . . . omnipotent' (*Trin.* 5.5), 'not a portion of God but whole God' (*Syn.* 69), so that 'God the Father and God the Son are clearly one, not by a union of person, but by the unity of substance' (*Trin.* 4.42). And if the Son is thus God from God and in His birth receives all that the Father has and is, obviously by His nature He is equal to the Father. And as the Church 'confesses the Father eternal' so it confesses that the Son is 'born from eternity' (*Trin.* 4.6) and 'is eternal' (12.34). There is no contradiction between being born and eternally existing, as the Arians think, for the Son is 'born from eternity,' and if His generation is not eternal 'then neither is the Father eternal' (12.25). For the Son 'there is no antecedent time' (12.17), and 'whatever transcends time is eternal' (12.26).

While Hilary declares that the Son 'is like the Father in might, honor and nature' (*Syn.* 69), with a 'wholly similar essence' and 'a similar substance in both Persons' (*Syn.* 64), he leaves no doubt that there is not only likeness but identity of substance between the Father and the Son. For the Son is 'God of God' and He has and is all that the Father has and is. 'In Him there is nothing new, nothing strange, nothing of recent origin so that . . . God the Father and God the Son are clearly one, not by a union of person, but by the unity of substance' (*Trin.* 4.42). Thus there is 'one substance of the Father and Son' (*Syn.* 69) and 'no distinction whatever between the essence and nature of the Father and the Son' since 'the whole exposition of faith makes no distinction between Father and Son . . . in time, or name, or essence, or dignity or domination' (*Syn.* 33). He uses the Nicene symbol of 'Light from Light' to inculcate this doctrine and says that 'the true faith asserts that God is born from God, as light from light, which pours itself forth without self-diminution, giving what it has yet having what it gave' (*Trin.* 6.12). He points to the oneness of operation of Father and Son in that they are one principle of operation (*Trin.* 4.21; 9.45, 48; 7.21, 22, 26) to further verify their identity of substance. He stresses the circumincession of the Father and Son, without using this word, and bases the mutual inexistence of Father and Son on their oneness of nature and essence (*Trin.* 6.19; 7.28, 41, 31, 39, 40; 3.23; 4.40; 5.37, 39; 8.54, 55, 25, 41, 53, 16).

From the fact that Hilary at times speaks of the Son's origin as if it were due to divine will (*Syn.* 58; *Trin.* 2.24; 3.3, 4; 6.21), and at times as if it were due to divine intelligence (*Trin.* 2.15; 7.11; 12.52), some have urged that for Hilary the principle of divine generation is the divine will while others have made it the divine intellect. But he certainly does not understand divine will in the Arian sense of a free, creative will. And even if he says 'that He who was born of the substance of God is born also of His purpose and will' (*Syn.* 37), it seems clear enough that for him neither will nor intellect was the principle of generation but that this divine generation is inscrutable.[77]

It has also been maintained that Hilary prefers *homoiousion* to *homoousion*. But it seems more correct to say that while he finds neither term perfect, and *homoiousion* less open to misinterpretation, he nonetheless definitely thinks that if one wishes to reject all Arianism, the only adequate term is *homoousion* if this is understood as directly signifying identity of substance or as insinuating this.[78]

The Holy Spirit receives much less attention in Hilary's writings, but he is not a Binitarist. He indicates the Holy Spirit's divinity in many ways. In his summaries of faith he coordinates Him with the Father and the Son: 'He commanded them to baptize in the name of the Father, the Son, and the Holy Spirit, that is, in the confession of the Origin, the Only-Begotten, and the Gift . . . God the Father . . . from whom are all things; and our Lord Jesus Christ . . . through whom are all things; and the Holy Spirit . . . the gift in all things. Nothing can be found lacking in that supreme consummation within which there is found in the Father, the Son and the Holy Spirit: infinity in the Eternal, form in the Image and the use in the Gift' (*Trin.* 2.1; cf. 12.57; 4.1; 3.27; 4.28; 5.29). He names the three in doxologies (Ps 143.23; Fragm. A I 1). He declares (*Trin.* 2.29): 'we are bound to confess Him, proceeding, who has Father and Son as His authors (*auctoribus*) . . . He does exist, inasmuch as He is given, received, retained. He is joined with Father and Son in our confes-

sion of the faith, and cannot be excluded from a true confession of
Father and Son; take away a part, and the whole faith is marred. . . .
He it is through whom all things exist, and from whom are all things,
and . . . He is the Spirit of God, God's gift to the faithful. If our
answer displease them, their displeasure must also fall upon the
Apostles and the Prophets, who spoke of Him exactly as we have
spoken (Gal 4.6; Eph 4.30; 1 Cor 2.12; Rom 8.9, 11).' He does not
call Him God explicitly, but Hilary denies that He is a creature: 'As
for me, it is certainly not enough to deny . . . that my Lord and God,
your Only-Begotten Jesus Christ, is a creature. I will not even permit this name to be associated with your Holy Spirit, who has proceeded from You and has been sent through Him' (*Trin.* 12.55).

To the question whether the Spirit Paraclete comes from the
Father or the Son (*Trin.* 8.20) he replies that 'He receives from the
Son . . . and proceeds from the Father. . . . But, if we must hold that
there is a difference between receiving from the Son and proceeding
from the Father, then, certainly, we shall have to admit that it is
one and the same to receive from the Son as it is to receive from the
Father. . . . [and the Son] teaches that what is to be received from
the Father must still be received from Him, because everything that
belongs to the Father is His' (*ibid.*). He does not seem to say
explicitly that the Holy Spirit receives the divine nature from the
Father and the Son, but this is what he means for he says that the
Holy Spirit 'did not receive anything from creatures' but 'from
those things which are wholly proper to God' (*Trin.* 9.73). He knows
that the Holy Spirit is not generated for the Son is the Only-Begotten,
but he does not know how to describe His origin and so he simply
says, 'I hold fast to the fact that your Holy Spirit is from You,
although I do not grasp it with my understanding' (*Trin.* 12.56). At
times, it is true, he seems to deny verbally that the Holy Spirit is
homoousion or *homoiousion* with the Father and the Son (*Syn.* 32).
But if he did not think that the Holy Spirit was equal to and one
with the Father and the Son, would he question whether the Holy
Spirit like the Son could be generated by the Father?[79]

Is the Holy Spirit a third Person? Sometimes Hilary applies the
term *Holy Spirit* (*Trin.* 8.23) to the Father or to the Son, apparently
to signify the 'divine nature' or the divinity of Christ (8.46), but he
also uses the term in contradistinction to the Father and the Son.[80]
He often calls the Holy Spirit 'Gift' (*Trin.* 2.29; 2.1; 34.47), and so
will Augustine later on and yet clearly regard Him as a person. He
never explicitly calls Him a Person. And yet he clearly distinguishes
the Holy Spirit from the Father and Son in his trinitarian passages
(*Trin.* 2.27; 1.36; Ps 143.23; Fragm. B II 9, 5). He approves the

synod of Antioch for rejecting the heresy that Father, Son, and Holy Spirit were only one Person and for declaring that 'there were three substances, meaning three subsistent Persons' (*Syn.* 32). He distinguishes the Holy Spirit from the Father and the Son and says 'the Paraclete Holy Spirit has the office and rank peculiar to His substance' (*Syn.* 55). He puts Him on the same level as Father and Son in terms of personality (*Trin.* 2.29, 5, 3; 1.33–34). He describes the Holy Spirit's origin as from the Father and through the Son (*Trin.* 12.55, 56, 57), not by creation or generation but procession (*Trin.* 12.55). He assigns Him personal functions, to divinize the faithful (*Trin.* 1.36; 2.29, 31), to enlighten 'all the patriarchs and prophets' (*Trin.* 2.32) and us (*ad Const.* 11), to teach the Apostles and faithful (*Trin.* 2.23), to inhabit faithful hearts with the Father and the Son (*Trin.* 8.26; Ps 118).

Thus Hilary leaves no real doubt that he considers the Holy Spirit truly divine, assigns Him personal functions, regards Him as a third in the divinity distinct from the Father and the Son, and thus considers Him a divine Person even though he does not explicitly call Him this.[81]

Hilary made an important contribution to the formulation of trinitarian doctrine in the West by his attempt at a true synthesis, something that neither Tertullian nor Athanasius had ventured to do. The Cappadocians produced a better analysis of the concepts of nature and person, and Augustine would far outstrip Hilary. But in his day and for his time and place Hilary produced an important trinitarian doctrine, especially in its anti-Arian aspects.

CHAPTER SEVEN

The Augustinian Phase

VICTORINUS

Marius Victorinus (d. *c.* 362), 'an African by birth, a Roman by long residence in the capital, a convert from Neoplatonism,'[1] was a lay contemporary of Hilary but more blunt and outspoken in his theological judgments. He has been called 'the most original and interesting figure in the middle decades of the fourth century,'[2] and some of his ideas seem to have influenced Augustine. He wrote three treatises against Arianism, *De generatione divini Verbi, Adversus Arium, De homoousio recipiendo* and three Hymns on the Trinity.

He presents a doctrine of eternal generation to refute the Arian objection that generation involves change. Candidus urged that generation implies motion and motion implies change, but change is impossible in God and so is generation. Victorinus replies that 'not every motion is change' (*De generat.* 30), that God's *esse* is equivalent to *moveri* (*Adv. Arium* 1.43) and that thus God is always in motion, and that as regards contingent beings His motion is a creation and as regards the Word it is an eternal generation (*De generat.* 29–30). At times he says the Father is 'older' and the Son 'younger' (*Adv. Arium* 1.20), but these rather unfortunate expressions do not negate his basic conviction that the Word is eternal and consubstantial with the Father, since he repeats that 'His Son always exists simultaneously,' 'immutable is the Father and immutable the Son,' 'always there is the Father and always the Son' (*Adv. Arium* 1.34), 'one and *homoousion* are God and the Logos' (*Adv. Arium* 1.30), 'one and simple are these two' (*De generat.* 22).

An interesting aspect of his doctrine is that God is '*tridynamos*, having three powers, being, living, understanding (*esse, vivere, intelligere*)' (*Adv. Arium* 4.21), and thus 'there is a triple singularity in each and unity in Trinity' (*ibid.*).

Then in Neoplatonic fashion Victorinus represents the relations between the Father and the Son as similar to those between the One and the Nous in the philosophy of Plotinus. The Father is the absolute, unconditioned, transcendent, unknowable and invisible One, who is 'prior to being' (*Adv. Arium* 4.20; *De generat.* 2). The Son is the 'form' through which the Father defines Himself, enters into relations with the finite and becomes knowable (*Adv. Arium* 3.7; 4.20). The Logos is, as it were, the term of the Father's will and since every will is, so to speak, a child, the Logos is Son; this Son proceeds 'not by necessity of nature but by will of the magnitude of the Father' (*Adv. Arium* 1.31), not so that this generation is free 'but that it has the will for its principle.'[3] The Son is also the term of the Father's understanding, the image by which the Father knows Himself (*Adv. Arium* 1.31) and as image He is both distinct from the Father and 'identical with the Father, because in Him the Father is represented to Himself.'[4] The Son is related to the Father 'as life to being, as act to potency, as spoken word to silence' (*Adv. Arium* 1.41). The Son is equal to the Father because the Father has given Him all that the Father has, but the Father is greater because He has given and the Son has received (*Adv. Arium* 1.13). In 'substance, power, dignity' (*ibid.*) the Son is equal to the Father, but as person, as Son, as receiver of life and substance He is less.

To the Holy Spirit Victorinus gives less attention, but he places Him on the same level of divinity and personality as the Father and Son. Thus he writes: 'If God is spirit, and Jesus Christ is spirit, and the Holy Spirit is spirit, there are three of one substance, or who in other words are consubstantial. But the Holy Spirit is from Christ, as Christ is from God; and so the Three are One' (*Adv. Arium* 1.12). Though he sometimes seems to confuse Him with the Son, because of the imprecision of the word *spiritus*, he distinguishes Him as the intelligence distinct from life, as the voice distinct from the mouth that emits it: 'the Father is eloquent silence, Christ is His voice and the Paraclete is the Voice's Voice' (*Adv. Arium* 3.16); 'Christ is life, the Spirit is understanding' (*Adv. Arium* 1.13). The Son and the Holy Spirit are produced by the Father by a unique movement but since by this movement the Father has given the Son all He has, even the power to communicate Himself, the Son in turn gives to the Holy Spirit (*Adv. Arium* 3.8). The Father remains thus the first source of the whole Trinity, the unique principle of the divine life. However, His gifts are communicated to the Spirit by the Son who is, in consequence, a secondary and subordinate principle (*Adv. Arium* 1.8).

In Hymn 3 Victorinus unites the three very closely: 'O blessed Trinity. . . . In substance Thou art God, in form Word, in knowledge

Holy Spirit; Being, Life, Knowledge; Fixity, Progress, Regress; First Entity, Second Entity, Third Entity; yet the three but one. Word, God, the Holy Spirit, Thou art the same, O blessed Trinity. Thou, Holy Spirit, art the connecting link . . . Thou dost first link Two, and art Thyself the Third' (PL 8.1143–1146). He seems to visualize the divine being 'as in a continuous process of unfolding and re-folding,'[5] in which the unknowable reveals Itself in the Son as image and in the Spirit the same Godhead knows Itself, and so returns back to Itself, with the Spirit linking Father and Son and completing the perfect circle of the divine being (cf. *Adv. Arium* 1.60).

Though the three are one with a unity that transcends number (*Adv. Arium* 3.1), and mutually inexist each in the others (*Adv. Arium* 1.16), yet they are distinct as 'three subsistences of one substance' (*Adv. Arium* 2.4). These 'three subsistences' (a term Victorinus prefers to person) are 'mutually related in the same way as being, life and intelligence: life, that is the Son, is a mere form of being, which is the Father, just as intelligence, that is the Holy Spirit, is a mere form of life, which is the Son.'[6] Thus in the soul of man with its consubstantial triad of *esse, vivere, intelligere* Victorinus finds (*Adv. Arium* 1.32; 1.62–64) the best analogy of the Trinity of which it is an image.

At times the language of Victorinus is crude and infelicitous, and his doctrine is excessively Neoplatonic, and yet by his zealous effort to present the Trinity 'in the more general categories of ontology, Victorinus shows himself to be the precursor, not only of St. Augustine, but of the boldest schoolmen.'[7]

AMBROSE

Ambrose (d. 397) was a great orator and after Hilary the most important opponent of Arianism and Macedonianism. He was not a great theologian but he wrote to satisfy the immediate needs of his people in a delightfully clear and simple style and his writings were very popular and influential. He produced three works against Arianism.[8] The first, *De Fide* was written at Gratian's request and deals with the divinity of the Word. The *De Spiritu Sancto* was the first separate work on the Holy Spirit of any magnitude in the West but it borrowed heavily from Didymus, Athanasius, and Basil. It shows that the Holy Spirit is consubstantial with the Father and the Son. The *De incarnationis dominicae sacramento* is a refutation of Arianism.

Ambrose follows the Eastern method of treating the Persons

before the nature, so that the Father is the principle of the other Persons. He is the 'source and root of the Son's being' (*De Fide* 4.133), but He did not exist before the Son, 'for if He began to be a Father . . . how, then, is God unchangeable? For if God was first God, and then the Father, surely He has undergone change by reason of the added and later act of generation. But may God preserve us from this madness. . . . The devout spirit affirms a generation that is not in time, and so declares Father and Son to be coeternal' (*De Fide* 1.59, 60); since 'the Son is called both the Right Hand and the Power of God . . . when did the Power of God not exist?' (*De Sp. S.* 3.18). To the Arian question 'whether it was of His own free will, or on compulsion, that the Father begat,' Ambrose answered that 'the putting forth of His generative power is neither of will nor of necessity,' 'just as the Father is not good because He wills to be so, or is compelled to be so, but . . . by nature' (*De Fide* 4.103–104).

The Son is eternally Son, for 'He it is whom the Father begat before the morning star, as being eternal, He brought Him forth from the womb as the Son; He uttered him from His heart, as the Word. . . . He is the Arm of the Father, for He is creator of all, and the Wisdom of the Father, for He proceeded from the mouth of God; the Power of the Father, because the fulness of the Godhead dwelleth in Him bodily. . . . He is the perfect Son of a perfect Father. . . . Love, then, Him whom the Father loves, honor Him whom the Father honors' (*De virg.* 3.3, 4). Generation does not separate Son and Father, for 'the Son according to the Godhead is One with the Father, One by natural substance . . . nor is the Father ever separated from the operation of the Son' (*De Sp. S.* 2.135). As God the Son is equal to the Father, as Man He is less: 'He, therefore, possessing the fulness of divinity and glory, is not, in respect of His divinity inferior . . . but inferior in taking upon Him of the flesh and in His sufferings as a man' (*De Fide* 2.65, 70). The enigmatic final subjection of the Son to the Father that St. Paul speaks of (1 Cor 15.28), does not mean that 'the Son will be reabsorbed into the Father,' as the Sabellians say, nor is it a subjection of Christ as God but of Christ in us, His members, 'when we have become, not many members but one spirit . . . that "God may be all in all" ' (*De Fide* 5.161, 166, 168). The generation of the Son cannot be explained by philosophy (*De incarn.* 7) nor by 'instances taken from the generation of earthly creatures,' for the divine generation is a 'mystery' that 'rises high above all thought and feeling' and is 'incomprehensible,' for 'the Father begets impassibly, and yet of Himself and in ages inconceivably remote hath very God begotten very God' (*De Fide* 1.66, 64, 63, 67).

At the time that Ambrose was writing, 'some theologians identified the Holy Spirit with the Word; others regarded Him as merely a divine power or gift; others, while ascribing to Him a distinct personality, maintained that He is subordinate to the Father and Son.'[9] Hence Ambrose was intent on showing that the Holy Spirit was a divine person, coequal and consubstantial with the Father and the Son. He relied heavily on the Scriptures to show this, though at times his exegesis was quite defective. To show that the Scriptures witnessed to the divinity of the Holy Spirit, he argued 'that the properties and activities ascribed . . . to the Holy Spirit are such as can be ascribed only to one who is God, and not to one who is a creature.'[10] The Holy Spirit is 'Light' and 'Life' and 'Creator' and 'Lord' (*De Sp. S.* 1.171; 2.32; 3.96), just as the Father and Son. He is 'eternal' (1.99), 'infinite' (1.82), omniscient (2.115), and omnipotent (3.169). He 'fills all things, possesses all things, works all and in all in the same manner as God the Father and the Son work' (1.88). He is the author of grace, regeneration, and the new man (2.64, 66). He forgives sins (3.137), reveals the hidden things of God (2.122), inspires prophets and Apostles (1.55), vivifies us (2.29), sanctifies us (1.74), divinizes us (1.80) and dwells in us (3.90). If He possesses 'all that pertains to God' (3.112), He is not a creature (1.8), He is God, for 'God has a temple, a creature has no true temple. But the Spirit, who dwelleth in us, has a temple' (3.90, 91).

The Holy Spirit is not merely a divine force but a divine Person just as the Father and Son: 'Cherubim and Seraphim . . . say "Holy, Holy, Holy is the Lord God of Sabaoth" . . . that . . . you may understand the distinction of Persons in the Trinity, and the oneness of the Godhead' (3.110). The 'Holy Spirit is distinct from the Father and the Son' (1.106). 'The Father is one Person, the Son another, and the Holy Spirit another' (*Expos. ev. Luc.* 2.12). Over and over the Scriptures ascribe to the Holy Spirit personal actions, for He knows (*De Sp. S.* 2.115), searches (2.126), is grieved (3.48), reveals (2.122), forgives sins (1.112, 113), commands (2.145), rebukes (3.35), is 'the Arbiter of His own freedom' (1.18).

Sometimes Ambrose seems to view the Holy Spirit's procession as from the Father through the Son (2.134), sometimes as from the Father and the Son. For he writes that 'the Holy Spirit also, when He proceeds from the Father and the Son, is not separated from the Father nor separated from the Son' (1.120; cf. 119), and that the Son 'is the Fount of Life. That is the Fount of the Holy Spirit' (1.172). But it is not entirely clear that he means 'eternal procession' rather than 'temporal mission.'[11]

The Holy Spirit is coequal with the Father and the Son, and not in any respect inferior or subordinate, for He 'shares in the kingdom with the Father and the Son, and He is of one nature with them, of one Lordship and also of one power' (3.158). If the Holy Spirit is called 'the finger of God,' as the Son is called 'the Right Hand of God' (3.11), Ambrose declares, 'let them learn . . . that not inequality but unity of power is signified by this testimony: inasmuch as things which are the works of God are also the works of hands . . . and the same are the works of fingers' (3.31). He adds that some think 'that God should be praised *in* the Spirit, but not *with* the Spirit' (2.70), but actually 'in the use of the expression no lessening of honor can be implied, and nothing ought to be deduced derogatory to the honor of the Godhead' (2.84).

In the three 'there is unity of authority, unity of appointment, unity of giving . . . oneness of majesty in the Father, the Son, and the Holy Spirit . . . the same operation and divine power . . . so that to have the same will and the same power does not arise from the affection of the will, but inheres in the substance of the Trinity' (2.153, 154). As each Person possesses the Godhead, so He possesses fully the same will and power (*De Fide* 4.75), the same holiness and lordship (*De Sp. S.* 3.107, 109). Every divine operation is the work of the three (1.40, 131). The three inexist in one another, for 'as the Father is in the Son, and the Son in the Father, so the Spirit of God and the Spirit of Christ is both in the Father and in the Son' (3.6). The three are coeternal (*De Fide* 4.147) and coequal, since 'the perfection of the Godhead does not admit of inequality' (*De virg.* 3.4).

If Ambrose does not compare favorably with Marius Victorinus in philosophical speculation, his solid and lucid presentation of trinitarian doctrine must have come as a breath of fresh air to his flock.

AUGUSTINE

Augustine (d. 430) has been called 'the greatest doctor of the Church,'[12] 'the greatest philosopher of the patristic age and probably the most important and influential theologian of the Church,'[13] the one who 'gave the Western tradition its mature and final expression.'[14] It has been said that 'what Origen had been for the scientific theology of the third and fourth centuries, Augustine became in a much purer and more profitable way for the whole life of the Church of the following centuries until modern times.'[15] On the other hand, it has also been affirmed that 'the Greek Fathers are more philosophical, alike in treatment and in aim, than their Latin contemporaries. Their doctrine is both more subtle and more profound,' and while Augustine's 'treatment of the subject is deeply religious, and makes a quite invaluable supplement to the Greek definitions, it seems to me to possess less philosophical cogency.'[16]

Augustine presents trinitarian doctrine in a number of his works, in his *Enchiridion ad Laurentium, De fide et symbolo, De doctrina christiana,* in his Anti-Arian writings such as *Contra sermonem Arianorum* and *Contra Maximinum,* in his tracts *On the Gospel of St. John,* in *Letters 2* and *170.*[17] But in the 15 Books of his magnificent *De Trinitate,* Augustine is not so much a controversialist as a theologian and contemplative, at once thoroughly traditional and intensely personal. This work has two parts: the first (Bks. 1–7) establishes the doctrine of the Trinity according to the Scriptures and the Fathers and answers objections to it; the second (Bks. 8–15) seeks in man analogies that will throw light on the mystery, and this part is much more original and rich in the new avenues of speculation it opens up.

The dogma of the Trinity involves two elements: numerical unity of nature and real distinction of the three Persons. Hence it can be presented in two ways, both perfectly orthodox but resulting in quite different attitudes toward the mystery. One way, that of the Greek Fathers and of the Latin Fathers before Augustine, starts from the plurality of Persons and proceeds to the assertion that the three really distinct Persons subsist in a nature that is numerically one. Their problem was how to arrive at 'one' from 'three,' how to move from the plurality of persons to the unity of nature, and the answer they gradually developed was in terms of the 'consubstantiality' of the Son and Holy Spirit with the Father. In this approach the danger to be avoided was subordinationism, for by concentrating too much on the real distinction of the Persons one could endanger the unity of nature and the perfect equality of the three (as Apologists and Origen and Arians did in varying degrees). The advantage of this way is that in it God is not simply the God of the philosophers or of the Old Testament, but the specifically Christian God: Father, Son and Holy Spirit. The other way starts out from the unity of nature and moves to the trinity of Persons. It first affirms that there is numerically one divine nature and then that this one nature subsists in three really distinct Persons. Here the unity of nature is in the foreground, the trinity of Persons in the background. Now the problem is how to arrive at 'three' from 'one' and how to show that 'three' are compatible with this 'one.' This approach immediately negates subordinationism and Tritheism, but the danger it must avoid is Modalism.

Augustine takes the second way and where the Greeks thought primarily of three Persons having the same nature, he thought

rather of one single divine nature subsisting in three Persons. Hence
he started his explanation of the mystery not from the Father considered as the source of the other two Persons, but from the one,
simple divine nature or essence which is the Trinity. Thus he writes
that there is 'one God, one good, and one omnipotent, the Trinity
itself' (*Trin.* 8 pref.), 'one God is this Trinity' (*Civ.* 11.10),
'the Trinity is the one, only and true God,' 'the Father, the Son, and
the Holy Spirit are of one and the same substance or essence' (*Trin.*
1.2.4); 'the Father, the Son, and the Holy Spirit constitute a divine
unity of one and the same substance in an indivisible equality'
(*Trin.* 1.4.7).

Never before had the divine unity been set in such strong relief in
its relation to the three divine Persons. God, for Augustine, does not
mean directly the Father, as *ho theos* did for the Greeks, but the concrete Godhead, the basic divinity unfolding itself into three Persons,
the Father, the Son, and the Holy Spirit. He stresses oneness rather
than threeness and starts from the one divine essence rather than
from the saving deed of God in Christ, which he assumes to be
known. This new starting point will be very influential in all subsequent Western trinitarian teaching, and will lead to a distinction
between the two treatises on God, *De Deo Uno* and *De Deo Trino*.

With this starting point there can be no question of the equality
of the three, for they 'constitute a divine unity of one and the same
substance, in an indivisible equality' (*Trin.* 1.4.7); 'The three have
the same eternity, immutability, majesty, power' (*De doctr. christ.*
1.5); 'Each Person of the Trinity is God, and all together are One
God. Each is the full essence, and all together are One essence'
(*ibid.*). And by presenting the divine essence with all its absolute
perfections as existing identically in each of the three Persons,
Augustine can even say, 'so great is the equality in this Trinity, that
not only is the Father not greater than the Son in that which pertains to the divinity, but neither are the Father and the Son anything
greater than the Holy Spirit, nor is each person singly . . . anything
less than the Trinity itself' (*Trin.* 8.1); 'and they are infinite in themselves. And so each is in each, all are in each, each is in all, all are
in all, and all are one' (*Trin.* 6.10.12); 'since, therefore, the Father
alone, or the Son alone, or the Holy Spirit alone is just as great as
the Father, the Son and the Holy Spirit together, He is not to be
called threefold in any sense' for 'He is a Trinity rather than threefold' (*Trin.* 6.9).

If the three have identically the same divine essence, then they
must have one sole will and one sole operation: 'the will of the
Father and the Son is one, and their operation inseparable' (*Trin.*

2.9); 'when one of the three is mentioned as the author of any work, the whole Trinity is to be understood as working' (*Ench*. 38); 'the Catholic faith holds that the works of the Father and Son are not separable . . . not only of the Father and the Son but also of the Holy Spirit . . . are the works inseparable' (*In Jo*. tract. 20.3); 'in relation to the creature, the Father, the Son, and the Holy Spirit are one Principle, as they are one Creator and one Lord' (*Trin*. 5.15). Does this obliterate the several roles of the three Persons? Augustine says that it does not; for it was not 'this same Trinity' that 'was born of the Virgin Mary' 'but only the Son'; it was not 'this Trinity' that 'descended upon Jesus in the form of a dove' 'but only the Holy Spirit'; it was not 'this same Trinity' that said from heaven: 'Thou art my Son' 'but this was the word of the Father only' (*Trin*. 1.7). But he adds, 'not that the voice could be produced without the work of the Son and the Holy Spirit (for the Trinity works inseparably) but that such a voice was produced as would reveal the person of the Father alone; just as the Trinity wrought that human form from the Virgin, but it is the person of the Son alone, for the invisible Trinity produced the visible person of the Son alone' (*Trin*. 2.18). What, then, is to be said of the theophanies of the Old Testament, which older Fathers tended to regard as appearances of the Son exclusively? Augustine rejects this tendency for he does 'not see a determined person of the Trinity singled out by any characteristic sign' (*Trin*. 2.26), and concludes from his study of the Scriptures 'that we may not rashly assert which person of the Trinity appeared to any of the Fathers or the Prophets, unless the context itself offers some probable arguments for a particular person. . . . But we must also believe that not only the Son, or the Holy Spirit, but the Father also could have made Himself known to our mortal senses in a corporeal form or likeness by means of a creature that has been made subject to Him' (*Trin*. 2.36). He adds 'that when God was said to appear to the Fathers of ancient times before the coming of the Savior, those voices and those corporeal forms were wrought by angels. . . . And in these angels the Father, the Son, and the Holy Spirit are certainly present. Sometimes the Father, at other times the Son or the Holy Spirit, and sometimes God without any distinction of persons, made Himself known by means of His angels' (*Trin*. 3.27, 26); but 'the essence of God, wherein we understand . . . the Father, the Son, and the Holy Spirit, since it is in no way changeable, can in no way be visible in its proper self' (*Trin*. 3.21).

In thus stressing the unity of operation of the three, Augustine differed considerably from Greek Fathers who spoke as if each person had a really distinct role in external activities. And his view, with the corresponding doctrine of 'appropriation,' will dominate the West for a long time to come, though recently it has been strongly criticized as too rigid and too little conformed to Biblical and patristic doctrine. But it must be remembered that Augustine was not unique in this matter, for Basil had said that all things 'are performed equally among the worthy by the Father and the Son and the Holy Spirit' (*Ep.* 189.7), and the Greek Fathers had also recognized that there is a unity of operation in God and had used it to prove the unity of nature of the three.

It was noted above that the Augustinian approach was open to the danger of Modalism, and Harnack maintained 'that Augustine only gets beyond Modalism by the mere assertion that he does not wish to be a Modalist, and by the aid of ingenious distinctions between different ideas.'[18] But 'this is an unwarranted assumption. There is no evidence that the reality claimed by Augustine for the distinction between the persons is in any way different from that claimed for it by other orthodox Fathers . . . in their opposition to Modalism.'[19] That Augustine affirmed a real distinction between the Persons is beyond doubt, for he wrote that by denying they were 'three somethings' 'Sabellius fell into heresy. From the Scriptures we learn with absolute certainty . . . that there is the Father, the Son, and the Holy Spirit, that the Son is not the same as the Father, and that the Holy Spirit is not the same as the Father and the Son' (*Trin.* 7.9). They are somehow three individuals of one essence (*Trin.* 7.11), if this essence is regarded not as genus or species but as substratum,[20] and hence they are 'three Persons of one essence but not as each individual man is one person' (*Trin.* 15.11). Augustine did not much like this term 'person' but he accepted it, since 'the formula *three persons* has been coined, not in order to give a complete explanation by means of it, but in order that we might not be obliged to remain silent' (*Trin.* 5.10); and as a matter of fact he used the term quite extensively in this treatise (5.12; 15.5, 7, 11, 42, 43, 45).

The Arians had presented a 'very cunning argument,' that 'what is said or thought of God is predicated of Him not according to accidents, but according to substance. Consequently, to be ungenerated pertains to the substance of the Father and to be generated to the substance of the Son. Now to be ungenerated and to be generated are two different things, and hence there is a difference in substance between the Father and the Son' (*Trin.* 5.4). Augustine answered that 'although to be the Father and to be the Son are two different things, still there is no difference in their substance, because the names, Father and Son, do not refer to the substance, but to the relation, and the relation is no accident because it is not changeable'

(*Trin.* 5.6). Similarly he said that 'if by the Holy Spirit is meant the person to whom it properly belongs, then it denotes a relation. For He is referred to both the Father and the Son, because the Holy Spirit is the Spirit of the Father and the Son. . . . For He is the gift of the Father and the Son . . . in a certain sense the ineffable communion of the Father and the Son' (*Trin.* 5.12).

It has been said that for Augustine 'the Three are real or subsistent relations,'[21] 'and relations that are not identical with the substance or nature, since they are not something absolute.'[22] But this does not seem to be entirely accurate. Augustine does not say that the Persons *are* relations, but rather that they are distinguished from one another by their unchangeable relations to one another (paternity, filiation, gift). They are 'three somethings' whose names 'do not refer to the substance but to the relation.' Father, Son, and Holy Spirit are named in the Scriptures and distinguished from one another not in terms of accidents, for in God there are no accidents, nor in terms of substance as if they were three substances, for there is only one substance, but in terms of unchangeable originational relations. Thus, to use a later terminology, the three Persons are three subjects of one divine activity who are not accidentally nor substantially but relationally distinct, or three relationally distinct subsistents in one intellectual divine nature. Basil had already (*Adv. Eunom.* 1.20; 2.22) described the distinction between the three in terms of their causal relation and used this causal relation as an argument against both Sabellians and Anomoians,[23] but it was Augustine's strong stress on these distinctive divine relations that most impressed subsequent Western theologians and influenced them in their attempts to develop and synthesize this doctrine of internal divine relations.

To the doctrine of the Son's generative procession from the Father, Augustine found little to add. He simply pointed out that 'the uncorrupt and catholic faith proclaims the eternality of the Power and Wisdom of God, who is the only-begotten Son' (*Enar. in Ps. 26*), and so 'the Father was never without His Son' but 'is always in the process of begetting and the Son is always in the process of being born' (*Ep.* 238.24). However, he adds that 'the expression "always born" (*semper natus*)' is better than 'always being born (*qui semper nascitur*)' since this 'implies that he was not yet born' (*De Div.* Qu. 83, Qu. 37). Against Eunomius who held that the Word was the Son of the will of God and not of His nature or substance or essence, Augustine maintained that He 'was the Son of God by nature, that is, begotten from the substance of the Father' (*Trin.* 15.38).

To the traditional doctrine of the procession of the Holy Spirit Augustine made a considerable contribution, especially by his teaching about the *Filioque* and about the Holy Spirit as 'Gift' and 'Love' and sanctifying Inhabitant of the just soul.

He maintains explicitly that the Holy Spirit proceeds from the Father and the Son; but 'principally' from the Father: 'He . . . from whom the Holy Spirit principally proceeds, is God the Father. I have added "principally," therefore, because the Holy Spirit is also found to proceed from the Son. But the Father also gave this to Him,' for 'He so begot Him . . . that the common Gift should also proceed from Him, and that the Holy Spirit should be the Spirit of both' (*Trin.* 15.29). Again he declares that 'just as the Father has in Himself that the Holy Spirit should proceed from Him, so He has given to the Son that the same Holy Spirit should proceed from Him, and both apart from time . . . which consists of before and after, because time does not exist there at all' (15.47). But he carefully adds that 'we have to confess that the Father and the Son are the Principle of the Holy Spirit, not two Principles; but as the Father and the Son are one God, and in relation to the creature are one Creator and one Lord, so they are one Principle, as they are one Creator and one Lord' (5.15). To the question, why is the Holy Spirit not a Son if He proceeds from the Father, Augustine replies that He 'came forth, not as one born, but as one given' (5.15). Here we can see Augustine's special contribution in the matter of the Spirit's procession in his teaching that the Spirit proceeds timelessly and simultaneously from the Father and the Son as one Principle, that the Son's power to principiate the Spirit was given to Him by the Father in His generation, and that thus the Spirit's procession from the Son did not negate the Father's 'primordiality.' As Augustine presents the *Filioque*, it 'is almost a necessary inference from the Homoousion.'[24] Later on, the Second Council of Lyons will declare that 'we confess that the Holy Spirit proceeds eternally from the Father and the Son, not as from two principles, but as from one; not by two spirations but by one' (Denz 850).

Augustine often views the Holy Spirit as the bond of the Father and the Son, as their common gift. Thus he writes that 'the Catholic Church holds and preaches that God the Holy Spirit is . . . the Spirit of the Father and the Son . . . their community . . . that which is common to them both . . . this Gift which both have in common, namely . . . the Holy Spirit, who is God and the Gift of God' (*Serm.* 71). He sees the Holy Spirit as the Gift of God in many passages of the Scriptures (Jn 7.37–39; 4.7–14; 1 Cor 12.13; Eph 4.7–11) but especially in Acts (2.37–38; 8.20; 10.44–46). To the question whether the Holy Spirit was Gift before He was given to us, he replies that 'the Spirit is a gift eternally, but has been given in time' (*Trin.* 5.17), and 'is so given as the Gift of God that He also gives Himself as God.' There is therefore, 'no subordination of the Gift and no domination of the Givers, but concord between the Gift and the Givers' (15.36). Why is 'the Spirit specially called the Gift?' 'For no other reason except love,' he declares (15.32).

And it is as 'Love' that Augustine loves to view the Holy Spirit. He admits that the Scripture 'has not said that the Holy Spirit is love' (*Trin.* 15.27), but he thinks that 'according to the Sacred Scriptures, this Holy Spirit is neither the Spirit of the Father alone, nor of the Son alone, but the Spirit of both, and, therefore, He insinuates to us the common love by which the Father and the Son mutually love each other' (15.27). What is more fitting, he asks, if 'anyone of these three is to be specially called love' than 'that this should be the Holy Spirit?' (15.29). For the Holy Spirit is 'something common . . . between the Father and the Son. But this communion itself is consubstantial and coeternal, and if this communion itself can be appropriately designated as friendship, let it be so called, but it is more aptly called love. . . . And consequently there are not more than three: the one loving Him who is of Him, the one loving Him of whom He is, and the love itself' (6.7). For 'love, then, which is from God and is God, is properly the Holy Spirit, through whom the charity of God is poured forth in our hearts, through whom the whole Trinity dwells in us. For this reason the Holy Spirit, since He is God, is also most rightly called the Gift of God (Acts 8.20). What else is to be understood by the Gift in the strict sense except charity which leads to God, and without which any other gift, no matter which, does not lead to God' (15.32). Through the Holy Spirit both the Father and the Son 'are joined together; through Him the begotten is loved by the begetter, and in turn loves Him who begot Him . . . in Him they preserve the unity of spirit through the bond of peace (Eph 4.3) . . . not by the gift of anyone superior to themselves, but by their own gift' (6.7).

It is in connection with man's spiritual life that Augustine mentions the Holy Spirit most frequently, for on Him this life depends. For 'as a man could not have wisdom, understanding, counsel, courage, knowledge, godliness, and the fear of God, unless he had received the Spirit of wisdom, understanding, counsel, courage, knowledge, godliness, and the fear of God; as he could not possess power, love, or a sound mind, unless he had received the Spirit of power, love, and a sound mind; so he cannot have faith, without receiving the Spirit of faith. Similarly, we cannot pray aright without the Spirit of prayer' (*Ep.* 194.18). The Spirit is the Spirit of sanctification: 'the first gift of the Spirit is the remission of sins in regeneration' (*Serm.* 71); 'in some of the saints the Spirit works miracles, in others He speaks the truth; in some He lives the celibate life, in others He preserves conjugal modesty; each fulfils his own proper work, but all are equally alive. What the soul is to the human body, such is the Holy Spirit to the Body of Christ' (*Serm.* 267). It is the Holy Spirit who 'makes us abide in God, and God in us, for this is the effect of love. He is Himself the Love of God . . . and when He is given to a man, He kindles in him the fire of love towards God and towards his neighbor. . . . There is no gift that can surpass this gift of God; it alone separates between the children of the eternal kingdom and those of eternal perdition' (*Trin.* 15.31, 32).

In his work *On the Trinity* Augustine touched on the divine indwelling in the just, but in his letter *On the Presence of God* (*Ep.* 187; PL 33) he developed this teaching to such an extent that he surpasses the Greek Fathers in some respects in exposition of this mystery. Basically he sees this indwelling as trinitarian, although the Holy Spirit has a special, introductory role: for 'love, then, which is from God and is God, is properly the Holy Spirit, through whom the charity of God is poured forth in our hearts, through which the whole Trinity dwells in us.' 'Who would dare to think,' he asks, 'unless he utterly ignores the inseparability of the Trinity, that the Father or Son could dwell in someone in whom the Holy Spirit does not dwell, or that the Holy Spirit could dwell in someone in whom the Father and Son do not dwell' (*Ep.* 187.16). This inhabitational presence is not universal, since God 'though He is everywhere in His entirety, yet does not dwell in all (1 Cor 3.16; Rom 8.9). . . . It must be confessed that God is everywhere by the presence of divinity, but not everywhere by the grace of inhabitation' (*Ep.* 187.16). Nor is this divine indwelling coextensive with knowledge of God, for 'God inhabits some who do not know Him,' such as 'infants sanctified by the sacrament of Christ, regenerated by the Holy Spirit,' who thus 'could have Him before they knew Him'; but 'He does not inhabit some who know Him,' but 'do not glorify Him as God' and who 'could thus know Him but not have Him' (*Ep.* 187.21). God does not 'equally inhabit those in whom He dwells,' for why are 'some saints more holy than others, unless they have the indwelling God more abundantly' (*Ep.* 187.17). This divine indwelling is an effective presence, a temple-making presence, and it begins with baptismal regeneration, for God dwells 'only in those whom He makes His most blessed temple or temples, by drawing them from the power of darkness and transferring them into the kingdom

of His Son's love; and this begins from their regeneration'
(*Ep.* 187.35), which is ascribed to the Holy Spirit (*Ep.* 187.21). This
indwelling is a dynamic presence aimed at making men an ever more
perfect temple of God and ever more perfect saints (*Ep.* 187.29,
17). In baptized infants an ontological sanctity is effected, for in
them anterior to any free act of theirs, God 'acts secretly to make
them His temple' (*Ep.* 187.27) and to regenerate them by the Holy
Spirit (*ibid.* 21). But in just adults God wants this sanctity to grow
and grow, so that they will be 'renewed from day to day,' justified
more and more, come to 'have God' more and more, know Him
more and more fully and perfectly, come to be more and more like
Him in love (29). For 'nothing is better for us than to go to God, and
we go not by walking but by loving' (*Ep.* 155.13). But man is not
meant to go to God alone, but as a Christian. And the sanctity of a
Christian is the sanctity of a member 'of the body of Christ.' So
Augustine moves spontaneously from the presence of God in the
just soul to His presence in the Church, itself the body of Christ and
also a temple of the Holy Spirit (*Ep.* 187.33). For Christ has died to
assemble in one same city, one same body, one same temple the
children of God, and as charity unites man to God, so it unites Him
to Christ and thus forms the 'mystical' body of Christ, and an
'immaculate temple for eternity' (*Ep.* 187.33, 29).[25]

Perhaps the most original element of Augustine's contribution
to the theology of the Trinity was his search for traces of the mystery in the world of creatures. This search was not new. For a long
time men had tried to find images of the Trinity in created things,
in the sun and its ray and warmth, in root and shoot and fruit. But
these were far from satisfactory. Since God was essentially triune,
Augustine thought there should be vestiges of the Trinity in all
creation,[26] and he 'discovered' them wherever he found the number
three (*De vera relig.* 13, PL 34). But since God had made man specially to His image and likeness (Gen 1.26), Augustine thought it
would not be surprising to find an image of the Trinity in man, and
especially in 'the mind itself,' for 'to it a certain insight into invisible
things has been granted . . . and there is no one above it except God
. . . by whom it is to be ruled' (*Trin.* 15.49; cf. *Serm.* 52.17–19;
Enarr. in Ps. 42.6; *Serm. de symb.* 1.2). Here he hoped to find analogies that would help to convey the unity of the divine nature and
the distinctness of the three who possess it. Of the many analogies
to the triune God that Augustine searched out, perhaps these five
are the best: (1) lover, beloved, their love (*Trin.* 8.12–9.2; 15.5, 10);
(2) being, knowing, willing (*Conf.* 13.11); (3) mind, (self-) knowledge,
(self-) love (*Trin.* 9.2–8); (4) memory, understanding, will (*Trin.*

9.17–19); (5) our remembrance of God, our understanding of God, our love for God (*Trin.* 14.15–20).

It has been thought that Augustine's principle analogy was that of lover, beloved, love, which started from the Johannine dictum that 'God is love' (1 Jn 4.8). But he considers this analogy rather as a transition to the more important analogy of the mind's activity of knowing and loving itself (*Trin.* 15.5, 10). Already in his *Confessions* (13.11) he had pondered the triad of being, knowing and willing (*esse, nosse, velle*). But in his great work *On the Trinity* he elaborated this and moved from the analogy of the mind and its knowledge and love of itself to that of the mind remembering and understanding and loving God (14.15–20). In these analogies Augustine saw three real elements that are coordinate and equal and at the same time essentially one. Each threw some light on the mutual relations of the divine Persons. Yet Augustine had no illusions about the limitations of these analogies, remote and imperfect as they were (*Trin.* 10.19), for he wrote that 'although this image of the Trinity is one person, while there are three Persons in the highest Trinity itself, yet this Trinity of three Persons is more inseparable than that trinity of one person' (*Trin.* 15.43). It was the fifth analogy, however, that Augustine found most satisfactory, for in it 'man, like God, is one substance and not three. When he is absorbed in his totality—imagery, thought, volition—with the divine Being, then he is most like that Being, who is triune.'[27]

In searching out these analogies Augustine 'laid the foundations for the psychological theory of the processions' that was completed by St. Thomas, and in which 'the mind tries to penetrate into the inner life of God and, contemplating the divine nature endowed with intellect and will, explains through these two operations the number and the nature of the processions concerning the origin of the Son and the Holy Spirit.' St. Thomas will say that 'the Son is born of the Father as the Word of the divine intellect, "after the manner of the act of understanding," ' and that 'the Holy Spirit proceeds from the Father and the Son as the substantial term of their love, "a procession of love" ' (ST 1a, 27.2.3). And 'with these two processions the cycle of what can be called the divine evolution is completed because only these two operations demand a substantial term. This is the profound metaphysical study which St. Augustine inaugurated by his subtle analysis of the human soul, which he liked to see as the most beautiful image of the Trinity.'[28]

There can be little doubt that Augustine produced a more profound, comprehensive and stimulating synthesis of trinitarian doctrine than anyone else had before him in the West or East. It summed up the work of his predecessors, laid the foundation for most all subsequent trinitarian theology, and became 'the high-school not only for the technico-logical culture of the understanding, but also for the metaphysics of the Middle Ages . . . so that the realistic scholasticism of the Middle Ages is not conceivable apart from this work.'[29]

SUMMARY

Among the Apostolic Fathers only 1 Clement and Hermas pertained to the early Western Church and neither left any notable trinitarian doctrine. Justin, one of the Apologists, who founded a school at Rome, made a notable if somewhat subordinationist attempt to explain the mystery of the Trinity by a twofold stage theory of the Logos. In the first stage the Logos had an eternal and probably personal existence with the Father as Someone with whom the Father could commune. In the second stage this Logos was generated as Son pre-creationally but not eternally by the will of the Father for the purpose of creation.

Irenaeus stands out for his refutation of Gnosticism, his rejection of the twofold stage theory of the Logos, his exposition of the Holy Spirit's work on the hearts and lives of men, and his view of the Son and Holy Spirit as the 'Two Hands of God.' Though he developed no technical language or formulas to express trinitarian doctrine, he solidly presented and defended the traditional doctrine of one sole God the Creator and Lord of all who is Father, Son, and Holy Spirit, without falling into subordinationism or Modalism.

Tertullian in his treatise *Against Praxeas* vigorously refuted the unitarian Monarchianism of Praxeas. Where Irenaeus had properly rejected the twofold stage theory of the Logos Tertullian apparently accepted it and thus denied the eternal generation of the Son. He went beyond Irenaeus in saying explicitly that the Holy Spirit 'is God' and 'proceeds from the Father through the Son.' He was the first in the West to use the word *trinity* of God and he indicated clearly enough that this 'trinity of one divinity' was not just an economic trinity but also an immanent trinity. He was one of the first, if not the first, to use the term *person* for the three, and he seems to have understood it not in the juristic sense of a title-holder but in the metaphysical sense of a concrete individual or a self. And when he said the three are 'one in substance' he seemed to mean by divine substance a rarefied form of spiritual matter. Many of his affirmations about the Son will appear later in the Symbol of Nicea, such as 'the Son is of the Father's substance,' is 'one in substance with the Father,' is 'begotten,' is 'God of God,' is 'light of light.' His chief doctrinal defects lay in his materialistic view of the divine substance and in his acceptance of the non-eternal generation of the Son. But his doctrinal contributions far outstripped these defects and gave him a good claim to the title of founder of Latin theology.

Thus through Irenaeus the Church of Lyons and through Tertullian the Church of Africa made important contributions to the development of trinitarian doctrine in the West. At Rome the outstanding theologians of the 3d century were Hippolytus and Novatian. Hippolytus strongly opposed Modalism and accused Popes Zephyrinus and Callistus of favoring it. He himself adopted a subordinationist three-stage form of the two-stage theory of the Apologists, and he seemed to regard the Holy Spirit more as a divine force than as a divine person. Novatian was the first theologian at Rome to write in Latin and his work *On the Trinity* became something of a dogmatic *vade mecum* in the West. He opposed Modalism and Ditheism but left traces of subordinationism in his writings. Two popes are often singled out, Dionysius and Damasus. Dionysius condemned Sabellianism and Tritheism and even Arianism by anticipation, and clearly affirmed the divine trinity and unity as the authentic teaching of Scripture. Damasus anathematized the Macedonians and set forth a sound trinitarian doctrine in agreement with the creeds of Nicea and Constantinople. Thus in the 3d and 4th centuries Roman bishops felt quite competent to present the traditional trinitarian doctrine of the Church authoritatively and to condemn bluntly the errors opposed to it.

Hilary of Poitiers, the 'Athanasius of the West,' wrote strongly against Arianism and stressed the Father and the Son more than the Holy Spirit. He clearly taught the eternal generation and the strict consubstantiality of the Son and the divinity of the Holy Spirit, and sufficiently indicated his belief in the distinct personality of the Holy Spirit. He was one of the very first to attempt a true synthesis of trinitarian doctrine.

Marius Victorinus, African by birth and Roman by long residence, strongly opposed Arianism. He regarded the Logos as the term of the Father's will, the Son as the term of His understanding. Though his doctrine was excessively Neoplatonic, yet in his effort to present the Trinity 'in the more general categories of ontology' he is regarded as a precursor of Augustine and the Schoolmen.

Ambrose of Milan followed the Eastern method of treating the persons before the nature and put forth a solid presentation of a strictly consubstantial Trinity. He strongly opposed Arianism and Macedonianism, and was the first in the West to produce a separate work of any magnitude on the Holy Spirit.

Augustine was at once thoroughly traditional and intensely personal in his magnificent *De Trinitate*. The Greeks in starting from the trinity of persons and moving to the unity of nature had faced the danger of subordinationism. Augustine took a different approach that immediately eliminated subordinationism and Tritheism but laid him open to the danger of Modalism. Instead of starting from the Father considered as the source of the other two persons, he began with the one simple divine essence that is the Trinity, and this new approach was destined to dominate most all subsequent Western trinitarian teaching. With this approach there is no question of the equality of the three for they have identically the same essence and will and operation. Thus external works such as creation and sanctification are common to the three and only appropriated to the Father and to the Holy Spirit. Here again we have a doctrine—of appropriation—that will dominate the West for a long, long time. Augustine was not a Modalist, as some have charged, for he bluntly affirmed the real distinction of the three and based it on their real originational relations of paternity, filiation, gift. Here too Augustine's stress on these distinctive divine relations will exercise a strong influence on subsequent Western theologians in their efforts to explain the Triune God. Augustine did not much like the term *person* but he accepted it and used it quite extensively. For him the three are 'three somethings,' three 'someones,' or to use a later terminology they are three subjects of one divine activity who are only relationally distinct, or three relationally distinct subsistents in one intellectual divine nature. Augustine contributed a great deal to Pneumatology by his explicit teaching about the *Filioque* and about the Holy Spirit as Gift and Love and sanctifying Inhabitant of the just soul. He maintained that the Holy Spirit proceeds from the Father and the Son although principally from the Father, and yet that Father and Son are not two principles but only one principle of the Holy Spirit, as they are but one Creator and one Lord. Later on the Second Council of Lyons will canonize this doctrine when it declares that 'we confess that the Holy Spirit proceeds eternally from the Father and the Son, not as from two principles but as from one, not by two spirations but by one' (Denz 850). In some respects Augustine surpassed the Greek Fathers in his exposition of the divine indwelling. Though he conceded to the Holy Spirit a special introductory role in this inhabitation, he maintained that it was a trinitarian indwelling, a special presence of the three that begins with baptismal regeneration, effects an ontological sanctity in baptized infants and a dynamic orientation aimed at making them become ever more perfect saints. Augustine's greatest originality, however, has been thought by some to lie in his search for vestiges and images and analogies to the Triune God in the world of creatures. He found many such analogies, but his best were in the mind of man whom God had made to His image and likeness. Two of these would especially captivate the minds of subsequent theologians: (1) that of lover, beloved, and their love; (2) that of the mind remembering, understanding, and loving God. In developing this second analogy he laid the foundations of the psychological theory of the divine processions that would reach its crest in St. Thomas. There can be no doubt that Augustine produced a more comprehensive and stimulating synthesis of trinitarian doctrine than anyone else had before him in the West or East. It summed up the work of his predecessors and laid the foundations for most all subsequent trinitarian theology in the West. But it left unanswered many questions: What is the nature of the two processions? How do they differ? Why are there only two processions and only three persons? These questions would fascinate theologians down the centuries and find a full if extremely rarefied metaphysical answer only in the writings of Thomas Aquinas.

CHAPTER EIGHT

The Post-Augustinian Phase

In the long period from Augustine to the Early Middle Ages Augustine's doctrinal influence will generally remain dominant. For hundreds of years after his death conditions will not favor the development of trinitarian doctrine, for the Roman Empire has fallen to invading Vandals, Goths, Lombards, Moslems, Franks. Only with the coronation of Charlemagne as Holy Roman Emperor in 800 will there begin to be a milieu somewhat favorable to theological development. Two Creeds will stand out for their trinitarian contributions, the 'Athanasian Creed' and the Symbol of the 11th Council of Toledo, and a few writers such as Pope Leo the Great, Fulgentius, Boethius, Cassiodorus, Peter Damian, Isidore of Seville, Bede and Alcuin, John Scotus Eriugena. And these generally will not be innovators but rather compilers and transmitters of their Biblical and patristic heritage.

POPE LEO THE GREAT

Leo I (d. 461) has been called 'the greatest pope of Christian antiquity,'[1] largely because of his wisdom and strength in ruling the faithful and his consummate diplomatic skill in dealing with the invading barbarians and with the Eastern and Western emperors. He was not a great theologian but both the Eastern and Western Church esteemed very highly his Christological and trinitarian doctrine for its solidity and clarity. His *Letters* and *Sermons* (PL 54–56) manifest one of the noblest literary styles that Christian Rome has known.

His most notable dogmatic work is the so-called *Tome of Leo*.[2] It is the Letter he wrote to Flavian, the patriarch of Constantinople, which was accepted as a rule of faith by the Council of Chalcedon (Denz 290–295, 300). It not only condemns Eutyches' monophysitic 'iniquity of asserting that there was but one nature in Him after "the Word became flesh" ' (6), but gives in very compact form Leo's Christological doctrine about the Son's divine and human consubstantiality, His eternal and temporal nativity, His unity of person and duality of nature and a denominational consequence of this which theologians will call *communicatio idiomatum*. Thus he writes that 'in the whole and perfect nature of true man true God was born, complete in what was His own, complete in what was ours . . . without detriment . . . to the properties of either nature and substance which then came together in one person,' for 'both natures retain their own proper character without loss' (3). So the Son of God is 'God from God,' 'born from the Eternal one' and 'coeternal with Him' (2), 'descending from His heavenly home and yet not quitting His Father's glory, begotten in a new order by a new nativity . . . because being invisible in His own nature He became visible in ours' (4).

In *Sermon 75* Leo tells of the Holy Spirit, His nature, origin and mission: 'as therefore we abhor the Arians who maintain a difference between the Father and the Son, so also we abhor the Macedonians who, although they ascribe equality to the Father and the Son, yet think the Holy Spirit to be of a lower nature' (4). For 'all things whatsoever the Father has, the Son also has and the Holy Spirit also, nor was there ever a time when this communion did not exist' (3). And 'while the Son is the Only-begotten of the Father, the Holy Spirit is the Spirit of the Father and the Son, not in the way that every creature is the creature of the Father and the Son, but as living and having power with both, and eternally subsisting of that which is the Father and the Son' (3). This Holy Spirit, the Advocate who pleads for us, is 'the inspirer of the faith, the teacher of knowledge, the fount of love, the seal of chastity and the cause of all power' and through Him 'the whole catholic Church is sanctified and every rational soul quickened' (5). In *Letter 15* Leo makes it clear that the Holy Spirit 'proceeded from both' the Father and the Son (2).

He left no doubt about his belief in a consubstantial Trinity: 'we confess this blessed Trinity to be one God for this reason, because in these three Persons there is no diversity either of substance or of power or of will or of operation' (*Serm.* 75.3). He added that 'the mercy of the Trinity divided for itself the work of our restoration in such a way that the Father should be propitiated, the Son should propitiate, and the Holy Spirit enkindle' (*Serm.* 77.2).

Although Leo's trinitarian doctrine manifests no great theological originality, it represents an advance over previous papal writings, even those of Damasus and Dionysius.

Fulgentius of Ruspe in Africa (d. *c.* 533), who has been called 'the greatest theologian of his time,' was a devoted but reflective follower of Augustine. Among his many trinitarian writings perhaps the most important are *De Trinitate, De Fide* and *Contra Fabianum* (PL 65).

His trinitarian doctrine is largely that of Augustine. Thus the Son is born 'God from God . . . coeternal Son from eternal Father' (*C. Arian.* obj. 1). He is always present to the Father, He is 'one with the Father because their nature is one, other than the Father because they are distinct persons' (*Serm.* 2.2), and because each has His own 'personal property' (*C. Arian.* obj. 1).

The Holy Spirit is God as the Father and Son (*De Trin.* 2), one with the Father and the Son, for in them there 'is one nature, essence or substance' (*De Trin.* 2). Though He is sent by them He is in no way less than the Father and the Son (*De Trin.* 6). He is equal to the Father and the Son because, as they, so He is the creator of all things (*Ep.* 8.18). He proceeds from the Father and the Son (*De Incarn. Filii* 3), and 'so proceeds from the Son as He proceeds from the Father' (*Ep.* 14.28). He 'proceeds wholly from the Father and the Son, wholly remains in the Father and the Son, for He so remains that He proceeds and so proceeds that He remains' (*ibid.*). So often does Fulgentius refer to the *Filioque* that it is obvious that he accepts it as a traditional doctrine. However he apparently gives no thought to the inner nature of this procession and its differentiation from that of the Son but is content with the Biblical and patristic doctrine that the Son originates from the Father alone by generation and the Holy Spirit from the Father and Son by procession.

Again and again Fulgentius speaks of the Trinity that is one God: 'faith . . . preaches one God Trinity, that is Father, Son, and Holy Spirit, so that the true God is a Trinity in persons and one in nature. Through this natural unity the Father is wholly in the Son and Holy Spirit, the Son wholly in the Father and Holy Spirit, the Holy Spirit wholly in the Father and Son. No one precedes another in eternity or exceeds another in magnitude or surpasses another in power. . . . As the Son is neither posterior or less than the Father, so neither is the Holy Spirit posterior or less than the Son' (*De Fide* 4). The Father and Son and Holy Spirit are 'three persons' (*Ep.* 8.3) and distinct because of their 'personal properties' (*C. Arian*. obj. 1; cf. *De Incarn. Filii* 4; *C. Fabian*. Fragm. 7). Father, Son, and Holy Spirit are relative names, for Father refers to Son, Son refers to Father, and Holy Spirit refers to Father and Son since Spirit 'is of someone spirating' (*aspirantis*) and both Father and Son spirate the Holy Spirit. Thus 'these relative names make the Trinity, but essentials are in no way triplicated' (*De Trin.* 2). Like Augustine and the Cappadocians Fulgentius finds the distinction of the three persons in their mutual originational relations, but he does not develop this doctrine either ontologically or psychologically. Most of this doctrine will reappear verbally in more authoritative statements such as those of the *Quicunque* (Denz 75), of Lateran IV (Denz 803–805) and of Florence (Denz 1330–1331).

Fulgentius also stresses the inseparability of the three and their unity of operation and of immensity-presence. The 'holy Trinity operates inseparably, nor is there a work that the Father does and the Son does not; or that the Son does and the Holy Spirit does not' (*C. Serm. Fastid.* 2, 5, 6). Hence as the Father vivifies and regenerates, so does the Son and so does the Holy Spirit (*Ad Tras.* 3.35). But Fulgentius is careful to point out that 'operational inseparability' need not mean 'acceptational inseparability':

> because the operation of the Trinity is inseparable, the whole Trinity made the servile form that the Only-begotten accepted; yet it is certain that this form that is made by the whole Trinity pertains only to the person of the Son of God. Though there is in it one operation of the whole Trinity, yet there is not in it a common acceptance by the whole Trinity. For personal property . . . shows that something made by Father and Son and Holy Spirit is nonetheless accepted by one alone' (*Ep.* 14.22).

Perhaps Fulgentius's most interesting contribution is in the matter of the mission of the Son and Holy Spirit to men. He distinguishes two advents of the Son but calls only one a mission. In His visible advent the Son comes once, sent by the Father at the plenitude of time as savior for all men and this coming brings resurrection to some men, ruin to those who refuse to believe in Him. Invisibly He comes with the Father not once but innumerable times, whenever someone loves Him (Jn 14.23), and this advent brings not ruin but resurrection (*De Incarn. Filii* 9). Later theologians will regard both comings as missions.[3]

With regard to the Holy Spirit Fulgentius also distinguishes two ways of 'coming,' one visible, the other invisible, but he regards both as 'missions' of the Holy Spirit by the Father and the Son. For he writes that the Holy Spirit, although He already was everywhere, was sent in that He came over Christ in the form of a dove and on the Apostles in fire (*De Trin.* 6). He appeared only in the dove and the fiery tongues, but He was sent often without appearing (*C. Fabian.* Fragm. 30). Since He proceeds from the Father and the Son, He is sent by the Father and Son whenever the effect of spiritual grace is given by the Trinity (*ibid.* Fragm. 29) and is present by grace whenever He confers charity (*ibid.* Fragm. 28).

Does Fulgentius really mean to call the Holy Spirit's invisible coming through grace a mission and the Son's invisible coming not a mission? It is hard to be sure. But his words raise a provocative question about the possibility of a non-missioned coming of the Son and Holy Spirit whenever 'anyone loves them.'

In Fulgentius's doctrine of a strictly consubstantial Trinity, of the procession of the Son from the Father alone and of the Holy Spirit from the Father and the Son, of the relational distinction of the persons, their circumincession, absolute equality and inseparability in substance and operation, the mission of the Son and Holy Spirit, we have a fine example of the trinitarian doctrine and terms that will generally prevail down to the Middle Ages.

THE 'ATHANASIAN' CREED

The 'Athanasian Creed' (c. 430–500), also called the *Quicunque* after its opening words, is an important document for in it 'the Catholic belief in the Trinity received its definitive expression'[4] in the early Western Church. At times it has been placed almost on a level with Holy Scripture, at other times it has been called a rock of offense because of its damnatory clauses. It has been said that only two things are certain about it, that it is not a creed and not by Athanasius. It is true that it 'does not conform to the classic credal type represented by the Apostles' and Nicene Creeds. Nor was it, like them, originally called a *symbolum* but instead "the faith of St. Athanasius" . . . or "the Catholic Faith." '[5] It has been called 'not so much a creed as a hymn,'[6] but it seems clear enough that it was originally 'drafted as a summary of orthodox teaching for instructional purposes.'[7] Toward the 9th century it was inserted 'along with the Apostles' Creed and the Lord's Prayer, into psalters.'[8] Gradually it was ranked alongside the Apostles' and Nicene Creeds, by Alexander of Hales in the 13th century, by the Lutheran Book of Concord in the 16th century, by the Great Hellenic Encyclopedia (Athens, 1933). However, its liturgical use at Prime has been drastically reduced by Popes Pius X and Pius XII.[9]

Its author, date, and source of origin are still matters of controversy. From the 7th century on it was generally ascribed to St.
Athanasius, but in the 17th century it was realized that it was later
than Athanasius and of Latin origin. Scholars have attributed it to
Vigilius of Thapsus, to Vincent of Lérins, to Venantius Fortunatus,
to Hilary of Arles, to Honoratus, to Ambrose, to Fulgentius, to
Caesarius of Arles.[10] The *Enchiridion Symbolorum* says simply that
'the view prevails now that the symbol originated in South Gaul . . .
between 430–500 from an unknown author' (Denz 75).

This 5th–6th-century Western statement of salvific faith declares
with remarkable clarity, precision, and balance that:

> Whoever wishes to be saved must above all keep the Catholic
> faith; for unless a person keeps this faith whole and entire he will
> undoubtedly be lost forever. This is what the Catholic faith
> teaches: We worship one God in Trinity and Trinity in unity;
> we distinguish among the persons, but we do not divide the
> substance. [Father, Son, and Holy Spirit are distinct persons,
> still they] have one divinity, equal glory and coeternal majesty.
> What the Father is, the Son is, and the Holy Spirit is. [Each, the
> Father, the Son, and the Holy Spirit, is uncreated, has
> immensity, is eternal, is omnipotent, is God, is Lord, yet there is]
> but one eternal being . . . one uncreated being, one being that has
> immensity . . . one omnipotent being . . . one God . . . one Lord
> . . . The Father is not made by anyone, nor created by anyone,
> nor generated by anyone. The Son is not made nor created, but
> he is generated by the Father alone. The Holy Spirit is not made
> nor created nor generated, but proceeds from the Father and the
> Son. There is, then, one Father, not three fathers; one Son, not
> three sons, one Holy Spirit, not three Holy Spirits. In this Trinity
> there is nothing antecedent, nothing subsequent to anything else.
> There is nothing greater, nothing less than anything else. But the
> entire three persons are coeternal and coequal with one another,
> so that, as we have said, we worship complete unity in Trinity
> and Trinity in unity. This then is what he who wishes to be saved
> must believe about the Trinity. It is also necessary for eternal
> salvation that he believe steadfastly in the Incarnation of our
> Lord Jesus Christ. The true faith is: we believe and profess that
> our Lord Jesus Christ, the Son of God, is both God and man.
> As God He was begotten of the substance of the Father before
> time; as man He was born in time of the substance of His mother.
> He is perfect God and He is perfect man, with a rational soul
> and human flesh. He is equal to the Father in His divinity but He
> is inferior to the Father in His humanity. Although He is God
> and man, He is not two but one Christ . . . because He is one
> person (Denz 75–76).

The damnatory clauses may seem somewhat surprising until we recall that an appendix of anathemas against deviationists was a regular feature of creeds in the early Church (Denz 126, 151). The main thrust of these damnatory clauses, however, 'that eternal life is the knowledge of God, and that eternal death is atheism, the being without Him'[11] is quite intelligible in the light of the Johannine text, 'this is eternal life, that they know thee the only true God' (17.3), but today more explicit allowance would be made for invincible ignorance.

Many things are noteworthy in this creed. The approach is unusual. For the creed does not suggest that 'catholic faith' is merely an intellectual assent but declares, 'now this is the catholic faith that we worship one God in Trinity and Trinity in unity.' Furthermore, the creed definitely rejects certain errors without mentioning them explicitly. For it warns against 'confusing the persons,' as Sabellians did, or 'dividing the substance,' as Arians did, and declares that Father, Son, and Holy Spirit are three distinct persons who have one identical Godhead. Each of the three is uncreated, is eternal, is omnipotent, is God, is Lord, and yet Tritheism is excluded for the three are only one God, one Lord, one increate, one eternal, one omnipotent being. Although the credal statements are strongly reminiscent of Augustine, yet the creed unhesitatingly uses the words *substance* and *person* to express the divine unity and trinity, even though those words were something of a problem for Augustine. Again, while Augustine relied heavily on the concepts and words *relation* and *relative* to explain the distinction of the three, the creed bases the distinction of the persons on their originational relations but does not use the word *relation*. It explains the distinction of the three by the fact that the Father originates from no one but generates the Son, the Son is generated by the Father alone but with Him produces the Holy Spirit and the Holy Spirit proceeds from the Father and the Son. The *Filioque* is simply presented as a fact, a datum and an object of faith. This is remarkable at this early date. It is hard to believe that this credal declaration of the *Filioque* does not betray the impact of Augustine.

When this credal doctrine is compared with that of the Cappadocians and of earlier Western treatises and creeds, another point stands out. For the Cappadocians the Father's distinctive property was 'ingenerateness' (Naz. *Or.* 25.16; 26.19; 29.2), while the earlier Western treatises and creeds generally placed it in the fact that the Father generates the Son. But in this creed what stands out is that the Father originates from no one (*a nullo*) while both the Son and the Holy Spirit originate from someone, from the Father, a point that had been made before perhaps only by Ambrose (*De incarn.* 100) and Augustine (*Serm.* 140.2).

Nowhere previously have we encountered a formula so balanced, so precise, so elaborate and so ingeniously contrived. And what is perhaps most amazing of all is the way this creed achieved dogmatic value in the Western Church equal to that of the Apostles' and Nicene creeds, and retained this even after it was realized that there was no certainty about its author or date or birthplace. Even in recent dogmatic manuals in the West the *Quicunque* has been regarded as a dogmatic formula of 'divine and catholic faith.'

BOETHIUS

Boethius (d. *c.* 525) exercised a decisive influence on the development of medieval scholarship, it has been said, 'second only to that of Augustine.'[12] The Scholastics of the 11th and early 12th century derived most of their knowledge of Aristotle's works and techniques from Boethius' translations of some of Aristotle's works and from his application of Aristotelian logic and methods to theological doctrine. He 'was the first to apply Aristotelian methods to theological problems and to the elucidation of dogmatic statements. His conception of the functions of philosophy in analyzing, defining and explaining doctrine approaches very nearly to that of the scholastics, who in fact were building on his foundations.'[13]

Among his writings easily the most important and influential was *On the Consolation of Philosophy.*[14] He wrote four theological treatises, *How the Trinity is One God*; *Whether Father, Son and Holy Spirit may be Substantially predicated of the Divinity*; *How Substances can be Good*; *One Person and Two Natures*; and probably a fifth, *Brief Summary of Christian Faith.*[15] There was some doubt about the author of these treatises but today they are generally ascribed to Boethius.[16]

His trinitarian doctrine is largely derived from Augustine (*Trin.* introd. 32) but it is notable for the 'new and unaccustomed words' (*Trin.* 1.1) which he used in presenting it and for the definitions and expressions that he introduced and which often became 'classical.'

The catholic religion, he declares, believes in 'the unity of the Trinity,' that the 'Father, Son, and Holy Spirit are one God, not three gods' (*Trin.* 1.7), are 'not three substances but one substance' that 'cannot be separated or divided' and is not made up 'of parts combined into one' (*Pat.* 5–32). The Son is generated by the Father by a 'substantial production' (*Trin.* 5.44) and the Holy Spirit proceeds from the Father and the Son but 'the manner of that procession we are no more able to declare clearly than the human mind is able to understand the generation of the Son from the substance of the Father' (*Fid*. 25–28).

Why are the three one? Because in their divine substance there is 'an absence of difference' (*Trin*. 1.10), an absence of 'otherness.' For 'the principle of plurality is otherness and apart from otherness plurality is unintelligible' (*Trin*. 13–15). Where 'there is no difference, there is no plurality and accordingly no number, but only unity' (*Trin*. 3.3–4).

Yet despite this absence of difference and otherness in the Godhead, there is not a total absence of difference in the Triune God. For 'the Father is not the same as the Son, nor is either of them the same as the Holy Spirit, although the Father, Son, and Holy Spirit are the same God' (*Trin*. 6.10–12). The 'Father, Son, and Holy Spirit are the same thing (*idem*) but they are not the same one (*ipse*). . . . There is not, therefore, complete absence of difference between them, and so number does come in . . . from the diversity of subjects' (*Trin*. 3.46–52).

How does number come in, how can there be trinity in this unity? Boethius turns to the Aristotelian categories, 'ten categories which are universally predicated of things, namely substance, quality, quantity, relation . . .' (*Trin*. 4.1–4). But he notes immediately that 'when these categories are applied to God they change their meaning entirely' (*Trin*. 4.7–9), since 'when we say God, we seem to denote a substance, but it is a substance that is supersubstantial. When we say of Him "He is just" we mention a quality, not an accidental quality but rather a substantial and in fact a supersubstantial quality' (*Trin*. 4.14–18). Substantial predication, he concludes, is pertinent with regard to God but accidental predication is not (*Trin*. 4.105–108). And since 'the diversity of persons made the Trinity, the Trinity does not pertain to the substance. Hence neither Father, nor Son, nor Holy Spirit, nor Trinity can be substantially predicated of God, but only relatively' (*Pat*. 60–65).

In pondering relative predication he concludes that we cannot affirm that 'relative predication in any way increases, decreases or changes anything in the reality of which it is predicated' (*Trin*. 5.17–19) and therefore, 'if Father and Son are affirmed relatively and differ in nothing but relation, then this relative predication will effect . . . only an otherness . . . of persons' (*Trin*. 5.33–40). Accordingly 'the numerosity of the Trinity is secured through the predication of relation, and the unity is maintained because there is no difference of substance or operation or of any substantial predicate. So substance conserves unity, relation multiplies Trinity' (*Trin*.

6.3–9). But he carefully adds that 'the relation of Father to Son, and of both to the Holy Spirit, is a relation of identicals (*eius quod est idem ad id quod est idem*)' and that such a relation 'is not to be found in other things' (*Trin*. 6.20–23). And he reminds us that in this matter we must not 'be led astray by any imagination but be lifted up by simple intelligence to whatever is intelligible' (*Trin*. 6.24–25).

In noting that Father and Son are predicated relatively and differ in relation alone, Boethius had declared that thus the only otherness is that of persons. But he had also indicated that in God this otherness of persons is hardly intelligible (*Trin*. 5.39). Now he had to seek a definition of person and he readily admitted that 'the proper definition of person is a matter of very great perplexity' (*Eut*. 2.1–2) and is closely bound up with the concept of nature. For 'since person cannot exist apart from nature and since natures are either substances or accidents, and we see that a person cannot be constituted by accidents, then person implies substance' (*Eut*. 2.13–18). Pondering substances that are corporeal or incorporeal, living or not living, sensitive or not sensitive, rational or irrational (*Eut*. 2.19–23), he concludes that person is not predicable of anything that lacks life or reason, hence only of man or angel or God (*ibid*. 29–37). Summing up his analysis he says 'if person pertains to substances alone, and these rational, and if every nature is a substance existing not in universals but in individuals, then we have found the definition of person: "an individual substance of a rational nature" ' (*ibid*. 3.1–5).

'By this definition,' he declares, 'we Latins have described what the Greeks call *hypostasis*' (*Eut*. 3.5–7) or '*prosopa*' (*ibid*. 22), but then somewhat inconsistently adds that '*ousia* is identical with essence, *ousiosis* with subsistence, *hypostasis* with substance and *prosopon* with person' (*ibid*. 69–71). And in line with this he states that if 'the language of the Church did not forbid us to say three substances in speaking of God, *substance* might seem the right term to apply to Him' (*ibid*. 95–97). He concludes, however, that 'the exact terms which should be applied in each case must be left to the decision of ecclesiastical usage' but that in the interim his distinction between nature and person should stand, so that 'nature is the specific property of any substance, and person the individual substance of a rational nature' (*ibid*. 4.3–9).

This definition of person was to become famous, to be widely adopted, highly praised, strongly criticized. Aquinas will accept it but with many subtle distinctions (ST la 29.1). Modern theologians will continue to discuss its meaning.[17] In recent times it has been called the 'best definition because it contains everything by which a person is constituted and distinguished from all else.'[18] On the other hand it has been said to make 'more difficulties than it solves. For if a person is an individual substance of a rational nature, three persons seem to be three substances, whereas in God there is only one substance.'[19] But all in all it seems better to say that although verbally the definition may leave much to be desired, yet intentionally it is unexceptionable for by it Boethius intended to indicate that three notes constitute a person: substantiality, intellectuality, and incommunicability.

Thus Boethius made no mean contribution to the development of trinitarian doctrine in the West. By his use of Aristotelian philosophy in the analysis, definition, and explanation of trinitarian and Christological data he laid a foundation on which Scholastics would build their more systematic expositions and explanations of theological data and problems.

CASSIODORUS, ISIDORE, AND THE CREED OF TOLEDO

Two other writers, Cassiodorus (d. *c.* 580) and Isidore of Seville (d. *c.* 636), are sometimes singled out, not because they were innovative theologians—their doctrine was largely that of Augustine—but because they were effective compilers and transmitters of the sacred and secular knowledge of the past. Cassiodorus's compilation was his *Institutiones divinarum et humanarum lectionum* (PL 70) while Isidore's encyclopedia is called *Etymologiae* or *Origines* (PL 82). By their many quotations from pagan and Christian writers they rendered an immense service both to their contemporaries and to those who followed them.

The creed ascribed to and probably elaborated by the 11th Council of Toledo (675),[20] is the most highly developed formula of faith that the West has thus far produced (Denz 525–541). Later on it will achieve high distinction in the Western Church and be placed by some theologians on almost the same dogmatic level as the *Quicunque*.

It opens somewhat differently from the *Quicunque*: 'We confess and believe that the holy and ineffable Trinity, Father, Son, and Holy Spirit is naturally one God, of one substance, one nature, one majesty and power' (Denz 525). It affirms belief in the Father who has origin from no one but is the origin of the divinity and from whom the Son had birth and the Holy Spirit procession. And in the Son of God who is uncreated, coeternal, coequal, consubstantial with the Father, generated by the Father not by will or necessity but from the substance of the Father without diminution or division of this substance, perfect Son of perfect Father. And in the Holy Spirit, the third Person in the Trinity, one God coequal and consubstantial with the Father and the Son, not begotten nor created but proceeding from the Father and the Son and the Spirit of both, the charity and sanctity of both, and sent by both (Denz 525–527).

It then sets forth the proper way to speak of and understand the three, their nature and names and relations and distinction and identity. They are to be spoken of as Trinity, not triple, as one God in Trinity and not Trinity in one God. Father, Son, and Holy Spirit are relative names that signify three persons and not three substances and refer not to themselves (*ad se*) but to one another, but the name God refers to Himself (*ad se*) and not to another (*ad aliquid*). Singly each person is God and omnipotent, yet the three are but one God, one omnipotent. There is no more, no less deity, majesty, power in one person than in three. This Trinity is neither removed from number nor contained by number, since the persons insinuate number when viewed relatively (*ad invicem*) but lack number when viewed substantially (*in divinitatis substantia*). And the Trinity has deigned to show through these relative names by which it wished us to identify the persons that the persons cannot be understood apart from one another since the name of one person insinuates the other persons. Though the Father, the Son, and the Holy Spirit are one God they are three persons inseparable in existence and operation but really distinct in terms of their personal properties, for the Father has eternity without birth, the Son eternity with birth, the Holy Spirit eternity without birth but with procession.

This credal formulation clearly goes well beyond the *Quicunque* in the amplitude of its trinitarian doctrine. It declares somewhat ambiguously that the Father is 'the font and origin of the whole divinity,' 'the Father of His own essence.' It affirms that the Son is Son by nature and not by adoption and is generated neither by will nor by necessity. It declares that the Holy Spirit not only proceeds from the Father and the Son but is sent by both and is the love of both. It stresses the relative names of the persons and their implications, the implications of relative and substantial predication for the Trinity, and the application of number to it. It emphasizes not only the distinction of the persons but also their inseparability in existence, operation, and cognition. It is not hard to see why it came to have a very privileged status in the Western Church.

BEDE THE VENERABLE AND ALCUIN

Two writers stand out in the 8th century. The Venerable Bede (d. 735) in his *De natura rerum* (PL 90) tried to do for England what Isidore did for Spain in his *Etymologiae*, i.e., to give the clergy a summary of the scientific and ecclesiastical writings of the past. In his *Homilies* he gave a solid presentation of a coeternal, coequal, and consubstantial Trinity (*Hom.* II. 10–11; PL 94) and an exhortation to love and praise the Father and Son and Holy Spirit (*Hom.* II. 12; PL 94). *Alcuin* (d. 804) first headed the Bishop's school at York and later the Palatine school for Charlemagne, and was the 'chief organizer of the Carolingian renaissance.'[21] He 'gave the final stamp to the work of Isidore and Bede; their encyclopedic method became the prevailing approach to knowledge.'[22] In his *De Fide Sanctae et Individuae Trinitatis* (PL 101) the words *substance, essence, person, trinity* and *unity, coeternal* and *consubstantial, substantial* and *relative names, procession* and *mission* are commonplace. In general his trinitarian doctrine repeats the salient points that have become traditional. In the Trinity there is unity of nature and substance and operation and inseparability of nature and operation and persons (*De Fide* 1.12, 13). Of the ten categories substance is predicated of God properly, Father, Son, and Holy Spirit relatively, the rest only translatively (1.15), but there is no accidental predication because 'nothing in God is mutable' (1.9). The Father's distinctive property is that He 'alone is not from another' (1.11), the Son's that He 'alone is generated from the Father alone, the Holy Spirit's that He proceeds equally from the Father and the Son and is the consubstantial and coeternal Spirit of both' (1.11). But the Holy Spirit's relation to Father and Son lacks the reciprocal convertibility of the relation of Father and Son, for while the Holy Spirit is the Spirit of the Father and of the Son, the Father is not the Father nor is the Son the Son of the Holy Spirit. Alcuin, however, offers no explanation of this difference. In his *Libellus de Processione Spiritus Sancti* (PL 101), which he wrote for Charlemagne, he put forth an elaborate 'proof' of the *Filioque* from Scripture and the Fathers, but often based on interpretations that would be strongly discounted today.

9TH-CENTURY THEOLOGIANS

In the 9th century 4 men are often singled out. Rabanus Maurus (d. 856), a pupil of Alcuin and possessed of vast learning, compiled an encyclopedia known as *De universo* (PL 111), on the plan of Bede and Isidore, but it shows little or no originality in its trinitarian doctrine. *Ratramnus* (d. 868), a monk of Corbie, wrote in response to a request from Pope Nicholas I[23] his *Contra Graecorum Opposita* (PL 121) to defend the *Filioque* and other Latin teachings against the objections raised by the Emperors Michael and Basil. He maintained that the *Filioque* was a doctrine of faith based on the teaching of Christ and handed down from the Apostles through the Fathers. His scriptural evidence he derived from Luke and Paul but mostly from John, his patristic evidence from Athanasius, Nazianzus, Didymus, Ambrose, Paschasius, Augustine, Gennadius and Fulgentius, but mainly from Augustine. Another response to Pope Nicholas' request came from Aeneas of Paris (d. 870), whose defense of the *Filioque* was entitled *Liber Adversus Graecos* (PL 121). Aeneas drew his arguments from Athanasius, Ambrose, Cyril, Jerome, Augustine, Popes Hormisdas and Leo and Gregory, Fulgentius, Isidore, Prosper, Vigilius, Cassiodorus, Alcuin, and Prudentius. Here we see the *Filioque* controversy that Photius stimulated beginning to produce that endless stream of theological blast and counter-blast that continues down to the present.

John Scotus Eriugena (d. *c.* 877) was the most important and the most singular personage of the learned world of the 9th century and the possessor of probably the most acute and original mind of his time. He was the director of the court school of Charles the Bald, a brilliant but daring thinker, well versed in the writings of St. Augustine and the Greeks. He has been termed a rationalist, a pantheist, a heretic. In his principal work, *De Divisione Naturae* (PL 122) he used philosophy to elucidate dogma and produced a bold philosophical-theological synthesis that was deeply tinged with Neoplatonism and at times confused the object of reason with that of faith.

The interrelation of reason and authority was a problem for Eriugena as it is for us today. He realized that 'true authority does not oppose right reason, nor right reason true authority. For it is not to be doubted that both come from one source, namely the divine wisdom' (*Div. Nat.* I, 66). How would he reconcile the two? By putting reason first, it seems, and by reading Scripture allegorically, not literally:

now we must follow reason which investigates the truth of things, and overpowered by no authority and in no way shackled sets forth and proclaims openly what it has studiously examined and laboriously discovered. To be sure the authority of Holy Scripture must be followed in all things, for in it we have the truth as it were in its secret haunts. Nevertheless, it is not to be understood literally as if in making the divine nature known to us it always called things by their own names. On the contrary, condescending to our infirmity it uses figurative and symbolical language, encouraging our as yet immature and infantile senses by simple doctrine (*Div. Nat.* 1, 63–64).

It is not too surprising that his doctrine of God brought him the charge of pantheism. For he wrote that in God 'are all things, nay He is all things' (*Div. Nat.* I, 72), for 'He alone truly is. All other things that are said to be are theophanies of Him, which truly subsist in Him' (*ibid.* III, 4). He added that 'everything that subsists, whether created or uncreated, is contained within Him' (*ibid.* III, 17). And yet he also wrote that God is above all things (*ibid.* III, 20; IV, 5) and that 'the divine nature, because it is superessential, is one thing (*aliud*)' and 'what it creates in itself is another thing (*aliud*)' (*ibid.* III, 17).

Perhaps the most notable point in his trinitarian vocabulary is his continuing use of the word *substance* where the Latin tradition had settled on *person*. Thus he could approve the statement that 'the paternal substance, which from itself generated the filiated substance and emitted from itself the proceeding substance, is not undeservedly called the principal substance' (*ibid.* II, 23).

His trinitarian position with regard to 'cause' and the *Filioque* is especially interesting. 'There is therefore,' he writes,

> a substantial cause, ingenerate and generating; and there is a substantial cause, generated and not generating; and there is a substantial cause, proceeding but not ingenerate nor generated nor generating, and the three substantial causes are one, and one essential cause. . . . The Father precedes the Son and Holy Spirit, for the Son is born from Him and the Holy Spirit proceeds from Him, and so the Father not incongruously is believed to be the cause of causes. For He is the cause of the generated cause and of the proceeding cause. . . . Hence the Father is greater than the Son, not according to nature but according to cause. For the Father is the cause of the Son, but the Son is not the cause of the Father (*Div. Nat.* II, 30).

To confirm this view he turns to Gregory the Theologian (*ibid.*). Then he adds that 'the nature of the Father is not the cause of the Son, since the nature of the Father and Son is one and the same, because the essence of both is one and the same. For all this is not predicated of the Father and Son according to nature, but according to the relation (*habitum*) of generator to generated and of preceding cause to consequent cause. The Father therefore is the cause of the Son and of the Holy Spirit' (*ibid.*).

Is the Father alone the cause of the Holy Spirit? Does the Holy Spirit have one cause, the Father, or two causes, the Father and the Son, or one inseparable cause, the Father and the Son? Over and over Eriugena runs the changes on this theme and he finally seems to conclude that, 'although we believe and understand that the Spirit proceeds from the Father through the Son, we must not hold that the same Spirit has two causes, but one and the same cause, namely the Father of the generated Son and of the Holy Spirit proceeding from Him through the Son' (*Div. Nat.* II, 32).

Eriugena's terminology and doctrine raise many questions. Does he understand *substance* to mean *person* or *substance* when he says 'the paternal substance . . . generated the filiated substance . . . and emitted . . . the proceeding substance'? It seems that he must intend it to mean *person*, since the three have one and the same essence and nature—but? When he says 'the Father is greater than the Son not according to nature but according to cause' does he mean only what St. John and Gregory meant—or something more? When he speaks of 'the Father of the . . . Son and of the Holy Spirit . . .' is this only a verbal slip? Why does he shy away from the Latin *Filioque* and prefer the Greek *dia hyios* ('through the Son')? Why did he not note Augustine's doctrine that Father and Son are not two principles of the Holy Spirit but only one? Down the years the enigma of John Scotus Eriugena will tantalize theologians and philosophers alike.

PETER DAMIAN

Peter Damian (d. 1072), a monk, a Cardinal Bishop and a Saint, is ranked theologically among the antidialecticians (*Div. Omnip.*; PL 145, 603), who asserted 'that reason has no teaching authority in Christianity' and considered 'any encroachment of dialects on the sacred text to be a sacrilege.'[24] His trinitarian doctrine of a coeternal, coequal, consubstantial Trinity of Father, Son, and Holy Spirit who are distinguished from one another by their originational properties (*Op.* 1.1, 5; 1.2) but are one sole simple substance or essence, is found in his 60 *Opuscula* (PL 145). Most notable perhaps is what Damian teaches about the Holy Spirit. Unlike Eriugena he clearly places the *Filioque* among the truths that must be believed, for this is what Augustine, Gregory, and other Catholic Fathers declare and what Scripture testifies (1.10). Hence 'to be a true and perfect Catholic one must believe in the Holy Spirit,' who 'proceeds simultaneously from the Father and the Son,' since 'the Father generated such a Son that the Holy Spirit proceeds from Him just as He proceeds from the Father Himself' (*ibid.*).

The *Quicunque* had placed the *Filioque* among the objects of faith (Denz 75). So had the symbol of Toledo XI (Denz 527). Now Peter Damian uses the same words that this council used and says that the Holy Spirit proceeds from the Father and the Son, 'not from the Father into the Son and from the Son to sanctify creatures . . . but simultaneously from both' (1.1). It seems clear that the Western Church is definitely pointed toward a formal definition of the *Filioque*.

PART FOUR

The Middle Ages

'From the 11th century to the end of the 14th, a single culture informed all education and a common language, Latin, transmitted it.'[1] Scholars became preoccupied with humane studies, with dialectic, with philosophical and theological study and speculation. Educational leadership would move from the monastic schools to the cathedral schools and then to the universities. Out of them would come Scholastics and Scholasticism, intent on producing a harmonious union of revelation and reason, of faith and of knowledge, a synthesis of the Word of God and the words of men. Scholasticism would produce long-lasting intellectual benefits. But it would always carry within it a danger of over-emphasis on authority or reason or dialectics or metaphysics or method, to the neglect of historical criticism and scientific developments; a danger of merely treating dogmas as objects for intellectual analysis and synthesis and neglecting them as divine revelations meant to permeate and perfect the daily life of the Christian.

To appreciate the contributions made to trinitarian doctrine in the Middle Ages, it may help to present them in four chapters, and to consider first Anselm and Abelard, Gilbert and Bernard, Hugh, and Richard; second, Lombard, Joachim, and Lateran IV; third, Albert and Thomas, Alexander of Hales and Bonaventure; and finally Scotus, Durandus, Ockham, and the Council of Florence.

CHAPTER NINE

From Anselm to Richard
of St. Victor

ANSELM OF CANTERBURY

Anselm of Canterbury (d. 1109) has been called 'the first great original thinker in the West, since John the Scot.' He followed Lanfranc as Prior of Bec and Archbishop of Canterbury. He was a pioneer in the difficult task of determining the proper role and value of dialectics in theology. He was intent on understanding the faith he had in God, the Trinity, the Incarnation, for his was a *fides quaerens intellectum*. Theologically he was in the direct line of descent from Augustine, and like Augustine he made faith his starting point and gave it the primacy. But he went beyond Augustine in one respect for he applied dialectics to Augustinian premises and thereby drew conclusions for which St. Augustine had not looked, so that 'possibly in no other scholastic author may be found such exhaustive reasoning or series of deductions so well adapted to draw out of a principle or a revealed truth everything reason can lay hold of.'[1] This dialectical facility added to his metaphysical gifts enabled him to set about verifying in a set of monographs his basic principle that there can be and is no contradiction between truths of revelation and truths of reason.[2] Though he is most widely known for his ontological proof of God's existence[3] and his treatise on the Incarnation,[4] he has also made some important contributions to trinitarian doctrine. His most important trinitarian works are the *Monologion* (PL 158), *De fide Trinitatis* (PL 158) and *De processione Spiritus Sancti contra Graecos* (PL 158).

The *De processione* is a defense of the *Filioque* that is built not on the Fathers but on Scripture and reason. It develops a solid Biblical argument from St. John, which includes the major points that later Latin theologians will make. But the dialectical argument based on 'unbreakable reasons' and 'opposition of relation' (2) is most noteworthy. Anselm looks for the cause of plurality in God and finds it in the 'insociable relations' of Father, Son, and Holy Spirit (1). To the question, how can unity and plurality be reconciled, he answered in the famous phrase that the Council of Florence would later canonize (Denz 1330): 'unity does not lose its consequence unless some opposition of relation stands in the way' (*ubi non obviat aliqua relationis oppositio*) (2). In other words, everything in God is identical except where there are opposed relations of origin (as there are in Father, Son, and Holy Spirit). Only where one proceeds from the other can there be two, for only then do we have a distinctive 'relation of opposition.' Then in a remarkable series of very close reasonings Anselm uses this principle to show that the Holy Spirit must proceed from the Son as well as from the Father. Thus the Son cannot be the Father, because He proceeds from the Father; the Holy Spirit cannot be the Father, because He proceeds from the Father. But are the Son and Holy Spirit really distinct? Only if one proceeds from the other. It is 'obvious from Catholic faith' (4) that the Son is not from the Holy Spirit. Therefore 'it follows by unassailable reason that the Holy Spirit is from the Son as He is from the Father' (4), for just as He cannot be really distinct from the Father unless He proceeds from the Father, so He cannot be really distinct from the Son unless He proceeds from the Son. What is more, the relation of Father and Son is such that if the Holy Spirit proceeds from one, then He proceeds from both (7). And just as Father, Son and Holy Spirit are not three principles of creatures, three creators, but one principle only, so Father and Son are not two principles of the Holy Spirit but only one (18). Though Anselm generally followed Augustine closely, he did not approve Augustine's statement that the Holy Spirit proceeds *principaliter* from the Father (24) any more than he approved the Greek view that the Holy Spirit proceeds from the Father '*per Filium*' (15).

The *De Fide Trinitatis* is a refutation of an error of Roscelin (d. 1120), a canon of Compiègne. Whether Roscelin actually taught or intended tritheism, whether he was actually condemned for tritheism by a council at Soissons in 1092, is still a matter of dispute.[5] To Anselm it seemed that he taught this at least by implication. For Roscelin maintained that if only the Son was incarnate, then the Father, Son and Holy Spirit must be 'three separate things (*res*) as three angels or three souls' (1). For if they were only one thing, then if one was incarnate so must the others be also. Since Roscelin held that only the Son was incarnate, his teaching seemed to imply tritheism, for three separate things would be three gods. Anselm declared that Roscelin should have begun with Scripture, not reason (1), but since he defended his error by reason he had to be refuted by reason (3). And so he set out to show that the error was based on inaccurate concepts of nature and person, absolute and relative, and in particular on a misunderstanding of the Incarnation. For Roscelin seemed to think that 'man was assumed by the Son of God more into a unity of nature than into a unity of person' (4). Anselm went so far in his rebuttal as to affirm that if the Son is incarnate, it is not only not necessary for the other persons to be incarnate, but it is impossible for them to be (4), since incarnation means assumption of 'man into unity of person.' Not all later theologians will agree to this.

The *Monologion* is a powerful rational exposition of the divine nature, probably the first genetic explanation of the Trinity in terms of supreme Spirit endowed with intelligence and love. It was the response to 'certain brethren' who asked him to write about the Being of God in such a way 'that nothing in Scripture should be urged on the authority of Scripture itself' but rather as the 'conclusion of independent investigation' and 'briefly enforced by the cogency of reason' (Preface).

Anselm's starting point is the supreme 'Nature' (9), 'Substance' (11), 'Being' (12), 'Spirit' (29). Through 'this Spirit's expression (*locutio*) all things were created' (29). But 'this expression of the supreme Spirit, since it cannot be a creature, is no other than the supreme Spirit. Therefore this expression itself can be understood as nothing else than the intelligence (*intelligentia*) of this Spirit by which he understands (*intelligit*) all things. . . . If, then, the supreme simple Nature is nothing else than what its intelligence is . . . it is nothing else than what its expression is . . . and this expression must be consubstantial' with 'the supreme Spirit,' 'so that they are not two spirits, but one' (29).

And this expression 'is one Word, through which all things were created' and 'by which all things are expressed' (31). But if there were no creature, would that Word still exist? (32). Yes, for that supreme eternal Spirit 'eternally . . . understands himself,' and 'if he understands himself eternally, he expresses himself eternally. If he expresses himself eternally, his Word is eternally with him' (32). And 'by one and the same Word . . . he expresses himself and whatever he has made' (33). But if He and His Word are 'but one creator' (37), how can it 'be explained why they are two' (38)?

Acknowledging that this is a strict mystery Anselm declares: 'it is, therefore, evident that it cannot be explained why they are two, the supreme Spirit and the Word, although by certain properties of each they are required to be two. For it is the property of the one to derive existence from the other' (38). Why must they be two? Because, as Anselm says also in the *De processione*, one proceeds from the other and thus between them *obviat aliqua relationis oppositio*. And what should be the relationship ascribed to the two, that of father and son or that of mother and daughter? That of father and son, for 'the first and principal cause of offspring is always in the father . . . and the son is always more like the father than is the daughter' (42).

Now Anselm turns to divine love, and declares that as the supreme Spirit remembers and understands himself, so he loves himself, so that 'if by the memory of the supreme Spirit we understand the Father, and by his intelligence . . . the Son, it is manifest that the love of the supreme Spirit proceeds equally from Father and Son' (49, 50). Thus 'the Father loves himself, the Son loves himself and the one the other,' and 'necessarily each loves himself and the other with an equal love' (51). How great is this love? It is equal to the supreme Spirit and hence it *is* 'the supreme Spirit,' 'the supreme Being,' and 'what inference can be more necessary than that the Father and Son and the love of both are one supreme Being?' (53). And that the love of the supreme Spirit emanates 'from Father and Son, not as two, but as one and the same whole' (54). Is that love of Father and Son their Son? No, for as 'the Word . . . declares itself to be the offspring of him from whom it derives existence, by displaying a manifold likeness to its parent, so love plainly denies such a relation since . . . it does not show so evident a likeness to him from whom it derives existence' (55). This is obviously not yet a perfect presentation of the psychological theory of intelligible divine emanations as we will find it in Aquinas, but it is a remarkable approximation to it for this period of theological history.

There can be no doubt that for Anselm the mystery of the Trinity 'transcends all the vision of the human intellect' (64). Yet he was so intent on finding for the truths of faith 'necessary reasons,' 'cogent proofs' that he has seemed to some theologians to give the believer's reason a greater power than it really possesses.[6] Perhaps he did not mean by 'necessary reasons' and 'cogent proofs' irresistible demonstrations, yet he does seem to have thought 'that the believer, meditating upon the truths of the faith, could come to see, not only their appropriateness but also their inevitability.'[7]

PETER ABELARD

Peter Abelard (d. 1142) has been called 'the dominant intellectual figure of his day,'[8] 'the founder of the scholastic method,'[9] a rationalist, an Arian, a Sabellian. His most famous works are perhaps his *Sic et Non* (PL 178) and his *Historia Calamitatum*.[10] His chief trinitarian works are *Tractatus de Unitate et Trinitate divina*,[11] *Theologia Christiana* (PL 178), and *Introductio ad theologiam* (PL 178). Of this trinitarian 'trilogy' the *Introductio* 'is substantially identical with the *Theology*, and this is only a development of the *Tractatus*.'[12]

In 1121 Abelard was summoned to a Council at Soissons, where he and his book on the Trinity were examined and judged. And there, although his accusers 'had nothing before them either of my words or writings which they could charge against me' (*Hist. Calam.* 41), he had to cast his book into the fire and recite the Athanasian Creed. What book was this? It has been thought to have been *Theologia Christiana*.[13] But it seems definitely established today that it really was the *Tractatus*.[14] What was awry in this book? Abelard said that when he came to Soissons the people almost stoned him, saying that he 'had taught and written that there are three Gods.'[15] But Otto of Freising said the charge was not Tritheism but Sabellianism, while a recent interpreter thinks it was contempt of the argument from authority.[16] As a matter of fact the *Tractatus* had been directed against Roscelin's Tritheism, often explicitly rejects Tritheism, actually relies little on patristic evidence, and does contain a 'Sabellian' passage: 'God is three persons in such a way as if we said that the divine substance is powerful, wise, and good' (1.3). Perhaps Abelard's estimate is the best, that the book was burnt only because 'it had not been approved either by the Roman Pontiff or any other ecclesiastical authority.'[17]

Sic et Non is a collection of opposed patristic quotations regarding 158 theological, historical, ecclesiastical, ethical topics. In its trinitarian portion Abelard quotes various Fathers as saying, for example (6), that God is and is not tripartite, (13) that the Father is and is not the cause of the Son, (14) that the Son is and is not without a principle, (17) that only the Father is and is not called ingenerate. For a long time *Sic et Non* was thought to be a completely original innovation but 'the researches of Fournier and Grabmann . . . showed that the juxtaposition of seemingly contradictory authorities was already a method in common use in Abelard's day by compilers of canonical collections.'[18] What was the aim of *Sic et Non*? Some scholars have said its aim was to discredit the Fathers or 'to demonstrate that the Fathers were fallible and were not to be followed without question.'[19] Since he himself often used patristic arguments in his other works, it seems clear enough that he did not intend to destroy the authority of the Fathers but to make men realize they were not infallible and then lead them to make a more careful study of the differing words and concepts of the Fathers so that gradually terms and arguments would be used more accurately.

In his *Introductio* and other theological works Abelard put such an emphasis on reason that he came to be regarded as a rationalist who maintained that understanding must always precede belief and who changed Anselm's *Credo ut intelligam* into *Intelligo ut credam*. But this latter phrase is found nowhere in his writings and it is far from evident that these words 'fairly represent his position.'[20] For he believed in divine revelation, recognized the authority of Scripture, maintained that what was clearly written in the Bible was to be accepted unquestioningly, and wrote that 'now it . . . remains for us, after having laid down the foundation of authority, to place upon it the buttresses of reasoning' (*Introd.* 980). Although he did put great trust in dialectics he did not maintain that no doctrine was to be accepted until it had been rationally demonstrated. He did say that 'preachers should stop preaching when they did not understand what they were saying' (1054).

Anselm had seemed to concede to reason (*De Processione*; PL 158.315–316) the power to deduce a dogma, e.g., the *Filioque*, from philosophical premises.[21] Later theologians would deny reason this power, and would also deny that God had actually revealed the Trinity to pagans and Jews before Christ. Abelard's position on these points changed and developed. In the *Tractatus* he said the Holy Spirit had deigned to reveal the Trinity to pagans and Jews before Christ, by the intermediary of the philosophers and prophets. When he was criticized for this he repeated this teaching in his *Theologia*, reinforced it by the authority of St. Jerome (1123B, 1126C, 1129B, 1162B, 1165CD, 1172B) and tried to justify the revelation to and through the philosophers by a somewhat incoherent appeal to Rom 1.20 (1141A). He even declared that Plato had not only taught faith in the Trinity but proved it was so (1012D). But while he affirmed over and over that God had revealed the Trinity (1126C, 1160D, 1166B, 1171A, 1172A, 1179C, 1288A) and that reason is radically incapable of attaining this knowledge (1241C), he yet seemed to say inconsistently that knowledge of the Trinity came not only by way of revelation but also by way of philosophical deduction.[22] But as he moved on to his *Commentary on Romans*, his *Ethica*, his *Dialectica*, and his *Dialogue* he finally abandoned the possibility of deducing the Trinity by reason, admitted that the Trinity was not known to pagans and maintained the absolute necessity of revelation for achieving knowledge of it.[23]

About 1140 Bernard of Clairvaux, who was ecclesiastically one of the most influential men of those times, began to ponder Abelard's writings and became very disturbed by them. He first talked privately with Abelard and won from him a promise of retractation or at least of prudence. But soon after Abelard challenged Bernard to a public debate in the Council of Sens. When he reached Sens Abelard found to his consternation that Bernard had come there not to debate with him but to have him and 19 of his propositions condemned by the Council. Abelard refused to justify himself before the Council and appealed to Rome. The Council and Bernard sent to Pope Innocent II a description of the affair and a list of the suspect propositions (Denz 721, Introd.; Bernard, *Ep.* 190, PL 182.1053–1072). In his *Testante Apostolo* sent to Henry, Bishop of Sens, the Pope declared: 'by the authority of the sacred canons we have condemned the chapters sent to Us by your discretion and all the dogmas of Peter together with their author, and we have imposed on him as a heretic perpetual silence' (Denz 721, Introd.; PL 182. 361). The sentence, however, was not carried out.[24] In condemning some of Abelard's propositions Innocent II did not specify the number, or the order or the content of these propositions. Various lists of these capitula have been found, some giving 14, some 17, some 18, some 19 capitula.[25] Abelard himself in the *Apologia*,[26] which he wrote after the Council of Sens, enumerates the 19 that are found in Denz 721–739 and blames their selection on Bernard. Today it seems to be solidly established that the 19 capitula enumerated in Denz 721–739 are the Abelardian propositions that the Pope condemned. But three questions have been raised. Are these propositions really heretical? Are they found in Abelard's writings? Was Abelard really a heretic?

Three of the 19 capitula concern Abelard's trinitarian doctrine: '(1) that the Father is full power, the Son some power, the Holy Spirit no power; (2) that the Holy Spirit is not of the substance of the Father, and is the soul of the world; (14) that omnipotence properly or specially pertains to the Father, since He is not from another, but not wisdom and benignity.' If we use as our measure of the orthodox faith of the Church the *Quicunque* (Denz 75–76) with its declarations that the Father, Son, and Holy Spirit have one divinity, equal glory, coeternal majesty, are coeternal and coequal, that what the Father is the Son is and the Holy Spirit is, that each is omnipotent and uncreated, that the Holy Spirit proceeds from the

Father and the Son, then these 3 capitula contravene this faith in the coequality and consubstantiality of the three persons. For (1) denies the omnipotence of the Son and Holy Spirit; (2a) denies the consubstantiality of the Holy Spirit with the Father; (2b) denies the coequality of the Holy Spirit with the Father and the Son, for the soul of the world was understood to be a creature (*Introductio* II, 1082); (14) denies the Father's coequality with Son and Holy Spirit in wisdom and benignity.

Are these 3 capitula found in Abelard's writings? In his *Apologia* he denies having ever written that God the Father is all power, God the Son specified power, and God the Holy Spirit no power, and adds that if anyone can find these words in his writings, 'rather diabolical than heretical,' which 'he detests and abhors and condemns with their author,' he is willing to be branded 'not only as a heretic but as a heresiarch.' Yet although these 3 capitula are not found in his works in these very words and in this precise form, they are there at least equivalently or implicitly. Thus we find (1) in this form: 'Let us posit God the Father . . . as divine power and God the Son as divine wisdom, and let us consider that wisdom is a certain power' (*Theol.* IV, 1288–1289) . . . 'the benignity that is demonstrated by this name (of Holy Spirit) is not some power or wisdom, since to be benign is not to be wise or powerful' (*Theol.* IV, 1299). We find (2a) in this form: 'generation differs from procession in that he who is generated is from the Father's substance' (hence he who proceeds is not) (*Theol.* IV, 1299–1300), and again: 'not unaware that some doctors of the Church consider that the Holy Spirit is from the Father's substance also, i.e. is from Him in such wise that He is of one substance with the Father; properly however, we do not say He is from the Father's substance: only the Son is to be so denominated' (*Introd.* II, 1072). (2b) is met in this form: 'Macrobius also declares that the soul of the world, which we think is understood to be the Holy Spirit' (*Theol.* IV, 1307; *Introd.* II, 1080–1082) and in this: 'therefore the same substance is called both Holy Spirit and soul, Spirit from goodness, soul from vivification, Spirit from affection, soul from effect, Spirit in his eternity, soul in temporal administration' (*Epitome* 18; PL 178.1721). That Abelard identifies the Holy Spirit here with Plato's *anima mundi*, or with a created soul of the world is far from evident.[27] (14) is found in this form: 'in that He is ingenerate God, God the Father has this characteristic properly and specially, that He is omnipotent . . . and this name Father . . . so expresses the divine power which is omnipotence that it does not have wisdom or benignity distinct in it' (*Theol.* 1, 1131).

Was Abelard a heretic? Some of his trinitarian statements if taken just as they stand are heretical. But if heresy means not only erroneous words but also pertinacity in error, it seems he was not. For in his *Introductio* he declared that 'if perchance I put forth anything erroneous, none of this shall I contemptuously defend. . . . So that if I do not lack the vice of ignorance, yet I shall not incur the crime of heresy. For ignorance does not make a heretic, but rather the obstinacy of pride' (981). And if heresy means not only heretical words but also heretical intent, then it seems again that he was not a heretic, for in his *Apologia* he repudiated one by one all the errors of which he was accused at the Council of Sens. His words on occasion could seem to be and even be very unorthodox, and yet when viewed in the larger context of the entire treatise or of his total writings they would be offset again and again by other statements on the same point that were entirely orthodox. A great part of his writings was devoted to the refutation of heresy, the old heresy of Sabellius and Arius, the more recent 'heresy' of Roscelin and Gilbert of Porrée. There is a certain irony in Abelard's condemnation. He had gone out of his way in his *Sic et Non* to gather together opposed statements of the Fathers, some orthodox, others not. Now others had gathered together some of his unorthodox statements and condemned them. What led him astray? It can seem that in his desire to make faith intelligible to reason and to infidels he occasionally forgot that the Trinity is a strict mystery, above the reach of unaided reason and beyond the demonstrative and illustrative powers of even the believer. To make the divine persons and processions more intelligible he looked for similitudes and analogies in created things, such as the famous analogy of the brass seal (*Introd.* 97)[28] and pressed them too far.

He was not one of the great original thinkers in trinitarian theology, but he did originate some ideas and methods that would have a long life. He stimulated theologians to be more careful and scientific in their use of patristic evidence and arguments, and to discuss and explain points of theology rather than merely assert or prove them. He helped pave the way for Scholasticism. He showed that dialectic could be a useful, a valuable, a dangerous instrument for the theologian in his efforts to defend and explain the deep mysteries of the faith.

GILBERT DE LA PORRÉE

Gilbert de la Porrée (d. 1154) was chancellor of Chartres and then Bishop of Poitiers. He has been called one of the most eminent teachers and thinkers of the century,[29] and 'no less a creative genius than St. Thomas,'[30] but also a tritheist.[31] He had many disciples and

his 'school' was important in the 12th century.[32] He is best known
for his trinitarian teaching which was reputedly condemned
solemnly at the Council of Rheims in 1148.

Various judgments have been made about what happened to
Gilbert at this Council: 'his theories were censured,'[33] 'at the instiga-
tion of St. Bernard' the Council 'condemned 4 propositions that
were ascribed to him.'[34] 'At the Council of Rheims he abjured the 4
propositions ascribed to him. . . . Thereupon the Pope on his apostolic authority and with the consent of all present condemned the
articles.'[35] On the other hand John of Salisbury, who was an eyewitness, and Otto of Freising both maintained 'that there was no
decision against Gilbert,'[36] while John added that there was no question of abjuration but that Gilbert was simply told to correct some
passages in his commentaries on Boethius.[37] Today it seems clear
enough that there was no conciliar decision against Gilbert,[38] no
papal condemnation of Gilbert, and that the Profession of Faith
(Denz 30th ed. 389–392) to which Gilbert subscribed and which
Bernard hoped would bring about Gilbert's condemnation by the
Pope but did not, 'is not an official document of the ecclesiastical
magisterium' (Denz 745, Introd.).

The Rheims episode is still not entirely clear. In 1148 a Council
was held at Rheims under the headship of Pope Eugene III, and at it
4 doctrinal charges were brought against Gilbert, that he taught '(1)
that the divine essence . . . the divinity of God . . . is not God but
the form by which He is God; (2) that the three Persons . . . are not
one God, one substance, one something; (3) that the three Persons
are . . . distinct by three properties which are not the same thing as
the Persons but . . . differ in number from one another and from the
divine substance; (4) that the divine nature is not incarnate nor did
it assume human nature' (Denz 745, Introd.). These propositions
were not copied literally from his works, and Gilbert indignantly
refused to admit them, and so successfully defended himself that
the Pope assigned no note of heresy to the 4 capitula, but only
declared that 'no reasoning in theology was to divide nature and
person, and that God should not be called the divine essence only in
the ablative, but also in the nominative' (Denz 745, Introd.). Thus
one must not only say that God is God by reason of the divine
nature but also that God is the divine nature. In the trinitarian
charges the basic points in dispute were: (1) did Gilbert put a real
distinction between God and His divinity, so that this divinity was
not God; (2) did he put a real distinction between the persons and
the nature so as to introduce a real quaternity into God? His
accusers said he did, he said he did not.

Gilbert's chief trinitarian work was his commentaries on Boethius' *Opuscula Sacra* (*De Trinitate, De Predicatione, De Hebdomadibus, De Duabus Naturis*), usually called *Commentaria in Librum de Trinitate* (PL 64, 1255–1412). Nowhere in this did he say explicitly that *divinitas non est Deus*.[39] And sometimes he tended to identify explicitly *divinitas* and *Deus* (1270A, 1303D, 1308D). But there is no doubt that he put a distinction between God and His divinity (1269D, 1285B, 1302D, 1303C, 1381B), between the persons and the substance (1309B, 1310B, 1308B, 1359C), between the properties and the substance (1269A, 1390B). And though he did at times use the divine essence in the nominative case (1368A), he regularly preferred to predicate the divinity of God in the ablative rather than in the nominative (e.g. 1290B). But whether this distinction was a real or a logical distinction, whether it implied an ontological or a dialectical quaternity, is still in dispute.

Gilbert begins his prologue to the *De Trinitate*[40] by stating that errors and heresies about the Trinity are due to the misapplication of natural reason to theology (PL 64, 1255). Arians assumed that identity in substance meant identity in all respects, Sabellians thought that where there was one substance there could not be distinct persons, while Tritheists held that where there were distinct persons there must be distinct substances or essences. These errors were due to the application of 'natural' reason to every aspect of the mystery. Only the Catholic faith makes the correct use of natural and theological reasoning, by applying 'natural' reasoning to the trinity of persons, theological reasoning to the simplicity and unity of God. Theological reasoning considers the 'principle of things.' According to this God is one, since He is the one and only cause or principle of things, and His essence is simple and incomposite. For whereas creatures are composed of several forms, He has only one form, and so there is no distinction in Him between *esse* and *id quod est*. The general principle of theological consideration is this: the principle of unity is indifference. Thus where there is no difference between the three persons, there they are one, and accordingly they are numerically one in essence. The general principle of natural reasoning is this: the principle of plurality is otherness. Hence to show how in this one God there are three persons Gilbert turned to natural reasoning and applied the distinction he found in creatures between the *quo est*, the *subsistentia* and the *quod est*, the *subsistens* (1278D, 1279CD). Sabellians should have applied natural reason here and seen that in God there is but one *quo est*, one *subsistentia*, but three *subsistens* and *quod est*.

That Gilbert held that God is utterly simple and incomposite is clear. Is there a much more accurate way of stating that God is absolutely simple than by saying 'the essence of God is utterly simple' (1368A), or by saying that Father, Son and Holy Spirit 'are one God, indeed one divinity' (1303D), or the divine essence 'is simply one, by which these three are one and simple and entirely what they are' (1306A; cf. 1304D–1305A). Whatever Gilbert may be, he is certainly not a Tritheist.

That Gilbert transferred the terms *quo est* and *quod est, subsistentia* and *subsistens* from creatures to God to show how there can be plurality in God is clear. In his day there was a prevalent grammatical rule[41] that a name signifies both substance (*id quod*) and quality (*id quo*). Natural science deals with the *id quod*, mathematical science with the *id quo*. In created things the *id quo* (e.g. whiteness) is the cause of the white *id quod* (1360B), so that *aliud est quod est et aliud quo est* (1278D). This meant that they were distinct, but obviously it did not mean that the *id quod* was one substance, the *id quo* another substance. With proper discretion (1381D) and proportion (1283ABD), Gilbert maintained, this terminology could be applied to God. And he believed that he had applied it properly, and made it clear that the divine *id quo, divinitas,* unlike the created *id quo,* is not really and causally distinct from the divine *id quod, Deus.*[42] But his adversaries judged differently. They claimed to see in his trinitarian doctrine a real distinction between the *id quo, divinitas,* and the *id quod, Deus.*[43]

Are his adversaries right? Geoffrey of Auxerre, an eyewitness of the Rheims affair, maintained that Gilbert did put a real distinction between the form of divinity and God Himself and introduced into God an ontological quaternity, while John of Salisbury, another eyewitness, 'seems to excuse Gilbert altogether.'[44] Among recent interpreters, Karl Barth[45] charges Gilbert with teaching a real distinction between God and His *divinitas,* and so does A. Hayen.[46] But Hayen adds that 'this was not a distinction of cause and its effect . . . but an "objective" distinction which did not introduce a quaternity since the essence and properties were not ontological but dialectical principles; and yet the theological error involved, fully justified a formal condemnation of Porretanism.'[47] M. E. Williams holds that Gilbert viewed the form of divinity as distinct from God 'but that . . . the question of real distinction . . . as we understand it, is not considered by Gilbert.'[48] Though Gilbert's precise thought and intent are still obscure, it seems reasonable to agree with J. G. Sikes' contention that 'Gilbert's differentiation between God as subsistens and divinity as subsistentia was . . . one of logic and not of metaphysics. . . . That he was charged with believing in a God-

head composed of three Persons with the addition of a divine substance was hardly his fault; such a doctrine certainly does not
represent his views.'[49]

Gilbert's doctrinal troubles had considerable value for trinitarian theology. For they highlighted the need for a more accurate
understanding and expression of the interrelation between the
divine essence and persons and thus pointed the Church toward the
definitive statements of the Councils of Lateran IV and of Florence.

BERNARD OF CLAIRVAUX

Bernard of Clairvaux (d. 1153) has been called 'the last of the
Fathers and the equal of the greatest.'[50] He was a sign of contradiction in his day, loved by many, hated by others, for 'at his worst . . .
he could be an out and out Pharisee, condemning others for minor
points while overlooking major issues.'[51] He combined the soul of a
mystic and a saint with an aggressive zeal for orthodoxy.

In matters trinitarian he is most famous for his controversies
with Peter Abelard and Gilbert de la Porrée and from his writings
on these controversies we can get the best conspectus of his trinitarian doctrine and method. His views on Abelard and his doctrine
can be found in *Letters* 187–193 and 330–338 (PL 182), and his
interpretation of Gilbert in *Sermon 80 on the Canticle* (PL 183).
The best presentation of his own doctrine is to be found in *De Consideratione libri quinque ad Eugenium III Papam* (PL 182).

Bernard took a very dim view of Abelard, for he believed that
'the life, the character, and the books of Peter Abelard already published show him to be a persecutor of the Catholic faith and the
enemy of the cross of Christ . . . a monk in outward appearance . . .
but a heretic within . . .' (*Ep.* 331). So he wrote to Pope Innocent II
that 'we have in France an old teacher turned into a new theologian,
who in his early days amused himself with dialectics, and now gives
utterance to wild imaginations upon the Holy Scriptures. He is
endeavoring again to quicken false opinions, long ago condemned
. . . and is adding fresh ones as well. . . . He is presumptuously prepared to give a reason for everything, even for those things which
are above reason' and says, 'what is the use of speaking of doctrine
unless what we wish to teach can be explained so as to be intelligible?' (*Ep.* 190.1).

Abelard and his writings rubbed Bernard raw in many ways. But
what he considered Abelard's 'Arianization' of the Trinity seemed
to disturb him most deeply. Again and again he wrote that 'this
theologian' 'distinguishes with Arius degrees and inequalities in the

Trinity' (*Ep*. 330, 331, 332, 336). In his letter to the Pope he wrote
that 'our theologian' has laid down 'that God the Father is full power,
the Son a certain kind of power, the Holy Spirit no power, and that
the Son is related to the Father as force in particular to force in
general, as species to genus, as a thing formed of material to matter,
as man to animal, as a brazen seal to brass. Did Arius ever go further? . . . He says also that "the Holy Spirit proceeds indeed from
the Father and the Son, but not from the substance of the Father or
of the Son." ' Bernard added, 'far be it from us to agree with him
who says that the Son is related to the Father as species to genus,
as man to animal, as a brazen seal to brass, as force to force absolutely. For all these several things by the bond of their common
nature are to each other as superiors and inferiors, and therefore
no comparison is to be drawn from these things with That in which
there is no inequality, no dissimilarity' (*Ep*. 190.1.2; 2.4).

That Abelard intended no Arianization, no inferiorization of
the Son and of the Holy Spirit, that he did not think he had really
taught any such inferiorization, Bernard did not, could not, or
would not see. He was such a staunch 'traditionalist' that Abelard's
audacious novelties of thought and dialectic and illustration could
only seem to him to be an endeavor 'again to quicken false opinions
. . . long ago condemned.' However proper or improper were the
judgments and actions of Bernard and Peter, their confrontation
had trinitarian value. Both men believed in and loved the Trinity.
But Abelard wanted to make it more intelligible to believers and so
he used every new illustration and argument that his reason could
conjure up and many expressions that were wide open to misunderstanding. Bernard loved the faith as it was, with all its certitude, its
mystery, its supra-rationality, and so he energetically opposed every
Abelardian novelty that seemed to him to taint it, to endanger it,
to destroy it.

In Bernard's estimate Gilbert de la Porrée was another 'teacher
of novelties' and a 'heretic' whose teaching differed 'from the rectitude of faith' (*Serm. 80 in Cant. 6, 8*). Gilbert seemed to him to put
in God a distinction that denied His simplicity and introduced a
quaternity. Bernard thought that Gilbert taught that 'the divinity
by which He is God, is not God' (*ibid*. 6) and he begged God to forbid 'that the Church Catholic should assent to the proposition that
there is any substance or anything at all by which God is, and which
is not God' (*ibid*. 8). He added: 'quaternity divides a circle, it does
not signify deity' so 'if it pleases you to add a fourth divinity, I am
persuaded that this divinity which is not God, is not at all to be
adored' (*De Consid*. V, 7).

There is no doubt that Gilbert put a distinction between God and His divinity, and in Bernard's eyes this was a real distinction and it introduced a real quaternity. The passages in which Gilbert declared that God is utterly simple and incomposite, that Father, Son and Holy Spirit 'are one God . . . one divinity . . . one substance . . . one essence' and that 'the essence of God is utterly simple'— these Bernard seemed to ignore. Instead he concentrated on the passages that distinguished God and His divinity and it must be admitted that some of them, if taken literally and out of their total context, easily lent themselves to Bernard's interpretation. Once again we have two men professing the same faith and yet at loggerheads over it. Gilbert felt it was not enough to believe in the Triune God. Some effort had to be made to explain this, to give some distinction that would help to show that a God who was one in nature and three in persons was not an open contradiction. So he took from created substances a distinction between *quo est* and *quod est* and applied it to God with the best of intentions but with some very disturbing results. Bernard, on the other hand, felt it was enough to believe and that no such explanation was either necessary or possible or compatible with the supra-rational character of the mystery of the Trinity.

Bernard's own trinitarian doctrine is simple and traditional: 'I believe the eternal and blessed Trinity, though I do not comprehend it' (*Serm.* 76.6); 'it is enough to know that it is so. . . . It is a great mystery, to be venerated but not scrutinized. . . . To scrutinize it is rashness; to believe it is piety; to know it is life and eternal life' (*De Consid.* V, 8.18). With Gilbert in mind he writes: 'God is God by His divinity, but that divinity is God' (*ibid.* 7.15), and he adds: 'But the heretic says: "What"? Do you deny that He is God by His divinity? No, but I maintain that the same divinity by which He is God is God Himself, that I may not be obliged to admit that there is anything more excellent than God' (*Serm.* 80.7). He goes on to say that 'God is not formed, He is form . . . He is not composite . . . He is simple . . . as simple as He is one. . . . He has nothing in Himself except Himself . . . and yet God is Trinity . . . the substance is one, the persons are three' (*De Consid.* V, 7.17). And what is more, 'the properties of the persons are not anything else than the persons' and 'if someone tries to divide either the persons from the substance or the properties from the persons, I know not how he can profess himself a worshipper of the Trinity' (*ibid.* 7.18). There are many unities but 'among all things that are rightly said to be one, the Unity of the Trinity, by which three persons are one substance, holds the heights' (*ibid.* 7.19). With Abelard in mind he wrote: 'if the Holy

Spirit does not proceed from the substance of the Father and the
Son, no Trinity remains, but a duality. For no Person is worthy to
be admitted into the Trinity whose substance is not the same as that
of the others' (*Ep*. 190.1.3). He lashed out against the Abelardian
similitudes that would liken Son to Father as species to genus:
'May that execrable similitude of genus and species be accordingly
as far from our minds as it is from the rule of truth. . . . For since
. . . species is less than and inferior to genus, far be it from us to
think of such diversity between the Father and the Son' (*ibid*. 2.4).
Communia must stay *communia* and *propria propria*:

> His own name is peculiar to each and not common to the other.
> . . . It is not so with power and many other attributes which are
> assigned to the Father and the Son in common, and not singly
> to each taken by Himself . . . let him cease to call attributes which
> are common, *propria*. . . . For . . . the godliness of the faith knows
> how to distinguish cautiously between the *propria* of the Persons,
> and the undivided unity of the essence, and holding a middle
> course, to go along the royal road, turning neither to the right
> by confounding the persons, nor looking to the left by dividing
> the substance (*ibid*. 3.3, 7).

If Bernard made no very great positive contribution to the
development of trinitarian doctrine, his criticism of Abelardian and
Gilbertian doctrines alerted the Church to the danger of an improper
use of reason in trinitarian theology and to the need of a better
harmonization of reason and faith.

HUGH OF ST. VICTOR

Hugh of St. Victor (d. 1141) has been called one of the greatest in
an age of the great.'[52] He was an outstanding teacher in the so-called
'mystical school of the Victorines' that had been founded by
William of Champeaux, and which showed the world that mysticism and Scholasticism were compatible and could mutually enrich
one another.

Hugh's most important works are his *Didascalion* (*De eruditione
docta*) and his *De sacramentis fidei Christianae* (PL 176, 739–812;
173–618). The *Didascalion* 'became a locus classicus for subsequent
writers on education and method.'[53] It embraced 'all the known arts
and sciences, including that of dialectics, in the curriculum of the
finished theologian,'[54] for in Hugh's view the student of theology
should 'learn everything' (*Didasc*. VI, 3.801). In this work Hugh

gives the student of theology some practical advice. So many books have been written, he says, and so many opinions advanced about the Trinity that it would be too difficult to encompass them all. So he should first learn briefly and clearly what must be believed about the Trinity. Then in the books he reads he will find some things clear, some obscure, some ambiguous. Those that are clear and apropos, let him add to his basic trinitarian knowledge. Those that are ambiguous, let him try to interpret, those that are obscure, to clarify. If he finds something contrary to what he has learned to believe most firmly, let him consult more learned men and the universal and infallible faith before he makes any decision (*ibid.* 4.803–804).

The *De sacramentis* was the most comprehensive system of theology that had been produced so far in the West and 'it became the grandmother of all the *Summae* of the following hundred years.'[55] It resembled Damascene's *De fide orthodoxa* but unlike John's work it was not a mere compendium of doctrines but a genuine system with one great controlling principle, the economy of redemption. Though Scripture was Hugh's 'authority,' he made such a large use of reason that he has been charged at times with trying to give a rational demonstration of some of the mysteries of faith.

The rational creature as image of God furnishes him such a clear 'demonstration' of the Trinity:

> For it sees that from it wisdom is born and is in it; and it loves its wisdom, and from it procedes love. . . . And so three appear in one: mind, wisdom, love. And there is mind, and wisdom from mind, and love from mind and wisdom. And so there arises a trinity but unity does not recede, so that there is at the same time trinity and unity. . . . And the mind rises from this . . . and considers that its creator is wise and has wisdom from himself . . . and was never without wisdom . . . and always loved his wisdom and had love for his wisdom, and thus there was love coeternal to the eternal one and to his coeternal wisdom. Again it considers that there can be in God nothing other than God, and that all that is is one, and therefore there is Trinity and unity remains. For there is one who is from no one, and one who is from him, and one who is from both and with both, and so there is Trinity [and neither of these three can be the other, and] so it is a true Trinity, and perfect unity remains since there can be in God nothing that is not God (*De sacr.* I, 3.21, 22).

To the question that arises, why the three in God are called persons but in the rational creature are not, the mind answers that in the rational creature what is in the mind is not the mind but separable from it at times, and hence it is not proper to it to be a person but to be in a person. But since in God there is nothing separable from God, whatever is in God is God, and so the three are God, and they 'are called persons because they are God, and the three are one God because there is one deity in the three' (*ibid.* I, 3.25).

Did Hugh intend to give a strict demonstration by pure reason? It might seem so, for he speaks of a 'clear demonstration' (I, 3.21) and of 'reason that would prove not only that God is, but that He is one and three' (I, 3.11). But this presentation, beautiful though it is, is obviously not a strict demonstration of the real Trinity, for it contains too many lacunae and leaps and assumptions, and Hugh had too keen a mind not to be aware of this. What is more, he wrote that 'things that are evident from reason cannot be believed since they are known' (I, 3.30), but he certainly held that the Trinity had to be believed. He declared that 'human reason unless it be illumined by the word of God cannot see the way of truth' (I, 3.21). He stated that 'true reason proves that God is one, and then it argues and recommends that He is not only one but also three' (I, 3.19) and adds that 'we have demonstrated some vestige of the supreme Trinity, as much as human reason can from the little that is its and from what has been given to it' (I, 3.28). All he aimed at then was a congruent and suasive argument that would help believers see how a truth, that was not the product of reason nor a contradiction of reason but above reason, was yet in accord with reason (I, 3.30).

In matters trinitarian Hugh set forth a clear teaching about divine appropriations (I, 2.7, 8) and missions (I, 1.2) but an inadequate doctrine about the divine persons and their relations. His development of the analogy between the Trinity and the human soul into a 'clear demonstration' of the Trinity is perhaps his greatest contribution to trinitarian thought. Through his writings and his disciples, especially Richard, he was very influential in the 12th century.

Among Hugh's works (PL 176) there is a mysterious treatise, called the *Summa Sententiarum*. It has often been ascribed to Hugh but today it seems very probable that he was not its author.[56] 'It was early ascribed to one of his pupils, Odo of St. Victor, and the ascription is probably correct.'[57] It has been said to mark 'a decisive moment in the history of the development of dogma'[58] in terms of its influence on the composition of Peter Lombard's famous textbook, *Sententiarum libri quattuor*.[59] It seems to represent a confluence of an Abelardian and a Victorine current. It differs from the *De sacramentis* in plan, in content, in its brief and rapid expository style, and resembles modern manuals of theology. It differs, too, in its trinitarian presentation. For it takes a more restrained view of a rational demonstration of the Trinity by reducing the role of reason and clarifying the primacy of authority. It also offers something that was missing in *De sacramentis*, short but precise explanations of the word *person*, of the equality and relations of the divine persons and of the divine operations.

Richard of St. Victor (d. *c.* 1173), the disciple of Hugh, has been called 'his continuation and the idea of Hugh elevated to its highest power.'[60] He was the greatest theoretical teacher of mysticism in the Middle Ages and exclusively 'a theologian of the spiritual life.'[61]

His most famous works are his two treatises on mystical theology, known as *Benjamin Major* and *Benjamin Minor* (PL 196, 1–192), 'which remained for long textbooks of the subject for all writers on contemplation.'[62] His treatise *De Trinitate* (PL 196, 887–992), one of the most learned of the Middle Ages, was both speculative and affective. In its prologue he eulogizes faith and aims to use it as his point of departure but adds that he will always strive 'as much as this is right or possible, to comprehend by reason what we hold by faith' (889). And it is on the attributes of love and goodness especially that he bases his explanations of the mysteries of faith. Thus there will be two great trinitarian theories in the medieval theological world, the Augustinian that St. Thomas will systematize, and the theory of Richard of St. Victor, whose principal representative will be St. Bonaventure.[63] In his trinitarian doctrine Richard stands out for his definition of person, his contention that the Trinity can be rationally demonstrated, and his metaphysical and psychological explanations of the Trinity.

In Boethius' famous definition of person, 'an individual substance of a rational nature,' the word *subsistence* had often come to replace *substance* in the interest of greater clarity. But Richard felt that word was much too obscure and if it were used to define *person* one unknown was explained 'by a more unknown.' It would be far from evident to one reading this word that 'there could be three subsistences where there was evidently only one substance' (*De Trin* IV, 4).

So Richard proposes a new definition: 'a divine person is an incommunicable existence of the divine nature' (IV, 22). On the score of immediate intelligibility this new definition hardly seems to be an improvement on its predecessor. But it does represent a solid attempt to define something transcendent and it has a value of its own once it is understood. Richard wants to give 'existence' a new meaning. He writes that, 'if usage permitted, we could say that as *essence* corresponds to *esse*, so *sistence* to *sistere* . . . and then just as essence so sistence would signify the *esse* of a thing . . . while *existence* signified this same reality with (*ex*) a certain property' (IV, 19), 'a personal property by which each is distinct from all others' (IV, 17). And 'because there are several having one and the same *esse* with a different property, so unity is there according to the *modum essendi*, plurality according to the *modum existendi*' (IV, 19). Theologians generally see little difference between Richard's formula and that of Boethius, for incommunicable is nearly the same as individual and for substance Richard merely substitutes existence in the case of divine persons. For he says that 'as true as it is that every created person is an individual substance of a rational nature, so true it is that every uncreated person is an individual existence of a rational nature' (IV, 22). But if we change Richard's wording just a little it can become an extremely interesting definition: 'an incommunicable *existent* in a rational nature,' for thus it conforms to Aquinas' later definition: 'a distinct subsistent in a rational nature' (*Pot.* 9.4). Such a definition, stressing 'existent' rather than 'subsistent' would not only be in keeping with Richard's dynamic view of the Triune God but also with our modern stress on 'existence.'

Richard seems to have been very intent on a rational demonstration of the Trinity. He wrote: 'and so it will be our intention in this work, to adduce as far as God will grant, not only probable but also necessary reasons for the things we believe. . . . For I believe without doubt that, for the explanation of all things which must necessarily be, not only probable but even necessary arguments are not lacking, though it may happen that in the meantime these escape our effort. . . . It seems altogether impossible that a necessary thing . . . lack a necessary reason' (I, 4). This passage became a classic[64] and later theologians used it to make Richard an adversary to the thesis that says the Trinity is a strict mystery,[65] and to point out that Richard failed to realize that while a necessary reason for a necessary truth would not be lacking to the divine intellect, it might well be lacking with respect to our intellect.[66] But there are other passages in which Richard seems quite aware that the Trinity cannot be proved or reached by pilgrim reason, for he writes: 'if your experience teaches you something in human nature is above your intelligence, should it not teach you that something is above your intelligence in the divine nature' (III, 10). And he asks, 'do you grasp by intelligence or prove by example that there can be unity of substance in plurality of persons and plurality of persons in unity of substance' (VI, 22)? What then did he mean by 'necessary arguments'? Probably not strict demonstrations by unaided human reason, but a faith-illumined argumentation by unaided human reason, but a faith-the truths of faith which 'seem not only above reason but even against reason' (I, 1) are not against it but in accord with it.⁶⁷ Why else would St. Thomas approve Richard's doctrine of 'necessary arguments' (*De ver.* 14.9 ad 1)?

Richard's 'demonstration' of the Trinity is not as concise and direct as it might be, but its general flow is clear and involves four stages. In the first (I–II) he proves the existence of one God from the existence of contingent beings, the existence of degrees in beings, and the existence of the power of being. He has been credited with being the first to attempt an *a posteriori* proof of God's existence with the aid of the principle of causality.⁶⁸ In the second stage (III) he proves the existence of a second and a third person, in the third (IV) the compatibility of the plurality of persons with the unity of substance, and in the fourth (V–VI) the number of processions and their difference.

The second stage is in many ways the most interesting and important, and it pivots on charity. In God there is the plenitude of goodness, of felicity, of glory, and hence there must be the plenitude of charity, for nothing is better or more perfect than charity and without charity there cannot be supreme goodness, supreme joy, supreme glory. To be charity, love must tend to another, for no one is said to have charity by reason of a private love of self. But a divine person must have supreme charity, and it cannot have this for a created person. Hence there must be in God a plurality of divine persons. Must there be only two? There must be a third. For 'in mutual love that is very fervent there is nothing rarer, nothing more excellent than that you wish another to be equally loved by him whom you love supremely and by whom you are loved supremely' (III, 11). 'When one loves another . . . there is dilection, but not condilection. . . . When two love one another mutually, there is dilection on both sides but not condilection.' There is condilection 'when a third is loved concordantly and socially by two, and the affection of the two flows together in the kindling of a third love.' 'Who can estimate how great is the dignity of this intimate and supreme concord'? It cannot 'be lacking in the supreme and all-perfect good, it cannot be had without a Trinity of persons' (III, 19). Can there be a fourth person? No. For in God there can be only one person who is principle only, one who is term only, one who is both term and principle; only one person who is from Himself, one who is from one other, one who is from both others; one who only gives, one who only receives, one who gives and receives (V, 15, 25). The third person must be the completion of the Trinity for otherwise there would be irrationally an infinite processional series (V, 11). It must be rather obvious that Richard's analysis of charity does not result in a cogent proof of the presence of three and only three persons in God. No more cogent is his attempt to show in terms of love how these three persons are one in substance (V, 23).

If we compare Richard's use of psychological theory to explain the Trinity with that of Augustine,[69] we note interesting differences. Augustine starts with nature rather than person. He looks into natural human love of self, and sees there a *lover*, a *beloved*, a *love*, but it is difficult to see the Trinity imaged there for when I love myself, lover and beloved are the same. He looks into God's intellectual nature and sees there intellect and will as productive principles of two terms, *word* and *love*, but it is difficult to see how this mental *word* and *love* are *persons*. And yet this word and love fit well with the traditional doctrine of the Son as Word and the Holy Spirit as Love. Richard also looks to man as made to the image of God. But he turns immediately to persons, to the personal love of one for another, to the unselfish love of friendship that can be so wonderful, and in this he sees a reflection of a divine love of friendship. But in this unselfish love of friendship whereby one gives himself wholly to another, there is still a tinge of selfishness, for it excludes a third from sharing this love and joy. Now he turns to God and sees that in God there must be charity in its supreme form. When analyzed this means that there must be in God one infinite love and three infinite lovers, in such a way that one (the Father) is the productive principle of a condign beloved (the Son) and these two are the single productive principle of an equal co-beloved (the Holy Spirit). It is a beautiful theory and it may be said to build on the Johannine teaching that 'God is love.' But it seems to make little of the Biblical stress on the Son as Word and as Wisdom. Could it be otherwise? Could any comparison ever hope to be adequate? And yet each comparison has value, that of Augustine, that of Richard, for each represents an effort of the human mind working at its highest level to give intelligible expression to some aspect of the One who is ineffable.

CHAPTER TEN

From Peter Lombard to Lateran IV

PETER LOMBARD

Peter Lombard (d. 1160) was the author of 'one of the most success-
ful text-books the world has ever seen.'[1] The work that made him
famous and won him the title of 'Master of the Sentences' was his
Books of Sentences (PL 192, 519–964). It was a theological summa
in four books, which dealt with the three Persons and the one God
(1), creation, angels, hexaemeron, the fall and grace (2), the Incarnation, virtues, sins, commandments (3), the sacraments, sacramentals,
and last things (4). It took up these traditional doctrines one by one,
proposed a doctrinal thesis, brought forward authorities for and
against this thesis from Scripture, the Councils, the Canons, the
Fathers, and then gave judgment on the issue. But where Abelard's
quotations of the Fathers in his *Sic et Non* had tended to destroy
confidence in the authority of the Fathers, Peter's use of the Fathers
tended to restore confidence in them and their authority. He aimed
to be traditional and orthodox rather than original, and to produce
a clear and systematic summary of the Catholic faith of his day. He
succeeded so well that for centuries his work was 'the great theological handbook of the West,' and innumerable commentaries on
it were written, some as late as the 17th century.[2]

Since trinitarian doctrine must build on a Biblical foundation,
it is important to see what this Biblical foundation was in the Lombardian textbook. Lombard looked for 'authorities, by which the
truth of the divine Unity and Trinity is demonstrated' (*Sent.* I d.2,
c.4), and found them in both the Old Testament and the New Testa-

195

ment. In the Old Testament he saw the unity of nature indicated in Deut 6.4, Ex 20.23, Ex 3.14, Ex 15.3, Ps 67.5, Ps 80.9; the unity of nature and plurality of persons in Gen 1.26, Gen 1.1; the trinity of persons in Ps 32.6, Ps 66.6, Is 6.3; the duality of Father and Son in Ps 2.3, Is 53.8, Prov 8.22–30, Sir 24.5, Mic 5.2; the Holy Spirit in Gen 1.2, Ps 138.7, Wis 1.5, Is 61.1. In the New Testament (I, d.2, c.5) he found the unity of nature and the plurality of persons in Mt 28.19, Jn 10.30, 1 Jn 5.7, Jn 1.1, Gal 4.6, Rom 8.11 and Rom 11.36. He did not offer more texts 'because almost every syllable of the New Testament concordantly insinuates this truth of ineffable Unity and Trinity' (I, d.2, c.5). Measured by the standards of his day this Biblical foundation was solid enough. But modern exegetes see no duality or trinity of persons demonstrated or declared in any of the Old Testament texts Lombard cited, and as for his New Testament citations, they reject outright 1 Jn 5.7 and turn a very critical eye on some of the others.

In his teaching about the Trinity and the processions he is strongly traditional. According to Scripture 'Father, Son, and Holy Spirit are of one substance and inseparable equality . . . so that there is unity in essence and plurality in persons.' (I, d.2, c1–2). The Father begot the Son not by will but by nature, not by necessity but willingly though not by a 'preceding or acceding will' (I, d.6, c.1). The manner of this generation he found 'ineffable and unintelligible' (I, d.9, c.3). That the Holy Spirit proceeds from the Father and the Son he 'proves' (I, d.11, c.1) from many testimonies of Scripture (Gal 4.6; Rom 8.9, 11; Jn 14.26, 15.26; Mt 10.20), and he points out that although the Greeks deny the *Filioque* there are many Greek Fathers who testify to it (I, d.11, c.2). But 'while we live here below we are unable to distinguish between the generation of the Son and the procession of the Holy Spirit' (I, d.13, c.3). It is somewhat surprising that at this late date in a work of this kind there is still no attempt to investigate the nature of this generation or to try to differentiate it from the procession of the Holy Spirit.

In I d.5 Lombard wrote that 'the divine essence did not generate the essence. Since the divine essence is a certain reality that is one and supreme, if the divine essence generated the essence the same reality would generate itself, which is altogether impossible; but the Father alone generated the Son, and from the Father and Son proceeded the Holy Spirit.' For this teaching Abbot Joachim of Fiore attacked Peter as an insane heretic and declared that Peter thus put into God 'not so much a Trinity as a quaternity of three persons with that common essence as a fourth.'[3] But the Fourth Lateran Council did something that 'is perhaps unique in the history of conciliar canons,'[4] when it adopted Peter's doctrine and involved him by name in its solemn declaration: 'we condemn . . . the booklet . . . which Abbot Joachim published against Master Peter Lombard . . . calling him an insane heretic because he said in his *Sentences* that "a certain supreme reality is the Father, Son and Holy Spirit and it is not generating nor generated nor proceeding," and asserting that Peter thus put into God "not so much a Trinity as a quaternity" . . .' (Denz 803). Rarely, if ever hitherto had a theologian's teaching received such approval from a general council.

A pneumatological teaching of Lombard's, that the Holy Spirit is the love or charity by which *we* love God and neighbor (I, d.17, c.1; cf. d.10, c.2) has been widely discussed. He declares that while the Holy Spirit operates acts of faith and hope through the medium of virtues of faith and hope, He 'operates the act of loving by Himself alone without the medium of any virtue' (I, d.17, c.6).[5] This opinion of Lombard's will be refuted by Aquinas (ST 2a2ae, 23.2) and generally rejected by theologians, and today it can be 'considered obsolete.'[6]

However, there can be no doubt that Lombard's *Sentences* 'exercised a great influence on the development of scholastic theology' and 'shaped the minds of some of the greatest theologians of the Church.'[7]

JOACHIM OF FLORA

Joachim of Flora (d. 1202), a Cistercian Abbot, is famous for his theory of the three ages of history and for his attack on Peter Lombard's trinitarian doctrine. He died with a reputation for sanctity which persisted even after his posthumous condemnation by the Fourth Lateran Council.[8] Three of many works attributed to him are definitely authentic, *Expositio in Apocalypsim, Concordia Novi et Veteris Testamenti, Psalterium decem chordarum.*[9] His *Libellus de unitate seu essentia Trinitatis* against Lombard and condemned by Lateran IV (Denz 803) has been lost.[10] A work called *Liber contra Lombardum* has been preserved in Ms. 296 of Balliol College at Oxford.[11] Its author very probably was not Joachim but one of his disciples,[12] but it seems to coincide 'perfectly' with the lost work of Joachim that was condemned by Lateran IV[13] and described by Aquinas (ST 1a, 39.5).

Joachim divided the history of the world into three epochs: 'three states of the world are called by one name . . . to the image and likeness of him who is three in persons and one in substance' (*Conc.* III, 1, c.1). And 'the first state is to be attributed to the Father, the second to the Son, the third to the Holy Spirit' and 'in the third state the Holy Spirit was to show his glory, as the Son in the second and the Father in the first' (*Conc.* II, 1, c.8). The time 'under the law is ascribed to the Father. . . . The time that followed under the gospel is ascribed to the Son. . . . The time that will be anon under spiritual intelligence is ascribed to the Holy Spirit because He will be given to men more abundantly and will teach those whom He will fill with all truth' (*In Apoc.* Introd., c.5). In the third state 'not only our souls . . . but our bodies also will be spiritual' (*ibid.*). The communication of the Holy Spirit is intended to divinize our nature and make us 'participants of His plenitude' (*Psalt.* II, fol. 260 rB). To do this there must be 'a substantial distinction of the divine Persons, for otherwise the whole system collapses.'[14]

That is why Joachim so strongly opposed Lombard. For if you made the divine substance something distinct from the three Persons, as he thought Lombard did, then you would have a quaternity; if you absorbed the Persons into one substance you would fall into Sabellianism. The only way out of the dilemma, he concluded, was to make the three Persons three really distinct but utterly like substances, and call them 'one substance *similitudinarie*' (*Psalt.* I, d.1. fol. 233 rA). Their unity would be an '*idemptitas*' (*In Apoc.*, Introd. c.12), an assimilative and collective unity. This was Tritheism and Lateran IV condemned it (Denz 803). The root of his Tritheism may have been his belief that divinizing grace was a real communication of the Holy Spirit Himself which entailed His substantial distinction from the Father and the Son.[15]

If we turn to the *Liber contra Lombardum* we find there a powerful presentation of the Joachimite case against the doctrine of Lombard and Lateran IV, that the divine nature is a supreme reality that is not generating nor generated nor proceeding but it is the Father who generates, the Son who is generated, the Holy Spirit who proceeds. In Part I it maintains that the conciliar doctrine has no Biblical texts that prove it (I A a) but has against it many patristic testimonies (I A b), from Augustine (*De Trin.* 7.2), Richard (*De Trin.* VI, 22), Anselm (*Monol.* 44), Hilary (*De Trin.* 5.37). In Part II, perhaps the most important part historically, Tritheism is vigorously defended. The author argues that since Dionysius, Damascene and Boethius affirm that Father, Son and Holy Spirit are three who are numerically distinct, 'therefore that reality which is at once Father, Son and Holy Spirit cannot be numerically one,' unless you hold Sabellianism (II A a). Further Augustine says (*De doctr. christ.* I.5) that Father, Son, and Holy Spirit are three eternal realities (*res*). And from Boethius' definition of person as an 'individual substance of a rational nature' (*De pers. et duab. nat.* 3), it follows that the three Persons are three particular, individual substances. Hence when the three Persons are said to be one substance, this does not mean they are numerically one substance, but 'one because of consonance of the supreme likeness, supreme equality, supreme idemptity of the three Persons toward one another' (II A d). Their unity is 'not a unity of singularity' but 'of idemptity' (*ibid.*). For 'if there were a singular unity of the three Persons, the three Persons would be distinct only in names and not in reality' (II A e). And this is the error into which 'Master Peter fell' (*Sent.* I, d.24). To avoid quaternity Lombard and Lateran IV identified the '*res nec generans nec genita nec procedens*' with the three Persons, but this is impossible for if the three Persons are '*generans*,' '*genita*,' and '*procedens*,' and there is a '*res nec generans nec genita nec procedens*,' then quaternity is inevitable (II D a–e). The authority of Lateran IV does not impress the author for he puts it—surprisingly—on a level with the non-ecumenical councils of Ephesus II and of Rimini (II B d e), in which 'those gathered together . . . erred' (*ibid.*).

There is here a strong defense of Tritheism out of a conviction that it is the only way to avoid Sabellianism or Quaternianism. From now on theologians will have to try to show more clearly that the traditional doctrine of the Triune God leads neither to Sabellianism nor to Quaternianism nor to Tritheism and try to explain how three Persons can be really identified with one simple supreme reality and yet be really distinct from one another. Lateran IV will point the way.

THE FOURTH LATERAN COUNCIL

The Fourth Lateran Council (1215), which the Western Church considers to be the 12th Ecumenical Council, has been called the most splendid council of the Middle Ages. It was convoked by Pope Innocent III, and invitations were sent to patriarchs, archbishops, bishops, abbots and priors in the West and East.[16] In trinitarian matters it was the most important council the Church had produced so far and it was the first ecumenical council to define that the Holy Spirit proceeds from both the Father and the Son.

The chapter *Damnamus* is a most important, if at times poorly worded, trinitarian chapter. First it condemns Joachim's book and doctrine (Denz 803), as we have indicated above. Then it sets forth its own trinitarian doctrine in greater depth and length than any ecumenical council had done hitherto:

> We, therefore, with the approval of the sacred council, believe and confess with Peter Lombard that there is one supreme

reality, incomprehensible and ineffable, which is truly Father, Son, and Holy Spirit; at once the three persons taken together and each of them singly; and so in God there is only a Trinity and not a quaternity, because each of the three persons is that reality, that is the divine substance, essence or nature: which alone is the principle of all things and beside it no other can be found. And that reality is not generating, nor generated, nor proceeding, but it is the Father who generates, the Son who is generated, and the Holy Spirit who proceeds: so that there are distinctions in the persons, unity in the nature (Denz 804).

Here perhaps the most noteworthy and provocative point is the adoption of the Lombardian teaching that 'that supreme reality is not generating nor generated nor proceeding, but it is the Father who generates, the Son who is generated, the Holy Spirit who proceeds.' Is there here not an open contradiction, as the *Liber contra Lombardum* maintained? If the Father is generating and the Father is really identified with this one supreme reality, is it not an open contradiction to say the Father is generating but this supreme reality is not generating? First of all it must be noted that the Council obviously saw no such open contradiction. Hence it believed that the one supreme reality had two objective aspects—one of nature and one of persons—that were somehow sufficiently distinct to enable the Council to define that according to one aspect—that of one nature—this supreme reality was not generating nor generated nor proceeding, while according to the other aspect—that of three distinct persons—it was generating, generated, and proceeding. It believed that there was some distinction that had an objective basis in the one supreme reality that is the Triune God. What kind of distinction this is the Council did not say. But it made it clear that it could not be a real distinction, because it identified the three persons and the one nature and rejected quaternity. Nor could it be a purely logical distinction whereby the three would not be really distinct from one another, because it declared that the persons are distinct. Further than this the Council did not go. It left to later theologians the task of trying to conceive and name this transcendent distinction that lies at the heart of the mystery of the Triune God.

In the third paragraph the Council adopts a Greek way of expressing and envisioning the distinction and consubstantiality of the three, when it declares:

Although the Father is *alius*, the Son *alius*, and the Holy Spirit *alius*, yet they are not *aliud* (Greg. Naz. *ep. 1 ad Cledon*, PG 37. 179): but what the Father is, that the Son is, that the Holy Spirit is, so that according to the orthodox and catholic faith they are believed to be consubstantial. For the Father in generating the Son gave Him His own substance. . . . And it cannot be said that He gave Him a part of His substance and retained a part for Himself, because the Father's substance is indivisible since it is altogether simple. Nor can it be said that in generating Him the Father transferred His substance to the Son, as though He gave it to the Son in such a way that He did not retain it for Himself, for if He had He would have ceased to be substance. It is clear therefore that in being born the Son received the substance of the Father without any diminution, and so the Father and the Son have the same substance; and thus the same reality is the Father and the Son and the Holy Spirit who proceeds from both (Denz 805).

The intent of this is clear enough but the form used to express this intent leaves much to be desired.

The Council takes up the Johannine text, 'that they may be one in us as we are one' (17.22) and declares that 'the word "one" applied to the faithful means a unity of charity in grace, but as applied to the divine persons, it indicates a unity of identity of nature . . . for between Creator and creature no likeness can be noted without noting greater unlikeness' (Denz 806).

Thus this Council in its trinitarian declarations goes well beyond Nicea I and Constantinople I. It explicitly affirms the consubstantiality, coeternity, coequality, co-omnipotence of the three persons, their distinction from one another and their identity of nature, the procession of the Father from no one, of the Son from the Father alone, of the Holy Spirit from both. To signify God's oneness it uses the words *essence, substance, nature, reality, aliud,* to signify His threeness it uses *person* and *alius.* It explicitly rejects a quaternity in God and a merely collective unity of the three, and carefully distinguishes between our oneness with the divine persons by grace and their own oneness by nature. But it will be left to the Council of Florence to canonize the doctrine that the distinction of the persons is rooted in their relational opposition.

CHAPTER ELEVEN

From Albert to Bonaventure

ALBERT THE GREAT

Albert the Great (d. 1280) was eminent as a writer, a philosopher, a theologian, a bishop, a saint, but he is probably best known as the teacher of St. Thomas Aquinas.[1] It was his merit to realize that, like Plato, Aristotle could also be pressed into the service of the Christian faith. He opened the way for St. Thomas by his teaching on 'the relations between science and faith . . . the introductory and persuasive function of science with regard to the faith, and the radical inability of reason to explain the mysteries, and to these elements of solution . . . the Angelic Doctor added nothing that was entirely new.'[2]

Albert's trinitarian doctrine is found in his *Commentary on the Sentences* and in his *Summa Theologiae*. The Trinity is beyond the reach of natural reason, he declares bluntly. Richard's 'necessary reasons' 'are supernatural and divine and so cannot be found by natural light alone' (STh I, tr.3, q.13, m.3). 'Aristotle did not understand the Trinity except through appropriations. . . . Plato learned of the Father and Son not by the lead of natural reason but in the book of Moses and the Prophets' (*In I Sent*. d.3, a.18). The soul is only a slight image of the Trinity 'because it so offers a likeness of the supreme Trinity that it is unlike in the greatest part' (*ibid*. a.34 R).

In God there is a divine 'communicability,' Albert maintains, that manifests itself *ad intra* in the generation of the Son and the spiration of the Holy Spirit. In his *Commentary on the Sentences* he says divinity can be communicated in only two ways, by way of intellect and by way of will, but not by way of nature, and he adds that communication by way of intellect expressing itself is genera-

202

tion (*In I Sent.* d.10, a.12). But in his *Summa* he says that 'procession
of a word from the intellect does not make the Son, but the Son's
substantial emanation from the Father according to the communicability of nature in perfect likeness of species and form, brings it
about that He is Son' (I, tr.7, q.30, m.2). Since the Holy Spirit does
not proceed by way of nature, as the Son does, but by way of love,
He is not generated, because 'the first reason of his procession is by
way of love or charity' (I, tr.7, q.31, m.2, Sol.). He notes that the
Holy Spirit is indeed produced in likeness of substance, but not
precisely by reason of his mode of emanation, for 'the mode of
emanation of love . . . does not signify an emanation of nature but
of will: and the fact that one produced by way of love is produced
in likeness of substance and species, is not by reason of the emanation but of the simplicity of nature' (*ibid.* ad 2). Here, perhaps without realizing it, Albert has touched on what later theologians will
consider the basic difference between divine generation and procession, namely that to be generated means not merely to be produced
in likeness of nature (as the Holy Spirit is) but in likeness of nature
by means of a likeness-producing operation (as the Son is but the
Holy Spirit is not). Albert goes on to say that the Spirit of Love proceeds not by way of love of fruition of one's own proper good, for
this is the essential love 'that belongs to the whole Trinity,' but by
way of love of friendship which tends to another, for this is the
notional love 'that belongs to the Holy Spirit alone' (*ibid.* ad 6). He
adds that the Father and Son spirate the Holy Spirit 'not inasmuch
as they are Father and Son . . . but inasmuch as they are . . . one spirative principle. . . . Thus although they are said to be two spirators of
the Holy Spirit . . . yet they are one spirative principle and one simple
Spirit is spirated by them' (*ibid.* m.3, ad q.1).

Albert realized that only relations of origin distinguished the
divine persons, for in God 'there is distinction only according to
the opposition of relation of origin' (*ibid.* tr.9, q.41, m.2, a.3), so
that persons are the same where 'opposition of such relation does
not distinguish them' (*ibid.*). But he could not find a satisfactory
definition of person. He noted four definitions that were current,
Boethius' an individual substance of a rational nature; Richard's an
incommunicable existence of an intellectual nature; Richard's a *per
se* alone existent according to some mode of rational existence, and
Abelard's a hypostasis that is distinct by an incommunicable
property pertaining to dignity. If properly understood, he declared,
all were acceptable. But he inclined to Richard's 'incommunicable
existence,' since 'incommunicable' excludes every kind of communion according to act and potency and hence neither a separated

soul nor the human nature of Christ would be persons since they were 'communicable' (*ibid*.). At times he used still other definitions of person: 'a hypostasis distinct by a personal property' (*ibid*. m.1, Sol.), and 'a singular existent according to the mode of singular existence.'

It is difficult to estimate Albert's contribution to the development of trinitarian doctrine. By his *Commentary on the Sentences* and by his *Summa Theologiae*, as well as by his teaching, he certainly exercised a very considerable influence on Aquinas and on Aquinas' own *Commentary on the Sentences* and *Summa Theologiae*. But it seems an extreme exaggeration to say that 'precisely on the doctrine of the Most Blessed Trinity Albert wrote better than any man before him and was not surpassed subsequently even by St. Thomas.'[3] Before him Augustine wrote much better on the Trinity and after him so did St. Thomas.

THOMAS AQUINAS

Thomas Aquinas (d. 1274), 'the clearest thinker and the boldest innovator in scholasticism,'[4] integrated 'Aristotelian philosophical principles with traditional speculative theology, and . . . created, by remoulding and rethinking existing materials and old problems, a wholly new and original Christian philosophy.'[5] As 'a devout and orthodox believer' his problem was to effect 'a combination of Christian faith and Aristotelian philosophy which should leave the former intact and yet make room for the principles, methods and points of view of the latter.'[6]

Thomas dealt with the Trinity in many works but most thoroughly in his *Commentary on the Sentences*, his *Summa against the gentiles*, and his *Summa theologiae*. The *Summa theologiae* constitutes a general system of theology that covers the whole range of Christian truth. It has been said of it that 'its comprehensiveness, its sanity and moderation, the thoroughness with which each subject is treated, the pertinacy with which every problem is traced to its source, the fairness and exhaustiveness with which all possible objections are stated and the care with which they are answered, the very sameness in order and method of treatment—all contribute to make it the most impressive system of theology of the Middle Ages if not of any age.'[7]

For Thomas natural reason can neither demonstrate nor know the Trinity: 'that God is triune is uniquely an object of belief, and one cannot prove it in any demonstrative way. Some reasons can be advanced but they are not necessitating, and they have probability only for the believer' (*In Boeth. de Trin.* 1.4). By natural reason 'we can know what belongs to the unity of the essence, but not what belongs to the distinction of the persons' (ST 1a, 32.1). Hence 'the philosophers did not know the mystery of the trinity of the divine persons by its proper attributes, namely, paternity, filiation, and procession' but 'they knew some of the essential attributes appropriated to the persons, as power to the Father, wisdom to the Son, goodness to the Holy Spirit' (*ibid.* ad 1). 'Nor is the divine image in the intellect,' he added, 'an adequate proof about anything in God, since intellect is not in God and ourselves univocally' (*ibid.* ad 2).

Turning to the Trinity itself, Thomas sets out to show that there are two and only two processions in God (ST 1a, 27), four and only four real relations in God (ST 1a, 28), three and only three persons in God (ST 1a, 29, 30), five notions in God (ST 1a, 32), and visible and invisible missions of the Son and of the Holy Spirit (ST 1a, 43).

The two origins, generation and procession, that the Catholic faith saw in God, Aquinas expounded in terms of intellectual nature: 'the divine processions can be derived only from actions which remain within the agent. These acts in a nature which is intellectual and divine are only two, the acts of understanding and willing. . . . It follows that no other procession is possible in God but the procession of the Word and of Love' (ST 1a, 27.5). 'There is no need to go on to infinity in the divine processions, for the procession which is accomplished within the agent in an intellectual nature terminates in the procession of the will' (ST 1a, 27.3 and 1). For 'God understands all things by one simple act, and by one act also He wills all things. Hence there cannot exist in Him a procession of Word from Word, nor of Love from Love: for there is in Him only one perfect Word, and one perfect Love. Thereby is manifested His perfect fecundity' (ST 1a, 27.5 ad 3).

Down the centuries the nature of the generation of the Son and its differentiation from the procession of the Holy Spirit was a problem that disturbed Fathers and theologians alike. Some Fathers, Athanasius (*Or.* 3) and Basil (*Hom.* 29) warned against investigating it. Augustine (*Contra Maximin.* 1.14) and Damascene (*De fid. orth.* 1.8) said they could not solve it. In the course of time Fathers and theologians suggested that the Holy Spirit was not generated because He proceeded from two, as given and gift, and not through nature but through will. But not one of these reasons was very satisfactory or went to the heart of the problem. For if to be generated meant that a living being originated from a living being in likeness of nature, then it seemed that the Holy Spirit was generated.

Thomas pondered all this and looked around to see where he

could find an analogy for divine generation (*C. gent.* 4.11). In the material, vegetable, or sensory worlds? No. Only in the sphere of intellectual activity 'according to intellectual emanation must the divine generation be understood' (*ibid.*). And so he concluded that the answer to this problem must be found in a more thorough analysis of generation and of procession by way of intellect and will. There must be some element in generation that was verified in one of the divine intellectual processions and not in the other. What was it?

Generation, he wrote, in its proper sense 'signifies the origin of a living being from a conjoined living principle . . . by way of likeness in the same specific nature' (ST 1a, 27.2). But the Word 'proceeds by way of intelligible action, which is a vital operation—from a conjoined principle by way of likeness, because the conception of the intellect is a likeness of the object conceived, and it exists in the same nature because in God understanding and being are the same. Hence the procession of the Word in God is called generation, and the proceeding Word is called Son' (ST 1a, 27.2). But the second procession, 'the procession of love in God ought not to be called generation,' for 'the procession of the intellect is by way of likeness, and so can be called generation because every generator generates its own like; whereas the procession of the will is not by way of likeness, but is rather by way of impulse and movement toward some thing. So what proceeds in God by way of love does not proceed as begotten or as a Son but rather as Spirit' (ST 1a, 27.4).

What then was the element in generation that was verified in one divine procession and not in the other? It was the production of one like in nature by what later theologians will call a 'formally assimilative operation.' In other words, a generative act is essentially a likeness-producing act. In God the intelligible operation that produces the Word is such a likeness-producing act and hence it is called generation. But in God the operation of the will that is—or results in—love is not a likeness-producing act but rather an impulse-producing act. Hence it is not called generation.

For the first time in trinitarian history there is a clear-cut differentiation of divine generation and divine procession in terms of the intimate life of the Triune God. How much of this clear-cut differentiation is due to St. Thomas alone, how much to his predecessors, is open to dispute. But certainly it is Thomas who has put this differentiation in clear light and to whom later theologians will generally look as its author. And down the centuries it will remain the only clear-cut differentiation.

Does all this *prove* that the Son's generation is by way of intellect, the Holy Spirit's procession by way of will, so that the Son is produced by a formally assimilative act of understanding, the Holy Spirit by a non-formally assimilative act of loving? No. Some later theologians will say, it is true, that it is 'proximately of faith that the Son proceeds from the Father according to intellectual generation, and that it is common doctrine that the Holy Spirit proceeds from the Father and the Son according to mutual love.'[8] But others will maintain that all this is only a theory or analogical explanation, which has no dogmatic foundation and which in no way represents the actual situation within the Triune God.[9] Still others say this theory 'is not a simple comparison but a true analogy of proper proportionality . . . and it is very probable that . . . it formally though very imperfectly attains to the divine reality . . and if we regard its connection with documents of faith and its place in theology, it is perhaps certain.'[10]

Very early in the Church it was realized that the names of the divine persons were relative names that implied real relations among the persons in the Godhead. Gradually Fathers and theologians came to teach more and more explicitly that the persons are distinguished from one another by interpersonal relations. Thomas set himself to show that in God there are four real relations, paternity, filiation, spiration, procession, which are identified with the divine essence in their *esse* and thus are subsistent, and that three of them, paternity, filiation, and procession (passive spiration) are really distinct from one another by reason of their mutual opposition (ST 1a, 28.1–4) and thus constitute the three persons. That there are these real relations in God he concluded from the Biblical and dogmatic fact that there are in God two real processions, generation and spiration, for 'when something proceeds from a principle of the same nature then both the one proceeding and the one from whom he proceeds communicate in the same order and have real relations to each other' (ST 1a, 28.1). But 'as in God there is a real relation, there must also be a real opposition. But the very nature of relative opposition includes distinction. Hence there must be real distinction in God, not indeed according to what is absolute—namely, essence, in which there is supreme unity and simplicity, but according to what is relative' (ST 1a, 28.3). Thus paternity and filiation 'import opposite relations and therefore are distinguished from each other' (ST 1a, 28.3 ad 1). When he applies this same reasoning to 'procession' it becomes manifest that it is really distinguished from paternity and filiation. Thus there are three real relations in God that are really distinct from one another but really identified with the one simple divine essence.

This brings Thomas face to face with a fundamental trinitarian objection that 'things identified with the same things are identified with one another.' He answers briefly that this argument 'holds if they are really and logically identified . . . but not if they differ logically' (*ratione*) (ST 1a, 28.3 ad 1). In God the really distinct relations are identified with the same essence really but not logically since they differ in concept, for as relations they denote a respect to another which essence does not say. Hence it does not follow from this principle of identity that they are really identified with one another. This rather tenuous answer can seem to be only an exercise of verbal or conceptual gymnastics and yet according to his principles and logic it is quite correct. For to affirm identity of two things with a third under one aspect, is not to affirm identity under every aspect. Some Thomists will try to bolster this distinction by the example of an equilateral triangle in which 'the three equal angles are actually the same as a fourth, namely, the surface of the triangle, but are really distinguished from each other because of relative opposition.'[11] Many theologians will find it extremely difficult to conceive how such really distinct relations can exist in an absolutely simple being, or how they can fail to involve limitation or defect in the opposed relation. What seems evident is that this abstruse doctrine of divine relations will help little to feed a simple believer's faith and love of the Triune God. But it can be of great help to one who is intent on showing a rationalist that he simply cannot demonstrate that the Trinity involves an open contradiction.

Next Thomas turns to the divine persons. Boethius had defined a person as 'an individual substance of a rational nature,' Richard of St. Victor as 'an incommunicable existence of a rational nature.' Somewhat surprisingly Thomas accepts Boethius's definition, but when he finishes qualifying all the words of the definition (ST 1a, 29.1) it can seem that he has corrected rather than approved it. But in another treatise he wrote that a divine person 'is nothing else than a relationally distinct subsistent in the divine essence,' or still more simply, 'a divine person signifies a distinct subsistent in the divine nature' (*De pot*. 9.4). And if this is broadened so that it becomes 'a distinct subsistent in an intellectual nature,' it is the best definition of person that has been produced so far. It is easy to see in it the three essential ontological notes of a person, incommunicability, substantiality, intellectuality. To the objection that the term *person* is not found in Scripture he answers that 'what the term signifies is found to be affirmed of God in many places of Scripture' (ST 1a 29.3 ad 1). To the question what does *person* signify when applied to God, he answers: 'person in any nature signifies what is distinct in that nature . . . and distinction in God is only by relation of origin . . . therefore a divine person signifies a relation as subsisting' (ST 1a, 29.4). To Thomas this is the logical, inevitable, ultimate answer. To someone who is convinced that a person is essentially a distinct center of consciousness, this answer that Thomas gives must seem very unsatisfactory.

The divine missions, for Thomas, turn on the divine processions. A divine mission involves two elements on the part of a divine person, a procession of origin and a new way of existing (ST 1a, 43). It is not 'a sending by command or counsel,' it is 'according to equality,' it involves no separation, it is only 'the procession of origin from the sender' and 'a new way of existing in another' (ST 1a, 43.1), that 'does not come from a change in the divine person, but from a change in the creature' (ST 1a, 43.2 ad 2). Since 'the Father is not from another, it is in no way fitting for Him to be sent, but only for the Son and the Holy Spirit' (ST 1a, 43.4). But 'the Father gives Himself in that He freely bestows Himself to be enjoyed by the creature' (ST 1a, 43.4 ad 1). The Son 'is said to be sent by the Father into the world, inasmuch as He began to exist visibly in the world by taking our nature; whereas He was previously in the world' (ST 1a, 43.1). The Holy Spirit 'is said to be sent visibly, inasmuch as He showed Himself in certain creatures as in signs especially made for that purpose' (ST 1a 43.7 ad 2). To the Holy Spirit, who proceeds as Love, 'it belongs to be the gift of sanctification, but to the Son, as the principle of the Holy Spirit, it belongs to be the author of this sanctification. Thus the Son has been sent visibly as the author of sanctification, the Holy Spirit as the sign of sanctification' (ST 1a, 43.7).

Since 'it pertains both to the Son and to the Holy Spirit to dwell in the soul by grace and to be from another, it therefore pertains to both of them to be invisibly sent. As regards the Father, though he dwells in us by grace, still it does not pertain to Him to be from another and consequently it does not pertain to Him to be sent' (ST 1a, 43.5). The created condition for an invisible mission is grace, for 'the soul is made like to God by grace. Hence for a divine person to be sent to anyone by grace, there must needs be a likening of the soul to the divine person who is sent, by some gift of grace. Because the Holy Spirit is Love, the soul is assimilated to the Holy Spirit by the gift of charity. But the Son is the Word . . . that breathes forth Love. . . . Thus the Son is sent not in accordance with every and any kind of intellectual perfection, but according to the intellectual formation or illumination which breaks forth into the affection of love' (ST 1a, 43.5 ad 2). Why is sanctifying grace necessary for an invisible mission? Because 'no other effect can be put down as the reason why the divine person is in the rational creature in a new way except sanctifying grace' (ST 1a, 43.3). Only according to this gift is God present not only 'in a universal way by His essence, power and presence' but in a special way 'as the object known is in the knower and the beloved in the lover' so that 'God is said not only to exist in the rational creature but also to dwell therein as in His own temple' (*ibid.*) 'Only according to sanctifying grace' can man have 'the power of enjoying the divine person' (*ibid.*), for 'by the gift of sanctifying grace the rational creature is perfected so that it can both freely use the created gift itself and also enjoy the divine person Himself' (ST 1a, 43.3 ad 1).

That Thomas produced the most perfect metaphysical synthesis of trinitarian doctrine that had appeared thus far is beyond doubt. He achieved 'a genuine system worked into a consistent whole by a great dominating principle, the doctrine of God, to which everything was made tributary and in the light of which all things were viewed.'[12] Some of his doctrine met violent opposition and was even condemned for a time. But his canonization in 1323 put an end to the first great onslaught against his teaching. Gradually all his fellow Dominicans closed ranks behind him. Gradually the power and harmony of his trinitarian doctrine won over more and more theologians and ecclesiastics until it almost became the official doctrine of the Church. Today it is in eclipse and is being widely criticized as irrelevant to the needs and mentality of today. How long it will be before the sun of appreciation shines again on this magnificent achievement it is hard to say, but shine it will.

ALEXANDER OF HALES

Alexander of Hales (d. 1245) was 'the first great theologian of the Franciscan order,'[13] a teacher of St. Bonaventure, and the 'fountainhead . . . of the Franciscan school of thought.'[14] Many works have been attributed to him that were not his. It has been affirmed that he wrote no *Commentary on the Sentences*, but it has been established[15] that he did write such a commentary, a *Glossa in 4 libros sententiarum.*[16] For a long time Alexander's authorship of a *Summa theologica*[17] was generally accepted. Then his authorship was called into question and even denied.[18] However in an impressive study of the matter, P. V. Doucet concluded that 'Alexander himself somehow produced the *Summa* but with the collaboration of others, and mostly from his own writings though also from others.'[19] Hence, although the *Summa* is thus not the work of Alexander alone, it seems clear that its trinitarian doctrine in Book I represents the teaching of 'the 13th century Franciscan school of theology at the University of Paris,'[20] and to a very considerable extent not only the thought but even the words of Alexander himself. This Franciscan trinitarian doctrine is noteworthy for its contrast to that of the Dominicans.

What is most notable is the synthesis of the divine processions in terms of the principle, *bonum est diffusivum sui*. Hales makes it clear that this principle is fundamental to his whole system, when he declares that the diffusion of divine goodness is twofold: 'personal, by which one person diffuses himself in the procession of another . . . and essential . . . in the communication of divine goodness to creatures' (ST 1 n.330 ad 4). 'On the part of divine goodness,' he says, 'there is intrinsic influence of goodness in the eternal emanation of the Son from the Father and of the Holy Spirit from the Father and the Son . . . and there is extrinsic influence as in the emanation of creatures from the Creator' (*ibid*. n.64 ad 4). This fundamental principle is the reason not only of the divine processions but also of the trinity of persons: 'the nature of supreme goodness demands that there be one person in which there is the term of diffusion, as there is one which is the principle of diffusion and a third which is the quasi medium of diffusion' (*ibid*. n.319 ad 4).

Revelation and tradition tell him that there is generation in God and that the second person is truly Son. But what does it mean 'to generate'? He answers simply that 'to generate is to give to another the nature one has' (*ibid*. n.297 ad 25), and that this 'communication of good . . . by way of nature . . . is generation' (*ibid*. n.319 Sol.). But he qualifies this by saying that 'generation is the univocal production of one like in nature from the whole substance according to the principal mode,' i.e. so that the one produced 'has the power and property of producing another from himself' (*ibid*. n.296 Sol.).

Revelation and tradition say also that there is a second procession in God and that it is not generation. Why not? Hales turns again to his basic principle of diffusive good: 'goodness communicates itself either by way of nature' and thus there is 'the generation of the Son by way of intelligence from the mind,' or by way of will or affection,' and thus there is the 'spiration of love' or 'the procession of the Holy Spirit by way of love' from the Father and the Son' (*ibid*. n.317 Sol.; n.306). In 'this production by way of will a consort is required for it to be joyful and delectable,' and 'so the production of the Holy Spirit necessarily requires that it be not from one alone, but from more than one by reason of the flow of charity from one to the other, which is the perfection of will' (*ibid* n.324 ad 3). Since 'in God there is perfect charity, there are necessarily three persons and not more,' for 'where there is perfect charity, there is dilection and condilection . . . and in this condilection there is . . . the Holy Spirit who is love loved, if I may so speak' (*ibid.* n.317 ad 1).

It has been said that 'no scholastic that I know of, so clearly establishes the distinction between the two notions of *quis habens* and *quid habitum*, i.e. between the person possessing and the nature possessed,'[21] Thus Hales writes, 'when I say the person of the Father, I say one having divine being not from another. . . . When I say Son, I say one having the same divine being from another through generation. . . . When I say . . . Holy Spirit, I say one having the same divine being from others, namely the Father and the Son through procession' (*ibid.* n.312 Sol.). What makes a 'distinction of persons in the divine being' is 'difference of relation or of mode of existing . . . by reason of origin' (*ibid.* ad 1). But where other Western theologians stressed the opposition-aspect of these relations, Hales emphasized the unitive and connective aspect of these relations, their liaison-aspect, for paternity, filiation, procession not only distinguished Father, Son, and Holy Spirit they also connected them and brought it about that 'in the supreme Trinity there was supreme *germanitas* and connection' (*ibid.* n.319 Sol; cf. nn.320–327). Some later theologians, both Latin and Orthodox, will adopt his point of view.

Alexander thus laid the foundations of 'Franciscan' theology, which greater Franciscans, Bonaventure and Duns Scotus, would develop and perfect, so that in many respects it would compare favorably with that of the Dominicans, and in some perhaps even excel it.

BONAVENTURE

Bonaventure (d. 1274), the 'Second Founder' of the Franciscans,[22] constructed a theological edifice that in many ways rivalled that of Aquinas. He has been praised by some, blamed by others for his Platonism and Augustinism. The most important source of his trinitarian doctrine is his *Commentaries on the 4 Books of Sentences*,[23] but he also treats the Trinity in his *Breviloquium*,[24] and in his *Itinerarium mentis ad Deum*.[25] His *Breviloquium* has been termed an almost incomparable 'exposition of all that is vital and significant in the Christian faith.'[26]

Bonaventure like Aquinas holds that the Trinity 'of persons in the unity of essence cannot be naturally known through creatures, for this is proper to the divine nature alone, and its like neither is

nor can be found in creatures, nor can it be rationally excogitated.
. . . So the philosophers never knew it' (*In sent*. 1, d.3, p.1, a.1,
q.4).

But faith tells us there is a plurality of persons in God. And
reason gives us a confirmatory argumentation based on the divine
simplicity, primacy, perfection, and beatitude. For 'by reason of its
simplicity the essence is communicable and able to be in several, by
reason of primacy a person is fit to produce from itself another, and
I call this primacy innascibility, and by reason of it . . . there is in the
Father a fontal plenitude for all emanations. . . . By reason of perfection he is apt and prompt for this and by reason of beatitude and
charity he is willing' (*In sent*. 1, d.2, a.1, q.2). 'And this plurality . . .
is not repugnant to simplicity but rather to solitude' (*ibid*. ad 3).

An interesting development of this argument leads to the conclusion that in God there are only three persons. In God there must be
'beatitude, perfection, simplicity, primacy. . . . If there is supreme
beatitude, then supreme concord, supreme germanity and supreme
charity. But if there were more than three persons there would not
be supreme germanity, if less not supreme charity' (*In sent*. 1, d.2,
a.1, q.4). If there is 'supreme perfection then the producing person
produces perfectly both as regards the mode of producing and the
one produced. But there are only two noble modes of producing, for
every agent either acts by way of nature or by way of will (Aristotle,
Phys. II. 6). . . . And the person produced by either of these two
ways is most perfect. But if everything beyond perfection is super-
fluous and everything less than perfection is defective, it is necessary
that there be only two emanating persons . . . and one from whom
they emanate and therefore only three persons' (*ibid*.). 'The reason
. . . why there cannot be fewer than three persons is supreme beatitude and supreme perfection. For supreme beatitude demands
dilection and condilection. Supreme perfection demands a twofold
emanation. . . of nature and of liberality, and for this at least three
persons are required' (*ibid*.). 'The reason . . . why there cannot be
more than three persons is supreme simplicity, which does not permit persons to be distinguished except according to modes of emanating; and principal fecundity which does not permit a person to
produce by some kind of emanation unless he is intelligibly prior to
this. Hence because the first person is innascible and unspirable he
generates and spirates; because the second person is unspirable but
generated he does not generate but he does spirate; because the third
person is spirated and proceeds from the one who generates he
neither generates nor spirates. And so it is impossible that there be
more than three persons' (*ibid*.).

If there are 'only two noble modes of producing' in God, one by way of nature, one by way of will, can reason give reasons why one of these should be generation? Bonaventure thinks so: 'I believe,' he says, that 'the most powerful reason' for putting generation in God is that 'every nature is communicable, and there is in God an aptitude for this by reason of His nobility . . . so that His nature must needs be communicated to several. But there cannot be several from one nature unless one of these is from the other or both are from a third. Since, however, before the divine persons there is nothing, one must be from the other. And since they are conformed in nature and generation is emanation according to conformity of nature, I believe that it is necessary to put generation in God' (*In sent*. 1, d.9 a.1, q.1). And in God alone where there is 'substance having supreme simplicity' can there be 'generation of absolute perfection' which communicates 'the same substance in its entirety,' and in which the supposit 'does not add to the essence . . . nor limit it nor multiply the form' (*ibid*.).

If the second person is Son, is He also Word? In God, Bonaventure says, 'to speak' is 'to conceive by understanding' and thus 'to generate an offspring like Himself, and to this "speaking" there corresponds a Word that is born . . . an eternal Word' (*In sent*. 1, d.27, p.2, a.1, q.1). To 'speak the Word' belongs only to the Father, not to the Son nor Holy Spirit because 'although they understand themselves, they do not conceive an offspring since generative fecundity is not in them' (*ibid*. ad 4).

Long ago Augustine had written *eo Filius quo Verbum et eo Verbum quo Filius*, a formula that fascinated theologians down the centuries. Son because Word and Word because Son, that is the way Augustine wrote it. Thomas chose the first part, Son because Word, and said that the first person's act of understanding terminates in a Word that has the characteristics of a Son, and so by producing this Word He generated a Son. Bonaventure takes the second part, Word because Son, since 'the word is nothing else than a likeness expressed and expressive, conceived by the force of intelligence contemplating itself' and thus this word *presupposes* 'knowledge and generation and image: knowledge in the intelligence that contemplates, generation in the interior conception, image in the total likeness to the object contemplated, and to all of this it adds the notion of expression' (*ibid*. q.3).

Faith tells Bonaventure that the Holy Spirit proceeds from the Father and the Son and that He is not Son nor is His procession generation. And reason tells him that of the 'two noble modes of producing' in God, the second is by way of will. And if production

by way of nature is generation, the production that is not by
way of nature is not generation. For in God generation is not
simply 'the production of a similar substance . . . but production by
way of fecundity of nature' (1, d.13, a.1, q.2), and 'this condition is
lacking in the production of the Holy Spirit' (*ibid.*), since he proceeds
by way of fecundity of will and not by way of fecundity of nature.
Must this person who proceeds by way of will also proceed by way
of love?

> This person must proceed by way of love. . . . For an emanation
> by way of love . . . is the first and noblest . . . emanation by way
> of will. . . . For the affection of love is the first among all affec-
> tions and the root of all the others, as Augustine shows (*Civ.*
> 14.7). And that affection is the noblest of all since it holds more
> of the element of liberality. This is the gift in which all other
> gifts are given. . . . There is nothing in creatures that is considered
> so delicious as mutual love and without love there are no de-
> lights. . . . If there is, therefore, emanation by way of liberality
> in God, this must be first and supreme and so by way of love
> (*ibid.* q.2).

Since 'love has the perfection of delight and union and rectitude
from mutuality . . . the person proceeding by way of love must proceed by way of mutual love' (*ibid.* q.3).

Like the Master of the Sentences on whom he is commenting,
Bonaventure accepts Boethius' definition of person (*In sent.* 1, d.25,
a.1, q.2). Like his other master, Alexander of Hales, he stresses that
nature is 'possessed' while person is the 'possessor': in God there is
'nature and one having the nature. And the nature we call substance
or essence and the one having the nature we call person. . . . And because there is only one nature that is had, so there is said to be only
one substance and essence; but because several have it, there are
several persons, without any repugnance whatever' (*In sent.* 1, d.23,
a.2, q.2). Since there are several distinct persons there must be something that distinguishes them 'and this we call property' (*In sent.* 1,
d.26, a.1, q.1). But 'the personal properties are respective, not
absolute' (*ibid.* ad 3) and necessarily are 'relations' (*ibid.* q.2), both
because they are incommunicable and pertain to only one and
because they really differ' (*ibid.*). He notes that a 'relative property
can import . . . both relation and origin' (*ibid.* q.3) and adds that in
God these properties not only manifest distinction but also distinguish the persons. Do they also constitute the persons? And if they
do, do they constitute them inasmuch as they are relations or
inasmuch as they are origins? Sometimes he seems to say that these

relations constitute the persons (*In sent.* 1, d.26, a.1, q.3; d.27, p.1, a.1, q.2), sometimes that they only manifest persons already constituted by origins (*ibid.*).[27]

In his *Itinerarium Mentis in Deum* Bonaventure gives a lofty discourse 'on contemplating God's Trinity in His Name "Goodness" ' (6.49–52):

As pure being is the root and basis for the contemplation of God's essential oneness . . . so pure goodness is the absolutely first foundation for the contemplation of the divine emanations. . . . Good is said to be self-diffusive and therefore the highest good is that which diffuses itself the most. But diffusion cannot stand as the highest unless it is intrinsic yet actual, substantial yet personal, essential yet voluntary, necessary yet free, perfect yet incessant. Thus in the supreme good there must be from all eternity an actual and consubstantial producing, the producing of a hypostasis as noble as the One who produces by way of both generation and spiration. . . . And thus there is the producing of One beloved and One co-beloved, of One generated and One spirated. So there are the Father, the Son and the Holy Spirit. . . . If then you are able to behold with your mental vision this pure goodness . . . such pure goodness . . . is a diffusion by way of the Word in whom all things are expressed and by way of the Gift by whom all other gifts are given.

Should you then be able to see with the eyes of your mind this pure goodness, you can also see that its supreme communicability necessarily postulates the Trinity of Father, Son, and Holy Spirit. Since goodness is supreme in them, so must communicability be; since communicability is supreme, so must consubstantiality be; since consubstantiality is supreme, so must likeness be, which necessitates supreme coequality and this in turn supreme coeternity; while all the above attributes together necessitate supreme mutual indwelling, with each person existing necessarily in the others by supreme circumincession and each acting with the others in utter indivision of substance, power, and operation in this most blessed Trinity.

But—beware of thinking that you comprehend the incomprehensible, for concerning these six attributes there are other things to be considered that will lead our mental vision to the heights of rapt admiration. Here indeed is supreme communicability together with individuality of persons; supreme consubstantiality with hypostatic plurality; supreme likeness with distinct personality; supreme coequality with orderly origin; supreme coeternity with emanation; supreme indwelling with emission. Who would not be lifted up in wonder on beholding such marvels? Yet if we raise our eyes to the supremely excellent goodness, we can understand with complete certainty that all this is to be found in the most blessed Trinity.

In many respects the Thomistic and the Bonaventuran syntheses agree but they differ notably in others. Thomas looks at the divine nature and sees there only two productive operations and hence only two processions. The first is by way of intellect and terminates in a Word, and because it is a formally assimilative operation it is generation and the Word is Son. The second is by way of will and terminates in a Spirit of Love, but because it is not a formally assimilative but rather an impulsive operation it is not generation and the Spirit is not a Son. Bonaventure sees in God only two noble modes of producing and hence only two processions. The first, by way of nature, is the production of one like in substance by way of fecundity of nature, and thus it is the generation of a Son who is the Word. The second, by way of will, is the production of a person who proceeds by way of mutual love, but because this production is by way of fecundity of will and not by way of fecundity of nature it is not generation and the person who proceeds is not a Son but a Spirit of Love. Thomas saw in God only two productive operations, one by way of intellect that is generation, the other by way of will that is spiration, and thus there are only three persons, Father, Son and Holy Spirit, constituted by the three distinct subsistent relations of paternity, filiation, and passive spiration. Bonaventure saw in God only two noble modes of producing, one by way of nature that is generation, one by way of will that is spiration, and thus there are only three persons, Father, Son, and Holy Spirit, constituted, it seems by their origins and distinguished by their originative relations.

It must be admitted, however, that we do not find in Bonaventure the clear-cut definition of generation and the clear-cut differentiation of generation and procession that we find in Aquinas, and in other matters we look in vain for the precision that is so characteristic of Thomas. Yet there is no doubt that Bonaventure's trinitarian contribution is very important, even though it was soon overshadowed by the greater contribution of Aquinas. And today when there is widespread dissatisfaction with the Thomistic presentation and an urgent need for a more relevant and intelligible trinitarian doctrine, it would be a mistake not to reconsider the more dynamic presentation of Bonaventure and not to study its potential value for our times.

THE SECOND COUNCIL OF LYONS

The Second Council of Lyons was opened by Pope Gregory X in May, 1274. Thomas Aquinas died on his way to this council on March 7th. Bonaventure died on July 14th while he was taking an important part in this council. Thus in one year we had the convocation of one of the great trinitarian councils and the death of two of the greatest of trinitarian theologians.

This General Council was a Reunion Council. The pope convoked it, presided over it, approved it.[28] In the first session on May 7th the pope set forth the purpose of the Council, to succour the Holy Land, to reunite Greeks and Latins, to reform morals. On June 24th the Greek delegation arrived, headed by the Patriarch of Constantinople and two high officers of the court of Michael Palaeologus.[29] In the fourth session on July 6th the reunion was accomplished. In the sixth and last session on July 17th, the pope expressed his satisfaction with what had transpired and declared his intention to finish the work the Council had not had time to accomplish and to publish a list of Constitutions. On November 1st he published a list of 31 Constitutions.[30] Of particular importance for trinitarian doctrine are the Constitution on the Procession of the Holy Spirit and the Profession of Faith of Michael Palaeologus, the Emperor.

Michael's Profession of Faith was read at the 4th session (Denz Introd. 850). With regard to the Trinity it declared:

> We believe in the Holy Trinity, Father, Son and Holy Spirit, one omnipotent God and deity entire in the Trinity; coessential, consubstantial, coeternal and co-omnipotent, of one will, power, and majesty, the creator of all creatures. . . . We believe that each single person in the Trinity is the one true God complete and perfect. . . . We believe in the Son of God, the Word of God, eternally born of the Father, consubstantial, co-omnipotent and entirely equal to the Father in divinity . . . And we believe in the Holy Spirit, complete, perfect, and true God, proceeding from the Father and from the Son, coequal, consubstantial, co-omnipotent and coeternal with the Father and the Son in all things. We believe that this Trinity is not three gods but one God, omnipotent, eternal, invisible and unchanging (Denz 851, 852, 853).

The Constitution on the Procession of the Holy Spirit reads:

> with faithful and devout profession we confess that the Holy Spirit proceeds eternally from the Father and the Son, not as from

two principles but as from one, not by two spirations but by one. This is what the holy Roman Church, the mother and teacher of all the faithful has hitherto professed, preached, and taught, this is what it holds, preaches, professes, and teaches. This is what the unchangeable and true judgment of the orthodox Fathers and Doctors, Latin and Greek equally, maintains. But because there are some men who through ignorance of this unshatterable truth have fallen into various errors, we desire to close the road to these errors and so with the approval of the holy council we condemn and reprobate those who presume to deny that the Holy Spirit proceeds eternally from the Father and the Son or those who rashly dare to assert that the Holy Spirit proceeds from the Father and the Son as from two principles and not as from one (Denz 850).

Thus Lyons II clearly goes beyond Lateran IV in its explicit profession of belief concerning the procession of the Holy Spirit. Lateran IV had merely said that 'the Holy Spirit is from both the Father and the Son equally (Denz 800) and that 'the Holy Spirit proceeds from both' (Denz 805). Lyons II, however, besides explicitly affirming the *filioque* makes important affirmations about the second procession. Thus it declares its belief that the Holy Spirit proceeds from the Father and the Son (1) not as from two principles but as from one, and (2) not by two spirations but by one. It further maintains that (1) this is what the holy Roman Church has hitherto professed and now professes, and that (2) this is what the true and unchangeable judgment of both Greek and Latin Fathers and Doctors maintains. And therefore it condemns (1) those who presume to deny the *Filioque* and (2) those who rashly dare to assert that the Holy Spirit proceeds from the Father and the Son as from two principles and not as from one, by two spirations and not by one. Here lies the trinitarian importance of this council. For it not only defines the procession of the Holy Spirit from the Father and the Son as from one principle and by one spiration, but it declares that this has always been the teaching of the Roman Church and of both Greek and Latin orthodox Fathers and Doctors. In the estimate of the pope and the conciliar Fathers this is the traditional doctrine of both East and West now solemnly presented for acceptance and belief by the entire Church of West and East.

One point about this Constitution (Denz 850) is still obscure. A few historians have held that this Constitution was promulgated by the Council after the arrival of the Greek delegation and in its presence and with its consent.[31] If they are correct, there is no problem. But most historians maintain that it was promulgated by the

council before the Greeks arrived.[32] This seems to be more probable
and it raises the question as to just how this Constitution was presented to the Greeks and just what was their response. There is no
definite historical answer to this question. But since there is no
record that the Greeks objected to it, it seems proper enough to
infer that they accepted it. There are testimonies also that the Greek
ambassadors on their arrival presented letters of adherence to the
articles of faith, that Georges Acropolita in the name of Michael
Palaeologus professed the faith of the Roman Church, and that when
the Pope chanted the *Filioque* in the Creed the Greeks repeated the
Filioque in their own language.[33] Furthermore there is evidence that
what was done at Lyons II was ratified later in the East in the presence of legates of the Holy See and that Michael publicly accepted
the Roman profession of faith and the primacy of Rome, even
though much of the Eastern clergy did not accept the addition of the
Filoque to the Symbol. [34]

Just why this Constitution should have been promulgated before
the arrival of the Greek delegation is not clear. Perhaps the conciliar
Fathers thought that by condemning not only the Greek error about
the *Filioque* but also the error of some Latins about two principles
and two spirations they would show the Greeks they were not an
acceptor personarum and thus make the Constitution more acceptable to them.[35]

In any event this Council ranks as a great trinitarian council
since it made several explicit dogmatic additions to Pneumatology
that would be formally accepted by both Greeks and Latins in the
Reunion Council of Florence (Denz 1300). With this Council we
reach the dogmatic high point of the 13th century.

CHAPTER TWELVE

From Scotus
to the Council of Florence

SCOTUS

Duns Scotus (d. 1308), became the official doctor of the Franciscans. Often called the 'Doctor Subtilis,' he produced a trinitarian synthesis of the teachings of Hales and Bonaventure within which Aristotelian theories play a large part. His chief work is his great *Commentary on the Sentences*, composed at Oxford.[1]

For Scotus, as for Hales and Bonaventure, there are only two processions in God because there are only two ways of producing, the way of nature and the way of will. These two are distinct because 'they have opposite ways of principiating,' i.e., 'determinately by way of nature,' and 'not determinately but freely' (*Oxon.* 1, d.2, q.7, n.18). The first productive principle is constituted by the divine essence as knowable object and by the divine intellect as knowing power and is called *memory*. This memory has two aspects, an operative and a productive aspect. In its operative aspect it operates intellection and is common to the three for all three have infinite intellection. In its productive aspect it produces diction and is proper to the Father, for only He 'says' or produces the Word. Hence it is dictive memory in the Father that is the productive principle of the Word (*Oxon.* 2, d.1, q.1, n.9, 13).[2] The second productive principle is constituted by the divine essence as lovable object and by the divine will as loving power. This will also has an operative and a productive aspect. In its operative aspect it operates dilection and is common to the three for all three have infinite dilection. In its productive aspect it produces an infinite Love and is proper to the Father and the Son because only these two spirate the Holy Spirit.

221

Hence it is spirative will in the Father and Son that is the productive principle of the Holy Spirit (*ibid.*).

For Scotus, as for Hales and Bonaventure, the production of the Word is generation because it is a natural production, a production by way of 'natural inclination,' and a communication of essence by 'way of nature' (*Oxon.* 1, d.13, n.20). Where Aquinas said the Word is Son because the diction of the Word is a formally assimilative operation, Scotus says the Word is Son because the diction of the Word is a natural production, a production by way of nature.

In spirating the Holy Spirit the Father and the Son 'are one principle of the Holy Spirit' (*Oxon.* 1, d.12, q.1, n.2). But 'the Father does not spirate the Holy Spirit inasmuch as He loves the Son first, nor the Son inasmuch as He loves the Father, but Father and Son [spirate] inasmuch as they have the divine essence present as the first object of the will . . . lovable . . . but not loved' (*ibid.* n.7). The spiration of the Holy Spirit is not generation because it is not a production by way of nature but by way of will, and it is both necessary and free' (*Oxon.* 1, d.2, q.7, n.18).

Scotus accepts Richard of St. Victor's definition of person, 'an incommunicable existence of an intellectual nature,' but he insists that the word 'incommunicable' negates all communicability, and hence 'a divine person not only involves a negation of actual and aptitudinal communication but also a repugnance to communication *ut quod* (as human nature is communicated to Peter and Paul) and *ut quo* (as in the human nature of Christ). But such a repugnance cannot be had except through a positive entity, and so it follows that a divine person is never without such an entity' (*Oxon.* 3, d.1, q.1, n.10).[3] The divine persons are distinguished by relative properties (*Oxon.* 1, d.26, q.1, n.4, 5, 37) and are constituted by relations as relations (*Oxon.* 1, d.26; 1, d.2, q.7; q.4 quodlib., n.4), so that the whole supposit of persons consists of essence and relation. But unlike the Thomists Scotus maintains that there are in God real relations not only of paternity, filiation, active and passive spiration, but also of identity, equality, and likeness (*Oxon.* 1, d.31, q.1).

Thomists maintained that only opposed relations distinguished divine persons, and hence if the Holy Spirit did not proceed from the Son He would not be really distinct from the Son. Against them Scotus insisted that not only opposite relations (as paternity and filiation) but also disparate relations (as passive generation and active spiration) distinguished divine persons (*Oxon.* 1, d.11, q.2, n.9). And so he vigorously affirmed that even if the Holy Spirit did not proceed from the Son, the two would still be really distinct both by their constitution and by their procession (*ibid.* n.6).

Scotus produced a powerful trinitarian synthesis that would perdure down the centuries and win for him numerous and devoted
followers and opponents. And if our age produces a new trinitarian synthesis it will not be surprising to find included in it many
trinitarian insights derived from Scotism as well as from Thomism.

William of Ockham (d. *c.* 1349) is considered 'the central figure of a
new movement, known as the school of the nominalists.'[4] 'His
positions,' it has been said, 'had been well prepared . . . and it remained for him to weld them into a devastating unity which, for
sheer destructive capacity, was unequalled during the thousand years
we have been examining. Yet . . . there was also much in Ockham's
thought that was positive and of great importance for the future.'[5]
He was an English Franciscan who taught at Oxford, was accused of
heresy, had 51 of his propositions censured by a papal commission
as heretical or erroneous,[6] and was excommunicated by Pope John
XXII.

In his chief theological work, his *Commentary on the Sentences*[7]
he put his 'razor' to work trimming away what he considered un-
justified multiplication of entities, distinctions, formalities. He
stressed reason and yet drastically limited its ability to know God
and things divine. Reason cannot say that God is one and infinite
(*Sent.* 1, d.3, q.2, M).[8] Reason left to itself 'would say that in God
there cannot be three persons with unity of nature' (*Sent.* 1, d.30,
q.1, B). Why, then, hold a trinity of persons in God and not in creatures? 'Because one is expressed in Scripture, and the other is not'
(*Sent.* 1, d.2, q.1, F). Are there real distinctions in God? Reason left
to itself would say no, 'because if essence and relation and person
are simply one thing indistinct in number, it is difficult to see how
there are several relations and several persons and yet not several
essences' (*Sent.* 1, d.2, q.11, B). But what if reason were to say that
something is false? 'I consider it to be dangerous . . . to force anyone
. . . to believe something which his reason dictates to him to be false,
unless it can be drawn from Holy Scripture or from a determination
of the Roman Church or from the words of approved doctors' (*De
corp. Christi*, ed. Birch, p. 126, 18–23).

Scotus had relied heavily on his formal distinction. Ockham
denied this distinction for creatures (*Sent.* 1, d.2, q.6, E) and between
divine attributes (*Sent.* 1, d.2, q.1, F). But he admitted it for the
Trinity and added: 'to say that the essence and the three persons are
distinguished formally . . . is not to say anything else than that the

essence is three persons and a person is not three persons' (*Summa Logicae*, p.2, c.2). Scotus had held that the Holy Spirit would still be distinct from the Son even if He did not proceed from the Son. This too Ockham denied, on the ground that if 'the Holy Spirit does not proceed from the Son, active spiration is not in the Son and therefore filiation is not in the Son, and hence the Son is not really distinguished from the Holy Spirit' (*Sent.* 1, d.11, q.2).

It is not too surprising then to hear it said of Ockham that 'in things divine he is both fideist and sceptic, placing all theological certainty in the tenets of faith and none in reason's power to elicit them.'[9] By putting such a deep opposition and gulf between reason and faith he made it impossible to show that the Trinity was in accord with reason and powerfully helped to shatter 'the already trembling fabric raised by the Christian Aristotelians.'

THE COUNCIL OF FLORENCE

The Council of Florence (1438–1445), an ecumenical and reunion council, was convoked by Pope Eugene IV 'for the purpose of restoring unity with the Greeks.'[10] 'The Patriarchs of Alexandria, Antioch, and Jerusalem sent envoys, and Isidore, Metropolitan of Moscow, acted in the name of the Russian Church.'[11] The Emperor came 'not only to achieve a religious reunion of East and West but also to gain Western aid against the new Mohammedan threat to Constantinople.'[12]

The main points on which the Latins and the Greeks were divided were Purgatory, the *Filioque*, the use of unleavened bread in the Eucharist, and the primacy of the pope. After a two-months' debate on Purgatory 'the Greeks agreed that what the Latins taught was what they too believed.'[13] Discussion of papal primacy took little more than a week. The debate on the *Filioque* 'was the most lengthy of the council's tasks.'[14]

In the *Filioque* discussions Mark Eugenicus of Ephesus was the protagonist of the Greeks. He argued that St. John, St. Paul, and Athanasius testified that the Holy Spirit proceeds from the Father alone. So did the Second Council, and the Third agreed with it and forbade any addition.[15] Giovanni Montenero, the Dominican Provincial of Lombardy, presented the Latin case for the *Filioque*, arguing from St. Paul and St. John, from Leo the Great and Damasus and Hormisdas, from Hilary, Jerome, Ambrose, Augustine, from Basil, Epiphanius, Didymus, Athanasius, Cyril of Alexandria.[16] It was Montenero's solid presentation of Latin and

Greek Fathers and not his 'display of metaphysical niceties' that impressed the Greeks.[17] For the Greeks saints could not err in matters of faith. But here the Latin saints were saying that the Holy Spirit proceeds 'from the Son,' while the Greek saints were saying He proceeds 'through the Son.' So they began to realize gradually that 'these two expressions must mean the same thing and no obstacle could remain to prevent union between East and West at least as regards the doctrine of the Blessed Trinity.'[18] And so on Sunday, July 5th, 1439, the Greeks (but not Mark of Ephesus) signed the decree, and the pope and 'the rest of the Latins added their signatures.'[19]

The next day the decree was solemnly promulgated:

> In the name of the Holy Trinity of the Father and Son and Holy Spirit, with the approbation of this holy general Council of Florence we define that this truth of faith be believed and accepted by all Christians, and that all likewise profess that the Holy Spirit is eternally from the Father and the Son, and has His essence and his subsistent being from the Father and Son simultaneously, and proceeds from both eternally as from one principle and one spiration; we declare that what the holy Doctors and Fathers say, namely, that the Holy Spirit proceeds from the Father through the Son, tends to this meaning, that by this is signified that the Son is also according to the Greeks the cause, and according to the Latins the principle of the subsistence of the Holy Spirit, as is the Father also. And since all things which are the Father's, the Father has given to the Son in generating Him —except to be Father—so the Son has eternally from the Father that the Holy Spirit should proceed from the Son. . . . In addition we define that the explicitation of those words *Filioque* has been lawfully and reasonably added to the Creed for the sake of declaring the truth and because of imminent necessity (Denz 1300–1302).

To a large extent this *Decree for the Greeks* merely repeated what had already been defined by Lyons II, but it also went further. For it declared (1) that the Holy Spirit has His essence and His subsistent being from the Father and the Son simultaneously, (2) that the patristic teaching that the Holy Spirit proceeds from the Father *through the Son* tends to mean that the Son as well as the Father is the cause or principle of the Holy Spirit, and thus this teaching is substantially equivalent to the *Filioque*. And when it defined that the *Filioque* had been lawfully added to the Creed for good and sufficient reasons, it made it clear to the whole Church that the

Greeks had finally agreed with the Latins on the legitimacy of this incorporation of the *Filioque* into the Creed.

Another group of Oriental Christians, the Copts of Egypt, sent representatives to the Council to discuss reunion with Rome. After 'long meetings with Cardinals Cesarini, Le Jeune and Torquemada . . . the Bull *Cantate Domino* [was] promulgated in solemn session on 4 February 1442, and accepted by the Egyptians in the name of their Patriarch and of their Church.'[20] This decree, called the *Decree for the Jacobites*, promulgated some important trinitarian doctrine. The Decree reads:

The holy Roman Church, founded by the decree of our Lord and Savior firmly believes, professes and teaches: There is one true God, all-powerful, unchangeable, and eternal, Father, Son and Holy Spirit, one in essence but three in persons. The Father is not begotten, the Son is begotten of the Father, the Holy Spirit proceeds from the Father and the Son. . . . These three persons are one God, not three gods, for the three persons have one substance, one essence, one nature, one divinity, one immensity, one eternity. And everything is one where opposition of relation does not intervene. Because of this unity the Father is entirely in the Son and entirely in the Holy Spirit; the Son is entirely in the Father and entirely in the Holy Spirit; the Holy Spirit is entirely in the Father and entirely in the Son. None of the persons precedes in eternity or exceeds in magnitude or surpasses in power any of the others. . . . Whatever the Father is or has He has not from another but from Himself, and He is principle without principle. Whatever the Son is or has, He has from the Father and He is principle from principle. Whatever the Holy Spirit is or has, He has at once from the Father and from the Son. Yet the Father and the Son are not two principles of the Holy Spirit, but one principle, just as the Father and the Son and the Holy Spirit are not three principles of creation but one principle (Denz 1330–1331).

Most all the trinitarian doctrine of this Decree has already been defined in Lateran IV or Lyons II. Three points, however, stand out more explicitly than ever before: (1) that the Father and Son are but one principle of the Holy Spirit *as* Father and Son and Holy Spirit are but one principle of creation, (2) that Father and Son and Holy Spirit mutually inexist in one another *because* of their unity of essence, (3) that in God everything is one where opposition of relation does not intervene. The third point is the most noteworthy for it represents the explicit climax of a long patristic and theological study of the root of distinction in the one simple God. Here we have the canonization of a principle enuntated by Anselm of Canterbury that 'unity does not lose its consequence unless some opposition of relation stands in the way' (PL 158, 288C). According to this principle everything in God is identical except where opposed relations (as in Father, Son, and Holy Spirit) stand in the way of identity. For only where one proceeds from the other can there be two, since only then do we have 'relations of opposition.' Where there is no such opposition of relation—as between persons and essence—there is identity so that three persons are but one essence.

Is this relational doctrine part of the definition of Florence? It has been asserted that it 'is not . . . although it is essential to its systematic exposition of the doctrine of the Holy Trinity—essential rather as the keystone than as the corner stone.[21] But it seems more correct to say that 'this part, which *is* of defined faith, expounds as it were a systematization of everything said thus far.'[22]

This Council is very important in the history of trinitarian doctrine for it will be the last General Council to concern itself with matters trinitarian. The Church's solemn formulation of its trinitarian faith, that began with Nicea I in 325, has now reached its climax in the Council of Florence in this *Decree for the Jacobites* in 1442. The work of dogmatic formulation has come to an end (unless some Post-Vatican II General Council should decide to make further trinitarian definitions). But the work of the theologian, who must study the trinitarian doctrine in its Biblical and patristic sources and in its dogmatic formulations, will go on and on—until the face-to-face vision of the Triune God brings rest to the restless mind of the pilgrim theologian.

SUMMARY OF DOGMATIC DEVELOPMENT IN THE WESTERN MAGISTERIUM

In the development of trinitarian dogma in the West two creeds, the *Quicunque*, or the 'Athanasian' and that of Toledo XI, and three ecumenical councils, Lateran IV, Lyons II, and Florence exercised the greatest influence.

Before the *Quicunque*, however, two 3d-century documents are noteworthy. One is the epistle of Pope Dionysius that condemned Sabellianism, Tritheism, and Arianism by anticipation (Denz 113). The other is the 'Tome of Damasus' that condemned Sabellian, Tritheistic, Arian, and especially Macedonian errors as heretical, and used the terms *person* and *substance* to describe the trinity and unity of the Triune God (Denz 152–180). These show that in the 3rd and 4th centuries Roman bishops felt quite competent to present the traditional trinitarian doctrine of the Church authoritatively and to condemn bluntly the errors that were opposed to it.

Sometime in the 5th-6th century the *Quicunque* appeared, an amazing credal document whose author, date, and birthplace are still in doubt. In its approach and form and terminology it is unlike the Eastern creeds. In setting forth the Catholic faith that one must keep if he wishes to be saved it used the words *trinity, unity, substance, divinity, person,* but not *relation.* It rejected Sabellianism, Arianism, Tritheism, without mentioning them explicitly. It proclaimed that one God is three distinct and coequal persons, that each of these is uncreated, immense, eternal, omnipotent, God, Lord, and yet that there is but one eternal, uncreated, omnipotent being, one God, one Lord. The Three are distinct in that the Father originates from no one, the Son is generated by the Father alone, and the Holy Spirit proceeds from the Father and the Son. The *Filioque* is simply presented as a fact and an object of faith, something that is very remarkable at this early date. Nowhere previously have we encountered such a balanced and precise summary of basic trinitarian faith. It will achieve dogmatic value in the Western Church equal to that of the Apostles' and Nicene Creeds and will be regarded as a dogmatic formula of 'divine and catholic faith.'

In the 7th century we meet the most highly developed formula of faith the West had produced so far, the Creed ascribed to the Eleventh Council of Toledo (Denz 525–541). Like the *Quicunque,* in speaking of the Triune God, it uses the words *trinity, substance, divinity, persons* and affirms the *Filioque.* Unlike the *Quicunque,* it uses the term *consubstantial* of the Son and Holy Spirit, says that Father, Son, and Holy Spirit are relative names, that the Father is 'the font and origin of the whole divinity,' that the Son is generated neither by will nor by necessity, that the Holy Spirit is sent by the Father and the Son and is the love of both. It declares that the three are distinct in terms of their personal properties and inseparable in existence, operation, and cognition. It goes far beyond the *Quicunque* in the amplitude of its trinitarian doctrine, and later some theologians of the Western Church will place it on almost the same dogmatic level as the *Quicunque.*

The Fourth Lateran Council of 1215 was the first ecumenical council to define that the Holy Spirit proceeds from both the Father and the Son and in its trinitarian declarations it went well beyond Nicea I and Constantinople I. It explicitly affirmed the consubstantiality, coeternity, coequality, and co-omnipotence of the three persons, their distinction from one another and their identity of nature, the procession of the Father from no one, of the Son from the Father alone, of the Holy Spirit from both. It indicated that in the one supreme reality that is the Triune God there is a distinction between its nature-aspect and its person-aspect so that as nature it does not generate, as Father it does, and that this distinction is neither real nor purely logical. To signify God's oneness it used the words *essence, substance, nature, reality, aliud*; to signify His three-ness it used *person* and *alius*. It explicitly rejected a quaternity in God and a merely collective unity of the three, and carefully dis-tinguished between our oneness with the divine persons by grace and their own oneness by nature. But it left to the Council of Florence the declaration that the distinction of the persons from one another is rooted in their relational opposition, and to later theo-logians the task of conceiving and expressing the transcendent dis-tinction between the one divine nature and the three divine persons that lies at the heart of the mystery of the Triune God.

The Second Council of Lyons in 1274, an ecumenical and re-union council, ranks as a great trinitarian council largely because of its explicit dogmatic affirmations about the Holy Spirit. It went beyond Lateran IV for it not only explicitly affirmed the *Filioque* but added that the Holy Spirit proceeds from the Father and Son as from one principle and by one spiration, and that this has always been the teaching of the Roman Church and the true judgment of both Greek and Latin orthodox Fathers and Doctors. Hence it con-demned those who presume to deny the *Filioque* and those who rashly dare to assert that the Holy Spirit proceeds from the Father and the Son as from two principles and by two spirations.

The Council of Florence in the 15th century, an ecumenical and reunion council, amplified the trinitarian declarations of Lateran IV and Lyons II, and became a very important trinitarian council. In its *Decree for the Greeks* (Denz 1300–1302) it declared that the Holy Spirit has His essence and His subsistent being from the Father and the Son simultaneously, and that the patristic doctrine of the procession of the Holy Spirit from the Father *through* the Son is substantially equivalent to the *Filioque*. It also defined that the *Filioque* had been lawfully added to the Creed and thus made it clear to the whole Church that the Greeks had finally agreed with the Latins on the legitimacy of this addition. In its *Decree for the Jacobites* (Denz 1330–1331) three points stand out more explicitly than ever before, that the Father and Son are but one principle of the Holy Spirit *as* Father and Son and Holy Spirit are but one prin-ciple of creation, that Father and Son and Holy Spirit mutually in-exist in one another *because* of their unity of essence, and that in God everything is one where opposition of relation does not inter-vene. This last point, which seems to be of defined faith, is extremely important for it represents the explicit climax of a long patristic and theological reflection on the root of distinction in the one simple God. According to this principle of relational opposition, where there is opposition of relation, as between Father, Son, and Holy Spirit, there is real distinction, but where there is no such opposition as between the divine persons and the divine essence, there is real identity and thus the three persons are but one essence.

With this Council the Church's solemn formulation of its trinitarian faith, that began with Nicea I, has now reached its climax. And the work of dogmatic formulation has come to an end (unless a future council should decide to take it up again).

In the development of trinitarian doctrine in the early Western Church four men stood out, Irenaeus, Tertullian, Hilary, and Augustine. Irenaeus (d. 202) refuted Gnosticism, rejected the twofold stage theory of the Logos and presented a solid doctrine of one sole God who is Father, Son, and Holy Spirit. Tertullian (d. *c.* 220) is notable both for the defects and the positive contribution of his teaching. He refuted Praxean Monarchianism but apparently accepted the twofold stage theory and subscribed to a materialistic view of the divine substance. But he went further than Irenaeus in saying explicitly that the Holy Spirit 'is God,' in using the terms *trinity* and *person* for the three, and in making affirmations about the Son that would later appear in the Nicene symbol. And he seems to have understood person in the metaphysical sense of a concrete individual or self. Hilary (d. *c.* 367), the 'Athanasius' of the West, taught the eternal generation and strict consubstantiality of the Son and sufficiently indicated his belief that the Holy Spirit was a distinct divine person. He was one of the first to attempt a true synthesis of trinitarian doctrine. But it was Augustine (d. 430) who was to dominate Western trinitarian teaching for a long time. Instead of starting, as the Greek Fathers had, from the Father considered as the source of the other two persons, he began with the one simple divine essence that is the Trinity and thus immediately eliminated Subordinationism and Tritheism. The three are absolutely equal for they have identically the same essence and will and operation, and external divine works such as creation and sanctification are common to all three and only appropriated to the Father and to the Holy Spirit. But the three are really distinct by reason of their originational relations of paternity, filiation, gift. They are three 'someones,' three relationally distinct subjects of one divine activity, three 'persons,' although Augustine did not much like the term *person*. He contributed a great deal to Pneumatology by his teaching about the Holy Spirit as Gift and Love and sanctifying Inhabitant of the just soul and by his insistence that although the Holy Spirit proceeds from the Father and the Son, yet the Father and Son are not two principles but only one principle of the Holy Spirit, as they are but one Creator and one Lord. Lyons II and Florence will later canonize this doctrine (Denz 850, 1331). Though he conceded to the Holy Spirit a special introductory role in the divine indwelling, he held that it was a trinitarian inhabitation that begins with baptismal regeneration, effects an ontological sanctity in baptized infants and a dynamic orientation aimed at making them become ever more perfect saints. Perhaps his greatest originality lay in his search for vestiges and images and analogies to the Triune God in the world of creatures in thus laying the foundations of the psychological theory of the divine processions that would reach its crest in St. Thomas. There can be no doubt that his magnificent synthesis of trinitarian doctrine laid the foundations for most all subsequent trinitarian theology in the West. But it left many questions unanswered: what is the nature of the two processions, why are there only two processions and only three persons, questions that would fascinate theologians down the years and find a rarefied metaphysical answer in Aquinas.

Between Augustine in the 5th century and Anselm in the 12th, two men stand out for their contributions to trinitarian doctrine, Boethius and Eriugena. Boethius (d. *c.* 525) was the first to use Aristotelian philosophy in the analysis, definition, and explanation of trinitarian and Christological data, and he thus laid a foundation on which Scholastics would erect their more systematic expositions. But he is best known for his definition of *person* as 'an individual substance of a rational nature,' a definition that would be widely adopted, highly praised, strongly criticized, and lead some of its adherents into heretical deviations. Eriugena (d. *c.* 877) produced a bold and original philosophical-theological synthesis that led some interpreters to charge him with pantheism, others with rationalism. Where Latin theologians usually stressed authority and used the terms *person* and *principle* in dealing with the Triune God, Eriugena stressed reason and used the words *substance* instead of *person* and *cause* instead of *principle*. Although both the *Quicunque* and the symbol of Toledo XI had affirmed the *Filioque*, Eriugena held that the Holy Spirit 'proceeds from the Father through the Son.'

In the 12th century there were many important trinitarian writers. One, Anselm of Canterbury, was one of the West's most original thinkers. Two, Abelard and Gilbert, were 'liberals' who ran afoul of Bernard, a strong 'traditionalist.' Two, Hugh and Richard of St. Victor, tried to 'demonstrate' the Trinity. Two, Lombard and Joachim, battled over a divine 'quaternity.'

Anselm used dialectics to draw out the implications of revealed truths and to show there is no contradiction between revelational and rational truths, but in his desire to find 'cogent proofs' for truths of faith he seemed to some to ascribe to reason more competence than it has. He refuted Roscelin's putative Tritheism and defended the *Filioque* by Scripture and reason. Perhaps his most important trinitarian contribution was his genetic explanation of the Trinity in terms of supreme Spirit endowed with intelligence and love, an explanation that somewhat prefigured Aquinas' psychological theory of intelligible divine emanations.

Abelard put such a strong stress on reason in matters trinitarian that he has been called a rationalist, an Arian, a Sabellian. In his earlier writings he held that the Trinity could be known by reason without the aid of revelation and that pagans had known it, but in his later works he abandoned this position. In his desire to make faith intelligible to human reason he occasionally seemed to forget that the Trinity was a strict mystery. Three of his trinitarian propositions, that do seem to deny the coequality and consubstantiality of the three divine persons, were condemned. But if heresy means not only erroneous statements but also pertinacity in these errors, Abelard probably was not a heretic. And he did stimulate theologians to be more careful in their use of patristic evidence and to discuss and explain points of theology instead of merely asserting or proving them.

Gilbert de la Porrée's trinitarian doctrine was once thought to have been condemned by the Council of Rheims and by the pope, but today it seems clear that it was condemned by neither. His accusers said he put a real distinction between God and His divinity and thus introduced a real quaternity into God. He said he did not, and even today his precise thought and intent are difficult to determine. But his doctrinal troubles indicated the need for a more accurate understanding and expression of the relation between the divine essence and persons, and thus pointed the Church toward the definitive statements of Lateran IV and Florence.

Bernard of Clairvaux is most famous in matters trinitarian for his controversies with Abelard and Gilbert. He loved the faith as it was, with all its certitude, its mystery, its traditionality, its suprarationality, and so he energetically opposed Abelard and Gilbert for their novelties and called them heretics. However proper or

improper were the judgments and actions of Bernard, Peter, and
Gilbert, their confrontation alerted the Church to the danger of an
improper use of reason in trinitarian theology and to the need of a
much better harmonization of reason and faith.

Hugh of St. Victor stands out for his attempt to develop the
analogy between the human soul and the Trinity into a 'clear demonstration' of the Trinity. Richard of St. Victor also aimed at a rational
'demonstration' of the Trinity from an analysis of charity. Augustine
had started with nature rather than person, but Richard turned
immediately to persons, and to their unselfish love for one another.
In this he felt there was a reflection of trinitarian love and life. From
a fascinating analysis of perfect charity he concluded that in God
supreme personal love must mean that there is one infinite love and
three infinite lovers. It is not a cogent proof but it is a beautiful
theory and one that has a special relevance today with our strong
stress on person and personal love.

Peter Lombard's *Books of Sentences* became the great theological handbook of the West. It took up traditional doctrines one by
one, proposed a doctrinal thesis, brought forward authorities for
and against this thesis and then gave judgment on the issue. When
Joachim of Flora attacked part of Lombard's trinitarian teaching as
Quaternianism, the Fourth Lateran Council did something 'perhaps
unique in the history of conciliar canons': it adopted Peter's doctrine and involved him by name in its solemn declaration (Denz
803). Lombard's famous pneumatological teaching that the Holy
Spirit is the love or charity by which we love God and neighbor will
be refuted by Aquinas, generally rejected by theologians, then re-
considered by some present-day theologians.

Joachim of Flora stands out for his attack on Lombard's
'Quaternianism' and for the posthumous condemnation of his
tritheistic doctrine by Lateran IV. But henceforth theologians will
face the task of showing more clearly why the traditional doctrine
of the triune God leads neither to Quaternianism, Sabellianism, nor
Tritheism. Lateran IV will help.

In the 13th century the Dominicans and Franciscans made the
greatest contribution to trinitarian systematization that the Western
Church ever had seen or would see. Four men stood out, Aquinas,
Alexander of Hales, Bonaventure, Scotus, and the greatest of these
by far was Aquinas.

Augustine had left many trinitarian questions unanswered. One
of these was: why are there two and only two processions in God?
Aquinas answered that the divine processions are grounded in
immanent actions and since there are only two of these in God,

understanding and willing, only two processions are possible, that of the Word and that of Love. Augustine had found it impossible to say why the Son is generated but the Holy Spirit is not. Thomas answered that the second Person proceeds by way of intelligible action which is a likeness-producing operation and thus is generation, but the third Person proceeds by way of dilection which is not a likeness-producing operation and hence is not generation. Augustine had not been able to give a clear-cut intrinsic reason why there are only three persons in God. Thomas suggested that there are only three persons because there are only two productive processions—of Word and Love—and only three distinct subsistent incommunicable relations, paternity, filiation, and passive spiration. Surprisingly Thomas accepted, if with many qualifications, the Boethian definition of person, but he suggested a much better one of his own: 'a distinct subsistent in an intellectual nature.' Metaphysically his definition is excellent, but it will not please one who views a person psychologically as 'a distinct center of consciousness.' There can be little doubt that Aquinas produced the finest metaphysical synthesis of trinitarian doctrine that had thus far appeared in the West or East.

The Franciscans developed a distinctive trinitarian synthesis of their own. Alexander of Hales takes as his fundamental principle, *bonum est diffusivum sui*, and uses this to explain why there are only two divine processions and only three divine persons. Thus goodness communicates itself in two ways: by way of nature, and thus there is the generation of the Son by way of intelligence; and by way of will or affection, and thus there is the procession of the Holy Spirit by way of love from the Father and the Son. Since in God there is perfect charity, there is in God dilection and condilection and in this condilection the Holy Spirit who is love loved. Thus there are three persons and only three.

Bonaventure uses much the same principle and procedure. The supreme communicability of the divine goodness postulates the producing of One generated and One spirated, and thus there is a Trinity of Father, Son, and Holy Spirit. There are only two noble modes of producing in God, by way of nature and by way of will, and thus there are only two emanating persons and one from whom they emanate. If production by way of nature is generation, then production that is not by way of nature is not generation but spiration.

Scotus substantially synthesized the trinitarian doctrines of Hales and Bonaventure but added many subtle distinctions of his own. There are only two processions because there are only two divine productive principles and only two divine ways of producing, by way of nature and by way of will. The first productive principle is constituted by the divine essence as knowable object and by the divine intellect not as operating intellection but as producing diction of the Word. The second productive principle is constituted by the divine essence as lovable object and by the divine will not as operating dilection but as producing or spirating the Holy Spirit. Because only the production of the Word is by way of nature, only this is generation. Thomists maintained that only opposed relations distinguish divine persons and accordingly if the Holy Spirit did not proceed from the Son He would not be really distinct from the Son. Scotus vigorously denied this and insisted, as the Orthodox Greeks would also insist, that even if the Holy Spirit did not proceed from the Son the two would still be really distinct by their constitution and their procession.

With Aquinas and Scotus we reach the high point of speculative trinitarian theology. Both the Thomist and the Scotist synthesis will find devoted, tenacious, and disputatious followers and perdure down the years. They will encounter intense criticism in modern times. But any new and more relevant trinitarian synthesis, if it wishes to stay in any historical continuity with traditional doctrine, will have to take into account the basic insights both of the more static Thomist synthesis and of the more dynamic Franciscan synthesis.

PART FIVE

Protestant Trinitarian Doctrine
from Luther to the Present

At the Council of Florence there was a reunion of Greeks and Latins and an agreement on trinitarian doctrine. This reunion was not very effective, not very long-lasting. In 1453 Constantinople fell to the Turks, and the great schism between the Latin and the Orthodox Churches became permanent. In the 16th century the Protestant Reformation brought about another break from the Roman Catholic Church. From then on we have three currents of ecclesial, religious, and theological life, one Protestant, one Orthodox, one Roman Catholic. It will be helpful to look at these three theological currents separately in terms of their attitudes and contributions to trinitarian doctrine. Consequently in this Part we will study the flow of trinitarian doctrine among Protestants, in Part Six among the Orthodox, and in Part Seven among Roman Catholics.

The sixteenth century witnessed the Protestant Reformation out of which came the Protestant Churches. Protestant Christianity largely began with the work of Martin Luther (1483–1546), Ulrich Zwingli (1484–1531), and John Calvin (1509–1564). Gradually it developed its own principles and practices, its own theologies, and varying attitudes toward the doctrine of the Trinity. Consequently we shall first see the trinitarian doctrine of the Reformers themselves, then of their successors in subsequent centuries, concluding with a summary of Protestant teaching on the Trinity and an indication of what it is today.

CHAPTER THIRTEEN

The Reformers

MARTIN LUTHER

Martin Luther (d. 1546) never constructed a theological system comparable to Calvin's *Institutes*, but he has exercised a tremendous influence down the centuries. His trinitarian doctrine remained largely a simple, devout expression of his belief in the traditional dogma. There were three trinitarian symbols that he loved, the Apostles' Creed, the 'Athanasian' Creed and the *Te Deum*. 'The Apostles' Creed was the most excellent, he felt, for it summarized briefly and correctly the articles of faith.'[1]

In *The Small Catechism* he declared: 'I believe in God the Father Almighty, Maker of heaven and earth . . . [who] has made me and . . . provides me richly and daily with all that I need. . . . And in Jesus Christ, His only Son, our Lord . . . true God, begotten of the Father from eternity, and also true man, born of the Virgin Mary. . . . I believe in the Holy Ghost . . . [who] has called me by the Gospel, enlightened me with His gifts, sanctified and kept me in the true faith, even as He calls, gathers, enlightens and sanctifies the whole Christian Church on earth.'[2] In *A Brief Explanation of the Ten Commandments, the Creed, and the Lord's prayer* he adds: 'I believe . . . that no one can come to the Father through Christ and His life, sufferings and death . . . without the work of the Holy Ghost, by which the Father and the Son teach, quicken, call, draw me and all that are His, make us, in and through Christ, alive and holy and spiritual, and thus bring us to the Father; for it is He by whom the Father, through Christ and in Christ, worketh all things and giveth life to all.'[3]

Thus 'he recognized more and more the Christological approach

to the doctrine of the Trinity as the only one that was compatible
with his theology. . . . In general, however, the doctrine of the Trinity
came to a standstill in his theology.'[4]

MELANCHTHON

Philip Melanchthon (d. 1560) 'wrote Protestantism's basic creed,
the *Augsburg Confession*, and defended it in his theologically acute
Apology of the Augsburg Confession, both of which have come to
symbolize Lutheranism.'[5] His 'genius in the Augsburg Confession
passed over into the Thirty-Nine Articles of the Church of England.'[6] His trinitarian doctrine was more highly developed than
Luther's.

In the *Augsburg Confession* he wrote:

> Our Churches, with common consent, do teach that the decree
> of the Council of Nicaea concerning the Unity of the Divine
> Essence and concerning the Three Persons, is true and to be
> believed without any doubting; that is to say, there is one Divine
> Essence which is called and which is God . . . and yet there are
> three Persons, of the same essence and power, who also are co-
> eternal, the Father, the Son and the Holy Spirit. And the term
> 'person' they use as the Fathers have used it, to signify not a part
> or quality in another, but that which subsists of itself. They con-
> demn all heresies which have sprung up against this article, as the
> Manichaeans . . . the Valentinians, Arians, Eunomians, Moham-
> medans, and all such. They condemn also the Samosatenes, old
> and new, who, contending that there is but one Person, sophistic-
> ally and impiously argue that the Word and the Holy Spirit are
> not distinct Persons, but that 'Word' signifies a spoken word and
> 'Spirit' signifies motion created in things.'[7]

In the *Apology of the Augsburg Confession* he added: 'This article
we have always taught and defended, and we believe that it has in
Holy Scripture sure and firm testimonies that cannot be overthrown.
And we constantly affirm that those thinking otherwise are outside
the Church of Christ, and are idolaters and insult God.'[8]

In the *Loci Communes of 1555* he treats further the divine
persons and the meaning of person. 'Person . . . is an essence, a living
thing in itself, not the sum of many parts but a unified and rational
thing which is not sustained and supported by any other being as if it
were but an addition to it.'[9] The Persons are essentially and functionally distinct:

the Father is the procreator, the Son is begotten of the Father
and out of the Father's being . . . the essential and full Image of
the Father. The Holy Spirit proceeds from the Father and Son
and is the love and joy in the Father and Son . . . each person has
his own distinctive work. . . . The Son is the person through
whom the eternal Father pronounces creation; the Son is the
distinctive proclaimer of the promise and the perpetual upholder
of the office of preaching . . . the Son took upon himself human
nature . . . The Son is Mediator and Redeemer and Savior. . . .
The particular work of the Holy Spirit is to strengthen us in
heartfelt joy and love toward God. . . . Through the Holy Spirit
we feel joy, know that we live in grace.[10]

JOHN CALVIN

John Calvin (d. 1564) was 'one of the key figures in the history of
Christendom' and his 'theological achievement was not to innovate,
but to integrate . . . to conserve and confirm the gains of his predecessors, Luther and Bucer . . . Melanchthon and Zwingli.'[11] His
magnum opus, *Institutes of the Christian Religion* 'came before the
world as a Reformed *summa theologica* and *summa pietatis* in
one.'[12]

In his trinitarian doctrine he maintains that 'there is one divine
essence, containing three persons, and that this is taught in the
Scriptures from the beginning.'[13] To those who objected that the
word *person* was a human invention he replied:

how very unreasonable it is to reprobate words which express
nothing but what is testified and recorded in the Scriptures . . .
Sabellius . . . considered the names of Father, Son and Holy
Spirit as little more than empty sounds . . . arguing that . . . the
Father is the Son and that the Holy Spirit is the Father, without
any order or distinction. . . . The good doctors of that age . . .
to defend themselves against his intricate subtleties . . . affirmed
that they truly subsisted in the one God, or, what is the same,
that in the unity of God there subsisted a trinity of Persons. If
then the words have not been rashly invented, we should beware
lest we be convinced of fastidious temerity in rejecting them.[14]

He defines a divine person as 'a subsistence in the Divine essence,
which is related to the others and yet distinguished from them by
an incommunicable property.'[15] He strongly affirms the unity of the
three and appeals to Augustine for confirmation: 'These distinctive appellations,' says Augustine, 'denote their reciprocal relations
to each other, and not the substance itself which is but one.[16] And he

adds: 'if we maintain what has already been sufficiently demonstrated from Scripture, that the essence of the one God which pertains to the Father and Son and Spirit, is simple and undivided, and on the other hand that the Father is by some property distinguished from the Son and likewise the Son from the Spirit, the gate will be shut not only against Arius and Sabellius but also against all the other ancient heresiarchs.'[17]

At the time of Calvin there were some energetic Anti-Trinitarians, of whom the best known is Michael Servetus.[18] He was burned at the stake as a heretic by order of the Genevan Council because 'you, Servetus, have for a long time promulgated false and thoroughly heretical doctrine . . . and divulged even in printed books opinions against God the Father, the Son and the Holy Spirit.'[19] Calvin was very influential in this condemnation but 'tried to change the mode of his death' from the stake to the sword 'but in vain.'[20] But 'murmurs of criticism so speedily reached Calvin that in the following year he issued his *Defense of the Orthodox Trinity Against the Errors of Michael Servetus.*'[21]

In his *Institutes* he called Servetus and his followers madmen and wrote that

> the word Trinity was so odious and even detestable to Servetus that he asserted all Trinitarians . . . to be Atheists . . . he maintained . . . that in the beginning there was no distinction in God, because the Word was once the same as the Spirit; but that after Christ appeared God of God, there emanated from him another God, even the Spirit. . . . In other places he . . . [says] that God in his eternal reason, decreeing for himself a visible Son, has visibly exhibited himself in this manner; for if this be true, there is no other divinity left to Christ, than as he has been appointed a Son by an eternal decree of God.'[22]

That Calvin was strongly attached to the traditional trinitarian doctrine and strongly opposed anyone who contravened it is quite obvious.

CHAPTER FOURTEEN

The 17th Century

Luther and Melanchthon, Zwingli and Calvin, the founders and for-
mulators of Lutheran and Reformed theology, subscribed to substantially the same trinitarian doctrine. They accepted the ancient
creeds as expressing the sense of Scripture but Scripture was their
primary authority in matters of belief. Luther, and to some extent
Calvin, appealed not only to authority and reason but also to the
experience of the Christian as a testimony of the Holy Spirit. Thus a
third principle, Christian experience, was given a place in theology
beside authority and reason. Gradually this third principle would
come to dominate if not almost eliminate the other two principles for
some Protestant theologians.

Already in the 17th century Protestants began to take different
attitudes toward traditional trinitarian doctrine. In Europe some
chose Scholasticism, some Pietism, some Socinianism. In England
there were Controversialists and Deists, in America Unitarians and
a few Deists.

PROTESTANT SCHOLASTICISM

Although the Protestant Reformation began to some extent as a
revolt from scholastic theology, the 17th century saw the growth of
both Lutheran and Reformed scholastic systems that aimed to con-
solidate the ideas of the Reformation. They ascribed absolute infallibility to the Bible in every field it touched. Their philosophy was
Aristotelian. They treated trinitarian doctrine with all the subtlety
and detail of the Middle Ages. Lutheran and Calvinist scholastic
theologians attacked not only Roman Catholic theologians but one
another: 'Lutheran theologians charged Reformed theologians with
Sabellianism, because they showed a dislike of the term 'person,'

preferring 'hypostasis' or still better *tropos uparxeos*, mode of subsistence.'[1]

PIETISM

Besides the great Protestant scholastic systems there developed a Pietistic movement which would contribute to the development of the Wesleyan Evangelical Revival and of the experiential theology of Schleiermacher. Pietistic tendencies appeared in both Lutheran and Reformed circles before the end of the 16th century, but they had their largest development in the late 17th and early 18th centuries. Led by Philip Jacob Spener (1633–1705) the Pietists accepted the orthodox Lutheran doctrine of the Trinity but they insisted that what matters most is spiritual experience and so they made doctrine secondary to experience. Spener maintained that personal piety was far more important than doctrinal soundness.[2] In helping to break the control of Scholasticism and in making religious experience the chief basis of theology Pietism led to the modern age of religious life and theology in Germany.

SOCINIANISM

On the continent the outstanding Anti-Trinitarians were the Socinians. Faustus Socinus (d. 1604) succeeded in gathering the Unitarians of Poland into the strong and compact sect of Polish Brethren. His writings, especially the Racovian Catechism, offer us the best presentation of the Socinian rejection of the Trinity. Socinus accepted Scripture as the supreme authority in matters of faith but he interpreted it by his own reason and not by the traditional creeds. Building on the Biblical texts that assert the unity of God, on a rationalized acceptance of the Biblical kerygma, on a rejection of the Pauline and Johannine theologies, and on a Boethian definition of person, his reason told him that God was one in essence and in person 'because the divine essence is single in number. Therefore there cannot be several persons in it, since a person is nothing else than an intelligent, indivisible essence.'[3] Where orthodox theologians carefully distinguished essence and person in God, Socinians equated them and boldly affirmed that God is a Person. Here they would exert their deepest influence on later Protestant theology. Orthodox theologians, Protestant and Roman Catholic, of course rejected Socinianism. Arminian theologians favored it somewhat, not by denying the Trinity but by rejecting technical terms not found in Scripture. Socinian theories transposed to England and America would become Unitarianism.

TRINITARIAN CONTROVERSY

In England in the last decades of the 17th century there arose a notable trinitarian controversy.[4] In his treatise, *A Vindication of the Holy and Blessed Trinity* Sherlock used Descartes' notion of self-consciousness to present the three divine Persons as three Infinite Minds or Self-Consciousnesses, really distinct from one another and yet each entirely conscious of the thoughts of the others, so that they may be said to be numerically one. South in his *Animadversions upon Dr. Sherlock's book* objected to Sherlock's 'new notions' and argued that if God is only Infinite Mind He is not a substance and if He is not a substance He is nothing. He added that person and self-consciousness are not equivalents, for self-consciousness presupposes personality and is different from it. Wallis in his *Letters on the Trinity* also disagreed with Sherlock and insisted that 'person' in the doctrine of the Trinity does not have the same sense as when it is applied to man, but simply stands for a distinction, such that one person is not another person and yet all are only one God. Sherlock's doctrine was condemned by the Heads of Colleges in Oxford, but his concept of person as equivalent to self-consciousness would be very influential in modern trinitarian theology.

DEISM

English Deism[5] aimed at banishing from religion all mysteries and miracles and at affirming a natural religion that would be a means to virtue. Lord Herbert of Cherbury (1583–1648) has been called its father. In his *De Veritate* (1624) and his *De Religione Gentilium* (1663), Lord Herbert maintained that God's perfection demands a way of salvation open and common to all. This therefore could not originate in a particular revelation but must be implanted in the natural reason of man in all ages and places. He found such a way of salvation in all peoples and it embraced five tenets which summed up Deism: 1. there is a Supreme Being; 2. He is to be worshipped; 3. piety and virtue are the chief elements of His worship; 4. sin is to be expiated by repentance and amendment; 5. there are divine rewards and punishments after death. John Toland in his book, *Christianity Not Mysterious* (1702), argued that objects of faith must somehow be present in our consciousness and hence cannot be absolutely transcendent. There can therefore be mysteries only in a relative and not in an absolute sense. Since the Christian doctrine of the Trinity involved mystery he inclined to reject it. Matthew Tindal in his book, *Christianity as Old as the Creation* (1730), maintained that natural and revealed religion, Christian law and natural law do not differ substantially in content. Religion is merely the recognition of our duties as divine commands. Christianity is true insofar as it is as old as the world, 'The deists . . . criticised, as the Socinians had done, the problems of biblical religion. All elements of criticism can be found in them which we now associate with liberal theology . . . the category of myth . . . was invented by the deists two hundred and fifty years before Bultmann's essay on demythologization.'[6]

Henry Dodwell, Jr. gave a deep wound to Deism by his book, *Christianity not Founded on Argument* (1742), in which he insisted that religion is absolutely out of the proper jurisdiction of reason. David Hume in *An Enquiry Concerning the Human Understanding* (1784) undermined Deism still further by insisting that the 'human nature' on which Deism based its natural religion was not a reality but a philosophical dream of the Deists. By 1760 the Deistic movement had practically come to an end in England. Voltaire became the leader of the French Deists. In Germany Lessing 'was easily the ablest and most influential of all German Deists.'[7] In America the outstanding Deists were Benjamin Franklin, Thomas Jefferson, and Thomas Paine.

CHAPTER FIFTEEN

The 18th Century

The 18th century is known as the age of the Enlightenment or *Aufklärung*. Socinianism was one of its sources.[1] It was 'secular in spirit and destructive in effect. It diffused a skepticism which gradually dissolved the intellectual and religious patterns which had governed European thought since Augustine. It proclaimed the autonomy of man's mind and his infinite capacity for progress and perfectibility. . . . The theology and ethics of the churches were subjected to a criticism more merciless than any which they had hitherto faced.'[2] Its ideal was naturalism and its method was rationalism, as opposed to the supernatural and to revelation. It had three roots, '(1) Protestantism, or more specifically the disruption caused by Protestantism; (2) Humanism; (3) the autonomous development of individualistic philosophy, built upon mathematic-scientific discoveries.'[3] Its contribution to the development of trinitarian doctrine was largely negative.

SPINOZA

Baruch Spinoza (1632–1677) had a considerable influence on the 18th century, for he 'was seen by the anti-Christian rationalists as a triumph of reason over religion; he had "put God in his place," which was that of a necessary principle rather than a meddling old monarch.'[4] He was 'solemnly excommunicated from the Jewish community in 1656 for his belief that extension is present in God.'[5] In him all the essentials of modern naturalism and philosophical determinism were already present. In his *Ethics Demonstrated According to the Geometrical Order* he constructed a system of thoroughgoing pantheism. In this he 'denied the existence of a personal Being transcending Nature,' since for him 'God and nature are the same.'[6]

LEIBNIZ

G. W. Leibniz (1646–1716) was influenced by Spinoza and like him gave God a dominating role in his thought. He was suspected of being a Roman Catholic at heart but his letters show that he never ceased to be a loyal Lutheran, even though he outgrew strict Lutheranism. In three works, *Defensio Trinitatis, Duae epistolae ad Loefflerum,* and *Remarques sur le livre d'un antitrinitaire anglais* he set himself to defend the Trinity against Socinians and Neo-Arians by showing its possibility. He used St. Thomas' explanation to show there is no contradiction in the Trinity. Through Christian Wolff (1679–1754), who built a rationalist scholasticism on his metaphysics, Leibniz came to have a great influence on the German Enlightenment. Wolff was not a 'rationalist in the sense of being anti-religious,' since 'he developed a complete rational system of philosophy which included metaphysics and natural theology,' and 'his ideas may be said to have dominated in the German universities until the rise of the Kantian criticism.'[7] Wolff's successor, J. S. Semler, was a pioneer in the Biblical criticism that dominated 19th-century evangelical theology. He maintained that much in Scripture was accidental, contingent and purely local in interest, without dogmatic value and that the Nicene Creed was the product of three centuries of speculation.

VOLTAIRE

Voltaire (1694–1778) was 'the most powerful influence in European thought for the better part of a half century,'[8] and the leader of the French Deists. He was opposed to all revealed religions, all revelations, miracles, prophecy, to the authority of Scripture and to all religious dogmas. He maintained that Newton's laws had emancipated man's mind from authority and revelation. He was not an atheist: 'I believe in God, not the God of the mystics and the theologians, but the God of nature, the great geometrician, the architect of the universe, the prime mover, unalterable, transcendental, everlasting.' But he was very hostile to Christianity: 'every man of sense, every good man, ought to hold the Christian sect in horror. The great name of theist . . . is the only name one ought to take. The only gospel one ought to read is the great book of nature, written by the hand of God and sealed with his seal.'[9]

LESSING

G. E. Lessing (1729–1781) 'was easily the ablest and most influential of all German deists.'[10] He 'was well versed in Lutheran doctrine' but he 'denied any abiding distinctiveness to Christianity' and in its stead 'proposed a Deistic philosophy of morality and of faith in a Supreme Being. Nothing was to be believed which could not be rationally validated.'[11] With regard to Christ he wrote, 'I must confess I regard him merely as a divinely inspired teacher' and he added, 'the orthodox conceptions of the godhead are no longer mine, I cannot accept them. . . . As a term of reference. . . . I can only name Spinoza.' Does this mean that 'Christianity, and even deism, were cast aside, in favour of pantheism?'[12] In his works, *Nathan the Wise* and *The Education of Humanity* he maintained that revelation gave nothing to man that human reason left to itself could not have reached. He published the *Wolfenbüttel Fragments* of H. Reimarus' *Vindication of the Rational Worshippers of God* which sharply criticized the historical evidences of Christianity and the ecclesial confessions of the Trinity.

KANT

Immanuel Kant (1724–1804), 'by far the greatest . . . representative of the Enlightenment,'[13] was also 'its own destroyer.'[14] By his *Critiques* he put an end to the *Aufklärung* but he opened the way for the modern theological situation. He rejected both the orthodox and the rationalist views of religion. He rejected any unique revelation of religious truths, any authoritarian Church as custodian and interpreter of such a revelation. Claims to knowledge must be limited to the experienced world, shaped by the rational structures of the mind, and hence claims to knowledge of God through 'pure reason' were impossible. He 'was the product of a Pietistic home'[15] and respected Christ as a moral example. But 'he regarded the doctrine of the Trinity as of no practical value . . . and mistrusted as fanatical all dependence upon the recreative power of the Holy Spirit.'[16] Rationalism and Pietism had undermined the rigidity of theological orthodoxy. By teaching that objects of faith can never become objects of knowledge, Kant did 'no harm to Luther's view of faith,'[17] but pointed the way to a reorientation of theology in the direction of faith. When 'the nineteenth century recast theology in terms of experience and morality . . . it did this on the basis of Kant's philosophy.'[18]

CHAPTER SIXTEEN

The 19th Century

In the 17th and 18th centuries Deists had proclaimed a natural religion that had no real place for a mystery of the Trinity. In the 18th century most Protestants still adhered to trinitarian orthodoxy, but some were attracted to a religion of reason rather than one of revelation. Thus 19th-century Protestants had two main options in theology—for the principle of authority or for the principle of reason. But Protestant scholasticism, with its concern for precision and subtlety and its endless disputes over theological minutiae, had fallen into disrepute. On the other hand Enlightenment rationalism, which had vaunted the full competence of human reason to solve all problems, had received a body-blow from Kant's *Critique of Pure Reason*. Would Protestants be given any other options? Schleiermacher would offer his 'theology of experience,' Hegel his 'idealistic theology,' and Ritschl and Harnack their 'liberal theology,' each in the hope of giving men a relevant synthesis of the Christian message and the 'modern mind.' But none of these offerings was destined to have a very long-lasting appeal.

SCHLEIERMACHER

Friedrich Schleiermacher (1768–1834) has been called 'the father of modern liberal theology'[1] and 'the Church Father of the 19th century.'[2] He is noted for his concept of religion and for his dim view of the ecclesiastical doctrine of the Trinity.

For him religion is 'the consciousness of being absolutely dependent, or, which is the same thing, of being in relation with God.'[3] It is 'neither metaphysics nor ethics, nor a combination of the two. It is some deeper, unique, special thing . . . that . . . belongs to the realm of "feeling." [4] It is rather 'piety . . . a distinctive type of experience.'[5] And 'Christianity is a monotheistic faith, belonging to the teleological type of religion, and is essentially distinguished from other such faiths by the fact that in it everything is related to the redemption accomplished by Jesus of Nazareth.'[6]

He relegates the doctrine of the Trinity to an appendix at the very end of *The Christian Faith*. There he declares that the ecclesiastical doctrine of the Trinity is unsatisfactory because 'it is not an immediate utterance concerning the Christian self-consciousness, but only a combination of several such utterances.'[7] What is essential is

> the doctrine of the union of the Divine Essence with human nature, both in the personality of Christ and in the common Spirit of the Church; therewith the whole view of Christianity set forth in our Church teaching stands and falls. For unless the being of God in Christ is assumed, the idea of redemption could not be thus concentrated in His Person. And unless there were such a union also in the common Spirit of the Church, the Church could not thus be the Bearer and Perpetuator of the redemption through Christ. . . . But the assumption of an eternal distinction in the Supreme Being is not an utterance concerning the religious consciousness, for there it never could emerge.[8]

This doctrine of the Trinity is unsatisfactory on another score, for 'it demands that we think of each of the three Persons as equal to the Divine Essence, and vice versa, and each of the three Persons as equal to the others. Yet we cannot do either the one or the other, but can only represent the Persons in a gradation, and thus either represent the unity of the Essence as less real than the three Persons, or vice versa.'[9] Hence he wonders whether the relevant 'passages of the New Testament could not also be explained by the Sabellian view set up in opposition to our ecclesiastical interpretation,' and whether the Sabellian hypothesis cannot render us as much service as the Athanasian hypothesis 'without involving us in equally insoluble difficulties.' In other words, 'the question is whether formulae cannot be devised which, without asserting eternal distinctions in the Supreme Being, are yet equally capable of exhibiting in their truth both unions of the Essence with human nature.'[10]

For Schleiermacher 'the Bible and the creeds are important, but as records and interpretations of the experience of Christians.'[11] He 'sought to establish theology as a strictly empirical discipline,' organized doctrine about a single principle, Jesus Christ, and reduced 'the Trinity to a doctrine of the second rank.'[12] He has been strongly critized for making religion fundamentally a state of feeling and for making this feeling itself the raw material of doctrine. But he 'was destined to grow into a major reformer of Protestant theology, eventually becoming one of the greatest theologians of the Evangelical Church.'[13] And 'the entire theology of the last half-century, as far as it seeks at all to remain in touch with critical thought, has been in some degree or other influenced by the theological system of Schleiermacher.'[14]

G. W. Hegel (1770–1831), the 'greatest of German idealists,'[15] developed a philosophical trinitarianism based entirely on philosophical premises and thought that the traditional doctrine of the Trinity was at least analogous to his. Hegel has often been attacked as a pantheist, but recently it has been solidly maintained that he was a panentheist who held that a God of love could not be immutable, that God is with, but not before creation, that in God the universe is 'in process of achieving ever more inclusive levels of perfection' but that God 'transcends the universe as the Whole transcending the sum of its parts.'[16]

Hegel took from his predecessors the general principle of thesis, antithesis, and synthesis and used it to explain the world and God. The doctrine of the Trinity lent itself readily to this process. Thus he wrote in *The Philosophy of Religion*[17] 'God, who represents Being in-and-for-self, eternally produces Himself in the form of the Son, distinguishes Himself from Himself . . . but has not gone outside Himself, and this is the form of love . . . it is as totality that God is Spirit. . . . The relation between Father and Son is expressed in terms of organic life, and is used in the popular or figurative sense. This natural relation is merely pictorial and, accordingly, never entirely corresponds to the truth that is sought to be expressed.'[18] He adds that 'God is Spirit, what gives itself an objective form and knows itself in that,' and 'He is the eternal Process.'[19] He declares that 'the Trinity has been reduced to a relation of Father, Son and Spirit, and this is a childlike relation, a childlike natural form' but 'merely pictorial. . . . The abstract God, the Father, is the Universal, the eternal, all-embracing, total particularity . . . the Other, the Son, is infinite particularity, manifestation; the third, the Spirit, is individuality as such. The Universal, however, as totality is itself Spirit; all three are Spirit.'[20] He holds that 'the nature of God is indeed not a mystery in the ordinary sense of the term, and least of all in the Christian religion, for in it God has communicated the knowledge of Himself; but it is a mystery for sense-perception . . . and for the Understanding.'²¹

Does Hegel's God correspond to the Christian concept of the Triune God? No. He is 'obviously something very different.'²² It is true that 'the distinctions which he sees in God are immanent in his Being, and some of Hegel's terminology is reminiscent of the traditional psychological analogy and of classical discussions of the generation of the Son and the unity of Father and Son in the Spirit. But at least two crucial differences must be noted. First, Hegel apparently means to equate the second person of his trinity with finite existence . . . with the force of particularization, and the kingdom of the Son . . . is physical nature and finite Spirit. . . . Second, the conception of an "economic" Trinity has been abandoned or altered beyond recognition.'²³ What is more, it seems that 'God becomes personal only in the Kingdom of the Spirit, not in that of the Father or in that of the Son.'²⁴ Today the Hegelian synthesis 'has broken down beyond all possible recovery . . . no one can accept this synthesis—Christian, post-Christian, or non-Christian.'²⁵

Liberal Protestantism also made a strong plea for the allegiance of Protestants in the 19th century, and reached its zenith in the early decades of the 20th century. It abandoned the traditional creeds and dedicated itself to the modern ideal of freedom of thought. It aimed to interpret and restate the Christian religion in terms of modern civilization. It rejected the revelation that orthodoxy defended, because it judged this to be based on a supernaturalist metaphysics that justified miracles and magic. It made its four basic principles, 'the authority of Christian experience,' 'the centrality of Jesus Christ,' 'criticism of the tradition from within,' and 'social idealism.'²⁶ It stressed God's immanence, the humanity of Christ, the dignity of man, the nature of religious authority as wholly subjective.²⁷ It used the methods of modern science to find and state the 'essence of Christianity' and to use this to satisfy the needs of the modern world. Two men stood out in this effort, Albrecht Ritschl and his disciple, Adolf von Harnack.

RITSCHL

Albrecht Ritschl (1822–1889) saw the weakness of Hegel's speculative rationalism and of Schleiermacher's excessive reliance on feeling, and he built a theology that was to be guided solely by the revelation in Christ in the New Testament. His chief work, *Christian Doctrine of Justification and Reconciliation* (Edinburgh, 1902) aimed to study matters of direct moment for the Christian life and subjects to which the believer attaches value, and since much of

traditional dogma and speculative philosophy failed on this score,
it provoked new questions in church history, Biblical exegesis, practical and dogmatic theology. His theology excluded all assertions
about God or the person of Christ that might be termed speculative
or metaphysical. It was interested not in what God is in His celestial
being but in what He means for us, not in what Christ is in Himself
but in what He means for our life.[28] It rejected the orthodox doctrine of the two natures in the one Person of Christ, and of the three
Persons in the one substance of the Godhead,[29] and substituted for
the former an original direction of the will of Christ which results
in the perfect identity in action of the divine purpose and the human
volition.[30] His Christology is noteworthy. It

> starts from the principle that in a personal life what is real and
> actual consists of spiritual effects and nothing else. By this
> means . . . not only the dogma of the two natures, but the whole
> metaphysical background of ecclesiastical Christology is thus
> got rid of, even more decisively than in Schleiermacher's theo-
> logy, and replaced by an historical view of the subject. In strange
> contrast with this, Ritschl nevertheless continues to speak with
> orthodox theology of the deity of Christ. It is true this term has
> for him an altogether different meaning. It is the expression of
> our estimate of Jesus, of our trustful acknowledgment of the
> unique value of what his life effected for our salvation, but is
> not meant to predicate any metaphysical characteristic of his
> nature whatever, or any transcendental unity of his nature with
> God. . . . Metaphysical attributes of deity cannot be ascribed to
> him for the simple reason that they are altogether outside the
> religious method of cognition, which is concerned only with
> judgments of value.[31]

Ritschl gave his theological support to the tremendous expansion of
Biblical scholarship and thus helped bring it about that 'agnosticism
in metaphysics and confidence in historical scholarship were characteristic of the generation.'[32]

HARNACK

Adolf von Harnack (1851–1930) has been called 'the greatest Protestant historian of the late nineteenth century.'[33] His greatest work
is his *History of Dogma*,[34] but his most famous book is *What Is
Christianity?*[35] In this he sought to find the essence of Christianity,
to 'employ the methods of historical science and the experience of
life gained by witnessing the actual course of history,'[36] to go behind
the dogmatic statements and 'find out what is essential,'[37] for in these

Christological and trinitarian formulas he saw an unacceptable 'Hellenization' of the essential Christian message. He stressed this over and over: 'The influx of Hellenism . . . and the union of the Gospel with it, form the greatest fact in the history of the Church in the second century.'[38] 'The most important step that was ever taken in the domain of Christian doctrine was when the Christian apologists at the beginning of the second century drew the equation: the Logos is Jesus Christ.'[39] 'The identification of the Logos with Christ was the determining factor in the fusion of Greek philosophy with the apostolic inheritance.'[40] 'Although the acute phase of Hellenisation was avoided, Christendom became more and more penetrated by the Greek and philosophical idea that true religion is first and foremost "doctrine." '[41] 'The elaboration of the Gospel into a vast philosophy of God and the world . . . the view of revelation as a countless multitude of doctrines and explanations, all equally holy and important—this is Greek intellectualism.[42] The subject of the God-Man nature of the Saviour is . . . indubitably the central point in the whole dogmatic system of the Church. It supplied the doctrine of the Trinity. In the Greek view these two doctrines together make up Christian teaching *in nuce*.'[43] 'The doctrines of the identical nature of the three persons of the Trinity—how the doctrine of the Holy Ghost came about, I need not mention—and of the God-Man nature of the Redeemer are in strict accordance with the distinguishing notion of the redemption as a deification of man's nature by making him immortal. Without the help of the notion those formulas would never have been attained; but they also stand and fall with it.'[44] 'The Greek Church still entertains the conviction today that in these doctrines it possesses the essence of Christianity. . . . Criticism of this contention is not difficult' for 'the notion of the redemption as a deification of mortal nature is subchristian . . . the whole doctrine is inadmissible, because it has scarcely any connexion with the Jesus Christ of the Gospel, and its formulas do not fit him; it is, therefore, not founded on truth.'[45] It is 'a palpable fact that in Greek dogma we have a fatal connexion established between the desire of the ancients for immortal life and the Christian message . . . this connexion has led to formulas which are incorrect, and introduced a suppositious Christ in the place of the real one.'[46]

What then is the essential message of Christianity? It is very simple, and 'it may be grouped under three heads. . . . Firstly, the kingdom of God and its coming. Secondly, God the Father and the infinite value of the human soul. Thirdly, the higher righteousness and the commandment of love.'[47]

But even though 'most liberal thinkers of his own day saw that this was too simple a rendering even of the teaching of Jesus, and that Harnack had eliminated much that is essential to the Christian gospel,'[48] '*Das Wesen des Christentums* reached a 5th edition in 1901 and under the title of *What is Christianity?* it was hailed in England as an epoch-making book.'[49]

CHAPTER SEVENTEEN

The 20th Century

The 19th century saw the rise of new attitudes toward traditional trinitarian doctrine. Since the Trinity of essence was beyond the reach of his theological method, Schleiermacher gave it little attention in his theology of feeling, and relegated it to an appendix at the end of *The Christian Faith*. Hegel regarded the traditional presentation of the Trinity as a pictorial representation of his own philosophical trinity of personality as subject, object, and the unity of both in Spirit. But his pantheistic or panentheistic trinity was not the Trinity of orthodox Protestantism. Ritschl was interested in what God means to us and not in what He is in Himself, and in consequence he rejected the orthodox doctrine of the Trinity as lacking in value for us. Harnack regards the traditional trinitarian formulas as not a part of the essential Christian message but as an unacceptable Hellenization of it.

These attitudes will continue to some extent into the 20th century, but the 20th century will produce strong theological protests against them. And it will produce developments of its own, especially in the areas of Biblical criticism, existential philosophy, philosophical analysis of language and symbol, that will deeply affect theological reflection on traditional trinitarian doctrine.

In the United States and Great Britain we find various attitudes among Protestant theologians in the first half of the century. Some reject the doctrine of the Trinity as 'the product of metaphysics,'[1] as 'irrational and religiously valueless,'[2] as 'not a primary affirmation of faith but an intellectual hypothesis.'[3] Some maintain the traditional doctrine but lean heavily on philosophy to illustrate if not to confirm it.[4] Some fundamentalists maintain that Scripture, the authentic and inspired revelation of God, explicitly teaches the doc-

trine of the Trinity and they add a proof that tripersonality is necessary for personal life and fulfilment in God.[5] Other theologians
insist that the doctrine of the Trinity is not a per se revealed doctrine,
obtained by piecing together Biblical proof-texts, but is the ultimate
and necessary synthesis of the data of Christian revelation and
experience.[6] Hodgson regards the three as three 'intelligent, pur-
posive centers of consciousness,' three complete persons in the
modern sense of the term and thus subscribes to the 'social analogy'
of God as a divine society, just as Thornton and Lowry do.[7] And he
thinks that the unity of the three is not a mathematical unity, but
an 'organic' unity, a unity of 'intensity,' an internally constitutive
unity, a dynamic unity that actively unifies their lives, a unity that
involves the abandonment of the classical trinitarian doctrines of
principium and processions.[8] Perhaps the best American Protestant
contribution to trinitarian doctrine, both as a historical survey and
as a constructive statement, is Claude Welch's *The Trinity in Contemporary Theology*. In this he maintains a solidly traditional doctrine of the Trinity that is based on a modern, analytical view of
the New Testament revelation of the Triune God. He rejects all
views 'which stop short of . . . the 'essential' or 'ontological' Trinity,
such as those of Modalists, Monarchians, Subordinationists and of
Knudson and Brunner.[9] He rejects any approach to the doctrine that
'rests on an uncritical view of the biblical revelation.'[10] He rejects
the 'synthetic' approach to the doctrine, because it 'rests on a false
and misleading separation of the "elements" of the Christian revelation.[11] He holds with Karl Barth[12] that 'the doctrine of the Trinity
is a necessary analysis of the' New Testament revelation,[13] and is
'grounded solely in the revelation of God in Jesus Christ.'[14] But
unlike Barth he holds that this revelational grounding of the doctrine is compatible with a 'general revelation,'[15] and with 'trinitarian
philosophizing'[16] but not with 'philosophical trinitarianism.'[17] He
finds the 'social analogy' unsatisfactory and prefers to regard
Father, Son and Holy Spirit not as three 'persons' or 'personalities'[18]
in the modern sense of 'distinct centers of consciousness,'[19] but as
three hypostases which 'are not less personal than the essence,'[20] as
three eternal, distinct, intrinsic 'modes of being'[21] so that God is
'threefold (not three) as He and one as Thou.'[22] With Hodgson he
agrees 'that the trinitarian conception of God involves a new conception of the unity of God,'[23] but instead of Hodgson's 'internally
constitutive unity' of three distinct 'persons' or 'selves,'[24] he prefers
a 'personal unity' whereby God is 'One Subject, One Thou, One
personal being,'[25] 'who subsists in these three modes, Father, Son
and Holy Spirit.'[26] So Claude Welch wrote in 1952. But more recently

he has said, 'I could not now . . . write as confidently of the trinitarian formulations as I could in 1952.'[27]

But the men who will be most eminent in this effort to make
trinitarian doctrine more solid and influential, more modern and
relevant to contemporary Christians, will be Karl Barth, Emil
Brunner, Rudolf Bultmann and Paul Tillich, and all of these will
draw on the lonely genius of 19th-century Søren Kierkegaard.

SØREN KIERKEGAARD

Søren Kierkegaard (1813–1855) was 'little noticed in his own day
outside his native Denmark, but destined to exercise incalculable
influence over the 20th century.'[28] In him 'Lutheranism produced a
philosopher whose thought has brought on a revolution in both
theology and philosophy.'[29] His 'radically individualistic Protestantism . . . exerted—principally through Karl Barth—a far reaching
influence on later Protestant theology.'[30] He 'directed his criticism
against . . . intellectualism—represented by the Hegelians, moralism
—by the Kantians, aestheticism by Schleiermacher. Kierkegaard's
sharpest criticism was directed against Hegelianism,'[31] because it
claimed to preserve the essential content of Christianity within the
framework of an all-embracing metaphysical theory. He

> contributed three principles that have played a prominent role in
> determining the methodology of much twentieth-century theo-
> logy. First, he stressed that God is radically beyond the grasp of
> reason and can be known only in faith, hence that the Christian
> affirmation of God has nothing in common with any philo-
> sophical affirmation whatsoever. Second, he stressed that Christ-
> ian faith is based upon the absolute paradox that God became
> man in Jesus, and that the concern of the thinker can be only to
> point to this affirmation and to show how it affects the human
> situation—never to explain or justify it. Third, he dissociated
> faith from the communal and sacramental life of the empirical
> church and affirmed it as a relation between the individual and
> God.[32]

KARL BARTH

Karl Barth (1886–1969) has been called 'the most important and
most influential Protestant theologian of our generation' and 'the
great opponent . . . of nineteenth-century Protestant theology and its
immediate antecedents.'[33] His *Epistle to the Romans* opened the new
era in Protestant theology, but his *Church Dogmatics* is his greatest
work.

While Schleiermacher had relegated the doctrine of the Trinity to an Appendix of his work, Barth put it in the 'Prolegomena' to the *Dogmatics*, as fundamental to all other aspects of Christian faith, for 'by consideration of the unity and variety of God in His revelation attested in Scripture . . . we are confronted with the problem of the doctrine of the Trinity.'[34] So he writes: 'God's Word is God Himself in His revelation. For God reveals Himself as the Lord and that according to Scripture signifies for the concept of revelation that God Himself in unimpaired unity yet also unimpaired difference is Revealer, Revelation, and Revealedness.'[35]

For Barth 'the way that the doctrine of the Trinity develops out of God's revelation in Jesus Christ is very simple. Apart from Revelation God is hidden and unknown.' The content of Scripture 'both in Old and New Testaments is Jesus Christ. In Him God is revealed as Lord. When this revelation is expanded we have the doctrine of the Trinity, and when that is expanded we have the whole of the Christian Faith. . . . Analysis of what is included in Revelation yields (1) the Revealer, (2) the act of Revelation, (3) the state of Revelation. These distinctions correspond to Father, Son and Holy Spirit in Scripture.'[36]

'God reveals Himself as the Lord' is the statement that Barth regards as 'the root of the doctrine of the Trinity.'[37] For 'that He reveals Himself as the Son is what is primarily meant by saying that He reveals Himself as the Lord. Actually this Sonship is God's lordship in His revelation. The Lordship of God here means His freedom to be the Son, to be God for us.'[38] But the statement refers equally to the Subject of Revelation, the Revealer, for 'revelation in the Bible means the self-unveiling, imparted to men, of the God who according to His nature cannot be unveiled to man.'[39] So in revealing Himself, God is both the Revelation and the Revealer, and reveals Himself as the Father of the Son, and thus is Lord in his freedom to reveal or not to reveal. But the statement also means that the self-unveiling is 'imparted to men,' and this is God's revealedness, His being imparted to men as the Spirit of the Father and the Son, and thus is Lord in his freedom 'to become the God of such and such men.'[40]

Does this mean that the doctrine of the Trinity is explicitly contained in the Bible? No: 'the Bible can as little explicitly contain the dogma of the Trinity as it explicitly contains the other dogmas . . . the doctrine of the Trinity is a work of the Church.'[41] But 'we regard dogma . . . as a necessary and relevant analysis of revelation.'[42] 'We simply do not confuse or equate the Biblical witness to God in His revelation with the doctrine of the Trinity, but, of course, we claim to see between the two a genuine and truly found connection,'[43] and we say that 'we come to the doctrine of the Trinity by no other way than by that of analysis of the concept of revelation.'[44]

Barth's position here is extremely interesting. Most other trinitarian theologians considered the doctrine of the Trinity as a necessary *synthesis* of fundamental elements of Christian revelation such as monotheism, the deity of Christ and the Spirit, and their unity with the Father. Barth sees it rather as a 'necessary and relevant analysis of revelation,[45] 'of the one central fact to which the Bible bears witness—the act of God in revelation—and is therefore indirectly identical with this witness to revelation.'[46] Barth goes a step further. He not only holds that this doctrine is rooted in revelation, he insists it is rooted only in revelation, and so he opposes search for *vestigia trinitatis* for he sees the danger of their becoming a second root of doctrine.[47]

Turning now to God's Three-in-Oneness Barth declares: 'the God who reveals Himself according to Scripture is One in three of His own modes of existence, which consist in their mutual relationships, Father, Son and Holy Spirit. In this way He is the Lord, i.e. the Thou who meets man's I and unites it to Himself as the indissoluble Subject, and who actually thus and thereby becomes manifest to him as his God.'[48] He goes on:

> In our proof that the doctrine of the Trinity is rooted in Biblical revelation, we started from and always returned again to the revealed name Yahweh-Kyrios, which binds together OT and NT. The doctrine of the Trinity itself neither is nor claims to be anything else than an explanatory confirmation of this name. This name is the name of an unique entity, of a single, unique Willer and Doer, whom Scripture designates as God. . . . We may unhesitatingly equate the concept of the lordship of God . . . with what in the language of the ancient Church is called the essence of God, the deitas or divinitas, the divine ousia, essentia, natura or substantia . . . the godhead of God. . . . It is to the one single essence of God, which is not to be tripled by the doctrine of the Trinity, but emphatically to be recognised in its unity, that there also belongs what we call today the 'personality' of God. . . . 'Person' in the sense of the Church doctrine of the Trinity has nothing directly to do with 'personality' . . . three personalities in God . . . would be the worst and most pointed . . . tritheism. . . . In view of the history of the concept of Person in the doctrine of the Trinity one may well ask whether dogmatics is wise in further availing itself of it in this connection. . . . The statement 'God is one in three modes of being, Father, Son, and Holy Spirit,' thus means that the one God, i.e. the one Lord, the

one personal God is what He is not in one mode, but . . . in the mode of the Father, in the mode of the Son, in the mode of the Holy Spirit. . . . His existence in these three modes of existence, is absolutely essential to Him. . . . There is no attribute, no act of God, which would not in like manner be the attribute, the act of the Father, the Son and the Spirit.[49]

Barth maintains most all the traditional trinitarian doctrine: that there is both an immanent and economic Trinity and conformity in content between the two;[50] that the Trinity is and remains a mystery;[51] that the lordship and personality of God are to be associated with His one single essence;[52] that *opera trinitatis ad extra indivisa sunt* yet such works can be properly appropriated to one or other Person;[53] that there is a mutual inexistence or perichoresis of the Three in one another which is not only a *Nebeneinander* (coexistence) but also an *Ineinander und Miteinander*[54] of the Three; that God's threeness in oneness is founded on the relations of origin or processions;[55] that the Holy Spirit proceeds from the Father and the Son,[56] He admits that 'in the essence or act in which God is God there is first a pure origin and then two different issues'[57] but he gives only a qualified approval to the concept of '*communicatio essentiae*'[58] and to that of 'generation of the Son' and 'procession of the Word,'[59] and to the use of the term *person*.

Thus 'Barth is at most points close to the classical and Catholic doctrine,'[60] and 'the chief problem . . . in relation to Barth's approach to the doctrine of the Trinity is . . . the connection between his view of the basis of the doctrine in revelation and his opposition to all claims for a general revelation or a natural theology.'[61] Perhaps Barth made his most significant contribution to trinitarian doctrine in concluding from an analysis of the statement 'God reveals Himself as the Lord' that 'the doctrine of the Trinity is grounded simply and directly in the self-revelation of God in Jesus Christ' and then adding 'impressive confirmation in the entire structure of' his exposition.[62]

Emil Brunner (1889–1966) was 'in the front rank of theological reformers'[63] and gave 'the classic contemporary expression of' the view that 'the doctrine of the Trinity' is 'necessary, but only in a defensive way.'[64] Thus he wrote in his dogmatics, *The Christian Doctrine of God:*

The ecclesiastical doctrine of the Trinity, established by the dogma of the ancient Church, is not a Biblical *kerygma*, therefore it is not the *kerygma* of the Church, but it is a theological doctrine which defends the central faith of the Bible and of the Church. Hence it does not belong to the sphere of the Church's message, but it belongs to the sphere of theology; in this sphere it is the work of the Church to test and examine its message, in the light of the Word of God given in the Church. Certainly in this process of theological reflection the doctrine of the Trinity is central.[65]

What is the actual content of the New Testament message? 'The God who makes His Name known. But He makes His Name known as the Name of the Father; He makes this Name of the Father known through the Son; and He makes the Son known as the Son of the Father, and the Father as Father of the Son through the Holy Spirit. These three names constitute the actual content of the New Testament message.'[66] So 'we must honestly admit that the doctrine of the Trinity did not form part of the early Christian—NT—message, nor has it ever been a central article of faith in the religious life of the Christian Church as a whole, at any period in its history.'[67]

How then did the doctrine arise? 'This doctrine . . . developed out of the process of defending the truth against certain doctrines which would eventually have destroyed this unity of the Nature and the Revelation of God.'[68] But was 'the doctrine which finally emerged from these conflicts really in accordance with the truth it desired to defend?'[69] 'Only in a very restricted sense.'[70] For 'the formula of the classical doctrine of the Trinity' places 'the Three Names as Three Persons "side by side" . . . thus creating a speculative truth, which is really an illusion.'[71] 'No Apostle would have dreamt of thinking that there are the Three Divine Persons, whose mutual relations and paradoxical unity are beyond our understanding. No "*mysterium logicum*" . . . no antinomy of Trinity and Unity, has any place in their testimony, but only the "*mysterium majestatis et caritatis*": namely, that the Lord God for our sakes became man and endured the Cross. . . . The mystery of the Trinity, proclaimed by the Church . . . is a pseudo-mystery, which sprang out of an aberation of theological thought from the lines laid down in the Bible, and not from the Biblical doctrine itself.'[72] 'The terms used in the Athanasian Creed, and from this source incorporated into the traditional doctrine of the Trinity taught by the Church, "*una substantia, tres personae*," must sound strange to us from the outset. What room is there for the idea of "*substantia*" in Christian theology? . . . Even the idea of "Three Persons" is to be regarded with misgiving. It is indeed impossible to understand it otherwise than in a tri-theistic sense.'[73]

Karl Barth 'places the doctrine of the Trinity . . . at the beginning of his Prolegomena to the *Dogmatics* . . . we do not begin our study of the doctrine of God with the doctrine of the Trinity, but with the doctrine of the Holiness and the Love of God. . . . Thus Barth assigns an importance to the Doctrine of the Trinity which does not legitimately belong to it, but only to the revelation itself.'[74] For 'the ecclesiastical doctrine of the Trinity is not only the product of genuine Biblical thought, it is also the product of philosophical speculation, which is remote from the thought of the Bible.'[75]

Brunner's theology has been highly praised and strongly criticized. It has been lauded as 'a theology which is more sound and fruitful, more nearly an authentic interpretation of the full Gospel message, than almost any other parallel efforts.'[76] It has been strongly criticized for its strong 'overtones of primitivism' in arbitarily and rigidly limiting the 'doctrines to be preached to those explicitly stated in the kerygma,' and for its subordinationism in appearing to say 'that while the Son is of the essence of the Father, he is *not* in *all* respects *like* the Father.'[77]

RUDOLPH BULTMANN

Rudolf Bultmann (1884–   ) has been called 'one of the three or four most creative and decisive theologians of the twentieth century,' whose 'work, in earlier years done by the form-criticism method and in his later years by the method of demythologizing, has effected the development of theology not only in Protestantism but in Roman Catholicism and Judaism as well.'[78] His effort to demythologize the gospel can be seen as a grand attempt at synthesis of the modern mind and the Christian spirit.'[79] His theology aims to discover the meaning of the New Testament and to communicate it to the men of today and for this 'he believes that an existentialist type of language is the most effective instrument.'[80]

Certain elements in the New Testament, such as miracles, the fall of Adam, the Pauline conception of the Spirit, he finds meaningless for the man of today. He 'calls the meaningless element in the New Testament "myth" ' and 'by "myth" he means a form of imagery in which "the other-worldly is expressed in terms of this world and the divine in terms of human life, what is above in terms of what is here below." ' [81] The New Testament has a mythical cosmology and many mythological ideas 'such as a preexistent divine being, a redeemer on the cross, a savior for men's sins, resurrection, the Son, the Logos, a church joined to Christ by baptism and the Eucharist.'[82] Demythologization is 'an attempt to express the content of myth in a non-imaginative form.'[83]

Bultmann is not primarily concerned with the Trinity. He is concerned with God in so far as he has revealed Himself in the Christ-event. The fundamental doctrine is the Incarnation of the Word and in John's Prologue the doctrine of the Word is a myth. When this is demythologized, instead of the Word as a divine being consubstantial with the Father through whom the world was made and who became man, we have a Word of Address (*Anrede*) that the Father speaks. 'In place of Christ as the Incarnation of divine being we are given Christ as the human figure through whom the Father's Word is spoken.'[84] When Bultmann reviews the various titles which the New Testament gives to Jesus—Messiah, Son of Man, Lord, Son of God, God—he says these mean 'that in what Jesus says, in what he is, God speaks to us, God acts upon us, God acts for us. They show how the advent of Jesus has placed man in a new situation, has called on him to decide for or against God. . . . The formula "Christ is God" is, therefore, incorrect if the word God is taken to be an objectifiable power in the Arian, Nicaean, orthodox or liberal sense. It is correct if God is understood as the event that is the outcome of God's action.'[85] He declares that Jesus' 'teaching is not new in its thought content, for in its content it is nothing other than pure Judaism, pure prophetism.'[86] And 'the fact that finds mythological expression in what is said of the pre-existence of Christ' is that 'there exists a divinely authorized proclamation of the prevenient grace and love of God.'[87]

If the Word is a myth, so is the Holy Spirit,[88] for the idea of the Spirit as a power 'indwelling the believer' describes God's act in language appropriate to the world of nature and deprives man of the capacity for free response.[89] Demythologized, 'the Spirit no longer signifies an indwelling power' but 'the possibility of a new life which must be appropriated by a deliberate resolve.'[90]

Bultmann has been widely criticized, for his definition of myth, for his demythologized gospel message, for his rejection of miracles, for his 'overemphasis on realised eschatology and subjective dialogue between man and God,'[91] for his 'pre-Copernican behavior' in making man himself and his 'pre-understanding' the measure of the understanding of God's word and revelation. And his pupils, Ernst Käsemann, Günther Bornkamm, Gerhard Ebeling, Ernst Fuchs 'though still in basic agreement with their master's point of departure' have realized 'that his reduction of the coming of Jesus to a bare fact is insufficient to describe the content of the kerygma and the basis of faith, and to identify the gospel as "Christian." '[92]

On the other hand he has been widely and deservedly praised for his deep concern to communicate intelligibly and relevantly the message of the Gospel to the men of today. It is not surprising that his 'brilliant and daring theological proposals have become the focus for much of the most creative theological work of our time.'[93]

PAUL TILLICH

Paul Tillich (1886–1965), 'perhaps the best-known Protestant theologian of our time,'[94] 'made "theologizing" an honored and respected activity at the chief seats of American learning.'[95] The 'liberals . . . have never thought him liberal enough. The orthodox . . . take scandal in the structures of his thought because they correspond to no traditional scheme.'[96] He 'has been named by some of the most radical thinkers of our time as one of the "fathers" of the "God is dead" theology; a charge he always refuted.' He 'produced a philosophical or ontological theology in which every doctrine, symbol, and concept is traced back to one of the structures of being itself' yet the Bible remains his 'primary source of revelation.'[97] He desired 'to interpret the great symbols of Christianity in terms of modern existentialist philosophy, so as to make the power of Christ's message available to men today.'[98] He aimed to do this by his method of correlation,[99] which recognizes that 'symbolically speaking, God answers man's questions, and under the impact of God's answers man asks them. Theology formulates the questions implied in human existence, and theology formulates the answers implied in divine self-manifestation under the guidance of the questions implied in human existence.'[100]

Tillich's description of God has proved controversial. For him God is 'the power of being in everything and above everything, the infinite power of being,'[101] 'being-in-itself,[102] 'the ground of being,'[103] 'the absolute,' 'man's ultimate concern,'[104] 'the "absolute participant." '[105] As being-itself God 'is the ground of the ontological structure of being without being subject to this structure himself.'[106] 'These elements make him a living God, a God who can be man's concrete concern.'[107] 'God lives in so far as he is the ground of life.'[108] 'The statement that God is being-itself is a non-symbolic statement. It does not point beyond itself. . . . However, after this has been said, nothing else can be said about God as God which is not symbolic.'[109] ' "Personal God" does not mean that God is *a* person. It means that God is the ground of everything personal and that he carries within himself the ontological power of personality. He is not a person, but he is not less than personal.'[110] In these and like statements Tillich has seemed to some to confuse the boundary between the reality of God and the reality of the world to such an extent that 'in Chicago in May 1960 . . . three prominent philosophers discussed in all seriousness the question: "Is Tillich an atheist?' '[111]

Tillich's Christology too has been widely criticized.[112] He wrote: 'Christianity is what it is through the affirmation that Jesus of Nazareth . . . is actually the Christ, namely he who brings the new state of things, the New Being.'[113] 'New Being is essential being under the conditions of existence, conquering the gap between essence and existence.'[114] But is Christ God? Tillich states that Jesus the Christ in St. Paul (Phil 2.5-11) 'is certainly not God himself, but a divine being.'[115] He is a 'divine being, either the heavenly man, or the pre-existent Christ, or the divine Logos . . . with human characteristics . . . who represents God and is able to reveal him in his fullness.'[116] Divine but not God! If Tillich understands the Incarnation 'as the self-manifestation of God in existence through a divine half-being, half-principle which belongs to God, and nevertheless shows some essentially human characteristics,'[117] the 'Council of Chalcedon and Tillich's reinterpretation of the Incarnation are utterly incompatible.'[118] Most of Tillich's writings, it has been said, 'try to define the way in which Christianity is related to secular culture.'[119] This would be an eminently worthwhile task if his idea of Christianity were more conformed to the reality.

If Christ for Tillich is 'certainly not God,' then Tillich's God cannot be the Triune God of orthodox Christianity. For Tillich 'trinitarian monotheism is not a matter of the number three. . . . It is an attempt to speak of the living God, the God in whom the ultimate and the concrete are united. . . . The answer—to the trinitarian problem—is given in every life process.'[120] Thus 'the idea of the living God requires a distinction between the abysmal element of the divine, the form element, and their spiritual unity. This explains the manifold forms in which Trinitarian symbolism appears in the history of religion. The Christian doctrine of the Trinity systematises the idea and adds the decisive element of the relation of the Christ to the Logos.'[121] In the light of all this it is not surprising that Sabellianism has been detected in Tillich's theology, for 'Father, Son and Spirit, or . . . Being, Existence and Life, or yet Abyss, Meaning and Unity . . . are God as Infinite, God as Finite, God as uniting in himself finiteness and infinity. But these are not three realities in God . . . only aspects of our knowledge of God, which is exactly the Sabellian heresy.'[122]

Tillich has been recently criticized for construing Scripture on an aesthetic mode, for 'if Scripture is to be interpreted on the model of a picture, then, like any important aesthetic object, it must be understood not to make any claims.'[123] But he has been deservedly praised too for 'hardly any other theologian has had as much dialogue with and cooperation from artists, scientists, writers and philosophers of the Old World as well as the New.'[124] And 'whereas Karl Barth looks up into the heights of heaven and contemplates the eternal interplay of the Trinity, Paul Tillich looks down into the depths of reality and is captivated by the constant flux of history.'[125]

SUMMARY OF PROTESTANT TRINITARIAN DOCTRINE

The trinitarian doctrine of the Reformers was that of the early Church and of the traditional creeds, that God is one in essence and three in person. They believed that this doctrine was meant not for idle speculation but to help men to know and love and praise the Triune God. And 'person' meant for them 'that which subsists of itself' (Melanchthon), or 'a subsistence in the divine essence, which is related to the others and yet distinguished from them by an incommunicable property' (Calvin).

In the 17th century Protestant theologians began to take different attitudes towards traditional trinitarian doctrine. In Europe some opted for Scholasticism and its systematic theology, some for Pietism and its primary stress on spiritual experience, some for Socinianism and its rejection of the Trinity. In England some chose Deism and its naturalistic opposition to miracles and revealed religion.

The 18th century, as the Age of Enlightenment, had naturalism as its ideal and rationalism as its method. Spinoza's pantheism appealed to anti-Christian rationalists as a triumph of reason over religion. Leibniz defended the Trinity against Socinians and Neo-Arians but through Wolff his metaphysics came to exercise a great influence on the German Enlightenment. Voltaire was the leader of the French Deists, and strongly opposed revealed religion, revelation, miracles, dogma. Lessing, the most influential German Deist, maintained that nothing was to be believed which could not be rationally validated. Kant, by his *Critiques*, put an end to the Enlightenment, rejected both orthodox and rationalist views of religion, regarded the doctrine of the Trinity as of no practical value, and opened the way to the modern theological mood.

The 19th century offered Protestants new options, Schleiermacher's theology of experience, Hegel's idealistic theology and the Ritschl-Harnack liberal theology. Schleiermacher developed a new approach to Christianity that made theology an empirical discipline based on the Christian experience of redemption. He gave the doctrine of the Trinity only secondary rank, for the immanent Trinity was beyond the reach of this empirical method. Hegel, a pantheist or panentheist, developed a philosophical trinitarianism that was independent of the ordinary Christian revelational basis and grounded entirely on philosophical premises. Though some of his terminology is reminiscent of traditional Christian trinitarian doctrine of the generation of the Son and of the unity of Father and Son in the Spirit, his trinitarian doctrine was definitely not the Christian doctrine of the Trinity nor even compatible with this. Liberal Protestantism rejected supernaturalism, the traditional creeds and all metaphysical assertions about God or Christ, and used the methods of modern science to find the 'essence of Christianity' and to present this to the modern world. Thus Ritschl rejected the dogma of the two natures in Christ and of the three Persons in God and the whole metaphysical background of ecclesial Christology, and concentrated on what Christ means for us as the perfect revealer of God. Harnack regarded Christological and trinitarian formulas of orthodoxy as an unacceptable 'Hellenization' of the essential Christian message. These formulas had been attained only by the help of the Greek notion of the redemption as a deification of man's nature. If the Hellenistic overlay is cut away, the essence of Christianity is very simple. First, the kingdom of God and its coming. Second, God the Father and the infinite value of the human soul. Third, the higher righteousness and the commandment of love. His book, *What is Christianity?*, was hailed in England as an epoch-making book.

The 20th century has produced strong theological protests against the theologies of Schleiermacher, Hegel, and the Protestant Liberals. But it has also produced developments of its own, especially in the areas of Biblical criticism and existential philosophy that will deeply affect theological reflection on traditional trinitarian doctrine. In the United States and Great Britain we find various attitudes among Protestant theologians in the first half of the century. Some reject the doctrine of the Trinity as the product of metaphysics and religiously valueless. Some maintain the traditional doctrine but lean heavily on philosophy to illustrate if not to validate it. Some maintain that Scripture, the authentic and inspired revelation of God, explicitly teaches the doctrine of the Trinity. Others say the doctrine of the Trinity is not a per se revealed doctrine obtained by piecing together Biblical proof texts, but that it is the ultimate and necessary synthesis of the data of Christian revelation and experience. Hodgson holds that the Father, Son, and Holy Spirit are three complete persons in the modern sense and that their

unity is an organic unity of intensity. The best American Protestant historical survey and constructive statement of the trinitarian
doctrine was made by Welch in 1952. In this he maintained a solidly
traditional doctrine of the Trinity based on a modern, analytical
view of the New Testament revelation of the Triune God. He held
that the doctrine is grounded solely in the Christian revelation but
that this revelational grounding of the doctrine is compatible with a
general revelation and with trinitarian philosophizing but not with
philosophical trinitarianism. He finds the social analogy unsatisfactory and prefers to regard the three as three modes of divine being
and not as three persons in the modern sense of distinct centers of
consciousness. Instead of Hodgson's internally constitutive unity of
three distinct selves, he prefers a personal unity whereby God is One
Subject who subsists in three modes of being, as Father, Son, and
Holy Spirit.

But the most eminent trinitarian theologians are Karl Barth, Emil
Brunner, Rudolf Bultmann, and Paul Tillich, who all drew on the
lonely genius of 19th-century Søren Kierkegaard. In Kierkegaard
Lutheranism produced a philosopher whose thought brought on a
revolution in both theology and philosophy. He criticized the
moralism of the Kantians, the aestheticism of Schleiermacher, but
most of all Hegelianism because it claimed to preserve the essential
content of Christianity within the framework of an all-embracing
metaphysical theory. He stressed that God is radically beyond the
grasp of reason and can be known only in faith, that Christian faith
is based upon the absolute paradox that God became man in Jesus,
and that faith is a relation between the individual and God.

Barth was perhaps the most influential Protestant theologian
of our age. His view of the Biblical basis of the doctrine of the
Trinity is important. He maintains that the dogma of the Trinity is
not explicitly contained in the Bible nor is it, as most theologians
maintain, a necessary *synthesis* of fundamental elements of Christian revelation. It is rather a necessary and relevant *analysis* of
revelation, and the root of the doctrine of the Trinity is the statement
that God reveals Himself as the Lord, for on analysis this yields the
Revealer, the act of Revelation, and the state of Revelation, and
these distinctions correspond to Father, Son, and Holy Spirit in
Scripture. He adds that this doctrine is rooted only in revelation,
and so he opposes all claims for a general revelation or a natural
theology and all search for *vestigia trinitatis*. He prefers to call
the Father, Son, and Holy Spirit three modes of being or of existence
rather than three persons. He maintains most all of the traditional
trinitarian doctrines, that there is both an immanent and an

economic Trinity, that the Trinity is a mystery, that lordship and personality pertain to the one single essence, that *opera trinitatis ad extra indivisa sunt* and yet can be properly appropriated to one or other Person, that there is a mutual inexistence of the three in one another, that God's threeness-in-oneness is founded on the relations of origin or processions, that the Holy Spirit proceeds from the Father and the Son. He gives only a qualified approval to the concept of *communicatio essentiae,* to that of generation of the Son, and to the term *person.* It is not hard to see why he would stand out as the great opponent not only of 19th-century Protestant theologians but of Brunner, Bultmann, and Tillich as well.

In Brunner's estimate Barth assigns to the doctrine of the Trinity an importance it does not deserve, since it is not only the product of genuine Biblical thought but also of philosophical speculation that is remote from the thought of the Bible. Three names, Father, Son, and Holy Spirit, not three persons, constitute the actual content of the New Testament message. Three persons side by side, an antinomy of Trinity and Unity, *una substantia, tres personae,* a *mysterium logicum,* none of this has any place in the testimony of the Apostles. Brunner's theology has been highly praised as sound and fruitful, but it has also been strongly criticized for its strong overtones of primitivism and subordinationism.

Bultmann, by his application of form criticism and demythologizing to the gospel, exercised a great influence not only on Protestant but also on Roman Catholic and Jewish theology as well. His theology aimed to discover the meaning of the New Testament and to communicate it intelligibly and relevantly to the men of today. In the New Testament he found a mythical cosmology and many mythological ideas, such as a preexistent divine being, a redeemer on the cross, the Son, the Logos. He was not primarily concerned with the Trinity but rather with God in so far as He revealed Himself in the Christ-event. When he demythologized the Johannine doctrine of the Word, in place of Christ as the incarnation of a divine being he gave us Christ as the human figure through whom the Father's Word is spoken. When he demythologized the Holy Spirit, the Spirit no longer signified an indwelling power but the possibility of a new life. He has been widely criticized for his definition of myth and for his extreme demythologization of the New Testament, but his brilliant theological proposals have become the focus for much of the most creative theological work of our time.

Tillich, perhaps the best-known Protestant theologian of our time, produced an ontological theology in which every doctrine, symbol and concept is traced back to one of the structures of being itself. His description of God, as being-in-itself, the infinite power of being, the ground of being, not a person but not less than personal, proved very controversial and led some philosophers to wonder whether he was an atheist. His Christology too was widely criticized for it seemed to make Christ not God but an enigmatic divine being. With such a Christology his God could not be the Triune God of orthodox Christianity. And when he finds the answer to the trinitarian problem in every life process, so that the idea of the living God requires a distinction between the abysmal element of the divine, the form element, and their spiritual unity, it is not too surprising that he should be charged with Sabellianism. But hardly any other theologian had as much dialogue with and cooperation from artists, scientists, writers and philosophers of the Old World as well as of the New as he.

Next we shall look at the development of trinitarian doctrine among Orthodox theologians and then among Roman Catholic theologians. And when we have summarized their attitudes and positions, we shall try to compare the status of trinitarian doctrine among Protestants with its status among the Orthodox and Roman Catholics, and wonder about what lies in the future.

PART SIX

Orthodox Trinitarian Doctrine

John of Damascus (d. *c.* 749), summing up the trinitarian doctrine of his great predecessors, maintained a strictly consubstantial Triad, viewed the persons metaphysically as 'modes of being,' and seems to have assigned the Son no causal role in the production of the Holy Spirit. 'His *De Fide Orthodoxa* has remained the summation of Greek theology, to which nothing was added and in which little change was made in subsequent centuries,' writes one historian.[1] Photius, 'the father of Byzantine theology,'[2] strongly opposed what he considered the *Filioque* innovation of some Latins, and in his *Mystagogia Spiritus sancti* he offered an arsenal of anti-*Filioque* arguments that would serve Greek polemicists down the centuries.

CHAPTER EIGHTEEN

From Photius to the Present

After the death of Photius there seems to have been substantial peace between Rome and Constantinople until the time of Cerularius,[1] though Nicetas Byzantius, the emperor Leo VI, and Euthymius, the Patriarch of Constantinople wrote against the Latin *Filioque* doctrine in the 10th century.[2]

CERULARIUS AND PSELLOS

In the midst of the 11th century the peace between East and West was ruptured by Michael Cerularius, the Patriarch of Constantinople (d. 1059). For reasons that are not quite clear he decided to wage war against the liturgical and canonical discipline of the Latin Church and its teaching about unleavened bread, baptism, the authority of the Roman See and the *Filioque*.[3] On July 16, 1054, some 90 days after Pope Leo IX's death, the papal legates laid on the altar of Saint Sophia a bull of excommunication against Cerularius and his followers.[4] 'On July 20 a council headed by Cerularius and composed of 2 archbishops, 12 metropolitans and 7 bishops solemnly excommunicated in turn those who had been responsible for the action of July 16.'[5] Thus began the great schism between the Orthodox East and the Catholic West that is still going on today.[6]

In the 11th century a Byzantine, Michael Psellos (d. 1078), strongly defended the Photian doctrine and praised Cerularius for opposing the Latin heresy, while several Russians wrote polemics against the Latins.[7] In the 12th century Theophylact (d. 1108), Metropolitan of Bulgaria, wrote that the Latin doctrine of the *Filioque* was false and derived from a confusion between the concepts of procession and mission.[8]

The most important trinitarian event of the 13th century was the Reunion Council of Lyons II in 1274, at which 'Constantinople was officially represented by three distinguished envoys sent by the Emperor.'[9] At this Council both the Profession of Faith of Michael Palaeologus and the Constitution on the Procession of the Holy Spirit explicitly affirmed the *Filioque*. And the Constitution added that the Holy Spirit proceeds from the Father and Son not as from two principles but as from one and not by two spirations but by one, and that this was what the true and unchangeable judgment of both Greek and Latin Fathers and Doctors had maintained. 'There was no great discussion; within a few weeks the Eastern representatives agreed to everything. Reunion was proclaimed.'[10] But Michael the Emperor 'died without being able to induce his Church and people to accept the agreement reached at Lyons, and his successor openly repudiated it.'[11]

In the 14th century Hesychasm came to the forefront.[12] This was a method of contemplation that would lead, it was believed, to a vision of a certain divine light shining within, a light that was uncreated but really distinct from the divine essence. This method claimed descent from Simeon the New Theologian (d. 1022) who was 'dedicated wholly to the description of' that 'communion with the Divine Light which had been the purpose of monastic asceticism from the start.'[13] But 'the opponents of Hesychasm felt that in the theology of "deification" or union with God, the bounds between creation and God were erased, that in its extremes the Hesychast doctrine of the uncreated Light on Mt. Tabor bordered on pantheism.'[14] Gregory of Palamas (d. 1359) took up the defense of Hesychasm and he and his disciples used this doctrine of a real distinction between a divine operation and the divine essence to explain the mission and inhabitation of a divine person.[15] It has been affirmed that Gregory's doctrine of 'divine energies that permeate the world . . . only completes and renews in a creative way the most authentic and basic tendency in the Orthodox view of Christianity.'[16] Many of Gregory's followers in the 14th and 15th century vigorously opposed the Latin doctrine of the *Filioque*.

At Florence in 1439 was held the greatest of the Reunion Councils, to which came envoys of the Patriarchs of Alexandria, Antioch, and Jerusalem, Isidore the Metropolitan of Moscow, the Patriarch of Constantinople, and the Emperor himself. And all the Greeks except Mark of Ephesus subscribed to the decree that not only defined the *Filioque* and declared that the procession of the Holy Spirit from the Father *through* the Son is substantially equivalent to the *Filioque*, but added that the *Filioque* had been lawfully added to the Creed for good and sufficient reasons. But it has been urged that 'in order to comprehend in human terms, if not justify, their cowardly error' it must be recognized that the Greeks 'were under great psychological pressure from the emperor and subjected to the intrigues of the Latinizers, who were determined to achieve union at any cost.' And 'when the Greeks returned to Byzantium, they immediately repudiated with horror the union that had been forced upon them.'[17]

In the 15th century, Gennadius II, Patriarch of Constantinople and an enemy of the Florentine Union,[18] put forth a *Confession of Christian Faith* for the use of Moslems, which is numbered among the Symbolic Books of Orthodoxy.[19] In the 16th century Jeremias II, Patriarch of Constantinople, engaged in correspondence with some Protestant theologians of Tübingen (1576–1581) and his *Three Answers*, which covered the whole range of Orthodox faith, are sometimes numbered among Orthodox Symbolic Books.[20] In the same century Maximus Margunius (d. 1602), in the hope of bringing about a reunion of East and West, wrote ironically about the Holy Spirit and declared that the *Filioque* had been added legitimately by the Latins in a Roman Synod under Pope Damasus in 381, but his effort was fruitless.[21]

SYMBOLIC BOOKS AND SYNODS

The 17th century is notable for its Symbolic Books and Synods. Metrophanes Kritopulos (d. 1641) wrote a *Confession of the Orthodox Church*, which compared doctrinal tenets of Orthodox, Catholic, and Protestant Christians. Peter Mogila (d. 1647) of Kiev in Russia wrote in Latin an 'Orthodox Confession of the Catholic and Apostolic Eastern Church.' These two Confessions are generally accepted as Symbolic Books of the Orthodox.[22] Among the Symbolic Books are also numbered the Acts of Four Orthodox Synods, that of Constantinople (1638), of Jassy (1641–1642), of Jerusalem (1672), and of Constantinople (1672). All of these arose out of the problems produced by 'Cyril Lucaris, who as patriarch of Constantinople published his *Confession of the Orthodox Faith* in 1629, a document which was completely Protestant in content and inspiration.'[23] The synod of Jerusalem insisted on all the doctrines denied by Cyril's Confession, declared that Protestants are patently heretics, and denied that Cyril wrote the Confession attributed to him. The *Confession of Faith* of Dositheus, who presided over the Jerusalem Synod, is numbered among the Orthodox Symbolic Books and together with the 'Acts of Jerusalem' constitutes 'the last of the official pronouncements of their Church.'[24]

EFFORTS AT REUNION

In the 18th and 19th centuries there were two attempts to effect a union between the Orthodox East and Western Protestants, and one effort to restore communion between Rome and the East. Some English Non-jurors used Peter the Great of Russia to further their project of union with the Orthodox (1716–1725), but nothing came of this.[25] The Conferences held at Bonn between Old Catholics, Anglicans, and Graeco-Russians were aimed at uniting the three groups in faith.[26] In both Conferences the main question was that of the procession of the Holy Spirit. In the first Conference they agreed that the *Filioque* had not been legitimately added to the Symbol and hoped that for the sake of peace the primitive form might be restored.[27] In the Second Conference they were able to agree only on six propositions taken verbally from John Damascene, e.g. (2) the Holy Spirit does not proceed (*ekporeuetai*) from the Son, (6) the Holy Spirit is intermediate between Father and Son and conjoined to the Father *through* the Son. But since the participants did not understand some of these propositions in the same way, the hoped-for union did not materialize. One of the outstanding Russians of the 19th century, Vladimir Soloviev (1853–1900) was intensely concerned to restore communion between Rome and the East.[28] To help bring this about he sent a remarkable 'memorandum' to Pope Leo XIII.[29] In this he stated that

> the Oriental Church never determined and never presented to the belief of the faithful as an obligatory dogma any doctrine contrary to the Catholic truth. The dogmatic decisions of the first 7 ecumenical councils represent the sum total of absolutely indubitable and unchangeable doctrinal truth, recognized as such at all times and universally by the Oriental Church in its entirety. Anything that goes beyond these limits is subject to controversy and can be considered as a particular doctrine of a certain theological school, or of an individual theologian of greater or lesser repute, which never received the sanction of the authority of an infallible magistry.[30]

In this connection it is interesting to find a present-day Orthodox theologian writing that 'later Byzantium tacitly acknowledged that the catholic truth of the Church had been formulated, once and for all, by the ancient Fathers and the seven ecumenical councils.'[31] But perhaps the most important trinitarian contribution in the 19th century was that of Vasil V. Bolotov (d. 1900), a distinguished Russian theologian.[32] In his famous 27 theses he maintained that the doctrine that the Holy Spirit proceeds from the Father is dogma, but the doctrine that the Holy Spirit proceeds from the Father alone, or from the Father and the Son or from the Father through the Son is only a theologoumenon.[33] These *Theses* split Russian theologians into factions, so that some were strict Photians while others went so far as to acknowledge publicly as true the Florentine decree that declared that Latin and Greek Fathers were in substantial agreement about the procession of the Holy Spirit.[34]

20TH-CENTURY ORTHODOX THEOLOGIANS

Vladimir Lossky, Frank Gavin, and Thomas Hopko have made noteworthy presentations of Orthodox trinitarian doctrine in the 20th century. Lossky sees the question of the procession of the Holy Spirit as the sole dogmatic ground of separation of Eastern and Western Churches.[35] And so he criticizes Bolotov for minimizing at the Bonn Conferences the doctrinal divergences between Latin and Greek Triadologies and failing to see that their distinctive formulas are '*a Patre et Filio*' and '*a Patre solo*,' and not '*a Filio*' and '*per Filium*.' The formula '*a Patre solo*,' 'while verbally it may seem novel, in its doctrinal tenor represents nothing more than a very plain affirmation of the traditional teaching about the monarchy of the Father, as the unique source of the divine Persons.'[36] Where the Latins based 'the personal diversity in the Trinity on the principle of *relations of opposition*,'[37] the Orthodox regard 'the diversity of the Three Persons as something absolute' and so they 'refuse to admit the conception of a relation of origin which *opposes* the Holy Spirit to the Father and Son as one principle of being.' They maintain that 'the absolute diversity of the Three cannot be based in their relations of opposition without admitting, implicitly or explicitly, the primacy of the essence over the persons,' and 'that is exactly what Orthodox theology cannot admit.' 'The very principle of relations of opposition is unacceptable to Orthodox Triadology,' for 'if this were admitted . . . the personal diversity in the Trinity would be made a matter of relations. . . . The relations only express personal diversity; they are not the basis of it. It is the absolute diversity of the Three Persons which determines their relations to one another, in their differences, and not vice versa. . . . It is not relations of opposition but relations of diversity about which we ought to speak here.'[38]

Do the Greeks 'fall into subordinationism, by their emphasis on the monarchy of the Father'? They do not, Lossky maintains, for when

> the Father is called the cause of the Persons of the Son and the Holy Spirit . . . this unique cause is not prior to his effects . . . He is not superior to his effects. . . . We have to confess not only the unity of the One Nature in the Three, but also the unity of the Three Persons of the one identical nature. . . . By defending the Personal procession of the Holy Spirit from the Father alone, Orthodoxy makes a profession of faith in the 'Simple Trinity,' wherein the relations of origin denote the absolute diversity of the Three, while also indicating their unity. [But if the Holy Spirit] proceeds from the Father and the Son, the relations of origin, instead of being signs of absolute diversity, become determinants of the Persons, from the starting point of an impersonal principle.[39]

'By the dogma of the *Filioque*,' Lossky maintains, 'the God of the philosophers and savants is introduced into the place of the Living God. . . . By the dogma of the procession of the Holy Spirit from the Father alone, the God of the philosophers is forever banished from the Holy of Holies.'[40]

Lossky opts for Palamism and says that 'because God is unknowable in that which he is, Orthodox theology distinguishes between the essence of God and his energies, between the inaccessible nature of the Holy Trinity and the "natural processions" of God.'[41] He adds that 'after the Councils of Lyons and Florence . . . in the West there was no longer any place for the conception of the energies of the Trinity; nothing was admitted to exist, outside the divine essence, except created effects, acts of will analogous to the act of creation. Western theologians must profess belief in the created character of the Glory of God and of sanctifying Grace and renounce the conception of deification or theosis.'[42]

What does Lossky think about reconciliation between East and West?

> Reconciliation will be possible and the *Filioque* will no longer be an 'impedimentum dirimens' at the moment when the West, which has been frozen for so long in dogmatic isolation, shall cease to consider Byzantine theology as an absurd innovation

and shall recognize that it only expressed traditional truth, to be found in a less explicit form in the Fathers of the first ages of the Church. . . . Then we shall with one mind confess our common Catholic faith in the Holy Trinity, who liveth and reigneth in the inapproachable light of his glory.[43]

In Frank Gavin's interesting summary of trinitarian doctrine in contemporary Greek thought[44] two points are notable, his comment on the use and meaning of *hypostasis* and his view of the *Filioque* controversy. 'The word "hypostasis," ' he writes, came

to be employed by the Greek Fathers to mean what we mean by Persons, that is . . . the mode of His Existence. . . . For this reason, the Church came to use 'hypostasis' . . . to 'express [one of] the three modes of existence of the One Divine Being.' 'Person' ('prosopon') came into use later; but since it means something different in modern philosophy from what the Fathers meant by it, it is more advisable to use 'hypostasis' for 'Person,' when discussing the teaching of the Greek Fathers and the Greek Church. 'Person' nowadays has come to signify 'a self-conscious and self-directing being,' but does not connote, as it did to the Fathers, a special mode of the existence of such a being. 'Person' in the Fathers meant an 'eternal mode of existence of the Divine Being.' Hence . . . 'hypostasis' better expresses the conception which the Fathers held of 'Person.'[45]

About the *Filioque* he is very forthright: 'All Orthodox theologians deny' the 'validity and truth' of the addition of the *Filioque* clause to the ancient creed.[46] 'Many of the Greek Fathers taught that the Holy Spirit proceeds from the Father *through* the Son, while none of them held that He proceeds from the Father *and* the Son.'[47] 'The arguments of Photius have formed the basis of the dogmatic teaching and controversial writings of subsequent Orthodox theologians.'[48] 'No single difference between East and West has aroused so much bitterness on the part of Orthodox writers as has the matter of the *Filioque*.'[49] 'In the main, the controversy has not been illuminated by any further contributions, save in acrimony and vilification, than those of Photius, beyond whom there has been no advance in theological acumen or insight.'[50]

Thomas Hopko stresses the Orthodox accent on the Spirit in the Church:[51]

The accent on the Spirit in the Church depends on and flows from the person of the Incarnate Word who sends his Spirit to his people from God his Father so that they may become cor-

porately his body, and individually members of it. The Spirit
completes the mission of Christ and makes him present to the
world in the unity of the one body, as well as in the multiplicity
of the 'brothers' who are anointed with him as 'christs' to be
also the sons of the heavenly Father: gods by the gracious unction
of the Holy Spirit. . . . The Holy Spirit is the hidden presence
among us of the kingdom of God . . . The Holy Spirit, the kingdom of God, comes to persons . . . who form the body of Christ
. . . the Spirit over whom no man or institution holds jurisdiction
is the same Spirit whom Christ has sent to those who consciously believe in him and who is given to men in the sacramental
experience of life in the Church. . . . The Church must remain—
this is the message of Orthodox theology and life—to bear witness to the mystery of Godmanhood, the mystery of the Spirit
in us, the mystery of the fulfillment of human destiny and the
destiny of the world in the gracious deification of human persons
in freedom and in truth.[52]

What is Orthodox trinitarianism today? It is substantially the
doctrine of the great Greek Fathers and of the first seven Ecumenical
Councils with the addition of Photianism and Palamism. It maintains
a consubstantial Triad of Father, Son and Holy Spirit, three distinct
hypostases of one identical *ousia*. Unlike Augustine's Western
approach to trinitarian doctrine which started from the unity of
nature and moved to the trinity of persons, the Orthodox approach
is that of the Greek Fathers which started from the Father as the
cause of the other two Persons and moved to the identity of their
nature. This approach is entirely orthodox and has many advan-
tages, but if ineptly handled it can easily involve subordinationism.
Orthodox theologians in using this method, with some few excep-
tions, avoided elaborate systematization of trinitarian doctrine and
preferred to present a 'simple Trinity' to their people as the object
of their faith and worship. And for this they deserve strong praise.
But their addition of Photianism and Palamism to their trinitarian
doctrine poses a problem. For by making these additions part of
their trinitarian doctrine they seem to be involved in a basic incon-
sistency. For the Photian doctrine '*a Patre solo*' and the Palamite
doctrine of uncreated divine energies are not expressed in the dogmatic decisions of the first seven Ecumenical Councils. And yet
many (all?) Orthodox theologians insist that their trinitarian doctrine is measured by and limited to that of these first seven Councils.
    Is there any hope of agreement between Orthodox East and
Catholic West in matters trinitarian? Anthimus VII, the Orthodox
patriarch, wrote in his reply to Pope Leo XIII that it is the *Filioque*

both as doctrine and as addition to the Creed, that really divides the two Churches in trinitarian doctrine.[53] Must it always? Both Churches have such a deep faith in and worship of the same Triune God. Does this Triune God they both love want this fraternal division to continue?

Are there any signs of reunion? 'Signs of a rapprochement, although slight as yet, are increasing year by year.'[54] A recent writer pointed out that 'these two Churches have much more in common between themselves than each of them has with the Protestant Churches,' but until recently

> there was not the proper climate for full-scale, peaceful cooperation. Now, however, such a climate has been created by John XXIII, that good, wise, and truly great pope. . . . The first step was the calling of the Second Vatican Council. . . . The second was the establishment of the Secretariat for Christian Unity, entrusted by that far-seeing man to the tested and experienced rector of the Pontifical Biblical Institute of Rome, Augustin Cardinal Bea.' Then 'the meeting between His Holiness Pope Paul VI and the Ecumenical Patriarch Athenagoras. . . . God grant that this meeting between the heads of the two sister Churches may be the beginning of a process which leads them closer together and eventually to reunion.'[55]

PART SEVEN

Catholic Trinitarian Doctrine from the 15th Century to the Present

Theologically, the West made its greatest contribution to trinitarian systematization through the Dominicans and Franciscans, Aquinas, Bonaventure, and Scotus. Aquinas was easily preeminent, and with him and Scotus the Western Church reached the high point of speculative trinitarian theology. Dogmatically, the Church's solemn formulation of its trinitarian faith, that began with the Council of Nicea in 325, reached its climax in the Florentine decrees for the Greeks and Jacobites in the 15th century.

What has happened since? Karl Rahner has written:

> since the Council of Florence there has been no official doctrinal declaration by the Church in which the magisterium might seem to sanction a real progress in the understanding of this mystery. Much has been done no doubt since then in the line of research into the history of this dogma . . . efforts have been made to link Christian piety more expressly and more vitally with this mystery. Theology too has shown instances of writers who are more consciously and keenly aware of the obligation of presenting the doctrine of the Trinity in such a way that it can become a reality in the concrete religious life of Christians. . . . But . . . one might almost dare to affirm that if the doctrine of the Trinity were to be erased as false, most religious literature could be preserved almost unchanged throughout the process.[1]

To evaluate this judgment properly it will help to look more closely at trinitarian theologians and doctrine from the 15th century to today.

CHAPTER NINETEEN

Principal Trinitarian Theologians

The Dominicans gradually lined up behind St. Thomas, and began to use his *Summa* as textbook instead of Lombard's *Sentences*, and to publish Commentaries on the *Summa*. Of these Commentaries on the *Summa* the principal ones were produced by Cajetan (d. 1534), John of St. Thomas (d. 1644), Contenson (d. 1674), Billuart (d. 1751). In 1637 the Carmelites of Salamanca made an important contribution to Thomist theology by their *Cursus Theologicus*. More recently E. Hugon, and R. Garrigou-Lagrange helped to transmit Thomist trinitarian doctrine by their works, *Le Mystère de la Très Sainte Trinité* (1912) and *The Trinity and God the Creator* (1952).

The Franciscans made their chief contributions to the presentation of Scotist trinitarian doctrine through F. Lychet (d. 1520), John de Rada (d. 1608), F. Henno (d. 1713), and especially through C. Frassen (d. 1711), whose *Scotus Academicus* largely became the authoritative manual of Scotist theology.

The Jesuits, theological newcomers compared to the Dominicans and Franciscans, made important contributions to the transmission and expansion of trinitarian doctrine in the 17th century through Suarez, Ruiz de Montoya, and Petau, in the 18th century through Kilber and the Wirceburgenses, in the 19th century through Franzelin and De Régnon, in the 20th century through Billot, D'Alès, Galtier, Lebreton, Lonergan and Rahner.

Other theologians who made notable contributions in the 17th century were Thomassinus, Gerbert, and Tournely, in the 19th century Ginoulhiac, Newman, and Scheeben, in the 20th century Hervé, Janssens, Van Noort, and Schmaus.

In the following chapter we shall look to the contributions that these theologians made to trinitarian doctrine in the areas of our knowledge of the Trinity processions, relations, persons, unity, missions and inhabitation, then summarize these developments and from them try to indicate what directions trinitarian doctrine may take in the future.

CHAPTER TWENTY

Our Knowledge of the Trinity

In regard to the natural and revelational knowability or cognoscibility of the trinitarian dogma there is general agreement among theologians that this dogma is a strict mystery, knowable only by revelation.[1] This position is based on a solid traditional interpretation of Biblical data, on papal condemnations of opposed semirationalist views of Hermes (Denz 2738–2740), Günther (Denz 2828–2831), Frohschammer (Denz 2850–2861), Rosmini (Denz 3225–3226), and on Vatican I's definitions regarding mysteries (Denz 3015, 3041). Hence it is maintained that reason alone (1) did not know this mystery anywhere, (2) cannot know it, (3) cannot positively demonstrate it even after it is revealed and known by faith.[2] But although the trinitarian dogma is a strict mystery, still 'reason illumined by faith can progress with God's help to some analogical and imperfect understanding of this mystery.'[3]

Recently some authors have been urging a special connection between creation and the Trinity. R. C. Neville presents creation theory as a model for interpreting the Trinity. The doctrine of the Trinity, he asserts, 'stems from both revelational and speculative roots,' and 'speculation about creation furnishes a general model for interpreting the Trinity,' so that 'the particularities and unique claims of the Trinitarian doctrine that stem from the revelation of God in Jesus Christ can be given general and critical, though not particular and demonstrative, articulation in the notions of the creation theory.'[4] Teilhard de Chardin sees creation as a replica of the Trinity. 'In regard to the relationship of God to the material world, Teilhard begins by saying that creation is a reflection, an image of the life of the Blessed Trinity. This is what imposes upon it that metaphysical structure by which it must necessarily move

from multiplicity to unity, and more precisely toward an ultimate
unity with God.' And Pleromization, the 'slow maturation of
the universe into this "mysterious synthesis" . . . of the created and
Uncreated . . . at the Parousia,' is thus 'the fruit of God's reflection
. . . outside himself; it appears somehow as a sort of replica or sym-
metry of Trinitisation.'[5] Thus Teilhard 'suggests that bound up with
the trinitarian movement by which God posits himself and affirms
himself in the communion of the persons, is a movement of loving
expansion, by which God, completely freely and gratuitously,
unites his creation with himself. . . . Thus creation, with its counter-
part of progressive unification, is seen to be a "sort of replica or
symmetrical copy of trinitisation." '[6]

If the Trinity is knowable and known only by revelation, where
and how is this revelation to be found? Catholic theologians today
maintain that neither a trinity nor a plurality of divine persons is
taught or revealed explicitly in the Old Testament.[7] But while some
insist that 'the OT does not contain suggestions or foreshadowings
of the trinity of persons,'[8] others more correctly hold that 'in the
Old Testament the divine Trinity is somehow adumbrated,'[9] and
that 'the Old Testament must be understood to contain a genuine
secret pre-history of the revelation of the Trinity' in that God is
present there 'in the unity of Word and Spirit.'[10]

How then is the Trinity revealed in the New Testament? Some
manualists affirmed that the Trinity is 'explicitly revealed in the
New Testament'[11] 'is proved from the New Testament,'[12] 'is certainly
and clearly contained in the New Testament,[13] and that 'all the
gospels . . . are permeated with the thought, now latent, now manifest, of the three divine Persons.'[14] But today there are new ways of
viewing and finding this New Testament revelation. Often it is
viewed as God's act of self-communication rather than as the communication of certain revealed truths, as the Father's going out
from Himself into man's history through His self-expressive Word
and life-giving Spirit.[15] Sometimes it is said that 'to be understood
completely, the NT revelation must be viewed as an existential
movement, inaugurated by "all that Jesus began to do and to teach"
(Acts 1.1) and brought to term by efficacious direction of the
ascended Christ and of His Spirit, which the NT authors have been
inspired to present as the history of the primitive Christian
Church.'[16]

For one theologian 'the study of these words—Father, Son,
Word, Spirit—and their background is the best way to arrive at an
understanding of the distinction of persons as it is stated in the
NT.'[17] For another 'the Father's revelation through the Son is found

in the Scripture and his revelation through the Spirit is found in tradition. . . . The history of the distinction between them is closely related to the historical developments of the Trinitarian formula.'[18] For still another 'the "visible mission of the Son' is the theologian's real field of activity, the sphere in which he can more precisely define the deeper meaning of the divine Sonship.'[19] A fourth writes that 'in thinking of the Trinity we may start without misgivings from the experience of Jesus and His Spirit in us in the history of salvation and faith. . . . The immanent Trinity as such confronts us in the experience of faith—a constitutive component of which is indeed the concrete word of Scripture itself.' Thus 'the Trinity takes place in us, and does not first reach us in the form of statements communicated by revelation. On the contrary, these statements have been made to us because the reality of which they speak has been accorded to us. . . . Every treatise should be built up from the start from the "sendings," even if for didactic reasons they are only treated explicitly at the end.'[20]

Most theologians no longer expect to find in the New Testament a formal trinitarianism, only an elemental trinitarianism: 'the dogma of the Trinity . . . was a late arrival, product of three centuries' reflection and debate,' but 'confession of Father, Son and Holy Spirit . . . and hence an elemental Trinitarianism—went back to the period of Christian origins.'[21] Another writes that 'the elements of the trinity of persons within the unity of nature in the Bible appear in the use of the terms Father, Son and Spirit' but 'the personality of the Spirit emerged more slowly than the personal reality of Father and Son.'[22] *A New Catechism* says that 'the message of scripture proclaims so vigorously both the distinct proprieties of the Father, the Son and the Holy Spirit, and their divine oneness, that we cannot but confess one God in three persons.'[23]

It seems that the way of the manualist is a thing of the past, and that these new ways of discerning the elements of the Trinity in the New Testament, after they have been more carefully studied and verified, are likely to be in force for quite some time.

CHAPTER TWENTY-ONE

The Divine Processions, Relations, Persons, and Unity

PROCESSIONS

All post-Florentine theologians teach that there are two processions in God, the generative procession of the Son from the Father, and the non-generative procession of the Holy Spirit from the Father and the Son, and they base this teaching on Biblical and patristic evidence and on the solemn declarations of Symbols and General Councils. Most of them also follow Aquinas in teaching that the Son's procession is by way of intellect, the Holy Spirit's by way of will, and they consider this position as theologically certain[1] M. T.-L. Penido maintains that the so-called psychological theory is a true metaphysical analogy of proper proportionality of the dynamic order and encompasses truly and formally, although imperfectly, the reality of the mystery of the Trinity, at least in certain points.[2] B. Lonergan declares it is the common opinion of theologians that the divine processions are to be conceived according to the psychological analogy and that this has a foundation in Scripture and tradition. He adds that it seems to be the opinion of St. Thomas that in this psychological analogy the likeness between the Triune God and our mind is found in intelligible emanations of word and love, i.e., in a fully conscious, fully intellectual, fully actual production of word and love.[3]

A few theologians, however, give this psychological analogy little or no value as an index of the inner reality of the divine processions. G. H. Joyce, who regards the intellectual procession of the Son merely 'as a theological opinion of great probability and harmonizing well with revealed truth,' says that 'the doctrine of the procession of the Holy Spirit by means of the act of the Divine will is due entirely to Augustine. It is nowhere found among the Greeks. . . . It harmonizes . . . with all the truths of faith. It is admirably adapted to assist us to a fuller comprehension of the fundamental doctrine of the Christian religion. It does not possess the sanction of revelation.'[4] Karl Rahner writes:

> This is not to say that such a psychological doctrine of the Trinity is only sheer—and not even successful—theological speculation. We can certainly say that the two divine processions, whose existence is guaranteed by revelation, have something to do with the two basic acts which we know belong to the spirit: knowledge and love. For this there is a foundation in Scripture. But though the basic starting point of the Augustinian psychological doctrine of the Trinity is certainly valid . . . we must also point out . . . that the biblical foundation is restricted to the fact that in the dispensation of redemption the divine knowledge is displayed as revealing itself and the divine love as giving itself in personal communication. [But if] one begins with a concept of knowledge and love taken from natural philosophy [and applies] these speculative concepts to the Trinity one has to admit that they do not work: for the good reason that knowledge and love remain 'essential' concepts. One cannot and may not evolve a 'personal,' 'notional' concept of the word and of the 'weight' of love on the basis of human experience. For then the Word of knowledge and the Spirit of love would demand that a Word and a Spirit should proceed from them, again as persons.[5]

In the light of these varying estimates it seems clear that it is not theologically certain that the Son proceeds from the Father by way of intellect and the Holy Spirit by way of will. But it seems excessive to say, as Rahner does, that these speculative concepts taken from natural philosophy and applied to the Trinity do not work. Obviously natural concepts could not be expected to work—perfectly—when applied to the Trinity. But this psychological doctrine 'worked' for Augustine and Aquinas and for an immense number of theologians; it gave and gives a better analogical answer to many trinitarian questions than any other theory that has been thus far presented. It fits better than any other into the dogmatic framework of the Trinity, and it has given yeoman service to theologians faced with the extremely difficult task of finding an intelligible analogy to explain the Biblical and dogmatic data about the Trinity.

RELATIONS

Since there are in God real processions—generation and spiration—there must be and are in God real relations. On this theologians are agreed, and they regard the existence of real relations in God either as a matter of faith,[6] or more commonly and properly as theologically certain,[7] since there is no definitive pronouncement on this point. Thus they declare that it is theologically certain that: (1) there are four real relations in God, paternity, filiation, active spiration, passive spiration; (2) three of these, paternity, filiation, and passive spiration are really distinct from one another, and (3) subsistent, i.e., really identified with the divine substance, but (4) logically or virtually distinct from the divine substance.[8] All these theologians lean heavily for their doctrine on the Florentine relational declaration that 'in God all things are one where opposition of relation does not intervene' (Denz 1330) but not all agree on the dogmatic value of this pronouncement. Some say that '*omnia sunt unum* . . . is not part of the definition of the Council of Florence, although it is essential to its systematic exposition of the doctrine of the Holy Trinity—essential rather as the keystone than as the corner stone.'[9] Others, however, say that the declaration of which '*omnia sunt unum* . . .' is a part, is 'of defined faith . . . and sets forth as it were a systematization of all that has been said so far . . . and a (conflational) corollary of (1) the divine monarchy, (2) the consubstantiality of the Three and (3) the distinctions founded in relative properties.'[10]

If there are in God three really distinct subsistent relations, paternity, filiation, and passive spiration, and three really distinct divine persons, Father, Son, and Holy Spirit, the question must arise as to the connection between these three relations and these three persons: do these relations merely manifest these persons or do they also constitute them? Orthodox theology views them as merely manifesting the personal diversity of the three, not as constituting it.[11] Catholic theologians, however, generally say that the divine persons are not only distinguished by these relations but are 'constituted by these relations,'[12] or 'are these relations.'[13] Thus one writes: 'In God Persons are relations and relations are Persons. . . . In God personality essentially has its centre of reference in another. The Father is Father, that is himself, only because he is so to another: *ad alium*. The Son is Son inasmuch as he is Son of the Father. And the Spirit is the Spirit only because he is the common Spirit of their perfect unity, dynamic and fruitful.'[14] Another declares: 'the personalities of the divine persons really consist in their relationships with one another.' Relationships of men

always take place on the edge of the ego. The divine relationships on the other hand are of such power that not only is the heart of the ego given by each of the persons to each of the others, but I and Thou are built up together. The divine persons are relationships whose power is in themselves, and which exist in themselves. Every divine person is therefore individual only in his giving of himself, his movement towards the others. . . . Existence as a person for each depends on his orientation towards the others. The existence of one person is therefore in the fullest sense existence with others.[15]

At first sight—and second and third—this doctrine that 'in God Persons are relations and relations are Persons' may not appear very intelligible or very attractive or very likely to inspire a man's love and adoration. Yet it is a logical doctrine and a corollary of the basic doctrine that in one same God there are three consubstantial divine persons who are really distinct relationally or by their relative properties. For if in God the three divine persons are really distinct from one another, and only the three subsistent relations of paternity, filiation, and passive spiration are really distinct from one another, then these three persons must be these three relations, since in God there is only Trinity and not quaternity or sexternity (Denz 804). And 'when we affirm that the Father and Son are alike identical with the Divine Essence, we are affirming that the Supreme Infinite Substance is identical not with two absolute entities, but with each of two relations. These relations, in virtue of their nature as correlatives, are necessarily opposed the one to the other, and therefore different.'[16]

This doctrine of incommunicable subsistent relations offers a great deal of metaphysical value, for it solidly negates both Tritheism and Modalism. And if it is true 'that the doctrine of the Trinity as interpreted in terms of relations presents the most perfect formula possible to men in this life,'[17] perhaps it should be quickly added that only a metaphysician can properly appreciate this doctrine and cope with the traditional objection brought against it, that if three divine relations are identified with one same divine substance, then they must be really identified with and not really distinct from, one another.[18]

PERSONS

Since the Council of Florence the Boethian definition of person as 'an individual substance of a rational nature' has been used by most theologians down to the present.[19] Some theologians have added or preferred to this definition that of Aquinas: 'a distinct subsistent in an intellectual nature,'[20] since the Boethian definition, although it

can be rightly expounded, yet taken as it sounds 'makes more difficulties than it solves.'[21]

A few theologians have developed interesting definitions of their
own. Thus F. Klein defines a person as 'an intelligent being which
makes up, by itself alone, a complete and non-communicable whole;
a being conscious and master of itself, which says *I* and *me*, which is
aware of what flows from itself and what it receives from elsewhere.
Spontaneous and free in its actions, an independent centre of rights
and responsibilities, the person is the highest form of being we know;
it must therefore be found in God, since He possesses all perfection
—but only analogically.'[22] M. Pontifex says that 'by the term person
we understand the subject who possesses the nature and uses it. . . .
If we analyse this notion of person, we see that it adds to the notion
of nature that of self-sufficiency, completeness as a source of activity,
a marking off from everything else, that is of full individuality.'[23] M.
Scheeben declares:

> in general we define 'person' as the bearer and possessor of a
> rational nature. But in God all the divine persons possess one
> and the same individual, indivisible and simple nature . . . but
> . . . in different manners . . . the First Person possesses this nature
> of Himself, the Second possesses it from the First, and the Third
> from the First and Second. Accordingly the internal distinction
> and also the inner being of these persons are constituted by the
> relations in which they stand to one another as possessors of the
> same nature. . . . Therefore in our definition we must take these
> relations into account, and say that the divine persons are rela-
> tive proprietors of the divine nature. . . . The divine persons are
> relative only among themselves. They are not dependent on any
> higher being outside themselves, since they all have the same
> supreme and independent nature. They are not even dependent
> on one another, because the person who gives origin to another
> is related as essentially to the latter as the latter is to the former,
> and mutual relations in the same order are equalized.[24]

To the question, what seems to be understood by the term person,
B. Lonergan answers:

> Five things. First, person is a common name by which we reply
> to one asking, three what? Then, person is according to the
> definition of St. Thomas, a distinct subsistent in an intellectual
> nature. Thirdly, a divine person is either a subsistent relation or
> a relationally distinct subsistent. Fourthly, a divine person is a
> subject that is distinct and conscious of itself, both as subject

and as distinct. Fifthly, the divine persons are not only referred to one another by interpersonal relations but also constituted as persons by interpersonal relations.[25]

A remarkable effort to indicate why there are three divine persons is made by M. Schmaus:

> The life and being of God is of such abundance, so overflowing with ability to know and love, that it cannot creatively display itself in the living, knowing and loving of a single person. It requires a threefold ego. Thus the tri-personality of God is a sign of life at its highest and richest potential . . . three persons use God's power, life-potential and faculties of knowing and loving to the full. There is no impersonal zone in God, but rather, in the sphere of the divine being, existence, life, knowledge and will are taken to the highest possible peak of personal existence. . . . The three divine persons exist in closest relationship with one another. There is continually being carried on an exchange of life between them. Indeed, it is in exchange that their life consists. . . . In the Father's giving of himself to the Son, and the Son's to the Father, there springs into being from the mightiness of their giving, a third divine Person. . . . Each of the divine Persons finds his existence and his joy in the personalities of the other two. . . . Each of the divine Persons continually receives from each of the others fulness of life in the eternal bloom of youth, fulness so perfect as to be incapable of any enrichment. . . . From the fact that God is tri-personal . . . the whole visible and perceptible reality is . . . a mirror of God. . . . The whole of the created world is therefore built up in threes . . . root, stem and branch . . . knowledge, will and love . . . memory, reason and will.[26]

Should the divine persons be called 'modes of being' rather than persons, as Karl Barth, Claude Welch and some of the Cappadocian Fathers seem to wish? Lonergan says No! For Father, Son and Holy Spirit are not modes of being but subsistents. Since God subsists and each of the three is God, each subsists. A subsistent is that which is, a mode of being is a way in which it is. Conceiving the Father through paternity, we conceive paternity as a mode of being, but in reality in God paternity is not a mode of being but it is God the Father. There are three in God to whom we can say 'You.'[27]

Should the Father, Son and Holy Spirit still be called 'persons' today, when psychology stresses that a person is a 'center of consciousness'? L. Dewart thinks they should not, it seems, since in his

estimate the Hellenic term *person* that served the Christian faith
admirably in the past, is inadequate today. For

> Person has long ceased to mean *prosopon* or *persona* and per-
> sonality cannot today remotely convey the idea of a *mode of
> subsistence.* . . . To him who is formed by the twentieth century,
> *person* means . . . a center of consciousness and, therefore, a
> center of *exercised* existence, life, presence, freedom and reality.
> A person is a being who does not merely *have* life and existence,
> but one who *exerts* himself towards life and existence; it is a
> being whose *being* is life and existence. A person, thus, cannot be
> a termination of nature. On the contrary, nature is a termina-
> tion of personality—and a person moreover, terminates itself
> and makes its nature in and through existing.[28]

And in a second book Professor Dewart declares that only a *meta-
metaphysical* mode of philosophical thought can 'effectively restore
the foundations of Christian belief today.'[29] B. Lonergan finds
Dewart's contention that 'person' is a concept taken over from Hellenic thought 'a rather inadequate account of the matter' and says
that 'when Dewart talks about the God of Greek metaphysics, one
wonders what Greek metaphysician he is talking about.' He maintains that 'It is unhistorical to suppose that Greek philosophy
supplied all the principal elements in which we have for centuries
conceptualized the basic Christian beliefs of the Trinity and the Incarnation.' He adds that Dewart wants 'not merely the demythologization of Scripture but the more comprehensive *dehellenization* of
dogma, and specifically that of the Christian doctrine of God,' and
wants the principal means for dehellenizing dogma and for obtain-
ing a mature theism to be a theory of knowledge which apparently
'involves a rather strong repugnance to propositional truth' and an
exclusion of 'the correspondence view of truth,' of 'correspondence
between meaning and meant.' He admits 'that Catholic theology today has a tremendous task before it, for there are very real limitations to Hellenism that have been transcended by modern culture
and have yet to be successfully surmounted by Catholic theology,'
but 'that task is not helped, rather it is gravely impeded, by wild
statements based on misconceptions or suggesting unbelief.'[30]
Lonergan apparently sees no great difficulty in considering the
divine persons as 'centers of consciousness' in an analogous sense,
for he writes that 'a divine person is a subject that is distinct and
conscious of itself, both as subject and as distinct' and adds that
'Father, Son and Holy Spirit through one real consciousness are
three subjects conscious of themselves and of the others and of their

act,' so that 'a conscious Father consciously understands, knows, wills; a conscious Son consciously understands, knows, wills; a conscious Spirit consciously understands, knows, wills.'[31]

Karl Rahner declares:

> it is undeniable that the doctrine of the three persons in God evokes the almost unavoidable danger . . . of thinking of three different consciousnesses . . . [a] basically tritheistic position, in which the three persons are thought of as three personalities with different centres of action. [He wonders why we should not] operate from the very start with a concept and a word—call it 'person' or anything else that seems fitting—which can be more easily adapted to the matter in hand and can render it with less risk of misunderstanding? This is not to affirm with Karl Barth that the word 'person' is not apt when speaking of the reality in question and that it should be replaced by some less ambiguous word in Church teminology. We may concede, however, that the development of the word 'person' outside the theology of the Trinity, after the definitions of the fourth century, took a very different direction from its originally near-Sabellian tone. It developed the existential meaning (as in Hermes) of the ego which is opposed to every other person in independent, proper and distinctive freedom. The ambiguity of the word was thereby increased. However, there it is, sanctioned by the usage of more than 1500 years, and there is no other word which would be really better, more generally understandable and less exposed to misconceptions. We must therefore continue to use the word, even though we know there is a history behind it and that strictly speaking it is not altogether suitable to express what is meant and has no great advantages. But . . . in approaching the mystery of the Trinity from the standpoint of the economy of salvation, there is as little need to operate with the notion of 'person' from the beginning as in the history of revelation itself. Starting from the presence of God the Father himself, communicated in the economy of salvation through the Word in the Spirit, one could show that the differentiation in the 'God for us' is also that of the 'God in himself,' and go on simply to explain that this threefold quality of God in himself may be called triune 'personality.' . . . All difficulties would not disappear . . . but the difficulties could be rendered less acute and the danger of a tritheistic misunderstanding lessened.[32]

Two theologians wish the word *person* to be applied analogously not only between God and men but also between the divine persons themselves. B. Cooke declares: 'We have employed the term "person" and must unavoidably do so, but hopefully we have indicated that this word should be used of Father, Son, and Spirit with full awareness of the analogous nature of this predication, therefore with stress on the radical distinctiveness of "person," not just differentiating divine from human personhood, but distinguishing the reality of personhood as it applies to Father, Son and Spirit.'[33] L. Cantwell writes that the word *person* 'is used analogically as between the three divine persons. The Father is not a "person" in univocally the same sense in which the Son is a "person." '[34]

UNITY

Only a few theologians contributed anything special to the consideration of the divine unity. Most of them seem content to repeat the declaration of Lateran IV that 'there is one supreme, incomprehensible, ineffable reality, which is truly the Father, and the Son and the Holy Spirit ... . the three persons taken together and each of them taken singly; and, hence there is in God only a trinity, not a quaternity, because each of the persons is that reality, namely, the divine substance, essence, or nature.' (Denz 804).

Scheeben gives an interesting presentation of the divine unity in terms of unity of nature, immanent processions, unifying relations and community of persons. He declares:

the divine Trinity . . . is thoroughly permeated and pervaded by the highest unity. . . . Unity rules throughout; the divine nature and substance is one in all 3 persons, and these in turn are one with the essence. . . . The communication of the essence from one person to the others involves no separation or partition of the essence. . . . Furthermore, the first principle . . . the original possessor of the divine nature is one; and the distinction among the persons proceeds from this one principle. . . . For the Second and Third Persons are distinct from the First Person only because they have their origin from Him and stand in relation to Him by virtue of this origin. But this is an interior origin, arising from the interior of the producing person and remaining within Him. The Son does not depart from the bosom of the Father at His generation; He remains dwelling therein; He is distinct from the Father, but is not separated from the Father. The Holy Spirit likewise does not retire from the heart of the Father and the Son at His origin; He remains inseparably united to them, as the flame to the fire from which it flares up. . . . The order of origins in God . . . establishes only a distinction among the persons. Even this distinction is purely relative, that is, it consists only in the relationship of the persons to one another, specifically of the Second and the Third to the First. It is this relationship which distinguishes one person from the others to whom He is related, but at the same time unites them with one another, both in reality and in our concept; for the relative as such can neither exist nor be conceived apart from the term to which it is related. Thus distinction in possession not only does not exclude common possession, but essentially requires it. This union and community among the persons appear in higher relief when we reflect that . . . each of the three persons is in His own way a center and focus to which the other two are related and in which they are united to each other. . . . The Father is the common principle of the Son . . . of the Holy Spirit. . . . the Holy Spirit unites the Father and the Son with and in Himself . . . as the product of their mutual love. . . . the Son . . . occupies a central position, and is thus a link which joins the other persons in Himself to form a golden chain. . . . Everything in the Trinity is unity, union, and harmony in the highest and most beautiful sense of the word.[35]

B. Cooke stresses community of persons:

Certainly, there can be no rejection of the traditional teaching about the unicity of the divine nature, but perhaps today we can move another step away from a static conception of divine being and gain further insight into the dynamic aspect of divine unity. It seems that a judicious application of the analogy of personal existence, coupled with what we have already discussed regarding the distinctiveness of the three divine persons, can provide some valid insight. . . . Another avenue is suggested by our increased modern insight into the social dimension of personal existence, into the unavoidable inter-dependence of individual and community, into the manner in which community is established by personal self-giving. Is it not possible to think of the divine being as being constantly 'constituted' by the dynamic personal communion of Father and Son in the Spirit? This would be the ideal realization of that total union in being towards which our human love vainly strives, but towards which it points. Community of persons, rather than unity in nature, would then be our approach to thinking about the unity of being in the Godhead.[36]

G. Salet views the divine unity from the standpoint of love:

Here then are three Persons . . . not selfish egoisms that confront one another . . . but bountiful beings who are constantly giving themselves. They possess the same divine nature, that infinite richness which can communicate itself entirely, since it is infinitely spiritual, and which forbids any idea of division and sharing, of joint ownership and participation, because it is infinitely simple. . . . Each of the divine persons possesses this richness only in an unselfish way, only in order to love the others in a total giving of himself. . . . It is in the others that he finds himself. Each of the persons is not a selfish withdrawal into himself, but a complete pouring out of himself toward the others. This plurality of persons loving each other, however, does not result in a plurality of gods. If God is subsistent Love, how could he help but be infinite unity? All love is unifying; it brings about 'unanimity' among the most dissimilar things. What should we say then of infinite Love? Is it not unity itself? . . . Since the Blessed Trinity is divine Love itself, the dogma of the Trinity is the revelation of this Love. . . . The love of the divine persons for each other is poured out toward us. They have given us themselves, their very being, no more, no less than that. . . . 'Are you looking for something to give to God?' asks St. Augustine. 'Give him yourself.'[37]

CHAPTER TWENTY-TWO

Divine Missions and Inhabitation

MISSIONS

Theologians generally consider it theologically certain that proceeding divine persons can be sent either visibly or invisibly, and that the mission of a divine person in itself is a work common to the entire Trinity but in its term regards only the person sent.[1] Trinitarian manualists have generally put these missions at the end of their treatise but today there is a good and growing tendency to go the way of Scripture and start with the mission of the Son and the Holy Spirit,[2] and then toward the end draw together a doctrine of the Trinity in terms of its Biblical origins and historical development. Two theologians in particular have made noteworthy contributions to the development of a more satisfactory doctrine of the divine missions.

The first of these was Scheeben, who felt that the classical trinitarian theology had somewhat neglected the divine missions, and hoped to remedy this by presenting a more inspiring doctrine of divine missions as prolongations of the eternal processions. 'In the view of all theologians,' he wrote, 'these missions must be regarded as a temporal prolongation of the eternal processions, and as the introduction of their products into the creature.'[3] But how are these missions to be understood and explained? If 'by virtue of their infinity and omnipresence, all the divine persons together are from eternity substantially present everywhere they can ever be,' how can the Son and the Holy Spirit become present 'in a new way to the creature in time, and in this sense begin to exist outside of God'?[4] By reason of a distinctive activity? 'But every external operation is absolutely common to all the divine persons. . . . Hence by reason of activity no divine person can step into the outer world exclusively by Himself.'[5] Yet 'it is no less impossible to perceive such a mission without divine activity for any coming of God or of a divine person to a creature can be apprehended as taking place only in terms of some operation proceeding from God.'[6] 'How, then, can a divine person be established in a creature in a special way and exist in the creature by Himself alone?'[7]

> This can be done if a divine person exhibits His hypostatic character in some symbol (as the Holy Spirit did in the dove appearing at the baptism in the Jordan). . . . This kind of mission . . . is merely symbolic, since the divine person is visualized by the creature only in a material symbol representing Him. . . . Obviously this type of mission is imperfect by its very nature, since a merely symbolic representation cannot properly be called an existence of the represented object in the image. . . . This sort of mission serves only to accompany and illustrate in a visible manner the other kinds of mission which are complete in themselves. Thus . . . the dove was meant to illustrate the union of the Son of God (who had been sent in His human nature) with the heavenly Father in the Holy Spirit; and the symbolic mission of the Holy Spirit on Pentecost Day, under the image of the rushing wind and the fiery tongues, was meant to emphasize His interior mission into the hearts of the apostles. The latter two kinds of mission—in the Incarnation and in grace—can consequently be called real, actual missions in contradistinction to the symbolic missions.[8]

Scheeben sees two kinds of invisible mission of Son and Holy Spirit in the gift of sanctifying grace. The first kind is by '*Impression and Expression of the persons sent*':

> only where the power and activity of the divine persons are manifested in a particularly sublime manner, in an effect by which the specific divine excellence of a person is communicated to the creature, and in the communication of which the procession of this person is reproduced in the creature according to His specifically divine character; where consequently this person appears as a seal which, stamped upon the creature, impresses in him the divine and hypostatic character of the person—can we say in the full and proper sense of the word that the person Himself, and not merely some gift derived from Him, is lodged in the creature, is given to the creature . . . and is present in the creature. . . . Then . . . the divine person Himself is sent into the creature. All this takes place in sanctifying grace, and in it alone.[9]

In the outpouring of supernatural, filial, divine love . . . into our hearts, the interior outpouring of the love between the Father and the Son that is consummated in the Holy Spirit is continued because it is reproduced. So we can say not only that the love is given to us and is poured out upon us, but that the Holy Spirit Himself is given to us and poured out upon us in this love. We should do even better to say that the habit and act of charity, poured forth by the Holy Spirit, come into our heart by the very fact that He Himself, the torrent of divine love, is given and drawn to our soul.

Similarly in the conferring of supernatural divine light and the reflection of the divine nature upon our soul, in the impress of the supernatural likeness of God, the eternal splendor of the Father, is irradiated over us, and His consubstantial image, the Son of God, is imprinted in our soul and is reborn in us by an imitation and extension of the eternal production. Thus God's Son Himself in His divine and hypostatic character is lodged in the creature as the seal of the creature's likeness to God. By the impress of this seal the creature is made conformable to the Son Himself, and by fellowship with the Son he receives the dignity and glory of the children of God.

The application to the creature of the divine love-flame flaring up in the Holy Spirit by the enkindling of a similar flame, and the reflection upon the creature of the divine glory shining in the Son by the irradiation of a similar splendor: these two images give us a striking illustration of the two divine missions as prolongations of the eternal processions and their entrance into the creature.[10]

But 'a further aspect in the communication of sanctifying grace . . . will show us still another kind of interior mission of the divine persons . . . so essentially bound up with the former and so closely interwoven with it that . . . in fact, the two form a single indivisible, organic whole.'[11]

For Scheeben the second invisible mission is called *Habitum et Habens*. He describes it as follows:

The process by which the divine persons and their processions are formed in rational creatures is not a dead process but a living one, living with a spiritual life. It consists in the habit and acts of supernatural knowledge and love. As a result of the mission explained above, the divine persons become present to the rational creature as object of a living, intimate possession and enjoyment; and this is the second kind of mission' (158).

Just how does this mission take place?

> When God graciously adopts us as His children and truly
> unites us to Himself in a most intimate manner by the grace of
> sonship . . . He gives us Himself, His own essence, as the object
> of our delight. . . . In consequence of this presence of the divine
> essence in the soul and the real union of the soul with God
> which is effected by grace . . . we enjoy God . . . as an object that
> is really and truly in us and is our own. We truly grasp Him with
> our knowledge and embrace Him with our love. . . . God be-
> comes the object of our possession and enjoyment in His entire
> essence. Evidently, then, all three persons come to us and give
> themselves to us, inasmuch as they are one with the essence,
> and in the essence with each other. Yet the individual persons,
> too, as distinct from one another and especially so far as one
> proceeds from another, can give themselves to us for our pos-
> session and enjoyment.
>
> This is the way, then, in which the Holy Spirit comes to our
> soul and becomes present in it formally in His own person, as
> the outpouring and pledge of the Father and the Son, and hence
> also as the outpouring and pledge of the fatherly love with which
> the Father loves us, His adoptive children. . . . And when we for
> our own part know and love the Holy Spirit thus dwelling within
> us in His own character, and rejoice at our possession of Him,
> we return God's kiss and taste His ineffable sweetness. In the
> Holy Spirit and through Him we embrace the Son and the Father,
> who had sent Him to us as the pledge of their love and happiness;
> with Him and through Him our thoughts and our love are raised
> to the enjoyment of those persons from whom He proceeds.[12]

B. Lonergan takes a different approach to these missions, studies
their order, purpose and nature, and gives special attention to their
constitution. He is not satisfied with the way some theologians
explain this 'constitution' either through 'the *ad extra* term' or
through 'a certain union of the infinite and finite' (such as created
actuation by Uncreated Act), and against these he puts his thesis
that 'the mission of a divine person is constituted by the relation
of origin but in such wise that it demands a fitting ad extra term by
way of consequent condition.'[13] Since God is being through intellect
and agent through intellect, by the very fact that Father, Son
and Holy Spirit conceive and will a certain person to be sent, the
mission is constituted and the fitting *ad extra* term is produced.[14]
Three conceive and will that the Father send the Son. Three conceive and will that the Father and the Son send the Holy Spirit.
Three produce the proper external terms. Thus the missions are
constituted and the terms produced.

Both missions, that of the Son and that of the Holy Spirit, regard adoptive sonship. The Son's mission was to be mediator and redeemer, to bring it about that the Father could love us as His own Son. And if the Father loves us as His own Son, then He loves us as if we were sons and from this love flows the adoption of sons. And when the Father loves us as His own Son, then you have the mission of the Holy Spirit.[15]

Lonergan continues:

It was fitting to a mediator that He be a divine person in a human nature: so that He could teach men, give them an example of a new life, lead them to reconciliation, love and eternal life; so that He could die for those whom God willed to die to self in order to live to God. It was fitting that the Son be the mediator and redeemer, since according to truth He proceeds from the Father and according to sanctity he spirates the Holy Spirit. It was fitting that the Holy Spirit, who proceeds from the Word spirating Love, should be sent to us because of the Son; that He who from eternity is Gift, should be given us as guest and pledge. It was fitting that we should be drawn toward the Father through the visible Son, and that we should be withdrawn from sensible things and in the invisible Spirit desire and hope for eternal life.

The ultimate end of these missions is the communication of the divine good through immediate vision of it. The proximate good is variously called the kingdom of God, the body of Christ, the Church, mystical marriage of Christ with the Church, the economy of salvation, the city of God. But the divine persons who from eternity proceed from the Father are also sent by the Father in time to inaugurate and confirm new personal relations of reconciliation and love with human persons, and bring it about that the divine persons are more clearly revealed and more ardently loved.

In a human mission you find seven elements: a transition from place to place; a particular operation, or a new series of operations, whether by the person sent, or by the ones to whom he is sent, according to the counsel or command of the sender, that is revealed and confided to the sendee or imposed on him. Which of these elements can we find in a divine mission? Transition from place to place adds little or nothing to our understanding of a divine mission, for with a divine person there is no such transition. Both the mission of the Son and of the Holy Spirit regard not a single operation but a whole new series of operations, for the Son is sent to restore and reconcile all things so that God may be all things in all; while the Holy Spirit is sent to preside over the entire Christian life of each of the just.

But the Son and the Holy Spirit operate differently, for the Son through His assumed nature can perform works that are proper to Him, but the Holy Spirit since He has only the divine nature operates nothing that the Father and Son do not likewise operate. Since the end of a mission includes the cooperation of others, a mission is aimed not so much at doing works as at instituting and confirming new personal relations, such as friendship. All anthropomorphism must be removed from a divine mission, and so neither counsel nor revelation plays a part in the constitution of a mission. The two missions have one total end, since the Son is sent to establish new personal relations between us and God the Father, while the Holy Spirit is sent to confirm these relations, make us temples in which He dwells so as to make us heirs of eternal life. Since there is one total end for both missions, and this is not achieved without the cooperation of men, different stages can be distinguished in the achievement of this total end.

Thus the Son's mission begins in the Incarnation because through the Incarnation He is constituted the mediator who is sent to us. This mission went on during His mortal life as the Son of man entered on personal relations with the sons of men. A principal element of this mission is consummated when dying on the cross He became the cause of eternal life for all who would obey Him. His mission is continued through the Apostles and their successors. Another principal element of his mission is achieved as often as someone who is unjust is justified, and someone who is just is justified still more, because He came that they might have life and have it more abundantly (Jn 10.10). All that is accomplished on earth by the man Christ whether through His historical influence or from heaven pertains to the visible mission of the Son. The ultimate term of this mission is reached in the beatific vision of the heavenly citizens, when He 'delivers the kingdom to God the Father'[16] (1 Cor 15.24).

DIVINE INHABITATION

The divine indwelling seems to have been easily the most attractive topic for study since the Council of Florence. Theologian after theologian brought out theory after theory to try to explain this fascinating mystery of the God who is everywhere present by immensity and yet becomes newly present by way of inhabitation in the souls of the just. Generally the theologians agreed that the just are inhabited and sanctified by the three divine persons, but they differed with regard to the precise role of the persons and the best way of explaining this inhabitational sanctification.

Most of them held that the three persons inhabited the just soul with equal immediacy and that sanctification was a work common to the three, a work which Scripture and the Fathers at times appropriated to the Holy Spirit. Petau, however, felt that it was more a matter of 'propriation' than of mere appropriation, since in our sanctification there was an element that was personal and proper to the Holy Spirit alone; that the Holy Spirit as First Gift enjoyed something of an inhabitational priority over the Father and the Son; and that the Holy Spirit was united to the just by a title and in a manner that was proper Him by a union somewhat like the hypostatic union of the word with His humanity.[17] Like Petau, Scheeben thought that the Holy Spirit possessed the just soul, not merely by way of appropriation, but in a special way much like that in which the Word possessed His sacred humanity.[18] De Régnon also was dissatisfied with the merely appropriational view, but instead of opting for an exclusively special union of the just with the Holy Spirit, he assigned a proper and peculiar influence to each of the three in the just soul, from which there arose in each of the just real and really distinct relations to each of the persons whereby they became sons of the Father, brothers of Christ, and spirituals in the Holy Spirit.[19]

Today many theologians, dissatisfied with a merely appropriational position, have rallied to De Régnon's view that each of the divine persons plays a special role in sanctifying the just soul and that the just soul thereby has a special and distinct relation to each of the divine persons.[20] They maintain that 'the common explanation which sees in the indwelling of the divine Persons only different degrees of appropriation, does not seem to harmonize sufficiently with the language of the Fathers and the Scriptures.'[21]

Many, many theologians have tried to explain this mysterious inhabitational presence of the three in the just soul. But they may be gathered into three general groups, those who view the inhabiting God as the principle of our supernatural life, those who view Him as the term of our supernatural life, and those who view Him as both principle and term of our supernatural life.[22] Those in the first group consider Him either as efficient cause of sanctifying grace,[23] or as exemplary cause of it[24] or as quasi-formal cause.[25] Those in the second group consider His objective presence through knowledge and love as the reason of His inhabitational presence.[26] Those in the third group feel that God must be viewed both as principle of supernatural life or more precisely as quasi-formal cause, in order properly to explain the ontological aspect of inhabitational presence, and as term of supernatural life, as object of special filial knowledge and love, in order properly to explain the intentional or psychological aspect of inhabitational presence.[27] Some of these theologians today

see the divine indwelling of the three persons as absolutely linked
with our incorporation in Christ, others as so linked only *de facto*.[28]
Some build their explanation of the divine indwelling on De
la Taille's theory of 'created actuation by Uncreated Act,'[29] while
others dislike this theory and opt for a more psychological
explanation.[30]

Two Dominican theologians, R. Garrigou-Lagrange and H.
Nicolas, produced somewhat different but complementary explanations of the divine indwelling that turned largely on God's psychological presence by way of knowledge and love. The 'special
presence of the Trinity in the just,' according to Garrigou-Lagrange,

> differs notably from the presence of God as preserving cause of
> all creatures. . . . According to the Angelic Doctor (Ia 43.3), the
> special presence of the Trinity in the just presupposes the general
> presence of immensity . . . but . . . God, by sanctifying grace, by
> infused virtues, by the seven gifts, becomes really present in a
> new and higher manner, as object experimentally knowable,
> which the just soul can enjoy, which at times it knows actually
> . . . in a manner quasi-experimental, with the vibrancy of infused
> charity, which gives a connatural intimacy with the inner life
> of God. If the Blessed Trinity lives in the just soul as in a temple,
> a living temple of knowledge and love even while the just
> man lives on earth, how wondrously intimate must be this in-
> dwelling of the Blessed Trinity in the blessed who form the
> temple of heaven.[31]

The trinitarian presence, according to H. Nicolas, is to be
explained

> by means of full supernatural knowledge. . . . God is present
> through His creative action, by which He is wholly in the interior
> of every being. . . . God is present also by reason of the personal
> relations of knowledge and love which grace establishes between
> the soul and Him . . . and that holds good for the just alone. . . . If
> we search the sphere of love, we shall discover nothing. . . . But it
> is otherwise where knowledge is concerned. Does grace produce
> an experimental knowledge of God? . . . It is through faith that
> we know God, and faith does not consist in an experimental
> knowledge. Moreover, the sinner may have faith; he may know
> that God is present in his interior, at the root of his being, and
> he may know that God is Trinity, without that fact giving him
> the Trinitarian presence. Thus, if supernatural knowledge
> merely brought faith into play, we should have to abandon the
> notion of regarding it as the origin of the Trinitarian presence.

. . . But the just man tends towards the God in whom he believes with his whole strength, and he loves Him. Love, then, penetrates knowledge and modifies it profoundly. . . . Thus the soul knows God with a knowledge of faith completely impregnated by love—the knowledge of connaturality.

What, indeed, does it lack in order to be experimental? Only that the thing known should be at its origin and at its end. . . . We find this . . . realized in supernatural knowledge: God is at its origin, effectively causing grace in the soul, together with faith and love, whose exercise He activates; God is at its end also, effectively united to the soul by this very action . . .

By virtue of this knowledge and of the love which animates it, the creative contact of the soul with God becomes a personal presence, the Trinitarian presence, on which, on its side, it confers reality. . . . Did we not see above that grace was, originally and above all, the privileged love with which God loves a spiritual being as His child. Under the radiation of this love, created grace flowers in the soul and becomes actual in this plenary supernatural knowledge composed of faith, love, and all the illuminations of the Holy Ghost, which knowledge insures the Trinitarian presence. . . . By thus loving the soul, God comes into it and begins to dwell in it without waiting until the soul has been able to begin loving Him in return. The Christian is never alone as long as he is faithful to grace. He has only to seek refuge through faith and love in that core of his soul where the three divine Persons . . . live in him and with him in unutterable friendship.[32]

Two Jesuit theologians, B. Lonergan and K. Rahner, by their contrasting explanations of the divine indwelling, which build heavily on psychological and ontological presence respectively, have perhaps made the most important recent contributions to inhabitational theology.

Lonergan's thesis is that 'the inhabitation of the divine Persons, although it rather consists and is cognized in acts, is nonetheless constituted by the state of grace.'[33] He insists that 'there is question here of the presence of a person to persons, not of a stone to stones. The divine Persons and the just mutually inexist as known in knowers and beloved in lovers. And hence this inhabitation consists rather in acts, for cognition and love are verified in acts rather than in a habit or power.'[34] The state of grace means more than the habit of grace.

Four persons are needed to constitute it: the Father who loves; the Son because of whom the Father loves; the Holy Spirit by

whom the Father loves and gives; and the just man who is loved
by the Father because of the Son in the Spirit and is in consequence endowed with Sanctifying grace, the infused virtues and
the gifts of the Holy Spirit, and thus is just and righteous and ex-
pedite for receiving and eliciting acts ordered to eternal life. By
this state there is constituted a certain interpersonal divine-
human situation and according to this state the divine Persons
and the just mutually inexist as known in knowers and loved in
lovers. . . . This state, on the part of the divine Persons, is always
in second act; on the part of the just it is always so in first act as
to go promptly into second act under the divine motion in proportion to the perfection of the just.[35]

For Rahner the inhabitational presence of the three is explained
by means of a quasi-formal causality. For

each of the three divine persons communicates himself as such
to man, each in his own special and different way of personal
being, in the free gift of grace. This trinitarian communication
(the 'indwelling' of God', the 'uncreated grace,' to be understood
not merely as the communication of the divine 'nature' but also
and indeed primarily as communication of the 'persons,' since
it takes place in a free spiritual personal act and so from person
to person), is the real ontological foundation of the life of grace
in man and (under the requisite conditions) of the immediate
vision of the divine persons at the moment of fulfilment. This
self-communication of the divine persons obviously takes place
according to their personal proprieties and that means also
according to and by virtue of their relation to one another. . . .
But this means further: these three self-communications are the
self-communication of the one God in the threefold relative way
in which God subsists. Hence the Father gives himself to us as
Father, that is, in and by the very fact that being essentially himself he expresses himself and *thus* imparts the Son as his own
personal self-disclosure: and also in and by the very fact that
the Father, and the Son who receives all from the Father,
affirming themselves in love . . . impart themselves in loving
acceptation, that is, as Holy Spirit. God's relationship to us is
threefold. And this three-fold . . . relationship to us is not merely
an image or analogy of the immanent Trinity: it *is* this Trinity
itself, even though communicated as free grace. . . . The one
God imparts himself as absolute self-utterance and absolute gift
of love. . . . God does not merely give his creature a 'share' 'in
himself' (indirectly) by creating and donating finite realities
through his all-powerful *efficient* causality: but he gives *himself*, really and in the strictest sense of the word, in a quasi-formal
causality.[36]

In what better way can we conclude than with the words of Pope Pius XII in his famous encyclical on the *Mystical Body of Christ*:

> We are well aware that many a veil shrouds this profound truth
> . . . of the Holy Spirit's dwelling within our souls and impedes
> our power to understand and explain it. . . . But let all agree
> uncompromisingly . . . to reject every kind of mystic union by
> which the faithful would in any way pass beyond the sphere
> of creatures and rashly enter the Divine, even to the extent of
> one single attribute of the eternal Godhead being predicated
> of them as their own. And besides let all hold this as certain
> truth, that all these activities are common to the most Blessed
> Trinity, in so far as they have God as supreme efficient cause.
> Let it be observed also that one is treating here of a hidden
> mystery which in this earthly exile can never be fully disclosed
> and grasped, and expressed in human language. The Divine
> Persons are said to be indwelling in as much as They are present
> to intellectual creatures in a way that lies beyond human com-
> prehension, and are known and loved by them in a manner tran-
> scending all nature and utterly singular and intimate.[37]

SUMMARY OF CATHOLIC TRINITARIAN DOCTRINE

Since the Council of Florence the only notable dogmatic contribution has been Vatican I's definition of mysteries beyond the reach
of unaided reason (Denz 3015, 3041). But theologically there have
been many interesting developments in trinitarian matters.

Until recently the three great theological schools of the Dominicans, Franciscans, and Jesuits largely dedicated themselves to the
production of manuals of theology that set forth trinitarian doctrine
in the Latin language and in the scholastic form of thesis, adversaries,
theological note, proof from Scripture and Fathers and Councils,
response to objections. This method helped greatly to maintain
orthodoxy and to bring about uniformity in seminary education,
but it did not seem to make the Trinity an influential factor in the
lives of most priests and of those they taught. Today this method of
indoctrination seems to be at an end.

In the area of the revelational cognoscibility of the Trinity there
has been development. Many manualists said the doctrine of the
Trinity was explicitly revealed in the New Testament and they
'proved' this by an accumulation of proof-texts drawn from Scripture, Fathers, Councils. Today few theologians would say this or
try to prove it this way. Instead theologians are finding new ways
of viewing and discerning this New Testament revelation of the

Trinity, ways that lead to an elemental rather than a formal New Testament trinitarianism. Probably these ways—and others still to be discovered—will be the guidelines in the future.

In the area of divine processions some theologians are assigning the psychological analogy little or no value as an index of the inner reality of the divine processions, and thus they are in agreement with modern Orthodox theology on this point.

Where Orthodox theology views the divine relations of origin as manifestative but not constitutive of the divine persons, Catholic theologians generally continue to regard them as both manifestative and constitutive and then go on to elaborate them in the rarefied metaphysical form that Aquinas developed. This doctrine has value for a metaphysician, but it is hardly likely to inspire anyone else with the understanding and love of the divine persons that is so vitally needed today.

Most theologians retain the Boethian definition of person but an increasing number has realized that the definition of Aquinas is far better. Theologians define or describe a person variously, as 'a being conscious and master of itself' 'a subject who possesses the nature and uses it,' 'a bearer and possessor of a rational nature,' 'a subject that is distinct and conscious of itself.' Dewart thinks that the Father, Son and Holy Spirit should no longer be called 'persons,' since 'person' today means a 'center of consciousness' and not what *prosopon* or *persona* meant. But most theologians still seem to think, and correctly, that although the word *person* is not ideal today, it should be retained, since 'there is no other word which would be really better, more generally understandable and less exposed to misconceptions.'

Only a few theologians contributed anything special to the consideration of the divine unity. Scheeben presented it in terms of unity of nature, immanent processions, unifying relations and community of persons. Cooke opts for a more dynamic presentation of the divine unity as a community of persons. Salet sees infinite Love as unifying the three Persons.

Scheeben felt that classical trinitarian theology had somewhat neglected the divine missions, and tried to remedy this by presenting a more inspiring doctrine of divine missions as prolongations of the eternal processions. Lonergan studied the end, nature, and unity of the divine missions, and in opposition to many recent theologians he put forth the thesis that 'the mission of a divine person is constituted by the relation of origin but in such wise that it demands a fitting *ad extra* term by way of consequent condition.'

The divine indwelling became perhaps the most attractive topic.

Theologians in general agreed that the just are inhabited and sanctified by the three Persons, but they differed with regard to the precise role of the Persons and the best way to explain this inhabitational sanctification. A few were dissatisfied with the merely appropriational view for they felt that it did not harmonize sufficiently with the language of the Fathers and the Scriptures, and so they went beyond it by assigning a special and proper role to the Holy Spirit. De Régnon went still further and urged that each of the Divine Persons has a special role in sanctifying the just soul and that the just soul thereby has a special and distinct relation to each of the Divine Persons. Recently many theologians have followed him, so that this position seems to be achieving a wider and wider acceptance. Very many theologians have tried to explain this mysterious inhabitational presence of the three in the just soul, either by viewing the inhabiting God as the principle of our supernatural life, or as its term, or as both its principle and its term. This latter view, in one form or another, seems likely to gain wider acceptance, since it takes into better account both the ontological and psychological aspects of this inhabitational presence. But the stress will probably be not on God's new presence to or in the just soul but on the presence of the three Divine Persons to this human person, in terms of mutual love and immanence.

Conclusion

The basic trinitarian dogmas are still substantially in possession today, and always will be. But some Catholic theologians feel they are in need of a reappraisal. They see problems everywhere: a tension between the outlook of the Biblical writer and that of the trinitarian theologian; a tension between the rigid Hellenic thought patterns of trinitarian theology and the much more elastic thought patterns of modern philosophy and psychology with their extremely (excessively?) heavy stress on function, evolution, process, history, relativity and contingency; a tension between the modern hermeneutic and valid knowledge of the transcendental reality that is called Trinity; a tension between the old ontological view of person in trinitarian theology and the modern psychological view of the human person as always in process of becoming more fully an authentic person; a tension between the classical, metaphysical, 'dead' way of presenting the doctrine of the Trinity and the modern tendency to see value only in knowledge that is 'alive' and relevant to the modern way of thinking and living.

There is thus little doubt that Catholic theology at present is at a critical juncture, so that 'the contemporary task of assimilating the fruits both of religious studies and of the new philosophies, of handling the problems of demythologization and of the possibility of objective religious statements, imposes on theology the task of recasting its notion of theological method in the most thoroughgoing and profound fashion.'[1]

What will the new theological method be? 'Bultmann,' it has been said, 'has shown that a theology of God must be anthropocentric,' while 'Rahner, Schillebeeckx, Metz, join with their younger American counterparts in calling for a theology which can be

316

described as a Christian anthropology, a Christian humanism.'[2] A theology is needed that 'no longer ignores the transcendental structure of knowledge, the form of the subconscious, the eventual as well as symbolic role of language, the pressure of economic system and social forms. . . . Just as the NT is for men (as Jesus Christ died and rose for men), so Christian preaching and reflection (theology) must be centered in man.'[3] But if this theology must be anthropocentric 'it must also be Christocentric' and 'Teilhard de Chardin's theology of the Christic divine milieu of our evolving cosmos includes both dimensions.'[4] Will it be Bultmannian? 'Bultmann's thought . . . is being corrected by theologies of process (Ogden), of history (Pannenberg), of the future (Metz, Moltmann), of society (Cox).'[5] 'Apart from Rahner's efforts (and Maréchal's and de Petter's lesser known but important epistemological contributions) on biblical theology, the evolution of dogma, Catholic theology has been at a standstill in the area of religious language for decades.' If the 'question of hermeneutic forms the focal point of theological problems today . . . because hermeneutics is translating the Bible's word so that it can be heard today,'[6] then it should not be impossible to find by exegetical methods a hermeneutical norm internal to the New Testament whereby the New Testament should be interpreted.

It is evident that these problems and tensions are very real and that trinitarian theology needs to be reviewed and up-dated in the light of these problems. But to be so disturbed by these tensions as to dash off into a nebulous nowhere 'Beyond Trinity' is a bit premature. God is not dead, and God is—was—and always will be—the Triune God who has revealed Himself and communicated Himself by His inhabitational presence. This is not the first time the Church has been in tension. It was in extreme tension at the time of Arius, and under the inspiration of the Holy Spirit it started at Nicea to formulate the doctrine of the Trinity, and it based its formulation not only on Hellenic but also on Biblical and patristic thought patterns and concepts. That same Holy Spirit is just as much alive today and He is eminently capable of inspiring and directing whatever re-formulation and re-expression He may consider necessary to meet the needs of the people of God of today and tomorrow. Certainly Catholic theology has a tremendous task before it, a task that will involve trial and error, confusion and disturbance for a time, perhaps for a long time. What urgently needs to be done will be done by the Triune God for and in the Christian people. For He is their God and they are His people, and as He knows and loves them and lives out His trinitarian life so He wants them to know and love Him and live out the trinitarian life He has granted them.

Every theology has the commission to serve the Eternal, but it can do this only when the commission is fulfilled by answering the questions which are posed by its time and by the *kairos* which works within the time. The message of God in Christ does not have to fear this trial. For it has the imperishable power to accomplish this, but this power must be awakened and unfolded. And it is just this that is the task of theology, Protestant and Catholic (and Orthodox) theology, which is pledged to the Logos of the eternal and incarnate God and whose unity and connectedness, despite all the divisions in details, is grounded in and should be expressed in their emulation of each other in the knowledge and love of the truth.[7]

Glory be to the Father and to the Son and to the Holy Spirit, as it was in the beginning, is now and ever shall be world without end. Amen.

Notes

NOTES TO THE INTRODUCTION TO PART ONE

1. J. Lebreton, *History of the Dogma of the Trinity,* trans. A. Thorold (New York, 1939), p. vii.

NOTES TO CHAPTER ONE

1. All direct scriptural citations are taken from the Revised Standard Version.
2. J. Guillet, *Themes of the Bible,* trans. R. Sullivan (Notre Dame, Ind., 1964), pp. 271–272.
3. E. Jacob, *Theology of the Old Testament,* trans. W. Heathcote and P. J. Allcock (New York and London, 1958), p. 134.
4. J. Lebreton, *History of the Dogma of the Trinity,* trans. A. Thorold (New York, 1939), pp. 93–94.
5. J. Piault, *What Is the Trinity?,* trans. (New York, 1959), p. 21.
6. Jacob, *Theology of the Old Testament,* p. 144.
7. J. L. McKenzie, *Dictionary of the Bible* (Milwaukee, 1965), p. 930.
8. A. W. Wainwright, *The Trinity in the New Testament* (London, 1962), p. 34.
9. Guillet, *Themes of the Bible,* p. 272.
10. Wainwright, *The Trinity in the New Testament,* p. 33.
11. Jacob, *Theology of the Old Testament,* p. 335.

NOTES TO CHAPTER TWO

1. J. Jeremias, *The Central Message of the New Testament* (London, 1965), pp. 18–21.
2. N. M. Flanagan, *The Acts of the Apostles* (Collegeville, Minn., 1960), p. 14.

3. J. L. McKenzie, *Dictionary of the Bible* (Milwaukee, 1955), p. 843.
4. A. W. Wainwright, *The Trinity in the New Testament* (London, 1962), pp. 200–201.
5. E. Stauffer, *New Testament Theology* (London, 1955), p. 252.
6. Wainwright, *The Trinity in the New Testament*, p. 252.
7. J. A. Fitzmyer, *Pauline Theology* (Englewood Cliffs, N.J., 1967), p. 32.
8. *Ibid.*, p. 33.
9. McKenzie, *Dictionary of the Bible*, p. 831.
10. *Ibid.*
11. L. Cerfaux, *Christ in the Theology of St. Paul*, trans. G. Webb and A. Walker (New York, 1959), p. 443.
12. D. E. H. Whiteley, *The Theology of St. Paul* (Oxford, 1964), p. 108.
13. O. Cullman, *The Christology of the New Testament*, trans. S. C. Guthrie and C. A. M. Hall (Philadelphia, 1959), p. 216.
14. Cerfaux, *Christ in the Theology of St. Paul*, p. 466.
15. M. E. Boismard, *Son and Saviour*, trans. (Baltimore, 1962), p. 111.
16. Cerfaux, *Christ in the Theology of St. Paul*, p. 475.
17. R. E. Brown, *Jesus God and Man* (Milwaukee, 1967), pp. 16–18, 20–25; Wainwright, *The Trinity in the New Testament*, pp. 54–60, 63–65; Cullmann, *The Christology of the New Testament*, pp. 310–314.
18. McKenzie, *Dictionary of the Bible*, p. 843; cf. Wainwright, *The Trinity in the New Testament*, pp. 215–220.
19. Fitzmyer, *Pauline Theology*, p. 42.
20. McKenzie, *Dictionary of the Bible*, p. 844.
21. J. Bonsirven, *Theology of the New Testament*, trans. S. F. Tye (Westminster, Md., 1963), pp. 238–240; R. Bultmann, *Theology of the New Testament*, trans. K. Grobel (New York and London, 1965) 1:155–157; Fernand Prat, *The Theology of St. Paul*, trans. J. L. Stoddard (London, 1927) 2: 142–146; Fitzmyer, *Pauline Theology*, p. 42; Wainwright, *The Trinity in the New Testament*, pp. 201–204; Whiteley, *The Theology of St. Paul*, pp. 127–129.
22. Cullman, *The Christology of the New Testament*, p. 326.
23. Whiteley, *The Theology of Paul*, p. 123.
24. C. K. Barrett, JTS. n.s. 10 (1959): 379.
25. Cullmann, *Christology of the New Testament*, pp. 265–267; Bultmann, *Das Evangelium des Johannes* (Göttingen, 1956), pp. 15–19.
26. Brown, *Jesus God and Man*, p. 28.
27. C. H. Dodd, *The Interpretation of the Fourth Gospel* (Cambridge, Eng., 1960), p. 207.
28. C. K. Barrett, *The Gospel According to St. John* (London, 1960), p. 292.
29. *Ibid.*, p. 60.

30. A. von Harnack, ZTheolKirch 2 (1892): 194–197.
31. J. L. McKenzie, *Dictionary of the Bible*, p. 276.
32. Wainwright, *The Trinity in the New Testament*, p. 72.
33. *Ibid.*, pp. 54–60, 63–65.
34. Brown, *Jesus God and Man*, pp. 12–13, 18–19.
35. *Ibid.*, pp. 25–28.
36. V. Taylor, *The Person of Christ* (London, 1958), pp. 147, 150.
37. W. F. Howard, *Christianity According to St. John* (London, 1943), p. 80.

NOTES TO CHAPTER THREE

1. J. Quasten, *Patrology* (3 vols. Westminster, Md., 1951–) 1:40.
2. *Ibid.*, pp. 42–53; J. Lawson, *A Theological and Historical Introduction to the Apostolic Fathers* (New York, 1961), pp. 21–62; R. M. Grant and H. H. Graham, *The Apostolic Fathers* (2 vols. New York, 1965) 2:3–106.
3. H. A. Wolfson, *The Philosophy of the Church Fathers* (Cambridge, Mass., 1956), pp. 187–188.
4. Quasten, *Patrology*, 1:63–76; Lawson, *A Theological and Historical Introduction to the Apostolic Fathers*, pp. 101–152.
5. J. N. D. Kelly, *Early Christian Doctrines* (New York and London, 1965), p. 92.
6. J. Tixeront, *History of Dogmas* (3 vols. St. Louis, 1910) 1:123.
7. Wolfson, *The Philosophy of the Church Fathers*, pp. 184, 191.
8. Quasten, *Patrology*, 1:92–105; Lawson, *A Theological and Historical Introduction to the Apostolic Fathers*, pp. 219–267; F. Glimm et al., *The Apostolic Fathers* (New York, 1947), pp. 225–350.
9. A. Grillmeier, *Christ in Christian Tradition*, trans. J. S. Bowden (New York, 1965), pp. 36–65.
10. *Ibid.*, p. 64.
11. See Quasten, *Patrology*, 1:99–11; Tixeront, *History of Dogmas*, 1:116; Wolfson, *The Philosophy of the Church Fathers*, pp. 188, 191.
12. Quasten, *Patrology*, 1:29–39; Glimm et al., *The Apostolic Fathers*, pp. 167–184; Lawson, *A Theological and Historical Introduction to the Apostolic Fathers*, pp. 63–100; R. A. Kraft, *The Apostolic Fathers* (3 vols. New York, 1965) 3:57–177.
13. Lawson, *A Theological and Historical Introduction to the Apostolic Fathers*, p. 68.
14. Quasten, *Patrology*, 1:76–82; Lawson, *A Theological and Historical Introduction to the Apostolic Fathers*, pp. 153–177; Glimm et al., *The Apostolic Fathers*, pp. 147–163.
15. Quasten, *Patrology*, 1:85–92; Kraft, *The Apostolic Fathers*, 3:1–57; Glimm et al., *The Apostolic Fathers*, pp. 185–222.
16. Wolfson, *The Philosophy of the Church Fathers*, p. 191.
17. Quasten, *Patrology*, 1:53–58; Lawson, *A Theological and Histori-*

cal *Introduction to the Apostolic Fathers,* pp. 179–193; Glimm et al., *The Apostolic Fathers,* pp. 61–79.

18. See Grant and Graham, *The Apostolic Fathers,* 2:120.
19. G. L. Prestige, *God in Patristic Thought* (London, 1952), pp. 17–19.
20. Wolfson, *The Philosophy of the Church Fathers,* p. 191.
21. Quasten, *Patrology,* 1:186–253; Tixeront, *History of Dogmas,* 1:203–227; B. Altaner, *Patrology,* trans. H. Graef (5th ed. Freiburg, 1960), pp. 114–137.
22. Quasten, *Patrology,* 1:196–219; Altaner, *Patrology,* pp. 120–127; Kelly, *Early Christian Doctrines,* pp. 96–98; Tixeront, *History of Dogmas,* 1:213–224; L. W. Barnard, *Justin Martyr* (Cambridge, Eng. 1967), pp. 75–110.
23. Barnard, *Justin Martyr,* p. 89.
24. Kelly, *Early Christian Doctrines,* pp. 97, 101; Barnard, *Justin Martyr,* p. 89.
25. Quasten, *Patrology,* 1:208–209; Altaner, *Patrology,* p. 125.
26. G. S. Sloyan, *The Three Persons in One God* (Englewood Cliffs, N. J., 1963), p. 35.
27. Kelly, *Early Christian Doctrines,* pp. 97, 101; Tixeront, *History of Dogmas,* 1:217–218.
28. E. R. Goodenough, *The Theology of Justin Martyr* (Jena, 1923), p. 176.
29. Barnard, *Justin Martyr,* p. 103.
30. Quasten, *Patrology,* 1:220–228; Altaner, *Patrology,* pp. 127–129.
31. Quasten, *Patrology,* 1:229–236; Altaner, *Patrology,* pp. 130–131.
32. Tixeront, *History of Dogmas,* 1:217–218; Sloyan, *The Three Persons in One God,* p. 35.
33. Kelly, *Early Christian Doctrines,* p. 100.
34. H. B. Swete, *The Holy Spirit in the Ancient Church* (reprint; Grand Rapids, 1966), p. 44.
35. Quasten, *Patrology,* 1:236–242; Altaner, *Patrology,* pp. 131–133.
36. Quasten, *Patrology,* 2:1–5; Altaner, *Patrology,* pp. 212–215.
37. Quasten, *Patrology,* 2:5–36; Altaner, *Patrology,* pp. 215–222.
38. J. Lebreton, 'La théologie de la trinité chez Clément d'Alexandrie,' RechScRel 34 (1947): 145.
39. Tixeront, *History of Dogmas,* 1:248; Kelly, *Early Christian Doctrines,* p. 127; Grillmeier, *Christ in Christian Tradition,* p. 160.
40. Wolfson, *The Philosophy of the Church Fathers,* p. 207.
41. Lebreton, 'La théologie de la trinité chez Clément d'Alexandrie,' RechScRel 34 (1947): 152, 157.
42. Quasten, *Patrology,* 2:37–101.
43. Kelly, *Early Christian Doctrines,* p. 130.
44. Prestige, *God in Patristic Thought,* pp. 197–199.
45. Quasten, *Patrology,* 2:109–111, 123–138.
46. *Ibid.,* pp. 101–109.
47. Tixeront, *History of Dogmas,* 1:379–386; Kelly, *Early Christian*

Doctrines, pp. 133–136; J. F. Bethune-Baker, *Early History of Christian Doctrine* (London, 1949), pp. 113–118.

48. C. L. Feltoe, *St. Dionysius of Alexandria, Letters and Treatises* (London, 1918).
49. Wolfson, *The Philosophy of the Church Fathers*, p. 202.
50. Prestige, *God in Patristic Thought*, pp. 162, 179.
51. *Ibid.*, p. 192.

NOTES TO CHAPTER FOUR

1. J. Lebreton and J. Zeiller, *The History of the Primitive Church*, trans. E. C. Messenger (New York, 1947), p. 1058.
2. *Ibid.*, p. 1054; C. Bardy, *Paul de Samosate, étude historique* Louvain, 1929) 3 : 427–520.
3. See Lebreton and Zeiller, *The History of the Primitive Church*, p. 1055; G. L. Prestige, *God in Patristic Thought* (London, 1952), pp. 202–204.
4. Lebreton and Zeiller, *The History of the Primitive Church*, p. 1058.
5. J. Quasten, *Patrology* (3 vols. Westminster, Md., 1951–) 3 : 6–13; B. Altaner, *Patrology*, trans. H. Graef (5th ed. Freiburg, 1960), pp. 310–311; J. Tixeront, *History of Dogmas* (3 vols, St. Louis, 1910–) 2 : 22–29; J. N. D. Kelly, *Early Christian Doctrines* (New York and London, 1965), pp. 226–281; J. F. Bethune-Baker, *Early History of Christian Doctrine* (London, 1949), pp. 155–165; Philip Hughes, *The Church in Crisis* (New York, 1960), pp. 23–33.
6. J. C. Murray, *The Problem of God* (New Haven, 1963), pp. 39–40.
7. *Ibid.*, pp. 40–43.
8. Quasten, *Patrology*, 3 : 13–19; Tixeront, *History of Dogmas*, 2 : 29–31; Kelly, *Early Christian Doctrines*, pp. 224–225.
9. Hughes, *The Church in Crisis*, pp. 23–39; Tixeront, *History of Dogmas*, 2 : 32–36; Kelly, *Early Christian Doctrines*, pp. 231–237 Bethune-Baker, *Early History of Christian Doctrine*, pp. 155–171.
10. Prestige, *God in Patristic Thought*, ch. 10.
11. *Ibid.*, p. 211.
12. Kelly, *Early Christian Doctrines*, pp. 233–237.
13. Prestige, *God in Patristic Thought*, p. 188.
14. Kelly, *Early Christian Doctrines*, p. 234.
15. *Ibid.*, p. 237.
16. B. Lonergan, *De Deo Trino* (Rome, 1961), p. 75.
17. Murray, *The Problem of God*, pp. 45, 51.

NOTES TO CHAPTER FIVE

1. K. Bihlmeyer and H. Tüchle, *Church History*, trans. V. E. Mills (3 vols. Westminster, Md., 1958–) 1 : 251–252; J. N. D. Kelly, *Early Christian Doctrines* (New York and London, 1965), pp. 237–238; cf. also the *Ecclesiastical Histories* of Socrates, Sozomen, and Theodoret.

2. B. Lonergan, *De Deo Trino* (Rome, 1961), pp. 66–68.
3. Cf. Epiphanius, *Haer.* 73; P. Galtier, *De SS. Trinitate* (Paris, 1933), p. 89; A. D'Alès, *De Deo Trino* (Paris, 1934), p. 34.
4. Athanasius, *De syn.* (PG 26:681–793); A. Hahn, *Bibliothek der Symbole und Glaubensregeln der alten Kirche* (Breslau, 1897).
5. J. N. D. Kelly, *Early Christian Creeds* (New York and London, 1950), pp. 279–283.
6. J. F. Bethune-Baker, *Early History of Christian Doctrine* (London, 1949), p. 180.
7. Lonergan, *De Deo Trino*, p. 65; Kelly, *Early Christian Doctrines*, pp. 248–249.
8. Hahn, *Bibliothek der Symbole und Glaubensregeln der alten Kirche*, p. 206; Bethune-Baker, *Early History of Christian Doctrine*, p. 184.
9. B. Altaner, *Patrology*, trans. H. Graef (5th ed. Freiburg, 1960), p. 312; A. Robertson, *Selected Writings and Letters of Athanasius, Bishop of Alexandria* (Grand Rapids, 1953), p. xiv.
10. Robertson, *Selected Writings and Letters of Athanasius, Bishop of Alexandria*, pp. lxiii–lxvi; Altaner, *Patrology*, pp. 314–317.
11. Lonergan, *De Deo Trino*, pp. 79–83.
12. C. R. B. Shapland, *The Letters of St. Athanasius Concerning the Holy Spirit* (London, 1951).
13. *Ibid.*, pp. 18–34, 85–86.
14. *Ibid.*, p. 142, n. 2.
15. F. Cayré, *Manual of Patrology*, trans. A. A. Howitt (2 vols. Paris, 1936) 1:350.
16. A. Schmemann, ed., *Ultimate Questions* (New York, 1965), p. 146.
17. Shapland, *The Letters of St. Athanasius Concerning the Holy Spirit*, p. 42.
18. J. Tixeront, *History of Dogmas* (3 vols. St. Louis, 1910–), 2:75.
19. See Altaner, *Patrology*, pp. 335–357.
20. Kelly, *Early Christian Doctrines*, p. 259.
21. Quasten, *Patrology* (3 vols. Westminster, Md., 1951–), 3:231–232.
22. See B. Lonergan, *Divinarum Personarum* (Rome, 1957), pp. 172–175; Claude Welch, *The Trinity in Contemporary Theology* (London, 1953), pp. 276–281.
23. A. von Harnack, *History of Dogma*, ed. B. Bruce; trans. N. Buchanan et al. (7 vols. London, 1897–), 4:84–89; Tixeront, *History of Dogmas*, 2:81–89.
24. ConOecDecr 18; Denz 150.
25. Kelly, *Early Christian Creeds*, p. 332.
26. ConOecDecr 27–31.
27. Tixeront, History of Dogmas, 2:64.
28. ConOecDecr 21, 25.
29. ConOecDecr 17.
30. Kelly, *Early Christian Creeds*, p. 297.
31. ConOecDecr 17–18; Kelly, *Early Christian Creeds*, pp. 296–331.

32. Denz 300.
33. ConOecDecr 101.
34. Kelly, *Early Christian Creeds*, p. 296.
35. Harnack, *History of Dogma*, 4:98.
36. ConOecDecr 24.
37. H. R. Percival, *The Seven Ecumenical Councils* (New York, 1900), p. 169.
38. Th. de Régnon, *La Sainte Trinité* (Paris, 1892) 1:410–420.
39. E. Mersch, *The Theology of the Mystical Body* (St. Louis, 1951), p. 349.
40. Ch. Baumgartner, *La grâce du Christ* (Tournai, 1963), pp. 52–54.
41. D. Petavius, *Dogmata Theologica* (Paris, 1865) t. 3, lib. VIII, c. VI.
42. P. Galtier, *De SS. Trinitate* (Paris, 1933), pp. 290–305.
43. Mersch, *The Theology of the Mystical Body*, p. 338.
44. F. Dvornik, *The Photian Schism* (Cambridge, Mass., 1948), p. 432.
45. Bihlmeyer and Tüchle, *Church History*, 2:88.
46. Dvornik, *The Photian Schism*, p. 420; Bihlmeyer and Tüchle, *Church History*, 2:99.
47. *Monumenta Germaniae Historica*, Ep. VII, 227–228.
48. N. Zernov, *Eastern Christendom* (London, 1961), p. 94.
49. Dvornik, *The Photian Schism*, p. 432.
50. Bihlmeyer and Tüchle, *Church History*, 2:100; S. Runciman, *The Eastern Schism* (Oxford, 1955), p. 22.
51. Mansi XIII, 978–979; PL 102, 1050–1051; P. Cavallera, *Thesaurus Doctrinae Catholicae* (Paris, 1936), p. 589; Lonergan, *De Deo Trino*, pp. 269–270.

NOTES TO THE INTRODUCTION TO PART THREE

1. B. Altaner, *Patrology*, trans. H. Graef (5th ed. Freiburg, 1960), pp. 84–85, 99.
2. *Ibid.*, p. 120.
3. H. Wolfson, *The Philosophy of the Church Fathers* (Cambridge, 1956), pp. 192–193.

NOTES TO CHAPTER SIX

1. J. Lawson, *The Biblical Theology of Saint Irenaeus* (London, 1948), p. 5.
2. B. Altaner, *Patrology*, trans. H. Graef (5th ed. Freiburg, 1960), p. 150.
3. Lawson, *The Biblical Theology of Saint Irenaeus*, p. 20.
4. H. B. Swete, *The Holy Spirit in the Ancient Church* (London, 1912), p. 85.
5. A. Roberts et al., *The Ante-Nicene Fathers* (New York, 1926) 1:309–567.
6. Hans Jonas, *The Gnostic Religion* (rev. ed. Boston, 1963); J.

Lebreton and J. Zeiller, *Heresy and Orthodoxy* (New York, 1962), pp. 23–47; J. N. D. Kelly, *Early Christian Doctrines* (New York and London, 1965), pp. 22–28.

7. Kelly, *Early Christian Doctrines*, pp. 105–106.
8. J. Tixeront, *History of Dogmas* (3 vols. St. Louis, 1910–) 1:233.
9. Wolfson, *The Philosophy of the Church Fathers* (Cambridge, Mass., 1956), pp. 200–201.
10. Swete, *The Holy Spirit in the Ancient Church*, p. 86.
11. Lawson, *The Biblical Theology of Saint Irenaeus*, p. 132.
12. *Ibid.*, p. 129.
13. *Ibid.*, p. 131.
14. K. Bihlmeyer and H. Tüchle, *Church History*, trans. V. E. Mills (Westminster, Md., 1958), p. 195.
15. J. Tixeront, *History of Dogmas*, 1:304.
16. J. F. Bethune-Baker, *Early History of Christian Doctrine* (London, 1949), p. 138.
17. G. L. Prestige, *God in Patristic Thought* (London, 1952), p. 97.
18. R. E. Roberts, *The Theology of Tertullian* (London, 1924), p. 45.
19. Lebreton and Zeiller, *Heresy and Orthodoxy*, p. 248.
20. E. Evans, *Tertullian's Treatise Against Praxeas* (London, 1948), p. 4.
21. J. Quasten, *Patrology* (3 vols. Westminster, Md. 1951–) 2:285.
22. Evans, *Tertullian's Treatise Against Praxeas*, pp. 6–7.
23. Roberts, *The Theology of Tertullian*, p. 17.
24. Wolfson, *The Philosophy of the Church Fathers*, p. 195; Kelly, *Early Christian Doctrines*, p. 112; Tixeront, *History of Dogmas*, 1:310.
25. Tixeront, *History of Dogmas*, 1:313.
26. Quasten, *Patrology*, 2:284.
27. *Ibid.*, 1:280, 290, 299.
28. Prestige, *God in Patristic Thought*, p. 93.
29. Kelly, *Early Christian Doctrines*, p. 113.
30. Quasten, *Patrology*, 2:325.
31. A. Grillmeier, *Christ in Christian Tradition*, trans. J. S. Bowden (New York, 1965), p. 149.
32. Prestige, *God in Patristic Thought*, p. 159; cf. A. von Harnack, *History of Dogma*, ed. B. Bruce; trans. N. Buchanan et al. (7 vols. London, 1897–) 4:122, n. 3.
33. Harnack, *History of Dogma*, 4:122, n. 3.
34. Tixeront, *History of Dogmas*, 1:313.
35. Evans, *Tertullian's Treatise against Praxeas*, p. 47.
36. Kelly, *Early Christian Doctrines*, p. 115.
37. Prestige, *God in Patristic Thought*, p. 159.
38. Tixeront, *History of Dogmas*, 1:310, 314.
39. Evans, *Tertullian's Treatise Against Praxeas*, p. 236.
40. Kelly, *Early Christian Doctrines*, p. 114.
41. Grillmeier, *Christ in Christian Tradition*, p. 141.

42. B. Lonergan, *De Deo Trino* (Rome, 1961), p. 147.
43. F. Cayré, *Manual of Patrology*, trans. A. A. Howitt (2 vols. Paris, 1936) 1:137.
44. *Ibid.*, p. 138.
45. A. D'Alès, *La théologie de Saint Hippolyte* (Paris, 1906), pp. 31–34; Kelly, *Early Christian Doctrines*, pp. 123–125; Tixeront, *History of Dogmas*, 1:293–297; Lebreton and Zeiller, *Heresy and Orthodoxy*, pp. 153–157.
46. J. J. I. von Döllinger, *Hyppolytus and Callistus* (Edinburgh, 1876), pp. 192–193.
47. Bethune-Baker, *Early History of Christian Doctrine*, pp. 108–109; Lebreton and Zeiller, *Heresy and Orthodoxy*, pp. 157–159.
48. Eusebius, *Hist. eccl.* 6, 43, 9; Lebreton and Zeiller, *Heresy and Orthodoxy*, p. 278: Cayré, *Manual of Patrology*, 1:253.
49. A. D'Alès, *Novatien* (Paris, 1924), pp. 111–115.
50. Kelly, *Early Christian Doctrines*, pp. 125–126.
51. *Ibid.*, p. 126.
52. Wolfson, *The Philosophy of the Church Fathers*, p. 195.
53. D'Alès, *Novatien*, pp. 123–124: Tixeront, *History of Dogmas*, 1:328.
54. D'Alès, *Novatien*, p. 126.
55. *Ibid.*, pp. 116, 119.
56. Cayré, *A Manual of Patrology*, 1:334.
57. These are found in PL8. 1365–1372; cf. Denz 138, 141–143; DTC 9.631–659.
58. Altaner, *Patrology*, p. 414; Denz 137.
59. Mgr. Duchesne, MAH 1908.
60. E. Amann, 'Liberius,' DTC 9.631–659.
61. Tixeront, *History of Dogmas*, 2:250.
62. X. LeBachelet, 'Saint Hilaire,' DTC 6.2413–2460.
63. S. McKenna, *Saint Hilary of Poitiers* (New York, 1954) pp. v–vi.
64. Cf. *Ibid.*, p. vii. The *De Synodis*, found in PL 10, is translated in NicPNicChFath, 9.4–31. The *De Trinitate*, PL 10, is translated in NicPNicChFath, 9.40–235.
65. NicPNicChFath, 9:xi.
66. J. E. Emmenegger, *The Functions of Faith and Reason in the Theology of Saint Hilary of Poitiers* (Washington, 1947), p. 29.
67. P. T. Wild, *The Divinization of Man According to Saint Hilary of Poitiers* (Mundelein, 1950), p. 23.
68. A. Antweiler, *Des heiligen Bischofs Hilarius von Poiters zwölf Bücher über die Dreieinigkeit* (BKV²; Munich, 1933). 1:29.
69. O. Casel, *Glaube, Gnosis und Mysterium* (JL 15; Munster, 1941), p. 164.
70. Le Bachelet, 'Saint Hilaire,' DTC 6.2461.
71. Wild, *The Divinization of Man According to Saint Hilary of Poitiers*, p. 22; see P. Smulders, *La doctrine trinitaire de S. Hilaire de Poitiers* (Rome, 1944), p. 82.

72. E. W. Watson, NicPNicChFath, 9:xxx.
73. McKenna, *Saint Hilary of Poitiers*, p. xv.
74. G. Bardy, 'Un humaniste chrétien: Saint Hilaire de Poitiers,' RHEF 27 (1941): 13.
75. Smulders,*La doctrine trinitaire de S. Hildaire de Poitiers*, pp. 82–83.
76. *Ibid.*, pp. 84–87.
77. *Ibid.*, pp. 153–164.
78. *Ibid.*, pp. 237–245.
79. *Ibid.*, pp. 265–268.
80. *Ibid.*, pp. 269–271.
81. *Ibid.*, pp. 275–279.

NOTES TO CHAPTER SEVEN

1. H. B. Swete, *The Holy Spirit in the Ancient Church* (London, 1912), pp. 305–306.
2. J. N. D. Kelly, *Early Christian Doctrines* (New York and London, 1965), p. 269.
3. J. Tixeront, *History of Dogmas* (3 vols. St. Louis, 1910–), 2:265.
4. *Ibid*, 2:266.
5. Kelly, *Early Christian Doctrines*, p. 271.
6. Tixeront, *History of Dogmas* 2:271; cf. Victorinus, *Adv. Arium* 1.13; 3.7–9; 4.21.
7. *Ibid.*, 2:271.
8. All these works are found in PL 16. The *De Fide* is translated in NicPNicChFath 10.199–314, the *De Spiritu Sancto* in NicPNicCh-Fath 10.91–153.
9. F. H. Dudden, *The Life and Times of St. Ambrose* (Oxford, 1935) 2:571–572.
10. *Ibid.*, p. 573.
11. Swete, *The Holy Spirit in the Ancient Church*, p. 322: Dudden, *The Life and Times of St. Ambrose*, 2:575.
12. Tixeront, *History of Dogmas* 2:352.
13. B. Altaner, *Patrology*, trans, H. Graef (5th ed. Freiburg, 1965), pp. 492–493.
14. Kelly, *Early Christian Doctrines*, p. 271.
15. Altaner, *Patrology*, p. 493.
16. G. L. Prestige, *God in Patristic Thought* (London, 1952), pp. x–xi.
17. The *Enchiridion ad Laurentium* is found in PL 40, *De fide et symbolo* in PL 40, *De doctrina christiana* in PL 34, *Contra sermonem Arianorum* in PL 42, *Contra Maximinum* in PL 42, *On the Gospel of St. John* in PL 35, *Letters 2* and *170* in PL 33, and *De Trinitate* in PL 42.
18. Adolf von Harnack, *History of Dogma*, trans. N. Buchanan et al. (7 vols. London, 1894–), 4:131 n.
19. H. Wolfson, *The Philosophy of the Church Fathers* (Cambridge, Mass. 1956), pp. 358–359.

20. *Ibid.*, pp. 350–359.
21. Kelly, *Early Christian Doctrines*, p. 274.
22. Tixeront, *History of Dogmas*, 2 : 363.
23. See Wolfson, *The Philosophy of the Church Fathers*, pp. 339–342.
24. Swete, *The Holy Spirit in the Ancient Church*, p. 333.
25. S. J. Grabowski, *The All-Present God* (St. Louis, 1953), pp. 179–182.
26. M. Schmaus, *Die psychologische Trinitätslehre des hl. Augustinus* (Munster 1927), pp. 190–194.
27. G. Sloyan, *The Three Persons in One God* (Englewood Cliffs, N.J., 1963), pp. 78–79.
28. E. Portalié, *A Guide to the Thought of Saint Augustine*, trans. R. J. Bastian (Chicago, 1960), pp. 133–134.
29. Harnack, *History of Dogma*, 4 : 130.

NOTES TO CHAPTER EIGHT

1. F. Cayré, *Manual of Patrology*, trans. A. A. Howitt (2 vols. Paris, 1936) 1 : 122.
2 T. H. Bindley and F. W. Green, *The Oecumenical Documents of the Faith* (London, 1950), pp. 159–167.
3. E.g., A. D'Alès, *De Deo Trino* (Paris, 1934), pp. 257–275.
4. J. Tixeront, *History of Dogmas* (3 vols. St. Louis, 1910–) 3 : 327.
5. J. N. D. Kelly, *The Athanasian Creed* (London, 1964), p. 1.
6. C. H. Turner, *The History and Use of Creeds and Anathemas in the Early Church* (London, 1906), p. 66.
7. Kelly, *The Athanasian Creed*, p. 109.
8. *Ibid.*, p. 43.
9. *Ibid.*, pp. 44, 48–49.
10. *Ibid.*, pp. 112–113, 123.
11. F. D. Maurice, *Theological Essays* (Cambridge, Eng. 1853), p. 482.
12. D. Knowles, *The Evolution of Medieval Thought* (Baltimore, 1962), p. 53.
13. *Ibid.*, pp. 53–54.
14. In PL 63. A good translation is that by H. F. Stewart, *Boethius, The Consolation of Philosophy* (London, 1926), pp. 128–411.
15. These are all in PL 64. A good translation is provided by H. F. Stewart and E. K. Rand, *Boethius: The Theological Tractates* (London, 1926), pp. 2–127.
16. Cayré, *Manual of Patrology*, 2 : 220; B. Altaner, *Patrology*, trans. H. Graef (5th ed. Freiburg, 1965), p. 581; M. A. Barrett, *Boethius* (Cambridge, 1940), pp. 141–144.
17. K. Barth, *The Doctrine of the Word of God* (Edinburgh, 1936), p. 409.
18. M. Daffara, *De Deo Uno et Trino* (Turin, 1945), p. 380.
19. B. Lonergan, *Divinarum Personarum conceptionem analogicam* (Rome, 1957), p. 133.

20. J. Madoz, 'Le symbole du XIe concile de Tolède,' SpicSacLov 19 (1938): 16–26.
21. G. Leff, *Medieval Thought* (Baltimore, 1958), p. 61.
22. *Ibid.*
23. Cayré, *Manual of Patrology*, 2 : 380.
24. Y. M.-J. Congar, *A History of Theology*, trans. H. Guthrie (New York, 1968), p. 64.

NOTE TO INTRODUCTION TO PART FOUR

1. G. Leff, *Medieval Thought* (Baltimore, 1958), p. 88.

NOTES TO CHAPTER NINE

1. J. Bainvel, 'Anselme de Cantorbery,' DTC 1 : 1343.
2. J. de Ghellinck, *Le Mouvement Théologique du XIIe Siècle* (Bruges, 1948), pp. 78–82; Leff, *Medieval Thought (Baltimore, 1962), pp. 98–100.
3. Given in the *Proslogion* (PL 158) and provided in English translation by S. N. Deane, *St. Anselm* (La Salle, Ill., 1954), pp. 1–34.
4. The *Cur Deus Homo* (PL 158); translated in Deane, *St. Anselm*, pp. 177–288.
5. F. Cayré, *Manual of Patrology*, trans. A. A. Howitt (2 vols. Paris, 1936) 2 : 391 : F. Picavet, *Roscelin* (Paris, 1911), pp. 46–50.
6. A. D'Alès *De Deo Trino* (Paris, 1934), p. 103.
7. D. Knowles, *The Evolution of Medieval Thought* (Baltimore, 1962), p. 101.
8. Leff, *Medieval Thought*, p. 107.
9. J. Cottiaux, 'La conception de la théologie chez Abélard,' RevHisEccl 28 (1932) : 249.
10. J. T. Muckle, *The Story of Abelard's Adversities* (Toronto, 1954), pp. 11–70.
11. The best edition is by R. Stölzle (Freiburg, 1891).
12. Cottiaux, 'La conception de la théologie chez Abelard,' 251–252.
13. A. J. Luddy, *The Case of Peter Abelard* (Dublin, 1947), p. 8.
14. Cottiaux, 'La conception de la théologie chez Abélard.' 256; G. Pare et al., *Les Ecoles et L'Enseignement* (Ottawa, 1933), p. 289.
15. Muckle, *The Story of Abelard's Adversities*, p. 40.
16. Cottiaux, 'La conception de la théologie chez Abélard,' 255.
17. Muckle, *The Story of Abelard's Adversities*, p. 44.
18. Knowles, *The Evolution of Medieval Thought*, p. 125.
19. A. C. McGiffert, *A History of Christian Thought* (2 vols. New York, 1954) 2 : 209.
20. *Ibid.*, p. 205.
21. Cottiaux, 'La conception de la théologie chez Abélard,' 276–280.
22. *Ibid.*, 550.
23. *Ibid.*, 533–551.

24. McGiffert, *A History of Christian Thought*, 2:204.
25. J. Rivière, 'Les "capitula" d'Abélard condamnés au concile de Sens,' RechThMéd 5(1933): 5–8.
26. P. Ruf and M. Grabmann, 'Ein neuaufgefundenes Bruchstück der Apologia Abaelards,' SBMünch (Munich, 1930), fasc. 5.
27. A. V. Murray, *Abelard and St. Bernard* (New York, 1967), pp. 110–111, 114–115.
28. *Ibid.*, p. 101.
29. R. L. Poole, *Illustrations of the History of Medieval Thought and Learning* (Oxford, 1920), p. 156.
30. N. M. Haring, 'The Case of Gilbert de la Porrée,' MedSt 13 (1951) 2.
31. Fr. Foberti, *Gioacchino da Fiore e il Giocchinismo antico e moderno* (Padua, 1942), p. 70.
32. A. Hayen, 'Le Concile de Reims et L'Erreur Théologique de Gilbert de la Porrée,' ArchHistDoctLitMA (1936): 24–37.
33. J. G. Sikes, *Peter Abaelard* (Cambridge, 1932), p. 147.
34. Cayré, *A Manual of Patrology*, 2:414.
35. W. Williams, *Saint Bernard of Clairvaux* (Manchester, 1952), p. 316.
36. M. E. Williams, *The Teaching of Gilbert Porreta on the Trinity* (Rome, 1951), pp. 4–5.
37. *Historia Pontificum*, c. 11.
38. Hayen, 'Le Concile de Reims et L'Erreur Théologique de Gilbert de la Porrée' 39. See also Haring, 'The Case of Gilbert de la Porrée,' 1.
39. Haring, 'The Case of Gilbert de la Porrée,' 14.
40. *Ibid.*, 1–2.
41. *Ibid.*, 5.
42. *Ibid.*, 11.
43. Bernard, *Sermo in Canticum* 80.8 (PL 183.1170D); *De Consideratione* V, 7, 15 (PL 182.797A).
44. M. E. Williams, *The Teaching of Gilbert Porreta on the Trinity*, pp. 124–125.
45. *Church Dogmatics* (Edinburgh, 1956) 2/1.
46. Hayen, 'Le concile de Reims et L'Erreur Théologique de Gilbert de la Porrée,' 85–86.
47. *Ibid.*
48. M. E. Williams, *The Teaching of Gilbert Porreta on the Trinity*, p. 127.
49. *Ibid.*, pp. 147–148.
50. Mabillon, in PL 182.26, the general preface to Bernard's *Opera*.
51. G. Webb and A. Walker, *St. Bernard of Clairvaux* (Westminster, Md., 1960), p. 3.
52. Knowles, *The Evolution of Medieval Thought*, p. 142.
53. *Ibid.*, p. 143.
54. *Ibid.*

55. *Ibid.*
56. J. de Ghellinck, *Le Mouvement Théologique du XIIe Siècle*, pp. 197–201; P. Claeys-Bouuaert, 'La "Summa Sententiarum" est-elle de Hugues de Saint-Victor?' RHE 10 (1909): 278–289, 710–719.
57. McGiffert, *A History of Christian Thought*, 2:248.
58. de Ghellinck, *Le Mouvement Théologique du XIIe Siècle*, p. 197.
59. H. Weisweiler, 'La Summa Sententiarum, source de Pierre Lombard,' RechThMed 6 (1934): 132, n. 75.
60. X. Rousselot, *Etudes sur la philosophie dans le moyen âge* (Paris, 1840) 1:330.
61. A.-M. Ethier, *Le 'De Trinitate' de Richard de Saint-Victor* (Paris and Ottawa, 1939), p. 8.
62. Knowles, *The Evolution of Medieval Thought*, p. 145.
63. Th. de Régnon, *Etudes de théologie positive sur la Sainte Trinité* (5 vols. Paris, 1892–), 2:235–335.
64. P. Vignaux, *Philosophie au Moyen Age* (Paris, 1958), p. 64.
65. P. Galtier, *De SS. Trinitate* (Paris, 1933), p. 130.
66. D'Alès, *De Deo Trino* (Paris, 1934), p. 104.
67. L. Jannssens, *Tractatus de Deo Trino* (Freiburg, 1900), p. 405; G. Fritz, DTC 13.2691–2693.
68. Fritz, DTC 13.2693.
69. de Régnon, *Etudes de théologie positive sur la Sainte Trinité*, 2:305–313.

NOTES TO CHAPTER TEN

1. A. C. McGiffert, *A History of Christian Thought* (2 vols. New York, 1954) 2:252.
2. D. Knowles, *The Evolution of Medieval Thought* (Baltimore, 1962), p. 182.
3. See Denz 803, Introduction; D. Petau, *Dogmata Theologica* (Paris, 1865) 3:258–259.
4. J. de Ghellinck, *Le Mouvement Théologique du XIIe Siècle* (Bruges, 1948), p. 266.
5. C. Boyer, *Tractatus de Gratia Divina* (Rome, 1938), p. 188.
6. A. D'Alès, *De Deo Trino* (Paris, 1934), p. 260.
7. F. Cayré, *Manual of Patrology*, trans. A. A. Howitt (2 vols. Paris, 1936) 2:459.
8. E. Jordan, 'Joachim de Flore,' DTC 8.1428–1429.
9. *Ibid.*, 1429: cf. E. Anitchkof, *Joachim de Flore* (Rome, 1931), pp. 162–163.
10. Jordan, 'Joachim de Flore,' DTC 8.1430.
11. C. Ottaviano, *Joachimi Abbatis Liber Contra Lombardum* (Rome, 1934), pp. 35–41.
12. *Ibid.*, p. 81.
13. *Ibid.*, pp. 81, 83, 85.
14. *Ibid.*, p. 58.

15. *Ibid.*, p. 61.
16. P. Hughes, *The Church in Crisis* (New York, 1960), pp. 235–246.

NOTES TO CHAPTER ELEVEN

1. T. M. Schwertner, *St. Albert the Great* (Milwaukee, 1932), p. 281.
2. Th. Heitz, *Essai historique sur les rapports entre la philosophie et la foi* (Paris, 1909), p. 144.
3. Schwertner, *St. Albert the Great*, p. 276.
4. G. Leff, *Medieval Thought* (Baltimore, 1958), p. 213.
5. D. Knowles, *The Evolution of Medieval Thought* (Baltimore, 1962), p. 257.
6. A. C. McGiffert, *A History of Christian Thought* (2 vols. New York, 1954) 2:259–260.
7. *Ibid.*, 2:292.
8. A. D'Alès, *De Deo Trino* (Paris, 1934), p. 183.
9. Th. de Régnon, *Etudes de théologie positive sur la Sainte Trinité* (5 vols. Paris, 1892–), 2:119–121, 145, 227; 3:395, 558; 4:110, 129.
10. M. T.-L. Penido, 'La Valeur de la Théorie "Psychologique" de la Trinité,' EphemThLov 8 (1931): 16.
11. R. Garrigou-Lagrange, *The Trinity and God the Creator* (St. Louis. 1952), p. 137.
12. McGiffert, *A History of Christian Thought*, 2:293.
13. *Ibid.*, 2:295.
14. Knowles, *The Evolution of Medieval Thought*, p. 235.
15. V. Doucet, 'A New Source of the "Summa Fratris Alexandri," ' FrancStudies (1946): 403–417.
16. BiblFranSchMA (1951): 12–15.
17. *Doctoris Irrefragabilis Alexandri De Hales Summa Theologica* (Quaracchi-Florence, 1924–1928).
18. See Prologomena to book 3 of vol. 4 of his *Summa Theologica*.
19. Doucet, 'A New Source of the "Summa Fratris Alexandri," ' 369.
20. A. Emmen, 'Alexander of Hales,' NCE 1.297.
21. De Régnon, *Etudes de théologie positive sur la Sainte Trinité*, 2:346–347.
22. Knowles, *The Evolution of Medieval Thought*, p. 237.
23. *Opera Theologica Selecta* (Quarrachi-Florence, 1934).
24. *Opera*, 5.199–291.
25. *Opera* 5.293–316.
26. J. de Vinck, *The Works of Bonaventure* (Paterson, 1960) 2:viii.
27. De Régnon, *Etudes de théologie positive sur la Sainte Trinité*, 2:479–493; R. Stohr, *Die Trinitätslehre des heil. Bonaventura* (Munster, 1923), pp. 114–124.
28. F. Vernet, 'Lyon, Concile de,' DTC 9.1379.
29. Hughes, *The Church in Crisis* (New York, 1964), p. 267.
30. Vernet, 'Lyon, Concile de,' DTC 9.1379.

31. M. Calecas PG 152.172; Vernet, 'Lyon, Concile de,' DTC 9.1383; ConOecDecr 281, 283 n. 2.
32. Hughes, *The Church in Crisis*, p. 268, n. 12; Vernet, 'Lyon, Concile de,' DTC 9.1382; Denz 850.
33. Vernet, 'Lyon, Concile de,' DTC 9.1378.
34. *Ibid.* 1935.
35. *Ibid.*, 1383.

NOTES TO CHAPTER TWELVE

1. *Commentaria Oxoniensia* (Quaracchi-Florence, 1912–1914).
2. C. Frassen, *Scotus Academicus* (Rome, 1900), pp. 91–94.
3. *Ibid.*, pp. 165–166.
4. P. Boehner, *Ockham* (New York, 1957), p. xi.
5. G. Leff, *Medieval Thought* (Baltimore, 1958), p. 279.
6. A. Pelzer, 'Les 51 articles de Guillaume Occam,' RHE 18 (1922): 240–270.
7. *Opera Plurima, Super 4 Libros Sententiarum* (London, 1962).
8. S. C. Tornay, *Ockham* (La Salle, Ill., 1938), pp. 182–187.
9. Leff, *Medieval Thought*, p. 280.
10. J. Gill, *The Council of Florence* (Cambridge, 1959), p. vii.
11. N. Zernov, *Eastern Christendom* (London, 1961), p. 127.
12. P. Hughes, *The Church in Crisis* (New York, 1960), p. 312.
13. *Ibid.*, p. 315.
14. *Ibid.*
15. Gill, *The Council of Florence*, pp. 207–210.
16. *Ibid.*, pp. 213–222.
17. *Ibid.*, pp. 229–230.
18. *Ibid.*, p. 231.
19. *Ibid.*, pp. 291–293.
20. *Ibid.*, p. 325.
21. P. Henry, 'On Some Implications of the "Ex Patre Filioque tamquam ab uno Principio," ' EChurchQ 7 (1948) Suppl. 19.
22. B. Lonergan, *De Deo Trino* (Rome, 1961), pp. 217–218.

NOTES TO CHAPTER THIRTEEN

1. L. W. Spitz, *Luther's Works* (Philadelphia, 1960) 34:199.
2. *Concordia or Book of Concord* (St. Louis, 1957), pp. 160–161.
3. *Ibid.*, pp. 369–373.
4. W. Elert, *The Structure of Lutheranism* (St. Louis, 1962), pp. 216–217.
5. C. L. Manschreck, *Melanchthon on Christian Doctrine* (New York, 1965), p. vii.
6. *Ibid.*, p. xxi.
7. *Book of Concord*, p. 12.
8. *Ibid.*, p. 28.
9. *Ibid.*, p. 11.

10. *Ibid.*, pp. 16–17.
11. G. E. Duffield, ed., *John Calvin* (Grand Rapids, 1966), pp. xi, 167.
12. *Ibid.*, p. 154.
13. J. Calvin, *Institutes of the Christian Religion*, trans. J. Allen (Philadelphia, 1936), p. 138.
14. *Ibid.*, pp. 138–141.
15. *Ibid.*, p. 144.
16. *Ibid.*, p. 160.
17. *Ibid.*, p. 164.
18. R. H. Bainton, *Hunted Heretic* (Boston, 1953).
19. *Ibid.*, pp. 208–219.
20. *Ibid.*, p. 207.
21. *Ibid.*, p. 214.
22. Calvin, *Institutes of the Christian Religion*, pp. 164–165.

NOTES TO CHAPTER FOURTEEN

1. R. S. Franks, *The Doctrine of the Trinity* (London, 1953), p. 140.
2. A. C. McGiffert, *Protestant Thought Before Kant* (New York, 1911), p. 158.
3. *Racovian Catechism*, qq. 21–23. Published in *Bibliotheca Fratrum Polonorum* (Amsterdam, 1956).
4. Franks, *The Doctrine of the Trinity*, p. 149–151.
5. J. Orr, *English Deism* (Grand Rapids, 1934), pp. 1–283.
6. P. Tillich, *A History of Christian Thought* (New York, 1968), p. 291.
7. Orr, *English Deism*, p. 197.

NOTES TO CHAPTER FIFTEEN

1. P. Tillich, *A History of Christian Thought* (New York, 1968), pp. 287–288.
2. G. R. Cragg, *The Church and the Age of Reason* (Grand Rapids, 1962), pp. 234, 237.
3. J. Lortz, *History of the Church* (Milwaukee, 1935), p. 444.
4. E. Gilson and T. Langan, *Modern Philosophy: From Descartes to Kant* (New York, 1964), p. 141.
5. *Ibid.*, p. 483.
6. F. Copleston, *A History of Philosophy* (8 vols. Westminster, Md., 1945–), 4 : 259, 244.
7. Copleston, *A History of Philosophy*, 6 : 105–106, 114.
8. Cragg, *The Church and the Age of Reason*, p. 240.
9. A. C. McGiffert, *Protestant Thought Before Kant* (New York, 1911), p. 244.
10. J. Orr, *English Deism* (Grand Rapids, 1934), p. 197.
11. J. Pelikan, *From Luther to Kierkegaard* (St. Louis, 1963), p. 90.
12. E. W. Zeeden, *The Legacy of Luther* (London, 1954), p. 148.

13. Gilson and Langan, *Modern Philosophy*, p. 451.
14. Pelikan, *From Luther to Kierkegaard*, p. 97.
15. *Ibid.*, p. 91.
16. R. Franks, *The Doctrine of the Trinity* (London, 1953), p. 159.
17. Pelikan, *From Luther to Kierkegaard*, p. 98.
18. *Ibid.*, p. 99.

NOTES TO CHAPTER SIXTEEN

1. J. Dillenberger and C. Welch, *Protestant Christianity, Interpreted through Its Development* (New York, 1954), p. 182.
2. K. Barth, *Protestant Thought* (New York, 1959), p. 306.
3. F. Schleiermacher, *The Christian Faith*, ed. H. R. Mackintosh and J. S. Steward (New York, 1948) p. 12.
4. Dillenberger and Welch, *Protestant Christianity*, p. 184.
5. J. H. Nichols, *History of Christianity* (New York, 1956), pp. 167–168.
6. Schleiermacher, *The Christian Faith*, p. 52.
7. *Ibid.*, p. 738.
8. *Ibid.*, pp. 738–739.
9. *Ibid.*, p. 742.
10. *Ibid.*, p. 750.
11. Dillenberger and Welch, *Protestant Christianity*, pp. 186, 188.
12. C. Welch, *The Trinity in Contemporary Theology* (London, 1953), pp. 8–9.
13. R. Otto, 'Introduction,' *On Religion*, trans. J. Oman (New York, 1958), p. x.
14. O. Pfleiderer, *The Development of Theology in Germany since Kant* (London, 1923), p. 122.
15. F. Copleston. *A History of Philosophy* (8 vols. Westminster, Md., 1945–) 7:159.
16. R. C. Whittemore, 'Hegel as Panentheist,' *Studies in Hegel* (New Orleans, 1960), p. 134.
17. G. W. Hegel, *The Philosophy of Religion*, trans. E. B. Speirs and J. B. Sanderson (London, 1895).
18. *Ibid.*, 3:12.
19. *Ibid.*, 3:21, 13.
20. *Ibid.*, 3:25.
21. *Ibid.*, 3:17.
22. Copleston, *A History of Philosophy*, 7:241.
23. Welch, *The Trinity in Contemporary Theology*, pp. 12–13.
24. R. Mackintosh, *Hegel and Hegelianism* (Edinburgh, 1903), p. 258.
25. E. L. Fackenheim, *The Religious Dimension in Hegel's Thought* (Bloomington, 1967), p. 12.
26. Dillenberger and Welch. *Protestant Christianity*, pp. 215–217.
27. *Ibid.*, pp. 217–223.
28. A. B. D. Alexander, *Shaping Forces of Modern Religious Thought* (Glasgow, 1920), p. 299.

29. A. E. Garvie, *The Ritschlian Theology* (Edinburgh, 1899), p. 284.
30. *Ibid.*, p. 285.
31. O. Pfleiderer, *The Development of Theology in Germany* (London, 1923), pp. 189–190.
32. Nichols, *History of Christianity*, p. 284.
33. Dillenberger and Welch, *Protestant Christianity*, p. 208.
34. A. von Harnack, *History of Dogma*, ed. B. Bruce; trans. N. Buchanan et al. (7 vols. London, 1894–1899).
35. Trans. T. B. Saunder (London, 1923).
36. *Ibid.*, p. 6.
37. *Ibid.*, p. 11.
38. *Ibid.*, p. 172.
39. *Ibid.*, p. 175.
40. *Ibid.*, p. 176.
41. *Ibid.*, p. 182.
42. *Ibid.*, p. 196.
43. *Ibid.*, pp. 197–198.
44. *Ibid.*, p. 201.
45. *Ibid.*, p. 202.
46. *Ibid.*, p. 203.
47. *Ibid.*, p. 44.
48. Dillenberger and Welch, *Protestant Christianity*, p. 211.
49. Drummond, p. 147.

NOTES TO CHAPTER SEVENTEEN

1. E.g., A. C. McGiffert and D. C. Macintosh.
2. E.g., F. R. Tennant.
3. E.g., D. M. Edwards. On these men see C. Welch, *The Trinity in Contemporary Theology* (London, 1953), pp. 49, 50, 58.
4. E.g., C. Hartshorne, L. Thornton, D. Sayers; see Welch, *The Trinity in Contemporary Theology*, pp. 77, 84, 86.
5. E.g., C. N. Bartlett, J. B. Champion; see Welch, *The Trinity in Contemporary Theology*, pp. 99, 96.
6. E.g., W. N. Pittenger, J. S. Whale, C. Lowry, L. Hodgson; see Welch, *The Trinity in Contemporary Theology* pp. 128–132.
7. Welch, *The Trinity in Contemporary Theology*, p. 152.
8. *Ibid.*, pp. 140–145.
9. *Ibid.*, p. 219.
10. *Ibid.*, p. 219.
11. *Ibid.*, p. 229.
12. *Ibid.*, p. 233.
13. *Ibid.*, p. 238.
14. *Ibid.*, p. 235.
15. *Ibid.*, p. 235.
16. *Ibid.*, p. 244.
17. *Ibid.*, p. 249.

18. *Ibid.*, p. 268.
19. *Ibid.*, p. 271.
20. *Ibid.*, p. 271.
21. *Ibid.*, p. 277.
22. *Ibid.*, p. 271.
23. *Ibid.*, p. 235.
24. *Ibid.*, pp. 255–256.
25. *Ibid.*, p. 268.
26. *Ibid.*, p. 278.
27. Welch, 'Theology as Risk,' *Frontline Theology*, ed. D. Peerman (Richmond, 1967), p. 52.
28. J. B. Cobb, *Living Options in Protestant Theology* (Philadelphia, 1962), p. 133.
29. J. Pelikan, *From Luther to Kierkegaard* (St. Louis, 1963), p. 113.
30. F. Thilly and L. Wood, *A History of Philosophy* (New York, 1951), p. 579.
31. Pelikan, *From Luther to Kierkegaard*, p. 114.
32. Cobb, *Living Options in Protestant Theology*, p. 137–138.
33. E. Wolf, 'Karl Barth,' *Theologians for Our Time*, ed. H. Reinisch (Notre Dame, Ind., 1964), p. 1.
34. K. Barth, *The Doctrine of the Word of God*, trans. G. Bromiley (Edinburgh, 1960) 1 : 1. p. 344.
35. *Ibid.*, p. 339.
36. R. S. Franks, *The Doctrine of the Trinity* (London, 1953), p. 180.
37. Barth, *The Doctrine of the Word of God*, 1 : 353.
38. *Ibid.*, p. 368.
39. *Ibid.*, p. 368.
40. *Ibid.*, p. 381.
41. *Ibid.*, pp. 356, 354.
42. *Ibid.*, pp. 355–356.
43. *Ibid.*, p. 357.
44. *Ibid.*, p. 358.
45. *Ibid.*, p. 356.
46. Welch, *The Trinity in Contemporary Theology*, p. 171.
47. Barth, *The Doctrine of the Word of God*, 1 : 398.
48. *Ibid.*, p. 400.
49. *Ibid.*, pp. 414–415.
50. *Ibid.*, p. 548.
51. *Ibid.*, pp. 422–423.
52. *Ibid.*, pp. 401–403.
53. *Ibid.*, pp. 426–429.
54. *Ibid.*, pp. 425–430.
55. *Ibid.*, pp. 416–421.
56. *Ibid.*, pp. 443–454.
57. *Ibid.*, p. 418.
58. *Ibid.*, p. 494.
59. *Ibid.*, pp. 496–501.

60. Welch, *The Trinity in Contemporary Theology*, p. 203.
61. *Ibid.*, p. 205.
62. *Ibid.*, p. 233.
63. W. Lohff, 'Emil Brunner,' *Theologians for Our Time*, p. 30.
64. Welch, *The Trinity in Contemporary Theology*, pp. 65–66.
65. E. Brunner, *The Christian Doctrine of God*, trans. L. Wyon (2 vols. London, 1949) 1 : 206.
66. *Ibid.*
67. *Ibid.*, p. 205.
68. *Ibid.*, p. 220.
69. *Ibid.*, p. 220.
70. *Ibid.*
71. *Ibid.*, pp. 224–225
72. *Ibid.*, p. 226.
73. *Ibid.*, p. 227.
74. *Ibid.*, pp. 235, 236, 237.
75. *Ibid.*, p. 239.
76. C. Kegley, ed., *The Theology of Emil Brunner* (New York, 1952), p. xii.
77. Welch, *The Trinity in Contemporary Theology*, pp. 71, 74.
78. J. C. Cooper, *The Roots of the Radical Theology* (Philadelphia, 1967), p. 77.
79. *Ibid.*, p. 78.
80. H. P. Owen, *Revelation and Existence* (Cardiff, 1957), p. 2.
81. H. Fries, *Bultmann-Barth and Catholic Theology* (Pittsburgh, 1967), p. 98.
82. H. Fries, 'Demythologizing and Theological Truth,' *Rudolf Bultmann in Catholic Thought*, ed. T. F. O'Meara and D. Weiser (New York, 1968), p. 30.
83. Owen, *Revelation and Existence*, p. 5.
84. *Ibid.*, p. 27.
85. H. Bouillard, *The Logic of Faith* (New York, 1967), p. 130.
86. R. Bultmann, *Glauben und Verstehen* (Tübingen, 1952) 1 : 265.
87. Bultmann, *Theology of the New Testament*, trans. K. Grober (New York, 1965), 1 : 305.
88. Bultmann, 'New Testament and Mythology,' *Kerygma and Myth*, trans. R. H. Fuller, ed. H. Bartsch (New York, 1957), pp. 21–22.
89. Owen, *Revelation and Existence*, p. 45.
90. Bultmann, 'New Testament and Mythology,' p. 121.
91. J. Moltmann, *The Theology of Hope* (New York, 1967), pp. 67–68.
92. H. Zahrnt, *The Question of God* (New York, 1969), p. 255.
93. Cobb, *Living Options in Protestant Theology*, p. 258.
94. Cooper, *The Roots of Radical Theology*, p. 84.
95. *Ibid.*
96. H. Burkle, 'Paul Tillich,' *Theologians of Our Time*, p. 66.
97. Cooper, *The Roots of Radical Theology*, p. 87.

98. *Ibid.*, p. 88.
99. P. Tillich, *Systematic Theology* (3 vols. Chicago, 1953–) 1 : 67–73.
100. *Ibid.*, p. 69.
101. *Ibid.*, p. 261.
102. *Ibid.*, p. 262.
103. *Ibid.*, p. 264.
104. *Ibid.*, p. 270.
105. *Ibid.*, p. 271.
106. *Ibid.*, p. 265.
107. *Ibid.*, p. 264.
108. *Ibid.*, p. 268.
109. *Ibid.*, pp. 264–265.
110. *Ibid.*, p. 271.
111. Zahrnt, *The Question of God*, p. 335; cf. Cooper, *The Roots of Radical Theology*, p. 92.
112. C. W. Kegley and R. W. Bretall, eds., *Theology of Paul Tillich* (New York, 1952), p. 28.
113. Tillich, *Systematic Theology*, 2 : 97.
114. *Ibid.*, p. 119.
115. Tillich, 'A Reinterpretation of the Doctrine of the Incarnation,' *Church Quarterly Review* (1949) : 135.
116. *Ibid.*, 136–137.
117. *Ibid.*, 137.
118. G. H. Tavard, *The Vision of Paul Tillich* (New York, 1963), p. 124.
119. Zahrnt, *The Problem of God*, p. 303.
120. Tillich, *Systematic Theology*, 1 : 252–253.
121. *Ibid.*, 2 : 143.
122. Tavard, *The Vision of Paul Tillich*, p. 119.
123. D. H. Kelsey, *The Fabric of Paul Tillich's Theology* (New Haven, 1967), p. 196.
124. Burkle, 'Paul Tillich,' p. 77.
125. Zahrnt, *The Problem of God*, p. 298.

NOTES TO INTRODUCTION TO PART SIX

1. A. Schmemann, *The Historical Road of Eastern Orthodoxy* (New York, 1963), p. 226.
2. *Ibid.*

NOTES TO CHAPTER EIGHTEEN

1. M. Gordillo, *Theologia Orientalium cum Latinorum Comparata* (3 vols. Rome, 1960), 1 : 170–171; A. Fortescue, *The Orthodox Eastern Church* (London, 1929), p. 171.
2. Gordillo, *Theologia Orientalium cum Latinorum Comparata*, 1 : 173–175.

Notes

341

3. *Ibid.*, 1:209; Fortescue, *The Orthodox Eastern Church*, pp. 178–180.
4. PG 120.781–796.
5. A. Schmemann, *The Historical Road of Eastern Orthodoxy* (New York, 1963), p. 250.
6. A. Michel, *Humbert und Kerullarios* (Paderborn, 1925) 1:11.
7. Gordillo, *Theologia Orientalium* . . . , pp. 227–228.
8. PG 126.229A-B, C–232B.
9. R. M. French, *The Eastern Orthodox Church* (London, 1951), p. 78.
10. *Ibid.*, p. 78.
11. *Ibid.*
12. *Ibid.*, pp. 141–143.
13. Schmemann, *The Historical Road of Eastern Orthodoxy*, p. 232.
14. *Ibid.*, p. 234.
15. M. Jugie, *Theologia Dogmatica Christianorum Orientalium* (Paris, 1933) 2:238–242; B. Krivosheine, *The Ascetic and Theological Teaching of Gregory Palamas* (London, 1954).
16. Schmemann, *The Historical Road of Eastern Orthodoxy*, pp. 234–235.
17. *Ibid.*, p. 254. See above, pp. 224–227.
18. Fortescue, *The Orthodox Eastern Church*, p. 241.
19. F. Gavin, *Some Aspects of Contemporary Greek Orthodox Thought* (London, 1936), p. 211.
20. *Ibid.*, p. 211; cf. French, *The Eastern Orthodox Church*, p. 88.
21. See DTC 9.2039–2044.
22. French, *The Eastern Orthodox Church*, pp. 88–89; Fortescue, *The Orthodox Eastern Church*, pp. 362–365.
23. Schmemann, *The Historical Road of Eastern Orthodoxy*, p. 285.
24. Fortescue, *The Orthodox Eastern Church*, p. 268; Gavin, *Some Aspects of Contemporary Greek Orthodox Thought*, p. 217; French, *The Eastern Orthodox Church*, pp. 89–90.
25. G. Williams, *The Orthodox and the Non-jurors* (London, 1868).
26. J. Reusch, *Bericht über die Unions-Konferenzen* (Bonn, 1874–1875).
27. Jugie, *Theologia Dogmatica Christianorum Orientalium*, p. 449.
28. N. Zernov, *Eastern Christendom* (London, 1961), pp. 199–201.
29. S. C. Gulovich, *Windows Westward* (New York, 1947), pp. 114–123.
30. *Ibid.*, pp. 114–115.
31. Schmemann, *The Historical Road of Eastern Orthodoxy*, p. 226.
32. Jugie, *Theologia Dogmatica Christianorum Orientalium*, pp. 460–467.
33. V. Bolotov, 'Thesen über das Filioque,' *Revue Internationale de Théologie* 6 (1898): 681–712.
34. Jugie, *Theologia Dogmatica Christianorum Orientalium*, pp. 467–481.

35. V. Lossky, 'The Procession of the Holy Spirit in the Orthodox Triadology,' EChurchQ 7 (1948): Suppl. 31–53.
36. John Damascene, *De Fide Orthodoxa*, 1.8 (PG 94.820–824A).
37. Lossky, 'The Procession of the Holy Spirit in the Orthodox Triadology,' 36.
38. *Ibid.*, pp. 36–38.
39. *Ibid.*, p. 45.
40. *Ibid.*, pp. 45–46.
41. *Ibid.*, p. 46.
42. *Ibid.*, p. 52.
43. *Ibid.*, pp. 52–53.
44. Gavin, *Some Aspects of Contemporary Greek Orthodox Thought*, pp. 107–143.
45. *Ibid.*, pp. 122–123.
46. *Ibid.*, p. 126.
47. *Ibid.*, p. 127.
48. *Ibid.*, p. 132.
49. *Ibid.*, p. 138.
50. *Ibid.*, p. 139.
51. T. Hopko, 'Holy Spirit in Orthodox Theology and Life,' *Commonweal* (Nov. 8, 1968): 186–191.
52. *Ibid.*, 187, 191.
53. M. Gordillo, *Compendium Theologiae Orientalis* (Rome, 1939), p. 49; M. Rinvolucri, *Anatomy of a Church* (New York, 1966), p. 184.
54. T. Ware, *The Orthodox Church* (Baltimore, 1964), p. 324.
55. P. Bratsiotis, *The Greek Orthodox Church* (Notre Dame, 1968), pp. 103, 106, 109.

NOTE TO INTRODUCTION TO PART SEVEN

1. K. Rahner, 'Remarks on the Dogmatic Treatise "De Trinitate," ' *Theological Investigations*, trans. K. Smyth (Baltimore, 1966) 4:77–79.

NOTES TO CHAPTER TWENTY

1. B. Lonergan, *De Deo Trino* (Rome, 1961), pp. 284–285; P. Galtier, *De SS. Trinitate* (Paris, 1933), pp. 120–134.
2. Galtier, *De SS. Trinitate*, pp. 120–134; Lonergan, *De Deo Trino*, pp. 287–290.
3. Lonergan, *De Deo Trino*, p. 298.
4. R. C. Neville, 'Creation and the Trinity,' ThST 30 (1969): 3, 4f.
5. C. F. Mooney, *Teilhard de Chardin and the Mystery of Christ* (New York, 1965), pp. 168–181.
6. E. Rideau, *The Thought of Teilhard de Chardin* (New York, 1967), p. 154

7. A. D'Alès, *De Deo Trino* (Paris, 1934), p. 6; Galtier, *De SS. Trinitate*, pp. 13–23.
8. J. L. McKenzie, *Dictionary of the Bible* (Milwaukee, 1965), p. 900.
9. D'Alès, *De Deo Trino*, p. 6.
10. K. Rahner, 'Remarks on the Dogmatic Treatise "De Trinitate," ' *Theological Investigations*, trans, K. Smyth (Baltimore, 1966) 4 : 100.
11. D'Alès, *De Deo Trino*, p. 15.
12. I. M. Dalmau, *Sacrae Theologiae Summa* (Madrid, 1958), p. 230.
13. J. Van der Meersch, *Tractatus de Deo Uno et Trino* (Bruges, 1928), p. 392.
14. F. Klein, *The Doctrine of the Trinity* (New York, 1940), p. 54.
15. Rahner, 'Remarks on the Dogmatic Treatise "De Trinitate," ' 84.
16. D. M. Stanley, 'Christian Revelation as Historical Process,' *Studies in Salvation History*, ed. Luke Salm (Englewood Cliffs, N.J., 1964), pp. 158–159.
17. McKenzie, *Dictionary of the Bible*, p. 900.
18. G. Tavard, 'Scripture and Tradition,' JournEcumStud 5 (1968): 308–325.
19. E. Schillebeeckx, *Revelation and Theology* (New York, 1968), p. 95.
20. Rahner, 'Remarks on the Dogmatic Treatise "De Trinitate," ' 70, 98, 99.
21. R. L. Richard, 'Trinity,' NCE 14.300.
22. McKenzie, *Dictionary of the Bible*, p. 899.
23. *A New Catechism* (New York, 1967), p. 499.

NOTES TO CHAPTER TWENTY-ONE

1. E.g. Lohn, Boyer, Lercher, Daffara, Tanquerey.
2. M. T.-L. Penido, 'La Valeur de la Théorie "Psychologique" de la Trinité,' EphemThLov (1931): 5–17; 'Le Rôle de l'Analogie en Théologie Dogmatique,' *Bibliothèque Thomiste* 15 (1931): 311.
3. B. Lonergan, *Divinarum Personarum conceptionem analogicam* (Rome, 1957), pp. 62–79.
4. G. H. Joyce, 'Trinity,' *The Catholic Encyclopedia* (New York, 1912) 15.55–56.
5. K. Rahner, 'Remarks on the Dogmatic Treatise "De Trinitate," ' *Theological Investigations*, trans, K. Smyth (Baltimore, 1966) 4 : 85–86.
6. M. Daffara, *De De Uno et Trino* (Turin, 1945), p. 366; L. Lercher, *Institutiones Theologiae Dogmaticae* (Barcelona, 1945), p. 162.
7. I. M. Dalmau, *Sacrae Theologiae Summa* (Madrid, 1958), p. 363.
8. Lonergan, *Divinarum Personarum conceptionem analogicam*, p. 93.
9. P. Henry, 'On Some Implications of the "Ex Patre Filioque Tam-

quam ab Uno Principio," ' EChurchQ 8 (1948) Suppl. 19.

10. Lonergan, *De Deo Trino*, p. 218.

11. See above, pp. 279, 280, 314.

12. A. D'Alès, *De Deo Trino* (Paris, 1934), p. 240; Dalmau, *Sacrae Theologiae Summa*, p. 392.

13. L. Lohn, *De SS. Trinitate* (Rome, 1931), p. 237; Joyce. 'Trinity,' 56; Lonergan, *Divinarum Personarum conceptionem analogicam*, p. 139.

14. Henry, 'On Some Implications of the "Ex Patre Filioque Tamquam ab Uno Principio," ' 21–22.

15. M. Schmaus, *The Essence of Christianity* (Dublin, 1961), p. 187.

16. Joyce, 'Trinity,' 56.

17. M. Pontifex, *Belief in the Trinity* (New York, 1954), p. 52.

18. Lonergan, *Divinarum Personarum conceptionem analogicam*, 116–121; R. Garrigou-Lagrange, *The Trinity and God the Creator* (St. Louis, 1952), pp. 137–142.

19. E.g., D'Alès, Daffara, Dalmau, Downey, Herve, Tanquerey.

20. E.g., Herve, Dalmau, Lonergan.

21. Lonergan. *Divinarum Personarum conceptionem analogicam*, p. 133.

22. F. Klein, *The Doctrine of the Trinity* (New York, 1940), p. 9.

23. Pontifex, *Belief in the Trinity*, p. 18.

24. M. J. Scheeben, *The Mysteries of Christianity*, trans. C. Vollert (St. Louis, 1946), pp. 80–82.

25. Lonergan, *Divinarum Personarum conceptionem analogicam*, p. 138.

26. Schmaus, *The Essence of Christianity*, pp. 185, 188, 189.

27. Lonergan, *Divinarum Personarum conceptionem analogicam*, pp. 172–175.

28. L. Dewart, *The Future of Belief* (New York, 1966), pp. 143, 146, 147.

29. L. Dewart, *The Foundations of Belief* (New York, 1969), pp. 8–19.

30. Lonergan, 'The Dehellenization of Dogma,' *The Future of Belief Debate*, ed. D. Callahan (New York, 1967), pp. 83, 81, 70, 71, 74, 85, 86.

31. Lonergan, *Divinarum Personarum conceptionem analogicam*, pp. 138, 165, 167.

32. Rahner, 'Remarks on the Dogmatic Treatise "De Trinitate," ' 101–102.

33. B. Cooke, *Beyond Trinity* (Milwaukee, 1969), p. 58.

34. L. Cantwell, *The Theology of the Trinity* (Notre Dame, 1969), p. 84.

35. Scheeben, *The Mysteries of Christianity*, pp. 114–116.

36. Cooke, *Beyond Trinity*, pp. 58–60.

37. G. Salet, 'The Trinity: Mystery of Love,' *The Idea of Catholicism*, ed. W. Burghardt and W. Lynch (New York, 1960), pp. 136–138.

NOTES ON CHAPTER TWENTY-TWO

1. A. D'Alès, *De Deo Trino* (Paris, 1934), pp. 257, 261.
2. See above p. 291; see also *A New Catechism* (New York, 1967).
3. M. Scheeben, *The Mysteries of Christianity*, trans. C. Vollert (St. Louis, 1946), p. 147.
4. *Ibid.*, p. 150.
5. *Ibid.*, p. 151.
6. *Ibid.*, p. 152.
7. *Ibid.*, p. 153.
8. *Ibid.*, pp. 153–154.
9. *Ibid.*, pp. 154–155.
10. *Ibid.*, pp. 156–157.
11. *Ibid.*, p. 158.
12. *Ibid*, pp. 160–161.
13. B. Lonergan, *Divinarum Personarum conceptionem analogicam* (Rome, 1961), pp. 207, 206.
14. *Ibid.*, p. 212.
15. *Ibid.*, p. 219.
16. *Ibid.*, pp. 218–222.
17. D. Petavius, *Dogmata Theologica* (Paris, 1865) 8 : 6.
18. Scheeben, *The Mysteries of Christianity*, pp. 165–167.
19. Th. de Régnon, *Etudes de la théologie positive sur la Trinité* (5 vols. Paris, 1952) 3 : 551–552.
20. R. T. d'Eypernon, *Le mystère primordial: La trinité dans sa vivante image* (Paris, 1941), pp. 109–128; G. M. Dupont, *Foundations for a Devotion to the Blessed Trinity* (Calcutta, 1947); M. J. Donnelly, 'The Inhabitation of the Holy Spirit: A Solution according to de la Taille,' ThSt 8 (1947): 445–470.
21. F. Prat, *Theology of St. Paul* (London, 1927), p. 291; see P. De Letter, 'Grace, Incorporation, Inhabitation,' ThSt 19 (1958): E. J. Fortman, *The Theology of Man and Grace: Commentary* (Milwaukee, 1966), pp. 369–370, 373–374.
22. J. Trütsch, *S. Trinitatis Inhabitatio Apud Theologos Recentiores* (Trent, 1949).
23. E.g. Vasquez, John of St. Thomas, Gardeil, Garrigou-Lagrange, Lange.
24. E.g., Galtier, Chambat, Retailleau.
25. E.g., de la Taille, K. Rahner, Gleason, De Letter.
26. E.g., Suarez, Froget, Delaye, Menendez-Reigada, Nicolas.
27. See Fortman, *The Theology of Man and Grace: Commentary*, pp. 372–374.
28. *Ibid.*, pp. 374–384.
29. P. De Letter, 'Contemporary Theology of Grace,' *Clergy Monthly* (1957): 288–295; see Fortman, *Theology of Man and Grace: Commentary*, pp. 367–370, 373–374.
30. Lonergan, *De constitutione Christi ontologica et psychologica*

(Rome, 1958), pp. 63–82; *Divinarum personarum conceptionem analogicam*, pp. 206–216.

31. R. Garrigou-Lagrange, *Reality* (St. Louis, 1950), pp. 156–158.
32. H. Nicolas, *The Mystery of God's Grace* (Dubuque, 1960), pp. 73–78, 81.
33. Lonergan, *Divinarum Personarum conceptionem analogicam*, p. 236.
34. *Ibid.*
35. *Ibid.*, pp. 237–238.
36. Rahner, Remarks on the Dogmatic Treatise "De Trinitate," ' 95–96.
37. Pius XII, *The Mystical Body of Christ*, as translated in *The Catholic Mind* (1943): 30, 31.

NOTES TO CONCLUSION

1. B. Lonergan, 'The Absence of God in Modern Culture,' *The Presence and Absence of God*, ed. C. Mooney (New York, 1969), p. 173.
2. T. F. O'Meara and D. M. Weisser, *Rudolf Bultmann in Catholic Thought* (New York, 1968), pp. 233, 236.
3. *Ibid.*, pp. 236–237.
4. *Ibid.*, p. 233.
5. *Ibid.*, p. 223.
6. *Ibid.*, p. 240.
7. H. Fries, *Bultmann-Barth and Catholic Theology* (Pittsburgh, 1967), p. 182.

Bibliography

1. THE OLD TESTAMENT

Eichrodt, W. *Theology of the Old Testament*, translated by J. A. Baker. 2 vols. London: SCM Press, 1961, 1967.

Gelin, A. *Key Concepts of the Old Testament*, translated by G. Lamb. London: Sheed & Ward, 1955.

Jacob, E. *Theology of the Old Testament*, translated by W. Heathcote and P. J. Allcock. London: Hodder & Stoughton, 1958.

McKenzie, J. L. *Dictionary of the Bible*. Milwaukee: Bruce, 1965. A work that stands out for its erudition, clarity, balance.

2. THE NEW TESTAMENT

Amiot, F. *The Key Concepts of St. Paul*. New York: Herder & Herder, 1962.

Barrett, C. K. *The Gospel According to St. John*. London: S.P.C.K., 1960. A valuable introduction with comment and notes on the Greek text.

Bonsirven, J. *Theology of the New Testament*, translated by S. F. Tye. Westminster, Md.: Newman, 1963.

Brown, R. E. *Jesus God and Man*. Milwaukee: Bruce, 1967. Gives a definite answer to the question: Does the New Testament call Jesus God?

———. 'The Paraclete in the Fourth Gospel,' NtSt 13 (1967): 113–132. A solid effort to bring together many of the best insights of recent commentators.

Bultmann, R. *Theology of the New Testament*, translated by K. Grobel. 2 vols. New York: Charles Scribner's Sons, 1952, 1955; London: SCM, 1952, 1955.

Cerfaux, L. *Christ in the Theology of St. Paul*, translated by G. Webb and A. Walker. New York: Herder & Herder, 1959.

Cullmann, O. *The Christology of the New Testament,* translated by S. C. Guthrie and C. A. M. Hall. Philadelphia: Westminster Press, 1959. Notable for its heavy stress on functional Christology.

Dodd, C. H. *The Interpretation of the Fourth Gospel.* Cambridge, Eng.: Cambridge University Press, 1960. Valuable for its study of the leading ideas of this gospel.

Fitzmyer, J. A. *Pauline Theology.* Englewood Cliffs, N.J.: Prentice Hall, 1967. A brief but excellent study.

Hermann, I. *Kyrios and Pneuma.* Munich: Kösel-Verlag, 1961. Important studies in Pauline Christology.

Lebreton, J. *History of the Dogma of the Trinity,* translated by A. Thorold. New York: Benziger Bros., 1939.

Schweizer, E. 'Spirit of God,' (Pneuma-Pneumatikos), *Theological Dictionary of the New Testament,* vol. 6, 332–445, ed. G. Friedrich, translated by G. W. Bromiley. 6 vols. Grand Rapids: W. B. Eerdmans Co., 1964–68.

Swete, H. B. *The Holy Spirit in the New Testament.* London: Macmillan, 1919.

Wainwright, A. W. *The Trinity in the New Testament.* London: S.P.C.K., 1962. Maintains that the doctrine of the Trinity already emerges in the New Testament and belongs to the New Testament message.

Whiteley, D. E. H. *The Theology of St. Paul.* Oxford: B. Blackwell, 1964. Contains a noteworthy study of the Lord and the Spirit.

3. EARLY EASTERN CHURCH

Altaner, B. *Patrology,* translated by H. C. Graef. 5th ed. Freiburg: Herder-Nelson, 1960. An excellent survey of Christian literature from the 1st to the 8th century.

Bethune-Baker, J. F. *Early History of Christian Doctrine.* London: Methuen & Co., 1949. Reaches to the time of Chalcedon.

Dvornik, F. *The Photian Schism.* Cambridge, Mass.: Harvard University Press, 1948. An exceptionally fine piece of historical rectification.

Grillmeier, A. *Christ in Christian Tradition,* translated by J. S. Bowden. New York: Sheed & Ward, 1965. An excellent historical study of ancient Christology.

Harnack, A. *History of Dogma,* translated by N. Buchanan, et al. 7 vols. London: Williams & Norgate, 1894–1899. A still valuable, if controversial work.

Kelly, J. N. D. *Early Christian Creeds.* London: Longmans, Green & Co., 1950.

———. *Early Christian Doctrines.* New York: Harper & Row, 1965; London: A. & C. Black, 1965. The best work of its kind.

Lebreton, J. and Zeiller, J. *The History of the Primitive Church,* translated by E. C. Messenger. New York; Benziger Bros., 1947.

Murray, J. C. *The Problem of God.* New Haven: Yale University Press, 1963. Especially noteworthy for its study of the Nicene Problem.

Prestige, G. L. *God in Patristic Thought*. London: S.P.C.K., 1952. An exceptionally fine study of the evolution of trinitarian theory.

Quasten, J. *Patrology*. 3 vols. Westminster, Md.: Newman Press, 1951–. Valuable for its lists of critical editions, English translations, articles and monographs. It ranges from the 1st to the 5th century.

Swete, H. B. *The Holy Spirit in the Ancient Church*. London: Macmillan & Co., 1912. Still one of the best treatments of the subject.

Tixeront, J. *History of Dogmas*. 3 vols. St. Louis: B. Herder, 1910–1916. An old but still useful history that ranges from the New Testament to Damascéne and the Carolingians.

Willis, J. R., ed. *The Teaching of the Church Fathers*. New York: Herder & Herder, 1966.

Wolfson, H. A. *The Philosophy of the Church Fathers*. Cambridge, Mass.: Harvard University Press, 1956. An important but controversial work.

4. EARLY WESTERN CHURCH

Bihlmeyer, K. and H. Tüchle. *Church History*, translated by V. E. Mills. 3 vols. Westminster, Md.: Newman Press, 1958–1966.

Cayré, F. *Manual of Patrology*, translated by A. A. Howitt. 2 vols. Paris: Desclée & Co., 1936, 1940. Ranges from the Apostolic Fathers to the great mystics of the 16th century.

Clarkson, J. F., et al. *The Church Teaches*. St. Louis: B. Herder, 1955. A useful English translation of many of the documents found in Denzinger.

D'Alès, A. *La Théologie de Saint Hippolyte*. Paris: G. Beauchesne, 1906.

Hahn, A. *Bibliothek der Symbole und Glaubensregeln der alten Kirche*. Hildesheim: 1962.

Jonas, H. *The Gnostic Religion*. Boston: Beacon Press, 1963.

Kelly, J. N. D. *The Athanasian Creed*. London: A. & C. Black, 1964. A valuable study of the origin and theology of this creed.

Lawson, J. *The Biblical Theology of Saint Irenaeus*. London: Epworth Press, 1948.

Paissac, H. *Théologie du Verbe. Saint Augustin et Saint Thomas*. Paris: Editions du Cerf, 1951.

Portalié, E. *A Guide to the Thought of Saint Augustine*, translated by R. J. Bastian. Chicago: H. Regnery Co., 1960.

Roberts, R. E. *The Theology of Tertullian*. London: Epworth Press, 1924.

Schmaus, M. *Die psychologische Trinitätslehre des hl. Augustinus*. Münster: Aschendorffsche, 1927.

Smulders, P. *La doctrine trinitaire de S. Hilaire de Poitiers*. Rome: Gregorian University Press, 1944.

Stewart, H. F. and E. K. Rand. *Boethius: The Theological Tractates*. New York: W. Heinemann, 1918.

5. MIDDLE AGES

Cottiaux, J. 'La Conception de la théologie chez Abélard,' RHE 28 (1932): 247–295, 533–551, 788–828.

DeGhellinck, J. *Le Mouvement Théologique du XIIe Siècle.* Paris: Lecoffre, 1914.

Ethier, A. M. *Le 'de Trinitate,' de Richard de Saint-Victor.* Publications de L'institute d'études médiévales d'Ottawa 9 (Paris, Ottowa 1939).

Frassen, C. *Scotus Academicus.* 12 vols. Rome: typ. Sallustiana, 1900–1902.

Garrigou-Lagrange, R. *The Trinity and God the Creator.* St. Louis: B. Herder, 1952. A solid Dominican presentation and defense of Aquinas' trinitarian doctrine.

Gill, J. *The Council of Florence.* Cambridge, Eng.: Cambridge University Press, 1959. An outstanding work in every respect.

Haring, N. M. 'The Case of Gilbert de la Porrée,' MedSt 13 (1951): 1–40.

Knowles, D. *The Evolution of Medieval Thought.* Baltimore: Helicon Press, 1962.

Leff, G. *Medieval Thought: St Augustine to Ockham.* Baltimore: Penguin Books, 1958.

McGiffert, A. C. *A History of Christian Thought.* 2 vols. New York: Charles Scribner's Sons, 1932–33.

Murray, A. V. *Abelard and St. Bernard.* New York: Barnes & Noble, 1967.

Pelzer, A. 'Les 51 articles de Guillaume Occam' RHE 18 (1922): 240–270.

Poole, R. L. *Illustrations of the History of Medieval Thought and Learning.* London: Macmillan Co., 1932.

Rivière, J. 'Les "capitula" d'Abélard condamnés au concile de Sens,' RechThMed. 5 (1933): 1–22.

Stohr, R. *Die Trinitätslehre des. heil. Bonaventura.* Munster, 1923.

Williams, M. E. *The Teaching of Gilbert Porreta on the Trinity.* Rome: Gregorian University Press, 1951.

6. PROTESTANT TRINITARIAN DOCTRINE

Barth, K. *The Doctrine of the Word of God,* translated by G. T. Thompson. 2 vols. Edinburgh: T. & T. Clark, 1960, repr. A work that was very influential for a time and still has great value.

Brunner, E. *The Christian Doctrine of God.* Dogmatics I, translated by L. Wyon. London: Lutterworth Press, 1949. Notable for its disagreement with Barth over the place of the doctrine of the Trinity in Dogmatics and its criticism of the orthodox doctrine of the Trinity.

Bultmann, R. *Essays Philosophical and Theological,* translated by J. C. G. Greig. London: Macmillan Co., 1955.

Calvin, J. *Institutes of the Christian Religion,* ed. J. T. McNeill, translated by F. L. Battles. 2 vols. London: S.C.M. Press, 1961.

Cobb, J. B. *Living Options In Protestant Theology.* Philadelphia: Westminster Press, 1962.

Cooper, J. C. *The Roots of the Radical Theology.* Philadelphia: Westminster Press, 1967.

Cragg, G. R. *The Church and the Age of Reason.* Grand Rapids: Eerdmans Co., 1962.

Dillenberger, J. and C. Welch. *Protestant Christianity, Interpreted through its Development.* New York: Charles Scribner's Sons, 1954.

Franks, R. S. *The Doctrine of the Trinity.* London: G. Duckworth Co., 1953.

Garvie, A. *The Ritschlian Theology.* Edinburgh: T. & T. Clark, 1899.

Gogarten, F. *Demythologizing and History.* London: S.C.M. Press, 1955.

Harnack, A. *What is Christianity?*, translated by T. B. Saunder. London: Williams' Norgate, 1923. An epoch-making book in its time—aimed at dehellenizing the Christian message so as to find its essence.

Hegel, G. W. *Lectures on the Philosophy of Religion,* translated by E. B. Speirs and J. B. Sanderson. 3 vols. London: Kegan Paul 1895. An influential exposition of philosophical trinitarianism.

Kant, I. *Religion Within the Limits of Reason Alone,* translated by T. M. Greene, H. H. Hudson. New York: Harper, 1960. This and other works of Kant exercised a strong influence on some Protestant theologians in their efforts to bring about a reorientation of Protestant theology.

Luther, M. *Luther's Works,* ed. J. Pelikan. 54 vols. St. Louis: Concordia Publishing Co., 1959–67.

McGiffert, A. C. *Protestant Thought before Kant.* London: Duckworth & Co., 1919.

Macquarrie, J. *An Existentialist Theology: A Comparison of Heidegger and Bultmann.* New York: Harper & Row, 1955; London: S.C.M. Press, 1955.

Orr, J. *English Deism: Its Roots and Its Fruits.* Grand Rapids: W. B. Eerdmans, 1934.

Pelikan, J. *From Luther to Kierkegaard.* St. Louis: Concordia, 1950.

Robinson, J. A. T. *Honest to God.* Philadelphia, Westminster Press, 1963. A very interesting but controversial work that is said to have sold more quickly than any new book of serious theology in the history of the world.

Schleiermacher, F. *The Christian Faith,* ed. H. R. Mackintosh J. S. Steward. Edinburgh: T. & T. Clark, 1948. This work of the 'father of modern liberal theology' that relegates the Trinity to an Appendix had a great influence on subsequent Protestant theologians.

Servetus, M. *The Two Treatises of Servetus on the Trinity,* translated by E. M. Wilbur. Harvard Theological Studies. Cambridge, Mass.: Harvard University Press, 1932.

Tillich, P. *Systematic Theology.* 3 vols. Chicago: University of Chicago Press, 1953. A very important work that aimed to interpret the great symbols of Christianity in terms of modern existentialist philosophy, so as to make the power of Christ's message available to men of today.

Welch, C. *The Trinity in Contemporary Theology.* London: S.C.M.

Press, 1953. An important study of contemporary attitudes toward the doctrine of the Trinity that closes with a constructive statement for the foundation of an adequate Trinitarianism.

Zahrnt, H. *The Question of God.* New York: Harcourt, Brace & World, Inc., 1969.

7. ORTHODOX TRINITARIAN DOCTRINE

Bolotov, V. V. 'Thesen Über das "Filioque" von einem russischen Theologen,' *Revue Internationale de Théologie* 6 (1898): 681–712.

Eckardt, H. von. *Russia,* translated by C. A. Phillips. New York: A. A. Knopf, 1930.

Every, G. *The Byzantine Patriarchate 451–1204.* London: S.P.C.K., 1947.

Fedotov. G. *A Treasury of Russian Spirituality.* New York: Harper, 1961.

Florensky, P. A. 'On the Holy Spirit,' translated by A. E. Moorhouse, *Ultimate Questions,* ed. by A. Schmemann, 137–172. New York: Holt, Rinehart & Winston, 1965.

Fortescue, A. *The Orthodox Eastern Church.* London: Catholic Truth Society, 1929.

French, R. M. *The Eastern Orthodox Church.* London: Hutchinson University Library, 1951.

Gavin, F. *Some Aspects of Contemporary Greek Orthodox Thought.* London, S.P.C.K., 1936. A brief presentation of trinitarian doctrine with a heavy stress on the *Filioque.*

Gordillo, M. *Compendium Theologiae Orientalis.* Rome: Pontifical Institute of Oriental Studies, 1939. A polemical study of the history and doctrine of the procession of the Holy Spirit with an excellent index of authors and their works.

Hopko, T. 'Holy Spirit in Orthodox Theology and Life,' *Commonweal,* (Nov. 8, 1968): 186–191.

Lossky, V. *Essai sur la Théologie Mystique de L'Eglise D'Orient.* Paris: Aubier, 1944.

———. 'The Procession of the Holy Spirit in the Orthodox Triadology,' *EChurchQ* vol. 7, suppl. issue (1948) 31–53. Valuable for its clear-cut presentation of the Orthodox view.

Seraphim, M. *L'Eglise Orthodoxe.* Paris: Payot, 1952.

Solovyev, V. S. *God, Man and the Church: The Spiritual Foundations of Life,* translated by D. Attwater. Milwaukee: Bruce, 1938.

Zernov, N. *The Russian Religious Renaissance of the Twentieth Century.* New York: Harper & Row, 1963.

8. CATHOLIC TRINITARIAN DOCTRINE

Cooke, B. *Beyond Trinity,* Milwaukee: Marquette University Press, 1969.

De Letter, P. 'Sanctifying Grace and Our Union with the Holy Trinity,' ThSt (March 1952): 33–58.

De Régnon, Th. *Etudes de théologie positive sur la Sainte Trinité.* 3

vols. Paris: Retaux, 1892–1898. A work of great value even today for its solid presentation of the trinitarian dogma and the Scholastic and Greek theories of the divine processions.

Dewart, L. *The Future of Belief.* New York: Herder & Herder, 1966. A dehellenizing effort to recast traditional Christian doctrine in the light of modern man's new self-understanding.

Fortman, E. J. *The Theology of Man and Grace: Commentary.* Milwaukee: Bruce, 1966.

———. *The Theology of God: Commentary.* Milwaukee: Bruce, 1968.

Fries, H. *Bultmann-Barth And Catholic Theology.* Pittsburgh: Duquesne University Press, 1967.

Gleason, R. W. *The Indwelling Spirit.* New York: Alba House, 1966. Presents the divine indwelling in terms of De la Taille's theory.

Henry, P. 'On Some Implications of the "Ex Patre Filioque . . ." ' *EChurchQ.* Vol. 7 suppl. issue (1948): 16–31. Gives a Catholic view of trinitarian doctrine over against Lossky's Orthodox view.

Lonergan, B. *Verbum: Word and Idea in Aquinas,* edited by D. B. Burrell. Univ. of Notre Dame Press, 1967.

———. *De Deo Trino.* Rome: Gregorian University Press, 1961. Noteworthy for its survey of trinitarian errors, its study of the evolution of trinitarian doctrine and its presentation of the basic trinitarian dogmas.

———. *Divinarum Personarum conceptionem analogicam.* Rome: Gregorian University Press, 1957. Notable for its presentation of the divine processions on the analogy of intelligible emanations of word and love.

Mooney, C. F. *Teilhard de Chardin and the Mystery of Christ.* New York: Harper & Row, 1966. Notable for its presentation of Chardin's concept of trinitization.

Neville, R. C. 'Creation And the Trinity,' *ThSt* 30 (March 1969): 3–26.

Nicholas, J.-H. *The Mystery of God's Grace.* Dubuque: Priory Press, 1960. Explains the trinitarian presence in terms of full supernatural knowledge.

Penido, M. T.-L. 'La Valeur de la Thoérie "Psychologique" de la Trinité,' *EphemThLov* 8 (1931): 5–17.

Rahner, K. 'Some Implications of the Scholastic Concept of Uncreated Grace,' *Theological Investigations,* vol. 1. 319–346, translated by C. Ernst. Baltimore: Helicon Press, 1961. Presents God's self-communication in the mode of formal causality.

———, 'Remarks on the Dogmatic Treatise "De Trinitate," ' *Theological Investigations,* translated by K. Smyth, vol. 4. 77–102. Baltimore: Helicon Press, 1966. Noteworthy for its effort to up-date the dogmatic treatise on the Trinity and its insistence that the Trinity of the economy is the immanent Trinity and vice versa.

Richard, R. L. 'Holy Trinity.' *New Catholic Encyclopedia,* vol. 14, 295–306. New York-Washington, McGraw-Hill, 1967.

Scheeben, M. J. *The Mysteries of Christianity,* translated by C. Vollert. St.

Louis: B. Herder, 1946. Valuable especially for its presentation of the significance of the mystery of the Trinity and of the divine missions.

Stanley, D. M. 'Christian Revelation as Historical Process,' *Studies in Salvation History*, edited by C. L. Salm, 147–159. Englewood Cliffs, N.J.,: Prentice-Hall, 1964.

Trütsch, J. *SS. Trinitatis Inhabitatio Apud Theologos Recentiores*. Trent: Mutilati & Invalidi, 1949.

Vagaggini, C. *Theological Dimensions of the Liturgy*. Collegeville: Liturgical Press, 1959. Noteworthy especially for Chapter 7: The Liturgy and the Christological and Trinitarian Dialectic of Salvation: From the Father, Through Christ, in the Holy Spirit, to the Father.

Additional Bibliography

The following books and articles listed under Additional Bibliography are also listed in the text or in the original bibliography.

Barnard, L. W., *Justin Martyr*.
Dewart, L., *The Foundations of Belief*.
Dupont, G. M., *Foundations for a Devotion to the Blessed Trinity*.
Evans, E., *Tertullian's Treatise Against Praxeas*.
Goodenough, E. R., *The Theology of Justin Martyr*.
Kegley, C. W., ed., *The Theology of Paul Tillich*.
Lebreton, J., 'La Théologie de la Trinité chez Clément d'Alexandrie.'
Picavet, F., *Roscelin*.
Pontifex, M., *Belief in the Trinity*.
Rivière, J., 'Les "capitula" d'Abélard condamnés au concile de Sens.'
Tavard, G. H., *Paul Tillich and the Christian Message*.

Arendzen, J. O., *The Holy Trinity*, London: Sheed & Ward, 1937.
Baillie, D. M., *God was in Christ*, London: Faber and Faber, 1948.
Barnard, L. W., *Justin Martyr*, Cambridge University Press, 1967.
Benz, E., *The Eastern Orthodox Church: Its Thought and Life*, Chicago: Aldine Publ. Co., tr. by R. & C. Winston, 1963.
Bishop, W. S., *The development of Trinitarian doctrine in the Nicene and Athanasian Creeds*, New York: Longmans, Green and Co., 1910.
Bouttier, M., *Christianity according to Paul*, tr. by F. Clarke, Naperville: Allenson, 1966.
Bulgakov, S. N., *The Orthodox Church*, London: Centenary Press, 1935.
Chadwick, H., *The Early Church*, Baltimore: Penguin Books, 1967.
Chevalier, I. S., *Augustin et la pensée grecque. Les relations trinitaires*, Fribourg en Suisse: Collectanea Friburgensia, 1940
Cooke, B. J., *The God of Space and Time*, New York: Holt, Rinehart and Winston, 1969.

Cousins, E., 'Teilhard and the Theology of the Spirit', *Cross Currents*, v. 19 n. 2 Spring 1969.

Cunningham, F. L. B., *The Indwelling of the Trinity*, Dubuque: Priory Press, 1955.

Daniélou, J., S.J., *The infancy narratives,* tr. Rosemary Sheed, New York: Herder and Herder, 1968.

Dewart, L., *The Foundations of Belief,* New York: Herder and Herder,1969.

d'Eypernon, F. T., *The Blessed Trinity and the Sacraments*, Westminster: Newman Press, 1961.

Dupont, G. M., S.J., *Foundations for a Devotion to the Blessed Trinity*, Calcutta: The Oriental Institute, 1947.

Duquoc, C., 'Le dessein salvifique et la révélation de la Trinité en S. Paul', *Lum Vie* n. 29 p. 67–94.

Evans, E., *Tertullian's Treatise Against Praxeas*, London: S.P.C.K., 1948.

Fedotov, G. P., *The Russian Religious Mind*, Cambridge University Press, 1946.

Flew, A., MacIntyre, A., eds. *New Essays in Philosophical Theology*, New York: Macmillan, 1955.

Gonzalez, J. L., *A history of Christian thought*, Volume I: *From the beginning to the Council of Chalcedon*, Nashville: Abingdon Press, 1970.

Goodenough, E. R., *The Theology of Justin Martyr*, Jena: 1923.

Grane, L., *Peter Abelard: philosophy and Christianity in the Middle Ages*, tr. by F. and C. Crowley, New York: Harcourt, Brace and Jovanovitch, 1970.

Hanson, R. P. C., *God: Creator, Saviour, Spirit,* Naperville: SCM Book Club, 1960.

Hartshorne, C., *The Divine Relativity*, New Haven: Yale Press, 1948.

Hedley, G. P., *The Holy Trinity: experience and interpretation*, Philadelphia: Fortress Press, 1967.

Henry, C. F. H., *The Protestant Dilemma*, Grand Rapids: Eerdmans, 1948.

Janssens, A., *The Mystery of the Trinity*, Fresno: Academy Library Guild, 1954.

Johansen, A., *Theological Study in the Rumanian Orthodox Church under Communist Rule*, London: Faith Press, 1961.

Johnson, L., 'The Spirit of God', *Scripture* 8 (1956) 65–74.

Jurgens, W. A., tr., *The Faith of the Early Fathers*, Collegeville: 1970.

Kaufman, G. D., *Systematic theology: a historicist perspective*, New York: Scribner's, 1968.

Kegley, C. W., ed., *The Theology of Paul Tillich*, New York: Macmillan, 1952.

Kegley, C. W., ed., *The Theology of Rudolf Bultmann*, New York: Harper & Row, 1961.

Knight, G. A. F., *A Biblical Approach to the Doctrine of the Trinity*, Edinburgh: Oliver and Boyd, 1953.

Labriolle, P. Champage de, *History and literature of Christianity from*

Tertullian to Boethius, tr. by H. Wilson, New York: Barnes & Noble, 1969.

Lafont, G., O.S.B., *Peut-on connaître Dieu en Jesus-Christ?* Paris: du Cerf, 1969.

Lebreton, J., 'La Théologie de la Trinité chez Clément d'Alexandrie', *RechScRel,* 34 (1947).

Lowry, C. W., *The Trinity and Christian Devotion,* New York: Harper, 1946.

MacIntyre, A., ed., *Difficulties in Christian Belief,* Naperville: W. B. Eerdmans, 1959.

Maier, J-L, *Les missions divines selon saint Augustin,* Paradosis XVI Fribourg en Suisse: Editions Universitaires, 1960.

Mascall, E. L., *Theology and the Future,* New York: Morehouse-Barlow, 1968.

May, P., *The Doctrine of the Trinity,* Mysore: Christian Literature Society, 1958.

McShane, P., S. J., 'The Hypothesis of Intelligible Emanations in God', *ThSt* 23 (1962).

Meyendorff, J., *Orthodoxy and Catholicity,* New York: Sheed & Ward, 1961.

Neufeld, V. H., *The Earliest Christian Confessions,* Grand Rapids: Eerdmans, 1963.

Newbigin, J. E. L., *Trinitarian faith and today's mission,* Richmond: John Knox Press, 1964.

Niebuhr, H. R., 'The Doctrine of the Trinity and the Unity of the Church', *Theology Today* III (October 1946).

O'Meara, T. F., O.P., Weisser, D. M., O.P., eds. *Projections: shaping an American theology for the future,* Garden City New York: Doubleday, 1970.

Picavet, F., *Roscelin,* Paris: Alcan, 1911.

Pollard, T. E., *Johannine Christology and the early church,* New York: Cambridge University Press, (Society of NT Studies, monograph series, 13) 1970.

Pontifex, M., *Belief in the Trinity,* New York: 1954.

Rahner, K., S.J., *The Trinity,* tr. by J. Conceel, New York: Herder and Herder, (Mysterium salutis) 1970.

Ratzinger, J., *Introduction to Christianity,* tr. by J. R. Foster, New York: Herder and Herder, 1970.

Richardson, C. C., *The Doctrine of the Trinity,* Nashville: Abingdon Press, 1958.

Richardson, H. W., *Theology for a New World,* London: SCM Press, 1968.

Rivière, J., 'Les "capitula" d'Abélard condamnés au concile de Sens', *RechThMed* V Louvain 1933.

Rou, Olivier du, *L'Intelligence de la foi en la Trinité selon saint Augustin. Genèse de sa théologie trinitaire jusqu'en 391,* Paris: Etudes Augustiniennes, 1966.

Schindler, A., *Wort und Analogie in Augustins Trinitätslehre*, Tübingen, 1965.

Sherrard, P., *The Greek East and the Latin West*, London: Oxford University Press, 1959.

Socrates, *Ecclesiastical History*, Oxford: Clarendon Press, 1878.

Sozomen, *Ecclesiastical History*, tr. by E. Walford, London: Henry G. Bohn, 1855.

Spicq, C., *The Trinity and our Moral Life according to St. Paul*, tr. by Sister Marie Aquinas, Westminster: Newman, 1963.

Stephens, W. P., *The Holy Spirit in the theology of Martin Bucer*, New York: Cambridge University Press, 1970.

Sullivan, J. E., O.P., *The Image of God. The Doctrine of St. Augustine and its influence*, Dubuque: Priory Press, 1963.

Tavard, G. H., *Paul Tillich and the Christian Message*, New York: Charles Scribner's Sons, 1962.

TeSelle, E., *Augustine the theologian*, New York: Herder and Herder, 1970.

Torrance, T. F., *Theology n Reconstruction*, Grand Rapids: Eerdmans, 1965.

Warfield, B. B., *Studies in Tertullian and Augustine*, New York: Oxford University Press, 1930.

Welch, C., 'The Holy Spirit and the Trinity', *Theology Today* VIII April 1951.

Wilmart, V. A., 'Le premier ouvrage de S. Anselme contre le trithéisme de Roscelin', *RechThMed* Louvain 1931.

Glossary

Abba—a familiar address used by children to their father. It was used by Jesus in invoking His Father (Mk 14.36) and by early Christians (Rom 8.15, Gal 4.6).

Ad alium, ad invicem—to another, to one another.

Adoptionist—one who held that Christ was only an adopted, not the natural, son of God.

Aeons—Gnostic emanations or phases of the supreme deity, e.g. *Nous*.

Agennesia—ingenerateness, the quality of not being generated.

Anomoeans—those who held that Christ was unlike (*anomoios*) the Father.

Apollinarians—followers of Apollinaris of Laodicea (d. 390 c.). He affirmed that Christ was the consubstantial Son of the Father but had no human soul, and that the human soul was replaced by the divine Word.

Apologists—those who wrote Apologies, i.e., vindications, explanations, defences of Christians and their ways.

Appropriation—the teaching that all exterior (*ad extra*) divine works are common to all three persons, but that one or other work may for good reasons be specially attributed or appropriated to one person, as 'sanctification' to the Holy Spirit, because of its affinity to His personal characteristic of sanctity.

Arianism—the doctrine that made the Son a creature, a more or less perfect creature. It had different forms with different proponents.

Arian sense—a Subordinationist in the full Arian sense viewed the Son as a creature.

Autotheos—very God, the true, real God, God Himself.

Basilides—an important Christian Gnostic, who was born in Syria and lectured at Alexandria 120–140 c.

Binitarism—a theory that admitted only two persons in God, the Father and the Son.

Boethius—was born in Rome about 470–480. He became eminent for his literary, philosophical and scientific achievements. He was executed by the Western Emperor as a partisan of Byzantium.

Bonum est diffusivum sui—good is self-diffusive.

Charismatic Spirit—the Spirit as the agent of extraordinary free gifts, such as prophetic discernment (1 Kg 22.28).

Christological—concerned with the study, theology, nature of Christ.

Circumincession—inexistence, interpenetration, co-inherence.

Constantius—son of Constantine the Great, who became an Arianizing Emperor of the East.

Consubstantial—of the same substance, *homoousios* in Greek.

Defined faith—proposed definitively by the Church to be believed as divinely revealed.

Demiurge—a creator or craftsman. Plato pictures a Demiurge fashioning the world out of pre-existent material. For some Gnostics the Demiurge was an aeon that went astray, became the creator of man and the material world, and was the God of the Jews, an evil genius to be resisted.

Ditheists—those who held that there are two gods.

Divine and catholic faith—and hence to be believed as divinely revealed and proposed by the Church to be so believed.

Divine dialogue passages—passages where Yahweh is apparently engaged in dialogue with someone, e.g., Gen 1.26: 'Then God said: "Let us make man in our image" . . .'.

Doxology—formula or hymn of praise, e.g., 'Glory to the Father . . .'

Economic understanding—an understanding of the Father, Son and Holy Spirit not in themselves but as manifested in creation, redemption, sanctification.

Economy—a word used by the Fathers to express God's plan, design, dispensation of grace, management of mundane affairs, providential order of creation, redemption, sanctification, etc.

Ekporeuetai—a famous Greek verb meaning 'He proceeds from' (Jn 15.26).

Ekporeusis—procession from, the quality of proceeding from.

Elective sonship—an adoptive sonship by reason of a special dilective election.

Enchiridion Symbolorum—its full title is: *Enchiridion Symbolorum, Definitionum et Declarationum de rebus Fidei et Morum,* i.e., a Handbook of Symbols, Definition, Declarations about matters of Faith and Morals. It is, or was, a very widely used work that lists in chronological order most of the major ecclesial documents. It was first edited by H. Denzinger, and most recently in its 32nd edition by A. Schönmetzer, S. J. Denz 75 refers to the number in this Denzinger–Schönmetzer edition where the quotation in question is to be found in Latin.

Endiathetos—immanent. Many Fathers spoke of a *Logos endiathetos,* immanent in the Father, and of a *Logos prophorikos,* uttered by the Father.

Eo Filius quo Verbum et Eo Verbum quo Filius—by what he is Word by that he is Son, and by what he is Son by that he is Word.

Esse, vivere, intelligere—to be (being), to live (life), to understand (understanding).

Essence—the quiddity of a being, that which makes it what it is.

Eudoxians—followers of Eudoxius (d. 369). He was an Arian bishop of Antioch and then of Constantinople, and leader of official Arianism.

Eunomians—followers of Eunomius, who was bishop of Cyzicus in 360 and the true leader of the Anomoians.

Eusebians—followers of Eusebius of Nicomedia, one of the most influential Arian leaders.

Eternal procession, temporal mission—from eternity the Holy Spirit is originated by the Son, in time He is sent by the Son into the world to sanctify men. Thus He eternally proceeds from Father and Son and is temporally sent by Father and Son.

Fides quaerens intellectum—faith seeking understanding.

Filioque—'and from the Son'. According to different views the Holy Spirit proceeds *a Patre solo* (from the Father alone), or *a Patre Filioque* (from the Father and from the Son). In the first view the Father alone is the cause or principle of the Holy Spirit, in the second Father and Son are one principle of the Holy Spirit.

Formally assimilative operation—an operation whose very nature it is to produce a likeness.

Functional Christology—a Christology concerned with Christ functioning for us, rather than with Christ in Himself and in His immanent relation to the Father and Holy Spirit.

Functional sonship—a sonship attributed to Christ because of the soteriological or salvific functions that He exercises towards us.

Generative procession—a procession or origination by way of generation. Thus though a father and son are of the same nature, the father is said to be greater than the son because he is the son's cause or principle.

Gennesis—generateness, the quality of being generated.

Germanitas—intimacy, affinity.

Godhead—the deity itself, the divinity, the divine nature.

Hierarchical—a graded order involving superior and inferior elements.

Homoeans—those who held that Christ was like (*homoios*) the Father.

Homoeousians—those who held that Christ was like in substance or being or essence (*homoiousios*) to the Father.

homoios, homoiousios, homoousios—like, like in substance, of the same substance.

Hypostasis—apart from theology this word had many meanings. In theology initially it meant about the same as *ousia* (being, essence, substance), but gradually it came to signify positive and concrete and distinct existence in the particular individual. Ultimately it was accepted in the East as the technical description of what the Latins called the *personae* of God.

Hypostatized—considered a person, not just a personification.

Innascibility—inability to be born or generated.

Insociable relations—unidentifiable or incommunicable relations, such as paternity and filiation in God.

Kurios—the Septuagint (LXX) uses *Kurios*, the Greek equivalent of *Adonai* (Lord), to translate Yahweh. Since this is the usual name for God in the LXX, Paul's application of it to Jesus raises Jesus above the level of common humanity and can make Him appear to be—and be—equal to God.

Logos—a Greek word with many meanings, e.g. reason, rationality, word, definition, principle, etc. For Gnostics a Logos was one of their aeons. For Stoics Logos was the rational principle immanent in reality, giving it form and meaning. For Philo (c. 30 B.C.—A.D. 45) God is so utterly transcendent that between Him and the world there are intermediary powers, among whom and most important of whom was the Logos, God's agent in creation.

LXX— a symbol for the Septuagint.

Macedonians—denied the divinity of the Holy Spirit. They were called 'Macedonians' after Macedonius (d. 362), the bishop of Constantinople, but whether Macedonius himself actually denied the divinity of the Holy Spirit is not clear.

Marcellians—followers of Marcellus of Ancyra (d. 374 c.). He was an extreme consubstantialist, a staunch defender of the Nicene symbol, but was accused by his Arian opponents of leaning toward Sabellianism.

Marcion—was cast out of the Church by his father, the bishop of Sinope in Pontus. He came to Rome about 135, maintained the substance of Gnosticism, and rejected the OT as the work of a cruel and vindictive God.

Messiah—transliterated from the Hebrew, and Christ, transcribed from the Greek, both mean 'anointed'. The term Messiah had many meanings and was applied loosely to many salvific figures who were expected to appear at the time of God's definitive intervention on behalf of Israel, e.g. Elijah, perhaps the Suffering Servant, the Son of Man. More strictly the term refers to the 'anointed king of the Davidic dynasty who would establish in the world the definitive reign of Yahweh'. In apostolic times this appellation became the proper name of Jesus.

Messianic sonship—a special dilective sonship assigned to the Messiah.

Mia ousia, treis hypostaseis—a Greek phrase for 'one being' (one substance), 'three hypostases' (three persons), which corresponds to the Latin, *una substantia* (one substance), *tres personae* (three persons).

Mission—a sending, e.g. of a Saviour, a helper.

Modalism—a theory in which Father, Son and Holy Spirit are not three distinct divine persons, but only three modes of manifestation or operation of one sole divine person.

Modum essendi, modum existendi—mode of being, mode of existing.

Monarchian—Monarchians were so called because of their concern for the divine unity or 'monarchy'. They were thus 'Unitarians', holding that God is only one person.

Montanist work—About 260 Tertullian joined the followers of Montanus, who had announced himself as the organ of the Holy Spirit and was the leader of a rigorist sect that involved an austere moral doctrine.

Natural sonship—the sonship of one who is son by nature, not just by adoption.

Nature—the term had and has various meanings. Perhaps its basic meaning is essence regarded as the ultimate principle of operation. In God nature, essence, and substance will be considered identical by Lateran IV (Denz 804).

Nebeneinander, Ineinander, Miteinander—German for next to, in, with, one another.

Obviat aliqua relationis oppositio—some opposition of relation intervenes. *See* Relation of opposition.

Oikonomia—a Greek word with many meanings. *See* economy.

Ontological categories—categories of 'being'.

Opera trinitatis ad extra indivisa sunt—the exterior works of the Trinity are undivided, i.e., common to all three persons.

Ophites—a strange Gnostic sect, called 'Ophites' from the serpent, *ophis*, which played a large part in their system.

Palamas—Gregory of Palamas, a Saint in the Orthodox Church, is said to have taught that the saints in heaven do not intuit the divine substance itself but only a certain divine splendour, uncreated yet distinct from God.

Passive generation—the relation of one generated to the one generating.

Passive spiration—the relation of one spirated to the one spirating.

Perichoresis—a Greek word that seems to have meant 'dancing around', 'rotation', 'reciprocation', etc. It came to be used to signify the 'interpenetration', 'mutual inexistence' of the three divine persons.

Personae—To the question 'Three What'? Tertullian answered *tres personae,* three persons, and this word *persona* became the accepted Western word to express the dogma and theology of the three, Father, Son and Holy Spirit. Its basic meaning for Tertullian seemed to be 'a concrete individual', a 'self', taken in a metaphysical, not a psychological sense. 'Person' has been variously defined as 'an individual substance of a rational nature' (Boethius), as 'a distinct subsistent in an intellectual nature' (Aquinas), as a 'center of consciousness' (contemporary psychologists).

Personification—the process of presenting something impersonal as a person.

Philosophical trinitarianism—a trinitarianism (e.g. Hegelian) that is independent of the ordinary Christian revelational basis and is grounded entirely on philosophical premises.

Photinians—followers of Photinus, Bishop of Sirmium, who defended the Nicene *homoousion* but was thought to be a Modalist and an Adoptionist.

Pleroma—the divine world constituted by the Gnostic aeons.

Plotinus—one of the great thinkers of the ancient world (d. 270). He was considered the real creator of Neo-Platonism, a Platonic system based on a new theodicy that involved a hierarchy of the One, and Mind, and Soul.

Pneumatology—the study, science, theology of the Holy Spirit.

Pneumatomachi—'Spirit-fighters'. They were those who denied full divinity to the Holy Spirit. They were also called 'Macedonians' after Macedonius, the Homoiousian bishop of Constantinople, but there is no clear evidence that Macedonius really was a 'Spirit-fighter'.

Praxeas—a shadowy figure, called a 'Patripassian-Monarchian', who appears to have taught that Father and Son were one identical person and that thus it was the Father who suffered, died, rose.

Pre-dogmatic stage—the stage in which this teaching had not yet become dogma, i.e., definitively presented as a revealed article of faith to be universally believed. The dogmatic stage would thus begin with Nicea I.

Pre-existent Christ—Christ as existing before creation or incarnation.

Procession—in God, means the origination of one divine person from another.

Proposopon—a Greek word that originally meant 'face', 'mask', 'type', 'a tragic personage', etc., and gradually came to mean a concrete presentation of an individual, an individual. Hippolytus was apparently the first to use it with reference to the Trinity and in the sense of 'individual'.

Proximately of faith—near to divine and catholic faith.

Ptolemaeus—an eminent Gnostic of the Valentinian school (d. 180).

Quis habens, quid habitum—someone having, something had.

Quo est, quod est—that by which it is, and, that which is.

Relation—the respect of one to another, the way in which one, e.g. father, stands to another, e.g. his son.

Relation of opposition—if one originates from another, he is not that other but is distinguished over against that other, and thus has a relation of opposition to that other, as a son to his father. Thus a son is in relational or relative opposition to his father in a metaphysical sense.

Sabellian—Sabellius was a 3rd century Modalist for whom God was not three really distinct persons but only one person who expressed himself in three operations.

Salvation—in the OT the word 'approaches the idea of liberation from all evil and the acquisition of complete security'. In the NT the word has various meanings, liberation from sin, coming to the knowledge of the truth, the Parousia, life, immortality, eternal glory, entrance into the eschatological kingdom.

Semi-Arians—half-Arians. They are usually equated with Homoeousians but should rather, it seems, be equated with Homoeans, since Homoeans like strict Arians held that Christ was a creature, but, unlike Anomoians, held that He was like the Father.

Septuagint—the name commonly given to the Greek version of the OT made in the pre-Christian period by a legendary group of 70 Jewish experts.

Single stage theory of the Logos—in this the Logos is eternally both Logos and Son eternally generated by the Father. *See*, Twofold stage theory.

Sirmium Blasphemy—a notorious Arian formula of faith issued by a council at Sirmium (Mitrovica in Jugoslavia) in 357.

Spiration—a word apparently derived from the concept of 'spirit' as 'breath'. Since the Holy Spirit is said to proceed as the 'breath' of the Father, his origination is by way of spiration or 'breathing'. Lyons II defined that the 'Holy Spirit proceeds eternally from the Father and the Son . . . not by two spirations but by one spiration' (Denz 850).

Spirit—the Hebrew word *ruah* (*pneuma*, spirit) had various meanings, 'breath', 'wind', 'principle of life'. Used of God it signifies at times divine form or stuff, at times the principle of deity, at times an impersonal divine force, at times the Third Person of the Trinity.

Subordinationism—a doctrine that makes the Son and/or the Holy Spirit an inferior deity or a creature.

Subsistences—an abstract term at times used to signify 'persons'.

Subsistent relations—relations in God, such as paternity and filiation, which are not in any way accidental or contingent but as eternal and unchangeable as the divine substance itself, with which they are really identified and from which they are virtually distinct.

Subsistentia, subsistens—subsistence, subsistent. Gilbert de la Porrée applied the distinction he found in creatures between 'subsistent', that which subsists, and 'subsistence', that by which it subsists.

Subsisting substance—another way of signifying hypostasis or distinct subsistent.

Substance—that which exists in itself or subsists. In God it signifies that which God is, with the emphasis on its concrete reality. *See* Nature.

Supposit—something which has the notes of substantiality and incommunicability, a distinct or incommunicable subsistent. A rational supposit is a person, i.e. a distinct subsistent in an intellectual nature.

Symbol of Nicea—more commonly called the Nicene Creed. As a 'symbol' it is a sign, an expression of objective faith.

Theophany—an appearance or manifestation of God.

Triadic pattern—a threefold pattern, involving Father, Son, Spirit.

Trias—triad, trinity.

Trinitarian dogma—truths about the Triune God that are to be believed because divinely revealed and proposed by the Church to be so believed.

Tritheists—those who regard Father, Son and Holy Spirit not as three distinct persons in one god but as three gods.

Tropici—a group of Egyptian Christians who admitted the divinity of the Son but not of the Holy Spirit. They were called Tropici (*tropos* = figure) because of their figurative exegesis of Scripture.

Twofold stage theory of the Logos—in this theory Christ is eternally
    Logos but not eternally Son. In the first stage the Logos is Logos
    from eternity, but not Son. In the second stage the Logos is generated
    as Son for the purpose of creation of the world.
Unitarians—those who hold there is only one person in God.
Unum, unus—one being but not one person.
Ut quo, ut quod—as that by which, as that which.
Vade mecum—a 'go with me', a handbook.
Valentinians—followers of Valentinus, a Christian Gnostic, who carried
    on the work begun by Basilides. He taught at Alexandria and later
    at Rome in the middle decades of the 2nd century.
Yahweh—etymologically has often been thought to mean 'He who is', or
    'I am who am', or 'the Eternal'. Other scholars think that it means
    'He brings into being whatever comes into being' and thus designates
    Him as creator. This became the personal name of the God of Israel
    and He was called by this more frequently than by all other titles
    combined.

Index of Persons

Abelard, 177–81, 185–6, 195, 232
Aeneas of Paris, 167
Albert the Great, 202–4
Alcuin, 166
Alexander, A. B. D., 254 n28
Alexander, bishop of Alexandria, 65
Alexander of Hales, 210–12, 221, 233, 234
Altaner, B., 44 n21, 44 n22, 47 n30, 48 n31, 49 n35, 52 n36, 52 n37, 63 n5, 72 n9, 72 n10, 76 n19, 99 n1, 99 n2, 101 n2, 124 n58, 139 n13, 139 n15, 161 n16
Amann, E., 124 n60
Ambrose, 126, 136–9, 151, 152, 161
Anitchkof, E., 197 n9
Anselm, 173–6, 227, 231–2
Anthimus VIII, Orthodox Patriarch, 282
Antweiler, A., 127 n68
Aquinas, xxi, 149, 153, 163, 176, 202, 204–10, 214, 217, 218, 233–4, 248, 285, 287, 295, 314
Aristotle, 202, 204, 221
Arius, xvii, 62, 63–5, 96, 181, 242
Athanasius, xvii, 59, 72–5, 71 n4, 97, 126, 133, 136, 151, 159, 205
Athenagoras, Apologist, 48–9
Augustine, xix–xx, 133, 134, 135, 139–50, 152, 153, 154, 156, 161, 164, 173, 205, 214, 230–1, 302

Bainton, R. H., 242 n19, 242 n20, 242 n21
Bainvel, J., 173 n1
Bardy, G., 127 n74

Barnabas, 42
Barnard, L. W., 44 n22, 45 n23, 45 n24, 46 n29
Barrett, C. K., 23 n24, 26 n28, 26 n29
Barth, K., 163 n17, 184, 250 n2, 258–62, 260 n34, 260 n35, 260 n37, 260 n38, 260 n39, 260 n40, 260 n41, 260 n42, 261 n43, 261 n44, 261 n45, 261 n47, 261 n48, 262 n49, 262 n50, 262 n51, 262 n52, 262 n53, 262 n54, 262 n55, 262 n57, 262 n58, 262 n59, 270, 297, 299
Bartlett, C. N., 258 n5
Basil, 59, 75, 76, 77, 78, 79, 80, 81, 82, 101, 136, 143, 144, 205
Baumgartner, Ch., 90 n40
Bea, Augustin Cardinal, 283
Bede the Venerable, 166
Bernard, 179, 182, 185–8, 184 n43, 232
Bethune-Baker, J. F., 58 n47, 63 n5, 66 n9, 72 n6, 72 n8, 108 n16, 118 n47
Bihlmeyer, K., Tüchle, H., 71 n1, 93 n45, 93 n50, 107 n14
Billot, L., 287
Bindley, T. H., Green, F. W., 154 n2
Boehner, P., 223 n4
Boethius, xx, 161–4, 191, 192, 208, 231, 295
Boismard, M. E., 19 n15
Bolotov, V., 279, 279 n33
Bonaventure, xxi, 212–18, 221, 233, 234, 285
Bonsirven, J., 21 n21
Bornkamm, G., 265
Bouillard, H., 265, n85
Boyer, C., 197 n5, 292 n1

367

Index of Subjects

Acts of Orthodox synods, 277, 278
Age, of Enlightenment, 247, 268; of Holy Spirit, 198
Alexandrine doctrine, 52–61; revelation and Platonic philosophy, 52; God in Platonic fashion, 52, 54–5; eternal generation of Son, 53, 55; single stage theory, 53, 55; subordinationism, 54, 56; summary, 60–1
Ambrosian doctrine, 136–9; Eastern trinitarian methodology, 136–7; strict consubstantiality of the Three, 137–9; stress on Holy Spirit, 138–9
American deists, 246
Analogy, metaphysical, 292; psychological 292–3; for divine generation, 206–7; for Trinity, 136, 148–9, 153, 181
Anglicans and Reunion efforts, 278
Anomoians, 71, 144
Anselmian doctrine, 173–6; dialectics and Augustinian premises, 173; 'necessary reasons', 174; unity and *ubi non obviat aliqua relationis oppositio*, 174; rejection of Roscelin's tritheism, 174–5
Antinomy of trinity and unity, 263
Anti-Nicene party, 71, 72, 97
Anti-Trinitarians, 242, 244
Apostles' Creed, 158, 239
Apostolic Fathers' doctrine, 37–44; one God creator, ruler, judge, Father of universe and especially of Christ, 39; divinity of Christ, 39; less clarity about Holy Spirit, 40, 41–2, 43; summary, 43–4

Apologists' doctrine, 44–51; unity and trinity, 50; two stage theory of pre-existent Logos, 46, 47, 48, 49; relation of Holy Spirit to Father and Son, 46–7, 48, 49, 51; unity of power, rule, monarchy, 51; 'trinity of God, His Word, His Wisdom', 50; summary, 50–1
Appropriation, 143, 190, 309
Arian creed, the 'Sirmium blasphemy', 72
Arianism, 62–70, 97, 126–9, 136–7, 151, 227–8; doctrine, 63–5; origin, 62; basic principle, 63; nature of Son, 63–4; biblical argumentation, 64; condemnation at Nicea, 66–8; life after condemnation, 71 ff., summary 68–70
Arianization of Abelard, 185
Arians, 59, 60, 96, 140, 160, 177, 183
Aristotelian logic and method, 161; categories, 162; philosophy, 164, 231, 243; principle, 204
Arminian theologians, 244
Athanasian Creed, xx, 154, 158–61, 177, 239, 263; creed itself, 159; damnatory clauses, 160; doctrine, 160–1; Filioque, 160; origin, date, birthplace uncertain, 158–9; dogmatic value, 161; impact of Augustine, 160
Athanasius' doctrine, 72–5; 'God one through the Triad', 72; Son's generation eternal, by nature, in identity of substance, mysterious, 73–4; full divinity and consubstantiality of Holy Spirit, 74
Attributes of God in OT, 3; in NT, 10, 16, 19, 31; in Apostolic Fathers, 37,

225; Filioque amplified, 225;
Filioque's addition to Creed, 225;
Decree for Jacobites, 226;
mutual inexistence of Three, 226;
unity and relation of opposition,
226-7

Council of Lateran IV, 199-201;
condemnation of Joachim, 199;
approval of Lombard, 199; Trinity
and not quaternity, 200; one supreme
reality which is Father, Son and Holy
Spirit, 200; that reality not generating,
nor generated nor proceeding, 200;
but Father generates, Son is generated,
Holy Spirit proceeds, 200; Filioque
defined, 201

Council of Lyons II, 218-20; Reunion
council convoked by Pope, 218;
Profession of Faith of Michael
Palaeologus, the Emperor, 218;
Constitution on the Procession of
the Holy Spirit, 218-19; Holy Spirit
proceeds from Father and Son, 219;
as from one principle, 219; and by
one spiration, 219; and this is and
has been the teaching of East and
West, 219

Council of Nicea I, 66-70; convoked by
Emperor Constantine, 66; Creed, 66;
rejection of Arianism, 66; definition of
Son's strict divinity and consubstantiality with the Father, 66; belief in
the Holy Spirit, 66; consubstantial,
homoousios, 67; generic or numerical identity of substance, 67-8

Council of Toledo XI, 164-5; ineffable
Trinity, 164; Father the origin of the
divinity, 164; Son generated by Father
and consubstantial, 164; Holy Spirit
from Father and Son as charity and
sanctity of both, 165; names of Three
are relative, 165; Three are equal,
inseparable in existence and operation,
165; and distinct in terms of personal
properties, 165; almost dogmatic
value for some theologians, 164

Creation, and generation, 91, 98; and
Trinity, 289; an image of the life of
the Trinity, 289; a model for interpreting the Trinity, 289-90; a replica of
the Trinity, 289

Created actuation by Uncreated Act,
306, 310

Creeds and Reformers, 243; and Liberal
Protestants, 253; Nicene, 66; Nicene-
Constantinopolitan, 85; Quicunque
or Athanasian, 158; Toledo XI, 164-5

Damnatory clauses of the Quicunque,
158
Decree for Greeks, 225, 229
Decree for Jacobites, 226, 229
Dehellenization of dogma, 255, 298
Deification, 74, 78, 89, 138, 255, 276, 280
Deism, 245-6, 250, 268
Definition of generation, 211; of
hypostasis, 80, 82; of person, 163-4;
of person by Richard of St Victor,
191-2; of person by Aquinas, 192; of
person, 203-4, 208-9, 215, 222, 231,
234, 295, 296, 314
Demonstration of Trinity from soul,
189-90; from charity, 193-4
Demythologization, 246, 265, 298, 316
Dialectics in theology, 169, 173, 178
Difference between generation and
procession, 57, 79, 88, 91, 203,
205-6, 211, 214, 222
Distinction, formal, 223; real, 207, 209;
neither real nor purely logical, 200;
between divine persons, 140, 143-4,
160, 200, 212, 222, 228
Ditheism, 117, 121, 151
Diversity of the Three, personal, absolute,
279-80
Divine energies, 276; light, 276;
operation, 276; unity, 26, 30, 40, 51,
61, 66, 75, 82, 92, 113-14, 130, 140-3,
159, 165, 199-200
Divinity and God, 184
Divinity of Christ in Synoptics-Acts, 11,
13, 15; Paul, 17, 18, 19, 23; John,
24-7; 1 Clement, 38; Ignatius, 39;
Polycarp, 42; Barnabas, 42; 2
Clement, 43; Justin, 46;
Athenagoras, 48; Theophilus, 49;
Clement, 53; Origen, 55-6, Nicea I,
66; Pope Dionysius, 59; Alexander, 65
Divinity of the Holy Spirit in
Synoptics-Acts, 3-14; Paul, 20-21;
John, 27-9; I Clement, 38; Ignatius,
40; Justin, 47, Athenagoras, 48;
Clement, 54; Origen, 57, Nicea I, 66;
Constantinople I, 85; Athanasius, 74;
Cappadocians, 77-9
Doctrine of Trinity and Christian life,
285; grounded in God's self-revelation
in Christ, 262; how it developed, 260;
necessary only in a defensive way, 262;
not a Biblical kerygma, 262; not
explicitly in Bible, 260; only a theological doctrine, 263; origin, 263-4;
rooted only in revelation, 261; and in
speculation, 289; work of the Church,
260; unsatisfactory, 251

Dogma of Trinity, 289; a late arrival, 291, 263
Dogmatic affirmations, 229; decisions, 278, development, 227; formula, 228; value, 228

Economic Trinity, 22, 32, 33, 49, 61, 113
Economy, 108, 109
Ecumenical councils, 62; first seven, 282; eight, 93; trinitarian Nicea I, 66–8; Constantinople I, 83–6; Lateran IV, 199–201; Lyons II, 218–20; Florence, 224–7
Ecumenical Patriarch Athenagoras, 283
Ekporeuetai, 78–9, 87, 94, 278
Elemental trinitarianism, 60, 95, 291
Emanations, intelligible divine, 176, 206, 292
Endiathetos Logos, 45, 47, 48, 49, 118
Energies and essence of God, 280
Eo Filius quo Verbum et eo Verbum quo Filius, 214
Equality of the Three, 140–1, 159, 164, 165
Essence, 141–4, 166, 184, 200, 207, 225, 228–9, 276, 279; essence does not generate but Father does, 200; essence and energies of God, 280; essence and substance and nature, 200
Eternity as norm of divinity, 114, 115, 118
Eternity of the Son in Clement, 53; Origen, 55–6, Bishop Dionysius, 58–9; Pope Dionysius, 58–9; Alexander, 65; Nicea I, 66
Evolution of dogma, 317
Existential philosophy, 257, 269
Experience, and trinitarian doctrine, 293; Christian, 243, 244, 250, 251, 253; of faith, 291; of Jesus and His Spirit, 291
Experiential theology of Schleiermacher, 244, 251

Faith, defined, 227–9; divine and catholic, 228; illumining reason, 289
Father is alone God in the strict sense, 55; is first source of Trinity, 135; is a fontal plentitude for all emanations, 213; is font and origin of whole divinity, 165; is greater than the Son, 135; is older, 134; is one person with the Son, 117; is Father of His own essence, 165; is the fontal principle of the consubstantial Triad, 71; is the primordial principle of divine life, 88; is the transcendent One, 135; Father and Son spirate Holy Spirit as one spirative principle, 203; Father generates the Son, the essence does not, 200
Fecundity, 213; of nature, 217; of will, 217
Filiation, 207, 212; in OT, 4; by the Holy Spirit, 88, 89
Filioque, 93, 98, 145, 152, 156, 159, 160, 166, 167, 168, 169, 170, 173, 174, 178, 196, 199, 201, 203, 207, 211, 214, 218, 219, 220, 224, 226, 228, 229, 262, 273, 275, 276, 277, 278, 280, 281, 282
Florentine Decree, 279, 285; union, 277
Formally assimilative operation, 206
French deists, 257–8
Fundamentalists, 257–8
Full supernatural knowledge and the divine indwelling, 310

Generation, analogy, 206; and spiration, 211; definition, 206, 211; generation of Son and Barth, 262; generation of Son and procession of Holy Spirit, 205–7, 211, 214, 222; generation of Son by way of nature, 203; ceaseless, 55; eternal, 53, 55, 58, 59, 65, 66, 127, 131; not by will or necessity but by nature, 73; philosophically inexplicable 137; why generation in God, 214
Genetic explanation of Trinity in terms of Spirit, 175, 253
Gennadius II, Patriarch of Constantinople, 277
Gifts of the Holy Spirit in the OT, 6; in Syn. Acts, 14; in Paul, 20–1
Gnosticism, 101–3, 114, 230
God, and divinity, 184; as a divine society, 258; as one and creator, 3, 16, 31, 37–8, 39, 40, 45, 48, 54–5, 66; as eternal Process, 252; as quasi-formal cause, 309; as Spirit, 252; as spiritual matter, 114, 150; as supreme efficient cause, 313; in continuous process of unfolding and refolding, 136 as inferiorized, 56, 63, 68; not as Father, 141; only as Father, 55; God of Christians, 140; of Greek metaphysics, 298; of Hegel, 253; of nature, 248, of Tillich, 266–7,
God's self-communication as Trinity, 312; self-revelation in Jesus Christ, 262
God is Father, 4, 10, 11, 16, 24, 37, 39, 41, 42, 43, 66; is Son, 20, 27, 39, 66,

109, 159; is Holy Spirit, 78, 111, 159; is Trinity, 141, 159
Grace, sanctifying, 210, 280; and inhabitation, 310–12
Greek, delegation to Florence, 224; to Lyons II, 218; dogma and Christian message, 255; Fathers and cause of Holy Spirit's subsistence, 225; and indwelling, 90, 92, 147; and trinitarian starting point, 76, 140

Hellenic Encyclopedia, 158
Hellenization of Christian message, 255, 298
Heresy, 182
Heretic, 167, 180, 181, 196–9, 242, 278; heretical, 179–80, 242, 276
Hesychasm, 276
Holy Spirit, and man's spiritual life, 146–7, 150; age of, 198; as consubstantial with Father and Son, 74, 78, 92, 94, 111, 136, 141; as demythologized, 265; as a distinct person, 21, 28, 38, 47, 54, 57, 58, 66, 78, 82, 85, 132, 159; as a divine force, 14; 21, 151; as Gift, 145–6, 152; as inferior to Son, 57; as Love, 145–6, 152; as pre-existent, 21, 28, 30, 38, 40, 42, 43, 48, 54, 57, 66; as principally from the Father, 145, 174; as proceeding from Father and Son, 219, 221, 222, 203, 225–6, 159, 165, 201; as Voice's Voice, 135; as soul of the world, 180
Homoians, 71, 74; *homoiousios*, 72, 131, 132
Homoousios, 55–6, 58–9, 66–8, 61, 62, 71–2, 74, 81, 96, 126–7, 131–2, 134
Hypostasis and *ousia*, 66, 282; and person, 58, 60, 79–82, 244; and substance, 59, 66; definition, 71, 75, 79, 80, 82, 85–6

Idealists, 252
Identity of substance, generis or numerical, 56, 67, 73, 78, 81, 82, 92, 228
Incorporation and inhabitation, 310
Inexistence of Three, 139, 226, 229, 262
Inhabitation, 88, 98, 147–8, 152, 276, 308–13; areas of agreement and disagreement, 308; 'propriation' vs. appropriation, 309; distinct relations to the Three, 309; 3 types of explanation, 309; inhabitation and

incorporation, 310; two Dominican explanations, 310–11; two Jesuit explanations, 311–12; Pius XII and inhabitation, 313; inhabitation as constituted by full supernatural knowledge, 310–11; by quasi-experimental presence, 310; by quasi-formal causality, 312; by the state of grace, 311–12
Inhabiting God as both principle and term of our supernatural life, 309; as principle of our supernatural life, 309; as term of our supernatural life, 309
Invisible mission of Son and Holy Spirit, 304–6. See Mission

Jesus Christ in John, as Word, 24; Son of God, 25–7; God, 27; less than the Father, 26–7; soteriological Son, 25; metaphysical Son, 26; pre-existent Son, 26; creative Word, 24; revelatory Word, 24
Jesus Christ in Paul, as Christ, 16–17; Son of God, 17–18; functional Son, 17; eternal Son, 17; as pre-existent, 17; as subordinate to the Father, 18; as equal to the Father, 18; as image of the invisible God, 17; as in the form of God, 18; as creator, 17–18; as sent by the Father, 17; as redeemer, 17
Jesus Christ in the Synoptics-Acts, as Son of God, 11; as unique Son, 11; as messianic Son, 11; as more than messianic Son, 11; as strictly divine Son, 11; as Son of Man, 12; with more than traditional messianic powers, 12; as Lord, 12–13; with a messianic lordship, 13; with a strictly divine lordship, 13
Jesus Christ in the Apostolic Fathers, God's child, 37; God's Son, 37; Christ, 37; Lord Jesus Christ, 37; called 'God' 14 times, 39; the Father's Word, 39; the mind of the Father, 39; the Eternal, the Invisible who became visible for our sake, 39; the Lord who has been active in creation, 42
Jesus Christ in the Apologists, the Logos, 45; adorable, 45; God, 45; the Father's intelligence, 45; numerically distinct from the Father, 45; eternal, 45; eternally a distinct person?, 46; eternally generated as Son?, 46
Jesus Christ as distinct from the Holy Spirit, in Paul, 17; 1 Clement, 37–8, 2 Clement, 43; Ignatius, 39; Hermas,

Socinianism, 244, 268; Socinians, 246, 248

Spirit, as impersonal divine force, 6, 9, 14, 15, 21, 23, 27, 32, 252; as principle of deity, stuff of divine nature, 43; as divine level of being, 21

Spiration, 57, 219, 222, 229, 203; by way of love, 203; and generation, 211

Subordination of Jesus, 11, 13, 15, 18, 56–7, 61, 68

Subordinationism, 61, 62, 106, 122, 123, 140, 141, 150, 152, 263, 280

Subordinationists, Justin, 46; Tatian, 47; Athenagoras, 48; Theophilus, 49; Origen, 56, 57, 61, 68; Arius, 63–4; contemporaries, 258

Substance, 162, 175, 180, 184, 295

Subsistence, 163; subsistences, 136

Subsistent, being, 225; relation, 144, 207, 217, 294, 295

Summa of Aquinas, 287; Commentaries 287

Synods, Orthodox, of Constantinople (1638), of Jassy (1641–1642), of Jerusalem (1672), of Constantinople (1672), 277

Synthesis of trinitarian doctrine, 133, 149, 151, 153, 210, 211, 217, 221, 253,

Systematization of trinitarian doctrine, 233, 282, 285

Theology, anthropocentric, 316; Christocentric, 317; idealistic, 250; liberal, 246, 250; ontological, 266; Orthodox, 280, 314; philosophical, 266; Franciscan, 234–5; Jesuit, 287; Thomistic, 233, 234, 287

Three ages of history, 197–8

Three Names constitute the NT message, 263

Three notes indicate a person, 164

Three Persons are distinct by originational relations, 157; and coequal, consubstantial and coeternal, 156, 164, 165; and mutually inexist, 226

Three personalities, 299

Three principles in Protestant theology, authority, reason, experience, 243

Three stage theory of the pre-existent Logos, 291

Treatise of the Trinity, 291

Trias first used by Theophilus for the Three, 50; Triad, 61, 66, 75; Triadic texts, patterns, ground plan, formula, 14–16, 21–3, 29–30, 32–3

Trinitarian, controversy, 245; doctrinal

origin, 251, 255, 268; dogma, 289; doxology, 42; errors, 125; formula, 255, 291; General Councils, 66–8, 83–6, 199–201, 218–20, 224–7; presence, 311; problem, 16, 22, 30, 32; problem answered, 267, 233; symbolism, 267; views of English and American theologians, 269; words, 228–9; elemental and formal trinitarianism, 291, 314

Trinitas first used of the Three by Tertullian, 112, 150

Trinitization, 290

Trinity, no formal doctrine in OT, 9; Synoptics, Acts, 14; Paul, 22; John, 29; Apostolic Fathers, 44; Apologists, 50–1; but elements, material for such a doctrine in NT, 14, 22, 29, 32–3; and Apologists, 49, 51

Trinity, essential or ontological, 258; of essence, 257; of one divinity, 112, 150; pantheistic or panentheistic, 257

Trinity and creation, 289; and revelation, 290

Trinity as analysis of NT, 258, 260; as explicitly revealed in the NT, 290; as a genetic explanation in terms of Spirit, 175; as economic and immanent, 113, 262; as immanent in experience of faith, 291; as an intellectual hypothesis, 257; as irrational and religiously valueless, 257; as a mystery, 262; as a product of metaphysics, 257; as a second rank doctrine, 251; as a synthesis of the data of Christian revelation and experience, 258

Tritheism, 59, 61, 117, 140, 151, 152, 160, 174, 177, 183, 198, 227, 228, 261

Tritheists, 58, 59, 181, 184

Twofold Stage theory of the pre-existent Logos, 45–6, 47–8, 60, 68, 100, 150, 230

Uncreated, Act, 310; grace, 312

Unity, divine, 16, 33, 51, 76, 100, 136, 140–3, 159, 166, 253, 258, 289, 300–2, 314; of essence, nature, substance, will, operation, 133, 141–2, 113, 156, 200; of power, rule, monarchy, 51

Unitarianism, 244; Unitarians, 244

Valentinians, 101, 108, 240

Vatican I, 289, 313

Vestigia trinitatis, 261